Tate Publishing

An Urban History
of Photography

Street & Studio

Edited by Ute Eskildsen
With Florian Ebner and Bettina Kaufmann

Foreword — 6 —

Introduction — 8 —
Ute Eskildsen

Staging: Early References — 16 —

Mobile Camera / Sophisticated Studio — 26 —

New Visions / New Public — 38 —

Postwar Flâneurs / Uncaged Fashion — 60 —

Provocation / Emancipation — 78 —

Revisiting Conventional Modes — 110 —

Index to Artists and Works — 145 —
Florian Ebner and Bettina Kaufmann

Essays

The Pose: Its Troubles and Pleasures — 171 —
Susanne Holschbach

La Foto Chiari: Some Thoughts towards a Neorealist Photography — 179 —
Jeremy Millar

Urban Characters, Imaginary Cities — 186 —
Florian Ebner

The Narrative City: Image, Glamour and Isolation — 195 —
Michael Bracewell

Typologies — 203 —

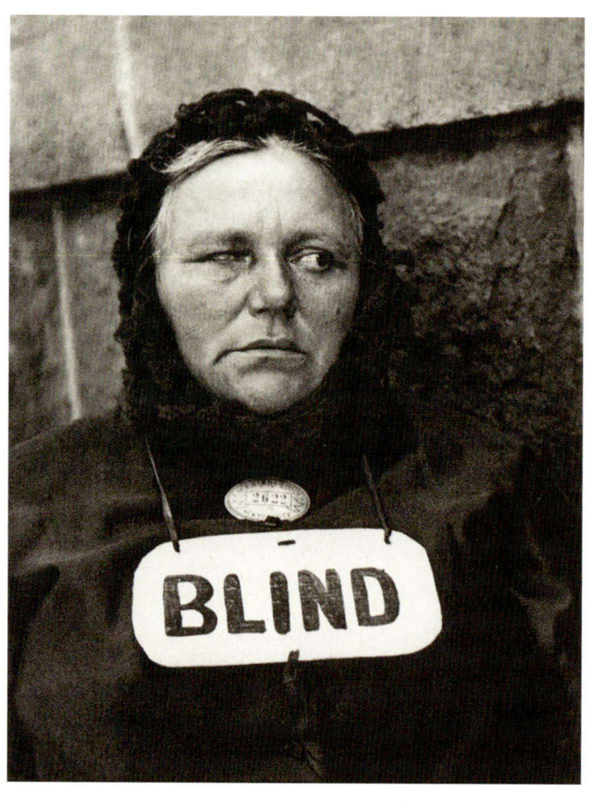

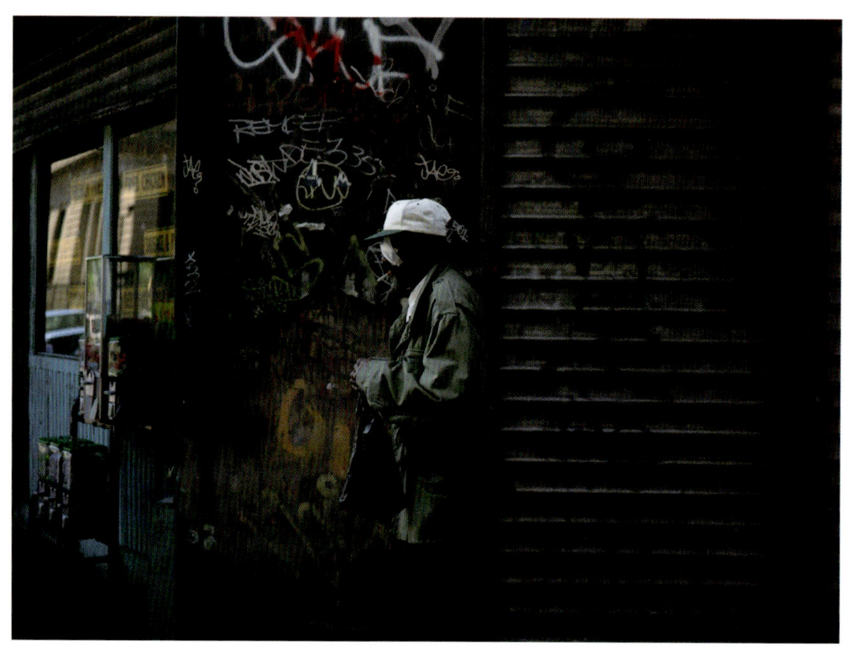

Blind

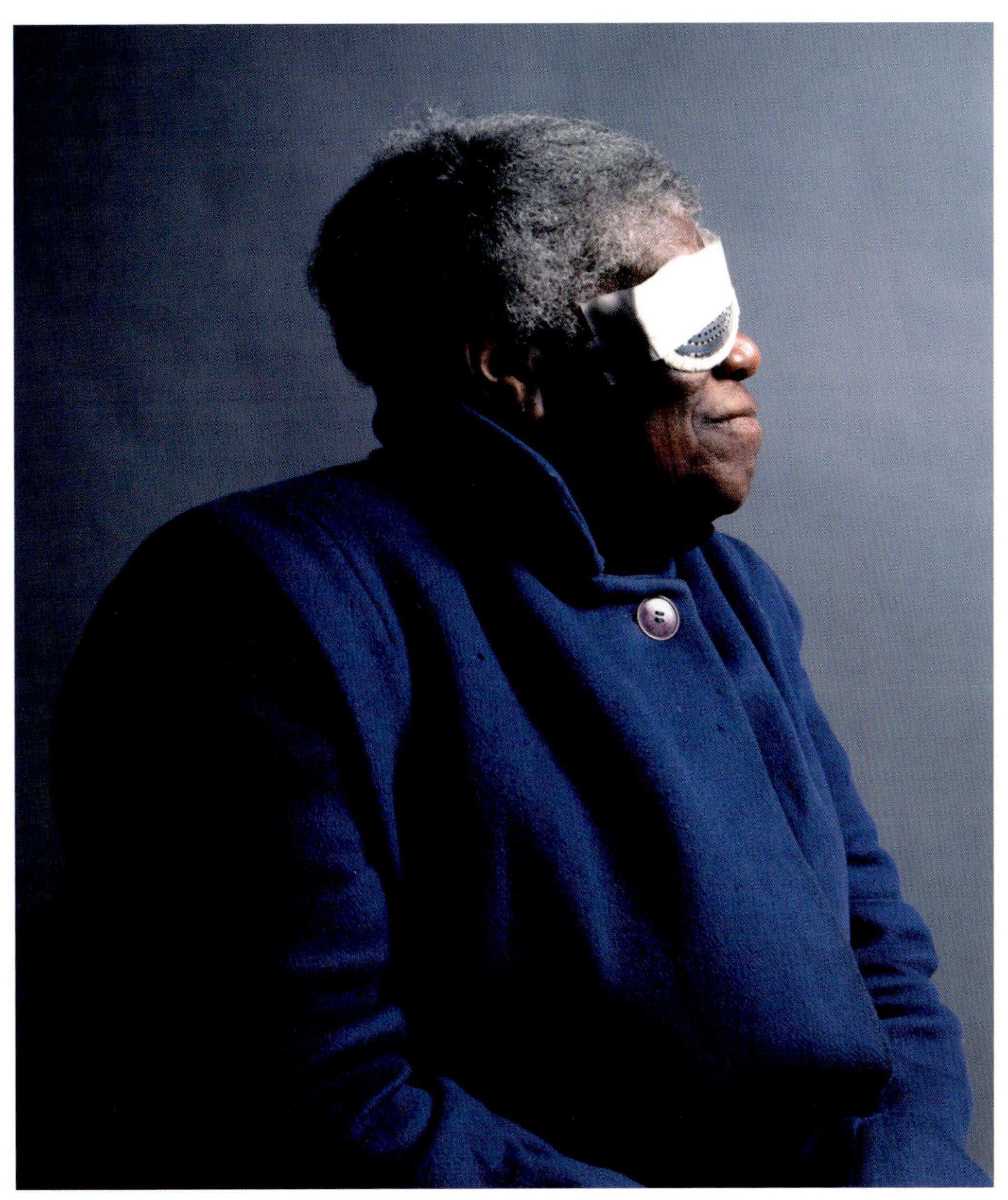

Foreword

Street & Studio: An Urban History of Photography is the first exhibition to examine the parallel evolution of two central sites of photographic practice. Since these two apparently divided image worlds of the street and the studio come from opposite perspectives, they combine different ways of seeing and representing the urban experience, focusing on the individual in a developing mass culture. But the exhibition does not follow the historical view that sees the two as separate, self-contained disciplines: without ignoring their discrete developments and differences, it engages with the works in a chronological and typological way, to look instead at the continual exchange, dialogue and crossover between the two.

In earlier times, photographic portrayals of urban culture were primarily understood as topographical views. The contemporary perspective – raising questions about the future of the city, life on the periphery of the urban agglomeration, and the urban demographic development – favours architecture and cityscape photography. However, *Street & Studio* shows how our visual concept of urban culture has been, to a considerable extent, shaped by different ways of representing the human being.

At the heart of the exhibition is the fundamental question of how these two approaches to the portrayal of the individual have been generated by the desires of the urban public. This aspect is explored through the inclusion of magazines and books that help to trace the mutual shift from the world of celebrity to everyday life, from the idealisation of the studio to the realism of the street – and vice versa. Furthermore, the show illustrates how inventions like the Photomaton reflect changes in society, and, in turn, changes in the status of the professional photographer.

Street & Studio is a collaboration between Tate Modern, London, and Museum Folkwang, Essen. Tate Modern's fourth exhibition dedicated to photography (following *Cruel and Tender*, and retrospectives of Jeff Wall and Robert Frank), it extends Tate's engagement with the variety of photographic practice. At Museum Folkwang, the exhibition continues a longstanding involvement with the history, practices and topics of photography. The idea for the exhibition emerged from an initial discussion between Ute Eskildsen at Museum Folkwang and Emma Dexter at Tate Modern, and it has been our pleasure to be involved at all stages of its subsequent development. Ute Eskildsen has shaped the concept and curated the exhibition in collaboration with Bettina Kaufmann in London and Florian Ebner in Essen. We are grateful for the extraordinary commitment they have shown in realising this project.

The catalogue, designed by Oliver Kimpel of Büro International, provides an exemplary accompaniment and guide to the exhibition. We are grateful to the contributors Ute Eskildsen, Florian Ebner, Susanne Holschbach, Jeremy Millar and Michael Bracewell, for their insightful essays; Florian Ebner and Bettina Kaufmann, for compiling the biographies and the informative context, the translators Ariane Kossack, Stefan Barmann and Daniela Friebel, Arne Reimer for checking and verifying the biographical and historical records, then to the editor Judith Severne for her management of the catalogue, as well as Roger Thorp, James Attlee, and

Beth Thomas, Katherine Rose and Roz Young for picture research, and Celeste Stroll, Sarah Tucker and Emma Woodiwiss in production, Melissa Larner and Hans-Jürgen Lechtreck for copy editing the English and German texts respectively.

We are also indebted to colleagues across a range of Tate functions who have contributed so enthusiastically to this exhibition, such as conservators, art handlers, communications, interpretation and education colleagues, fundraisers and many others: Registrars Hillary Taylor and Juleigh Gordon-Orr and Exhibitions & Displays Coordinator Stephen Mellor and Curatorial Programme Manager Helen Sainsbury; intern Sarah Fletcher for her dedication to the project; Press Officer Daisy Mallabar and Sarah Harrison; Jane Burton, Louise Ramsay and Pete Gomori in Marketing, Communications and Merchandise; Phil Monk, Sam Clarke, Marcia Creppo and the art handling team; Paper Conservators Katharine Lockett, Rachel Crome and Rosie Freemantle; Gabriela Salgado, Gillian Wilson, Simon Bolitho, Sarah Hyde, Sophie Howarth, Kirstie Beaven in Education and Interpretation; Fernando Gutiérrez at Pentagram for design work in the exhibition. We are equally indebted to Robert Knodt, Christiane Schneider, Hendrik von Boxberg, Jens Nober, Hella Nocke-Schrepper and Christiane Kuhlmann, for their contributions to the success of the exhibition at Museum Folkwang. We would particularly like to thank Sheena Wagstaff, Chief Curator at Tate Modern, for her role in the realisation of the exhibition at both museums.

To create an exhibition on this scale and complexity, with nearly 400 works, we relied upon support from a great number of organisations and individuals. We are indebted to numerous public and private collections who have lent so generously to the exhibition. Many of the works are becoming increasingly delicate, and we are deeply grateful to all those owners, both public and private, whose enthusiasm for the project has encouraged them to entrust their precious photographs to our care.

Vicente Todolí   Hartwig Fischer
Director, Tate Modern   *Director, Museum Folkwang*

Introduction
Ute Eskildsen

Let us compare two photographs: the first, Paul Strand's snapshot of a bowler-hatted man in the street, taken at the moment when he turns round to face the camera. The second, a portrait of the poet Ezra Pound, his silhouette barely discernible, by Alvin Langdon Coburn. Both photographs, executed or published around 1917, mark a break with the representational conventions of their time.

The photo of the man in the street conveys an unusual closeness and intimacy. His body occupies the entire picture in a manner hitherto exclusive to studio photography. At the same time, it is caught with a directness of movement that seems to characterise the instant in which it was taken more than the person himself. Indeed, the turn of the body signifies the authenticity of the moment shown. A similar formal reduction appears in Coburn's photograph, more a compositional study than a portrait. Coburn called his series of portraits 'Vorticist photographs'; using mirrors and other means of photographic manipulation, they experiment with the dynamic dissolution of the defined (pictorial) space in which the model is seated. The portrait of Pound is remarkable not in its verisimilitude, but rather in its formal modernity, which interprets both the poet and his work. Taken at different sites – in the street and in the studio – both photographs display a formal radicality that reflects a time of upheaval.

As a medium that records images, photography is exclusively tied to the places in which it is created. Over the course of its development, diverse genres and approaches have evolved, each defined by their circumstantial and spatial contexts. Since the invention of the medium, both portrait and studio photography have taken centre stage. Current theories maintain that the popularity of portraiture was inextricably related to the need of the bourgeoisie to represent itself. A more mobile photographic practice and an aspiring amateur photography meant that portraiture further developed ways of depicting the human subject: the controlled pose under the studio spotlight contrasted with the directness of life in the daylight of the street. *Street & Studio* focuses its attention on the beginning of this juxtaposition. Following many exhibitions presenting either street photography or studio portraiture in the context of nineteenth-century photography, *Street & Studio* simultaneously investigates these two central sites of photographic practice, with a special view to their divergent visual worlds and their dynamic interaction.

The subtitle of the exhibition, 'An Urban History of Photography', indicates that from its beginning photography has been a medium of the city, and refers to the modern metropolises that grew and developed, first in the West and later worldwide. The city is the social milieu in which the studio, followed by the street, became prospering sites for taking photographs of the human subject. From different perspectives, the studio and the street reveal contrary aspects of the city: the representational facade of the bourgeois subject and the common face of the man or woman in the crowd.

The popularity of studio photography in the nineteenth century was primarily characterised by a formalised and standardised production format, such as the *carte de visite*. In the shelter of the studio, and with the help of props and backdrops, the model's pose evolved into a general cultural practice. At the same time, ambitious photographers saw it as an artistic challenge to 'construct' the portrait rather than yield to the natural expression of the sitter. In the 1920s and the 1930s, the portrait studio as well as the fashion atelier became exclusive sites where visual fantasies and sophisticated arrangements could be realised.

At the same time, itinerant and improvised portrait studios appeared in the streets or in market places worldwide – long forgotten in the Western world today. Without wanting to present a comprehensive social history of the photo studio, the exhibition documents a multitude of ways in which the portrait studio has both exercised visual habits and fostered different photographic approaches – deriving from the expectations of the public as well as the whim of the photographer.

In the early days of the medium, street photography was still primarily a matter of staging: it was the introduction of smaller and less conspicuous cameras at the end of the nineteenth century that turned a new page in the history of photography. These cameras offered the possibility of observing people in unexpected, fleeting, even intimate moments. In this way, the street became an extension of the studio and, at the same time, provided the ground for visual adventures and experiments in everyday life. In the years following the First World War, the city, together with the new technologies of communication and public transport, became the centre point of an ever more accelerating modern life. Until the late 1930s, a widespread faith in the modern city prevailed, but after the Second World War this social, modernistic utopia gave way to disillusionment and visual accounts of isolation, as well as to a humanistic search for an encounter with the other. From that time on, many photographers saw the street as an indicator of the condition of society.

Street and studio photography have each developed their own stories and modes of representation. Even whilst acknowledging their fundamental geographic difference, the diverse contexts and functions of the images, and the technical conditions of their production, it is possible to see that they do nonetheless share some similar themes and comparable approaches. *Street & Studio* shows the interrelation of these two centres of photographic production: how the street has become a site of performativity and the studio one of authenticity. Where photographers adopted with a new and original vision – in artistic, journalistic and documentary projects as much as fashion photography – parameters were transgressed.

The exhibition looks at the representational appearance of the common man in the studio; as well as the growing number of fashion photographers who, since the 1950s, have preferred to work outdoors, in the streets. It also traces the strategies of photographers who, since the 1980s, have tended to direct their work in a very deliberate and almost cinematic manner or whose documentary approach follows meticulous plans. While the structured work of certain street projects may be seen to reflect studio portraiture, the dynamic pose of some studio works is in turn reminiscent of the rhythm of the street. It is no coincidence that the specificities of both sites – the noncommittal anonymity of the street and the spatial privacy of the studio – led, in the 1920s, to a rapid spread of the Photobooth. The Photomaton was initially an inexpensive and useful machine to make photos for the identity card required by the State; later, it turned into a playful instrument for producing images.

The theoretical perspectives guiding this exhibition are the notions of visibility and character typology. The question of visibility refers to the self-confident representation of the individual in front of the studio camera – who, if at all, is able to represent themself? It also refers to the exposure of hitherto ignored and overlooked subjects in the street. This is why the desire for *emancipation*, a crucial aspect of urban culture, is one of the most important socio-artistic concepts behind the form and function of many photographs. This social emancipation – in the sense of civil rights, racial and sexual liberation and self-determination – is expressed through different forms of posing and through an appropriation of both sites as stages for the human subject's self-portrayal and transformation. Photo portraits by photographers as varied as James van der Zee, Madame Yevonde, Malick Sidibé, Samuel Fosso, Peter Hujar, Robert Mapplethorpe, Laurie Anderson, Andres Serrano and Sunil Gupta provide examples of the different facets of portrait photography.

The notion of character typology refers to a more documentary approach to photography that has given vivid expression to the urban figures shaping our image of the city. Photography has greatly influenced our conception of the metropolis and its inhabitants; it has stimulated our imagination and awakened an interest in odd characters and 'freaks'. Typological modes of representation are inherent to photography – and are particularly relevent for the portrait photography included in this exhibition. Beyond the individual approaches, methods and perspectives of certain photographers – among them August Sander, Walker Evans, Brassaï, Lisette Model, Cindy Sherman in her early works, as well as less renowned names like Louis Vert or Friedrich Seidenstücker – the overview provided by this exhibition gives a comprehensive typological account of the photographic figures of the city.

City photographs often show unpretentious sites, views of buildings and monuments, everyday situations and disastrous changes – they document times of prosperity, times of stagnation and traces of disappearing urban spaces – but they also show people, inhabitants, the actors of urbanisation. *Street & Studio* commences at the turn of the nineteenth century. Back in 1903, the New York critic Sidney Allan could not imagine a better place with more artistic potential for 'out-door' photography than the city's Jewish quarter: 'The settings for a picture are ready at every moment of the day.'[1] The idea of the city as a self-generating source of images and the vision of being able to grasp every moment as an image became a reality after the invention and general use of instantaneous photography in the late 1880s.

Pictorialist photography around 1900, with its nature-oriented motifs and private worlds, took little interest in the urban sphere. However, in contrast to the increasingly fashion-oriented studio photography, several European photographers came to discover and appropriate the vitality of the street. In their motifs and approach, the photographs of Henri Rivière and Jacques Henri Lartigue, taken between 1890 and 1910, already reveal those aspects that would fascinate a future

1 Sidney Allan, 'Picturesque New York in Four Pages: The Esthetic Side of Jewtown', in *Camera Notes*, vol.6, no.3, 1903, p.146.

generation of street photographers. And the self-promotion of professional European photographers in the early years of the twentieth century clearly reveals an entire thematic spectrum of transition and crossover – between studio and documentary photography, between large-format and instantaneous photography, between portrait, urban and industrial photography.

After the First World War, urban space was, for the most part, visually defined by photography and film. According to Béla Balász, the mobile camera 'not only [produces] new things, but always also new distances and perspectives'.[2] This was, for him, the novelty of an art that was technologically determined. The mobility of the camera could be equated with urban perception. From light portable apparatuses to even smaller ones and the first 35mm camera with a mechanical film-advance lever and higher film sensitivity, the camera offered new ways of observing and interpreting the subjects of everyday urban life. 'The adventure of using the camera to penetrate areas and record events never before captured as images became a source of fascination for early photo journalism, a career which attracted a large number of intellectuals.'[3]

The further formal development of photographic images in the twentieth century must be seen in the wider context of public printed images – the booming illustrated magazines, the popular postcards, the prosperous market for photo books and the exhibitions of modern photography, a particular trend in Germany's Weimar Republic. These times of social change paved the way for a wide-ranging press photography and, along with it, new possibilities emerged for studio photography and for the fashion and advertising industries. For this reason, the late 1920s were a time in which the two sites central to photography – the street and the studio – became increasingly dependant on a growing print market.

The important role of the media should not be underestimated when considering the representation of the middle classes developing at the same time. Cecil Beaton intended his lavish studio photographs to be distributed in the media. Glamour had become a visual currency of modern society. And quite a few photographers have since unveiled the darker sides and the discreet charm of the bourgeoisie. Model's portraits show middle-class characters in the street in emphatic bodily poses that are at variance with their social typecasting.

The later figure of the paparazzi-photographer, who preys on urban celebrity culture, is part of the iconographic context of the bourgeoisie. He is a player in the subtle game revolving around the presence of the star who, in turn, seeks to control his or her public appearance. The *image* of the star created in the studios of famous photographers is tested in the street for its authenticity. The street can be seen as a site of unmasking, whereas the 'paparazzi look' has progressed into a style of fashion photography. The digital age has cultivated a new ubiquity for celebrities. This is shown in the work of the young Icelandic artist Kristleifur Björnsson, who uses internet images of famous stars, including official press photos as well as amateur snapshots taken by fans. Here, internet forums follow the tradition of journals and illustrated magazines.

2 Béla Balász, *Der Geist des Films*, Halle 1930, p.9.

3 Herbert Molderings, *Fotografie in der Weimarer Republik. Stationen der Fotografie II*, Berlin 1988, pp.11 et seq.

In the words of Rem Koolhaas, the renowned Dutch architect, 'The great singularity of the characterless city (of today) is its ability to do without everything that lacks function – to discard everything that is no longer useful – in order to crack open the asphalt layer of idealism and to accept everything that comes up from the ground instead … The characterless city is all that remains of what was once the city.'[4] Today, many young photographers direct their attention to the obvious signs of a globalised culture in the Western world. The Swiss photographer Beat Streuli has commented: 'The young people I photograph in European and American cities do not really seem to differ much from one another. I think there is a kind of stereotypical look to young people all over the Western world. I am always particularly interested in normality and its traces.'[5] But could photographs taken in Brussels, like those shown in the exhibition, also have been made in Istanbul? Streuli is 'in no way [interested] in a kind of "global conformity" … First and foremost, I want to show that similarities and resemblances between different cultures or people are as important and "worth seeing" as the differences are.'

It remains to be seen in which way the booming megalopolises in many parts of the world will expand urban iconography: 'There is a lot happening in cities these days', the American sociologist Saskia Sassen believes, 'but gone is the idea of the agora as a place where these developments intersected. Nowadays instead of public space you often have only public access.'[6]

The scope of *Street & Studio* is far-reaching and dialogically conceived. It follows a chronological order and makes connections between what is separated by time and space, reflecting continuities and ruptures in photographic portrayals. Divided into fourteen sections, the exhibition showcases approximately 350 works, including photographs in the form of prints, projections and images published in books and magazines. The catalogue has two main sections – comprising images and textual contributions – that define the programme of *Street & Studio*. The essays by Susanne Holschbach and Florian Ebner introduce central questions of photography; the essays by Michael Bracewell and Jeremy Millar further contribute to aspects of historico-cultural reflection. Taking the portrait studio as a departure point, Susanne Holschbach comments on the myriad aspects of the pose, including particular aspects of mobile photography of the street. Florian Ebner traces our fascination with the character types of urban life from the perspective of the observant pedestrian. Michael Bracewell's text discusses the development of urban culture through the agency of modern writers and a pop-culture *bohème*. Assuming that the street was always also a studio, Jeremy Millar draws parallels between photography and film, as well as the image of photography in film. The comprehensive index, compiled by Florian Ebner and Bettina Kaufmann, provides information and commentaries on the works exhibited, including technical data on the photographs as well as biographies of their authors, and the specific contexts of their aesthetic evolution. As a supplement to the chronological section of images, an overview of diverse character types that can be traced through different eras can be found at the front and end of the catalogue.

4 Rem Koolhaas, 'Die Stadt ohne Eigenschaften', in Theodora Vischer (ed.), *Dan Graham: The Suburban City*, exh. cat., Museum für Gegenwartskunst, Basel 1997, p.15.

5 Beat Streuli, from a text based on the lecture 'Photography into the Museum' at the Museum for Contemporary Art, Barcelona, May 1996.

6 Taken from an interview with Petra Steinberger, 'Verzweifelte Massen. Die US-Soziologin Saskia Sassen über die Zukunft der Stadt', in *Süddeutsche Zeitung*, 25 February 2008, p.12.

I would like to extend a special word of thanks to the assistant curators, Florian Ebner and Bettina Kaufmann, for their dedicated and trusting cooperation in this project. My thanks also go to all participating staff at Tate Modern, the Museum Folkwang and Tate Publishing.

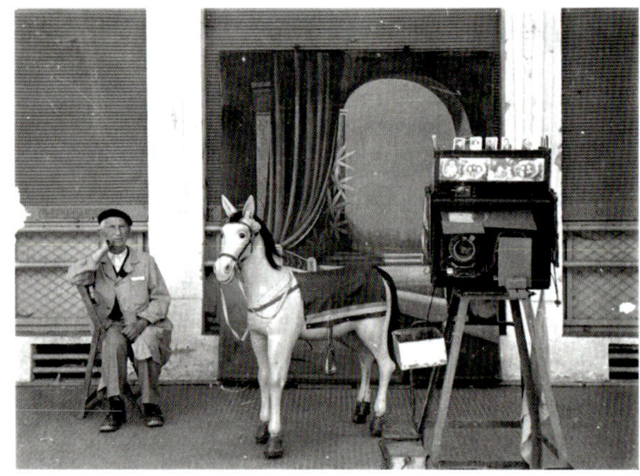

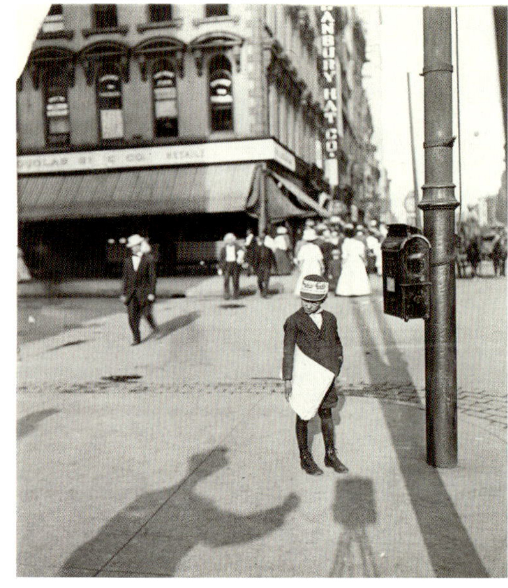

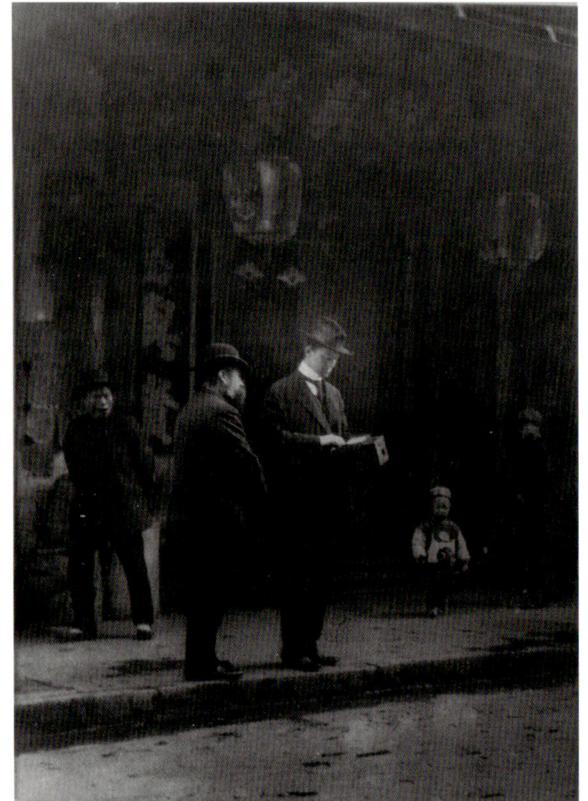

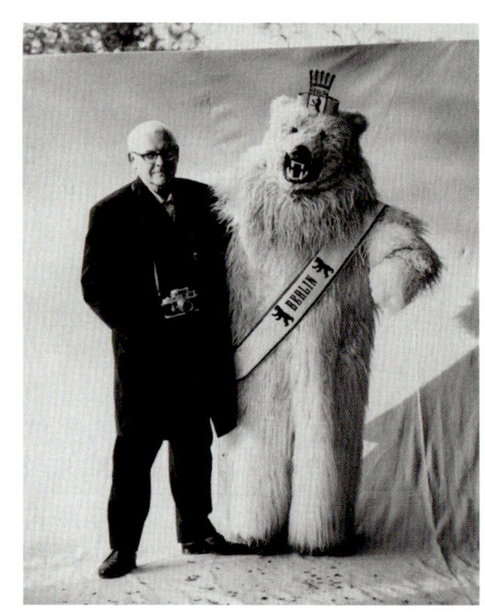

Photographers at Work

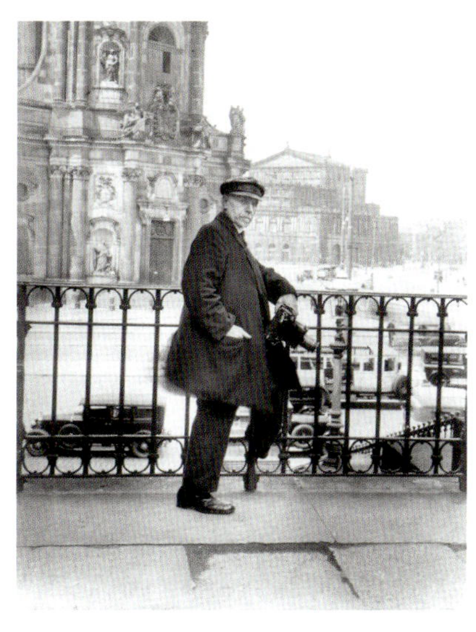

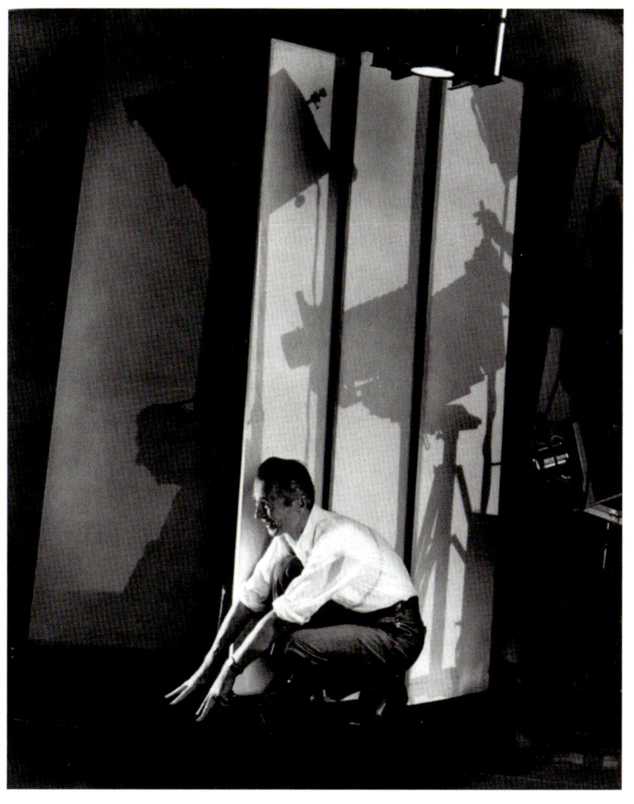

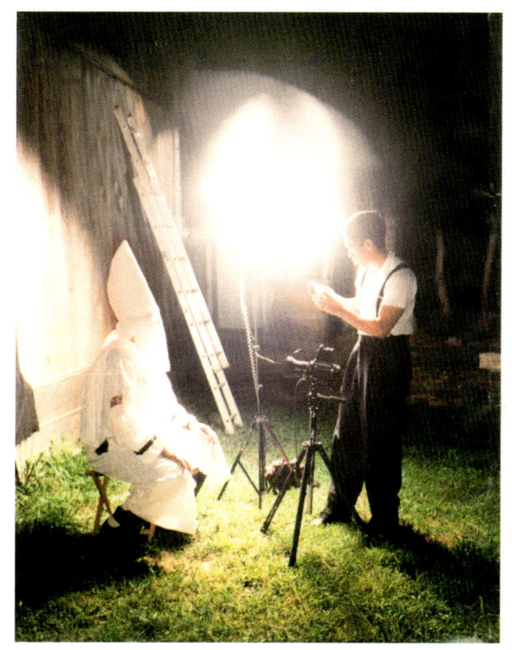

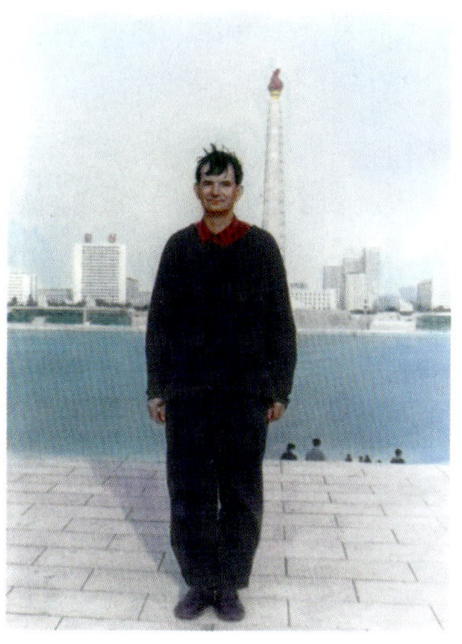

Carl Durheim
Edizioni Brogi
Galerie Contemporaine
Charles Nègre
Henri Rivière
Camille Silvy
Giorgio Sommer
John Thomson
Louis Vert

Camille Silvy, *Déclaration. L'Ordre du jour de l'Empereur à l'armée pour aller en Italie* (Declaration. The Emperor's Order of the Day for the Army for Italy), 1859

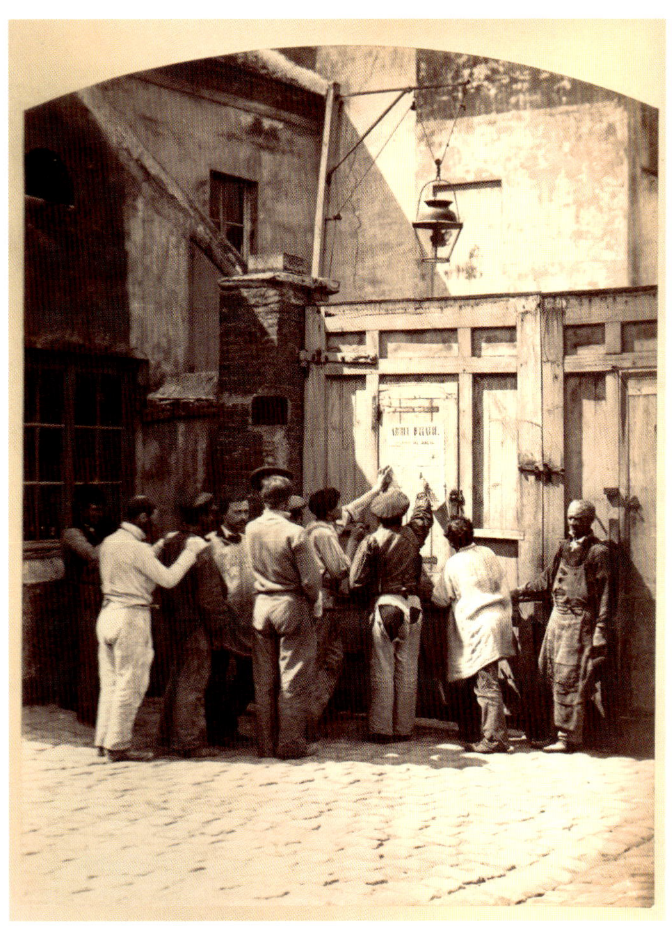

Charles Nègre, *Les Ramoneurs en marche* (Chimney Sweeps Walking), before May 1852

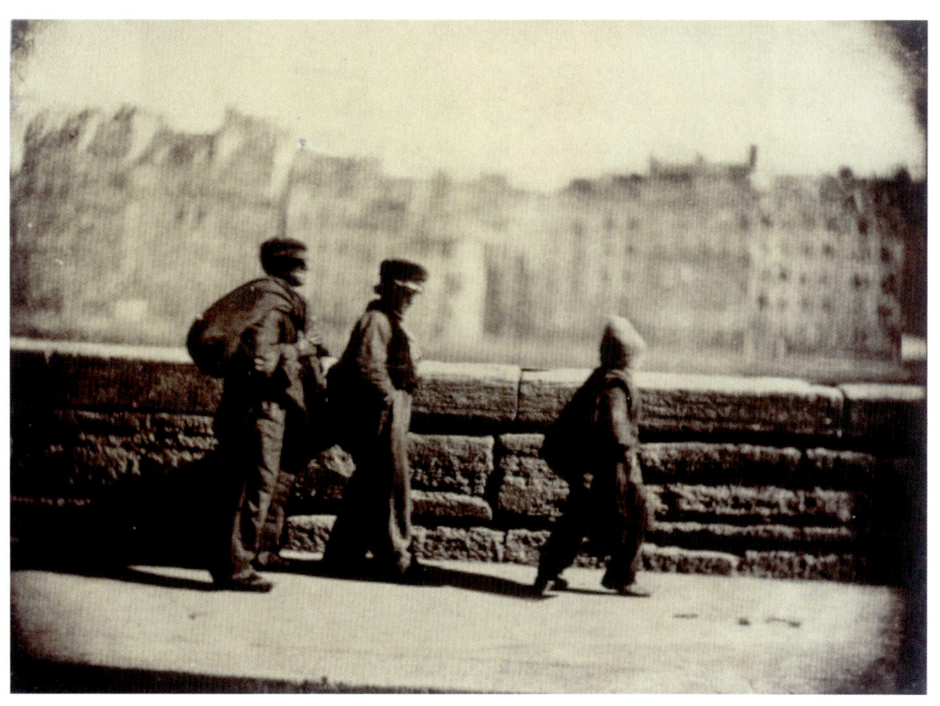

Henri Rivière, *Un Couple rentrant dans un bâtiment public*
(A Couple Entering a Public Building), 1885–95

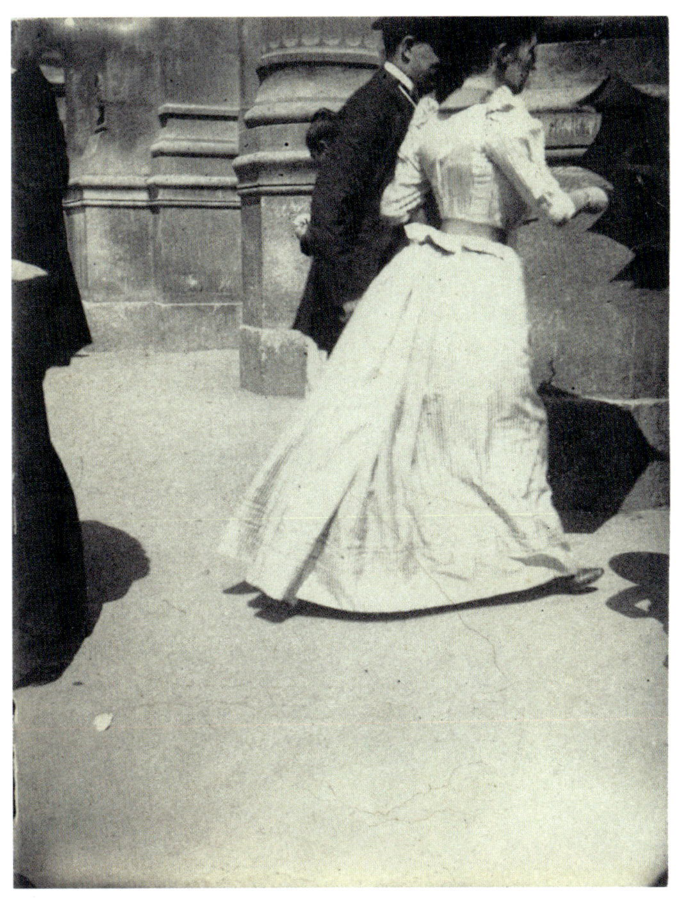

Henri Rivière, *Un Couple rentrant dans un bâtiment public*
(A Couple Entering a Public Building), 1885–95

Carl Durheim, *Joseph Ackermann, 37 Jahre alt* (Joseph Ackermann, 37 Years Old), 1852–3

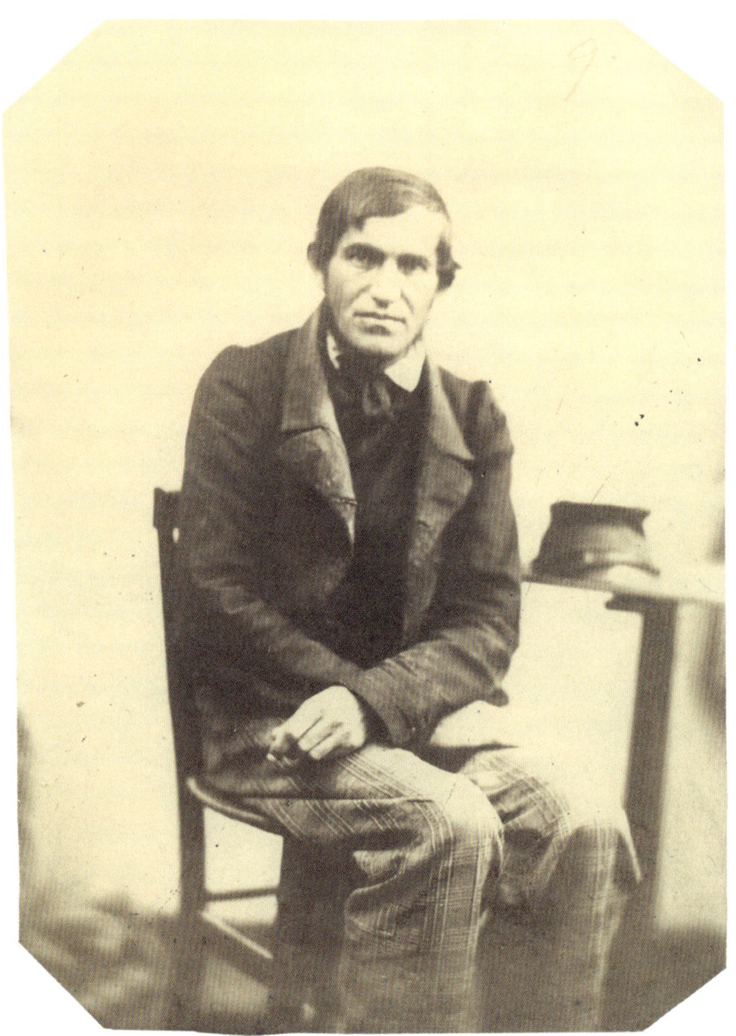

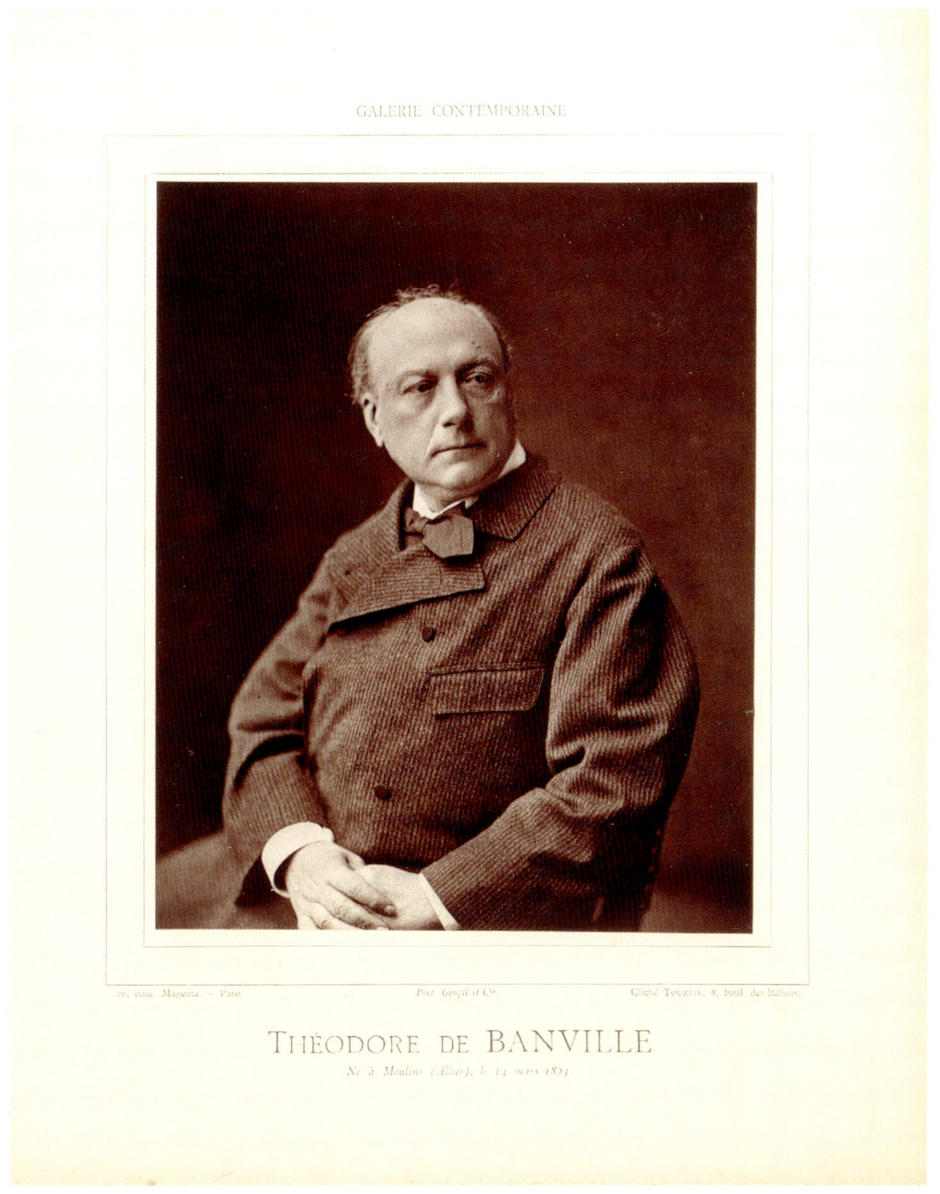

GALERIE CONTEMPORAINE
THÉODORE DE BANVILLE

Giorgio Sommer, *Mangiatori di maccheroni, Napoli* (Macaroni Eaters, Naples), c.1885

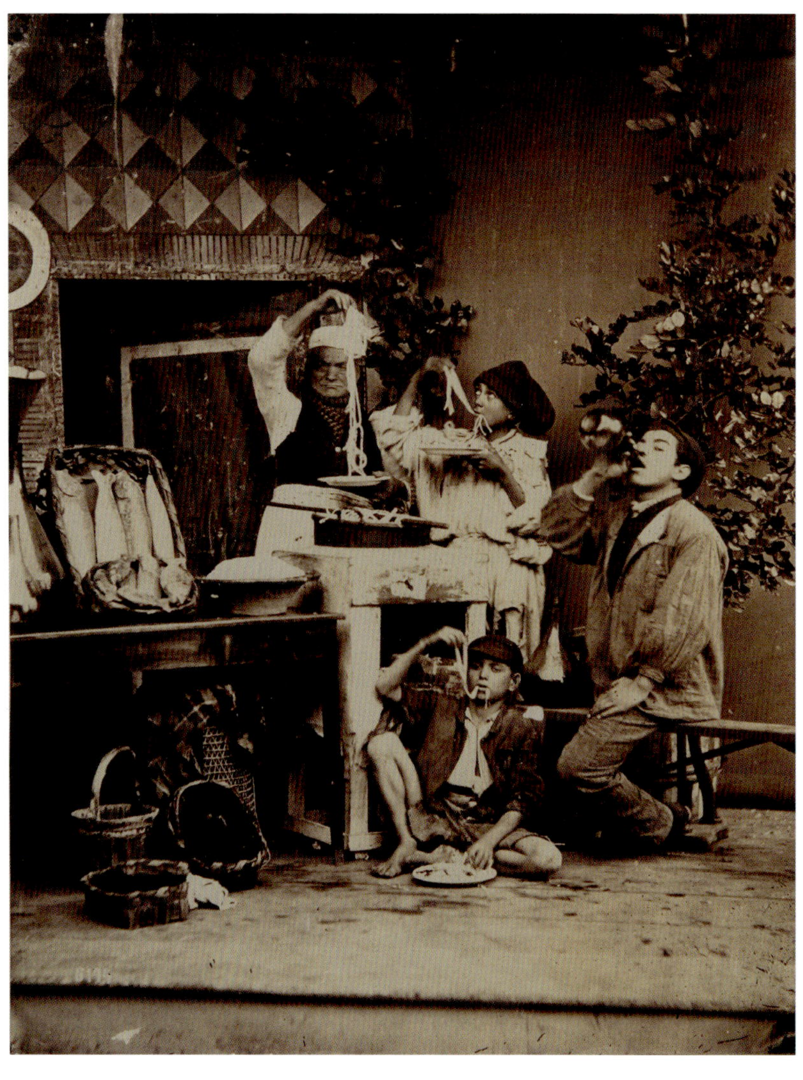

Edizioni Brogi, *Maccheronaio, Napoli* (Macaroni Factory, Naples)
1880

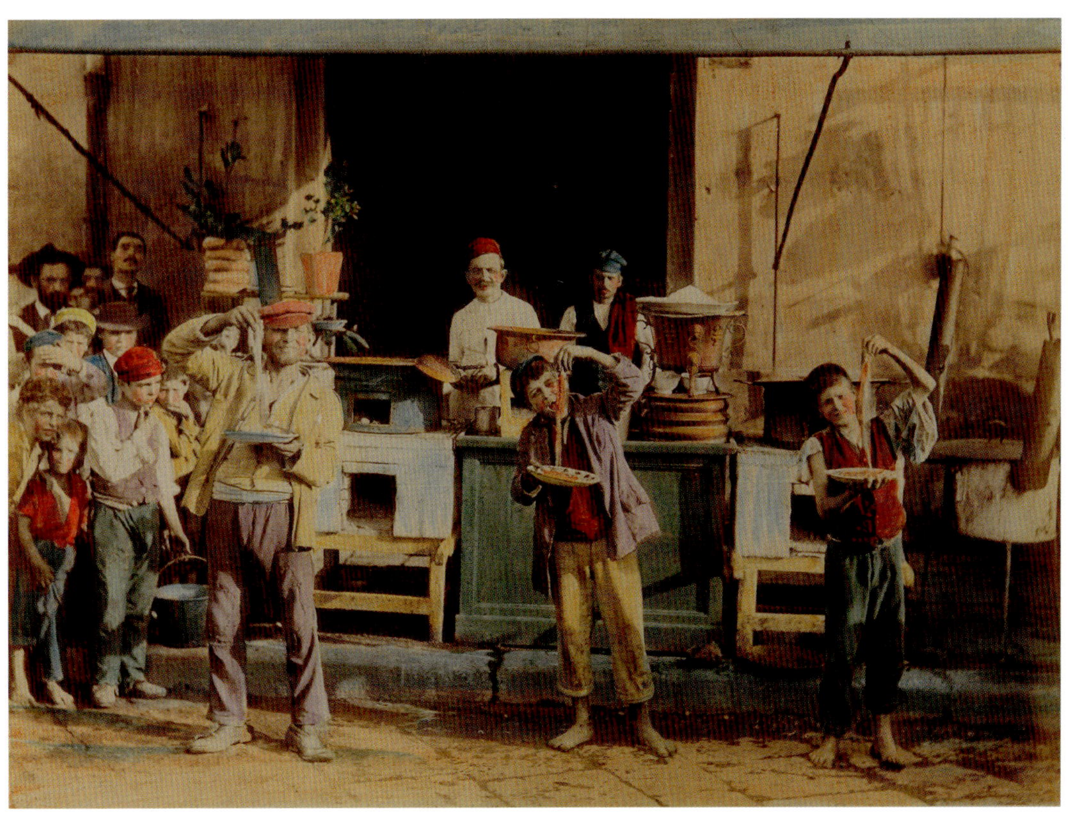

John Thomson, from *Street Life in London*, *The Temperance Sweep*, 1877

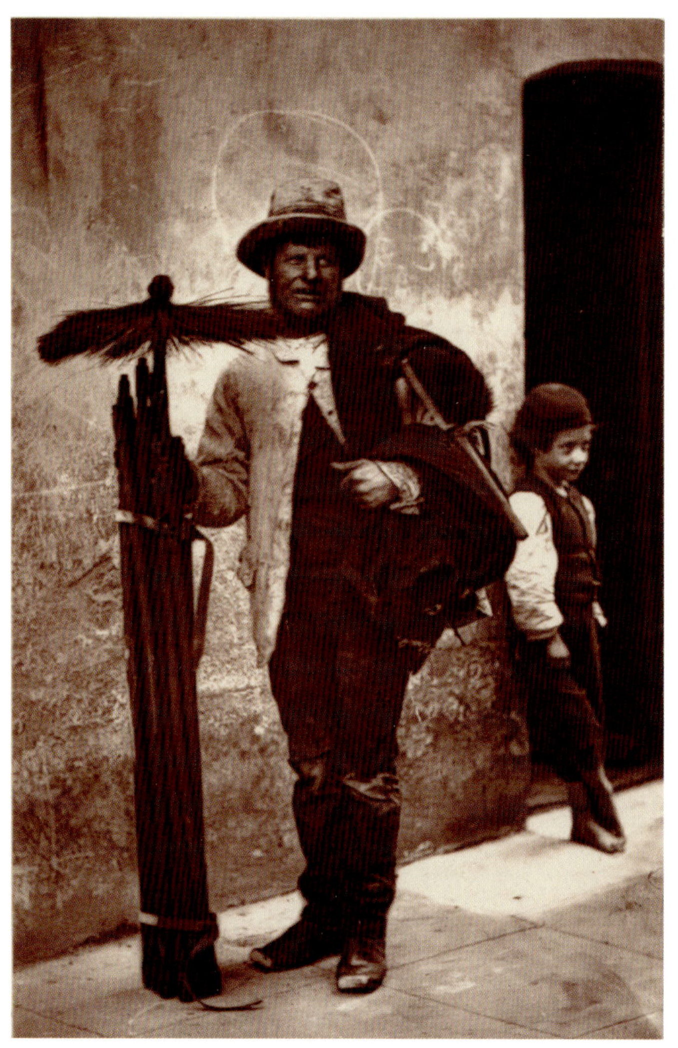

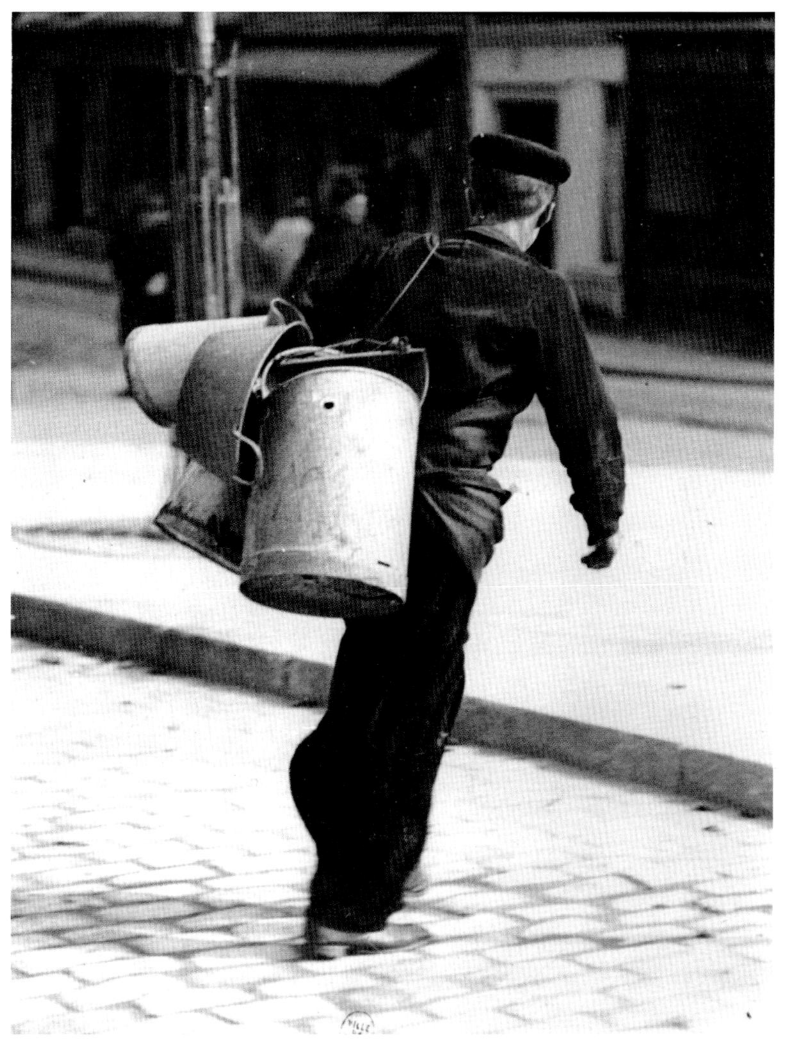

Alvin Langdon Coburn
Baron Adolf de Meyer
Hugo Erfurth
Jacques Henri Lartigue
Arnold Genthe
Lewis Hine
Madame d'Ora
Alfred Stieglitz
Paul Strand
Street Photographers

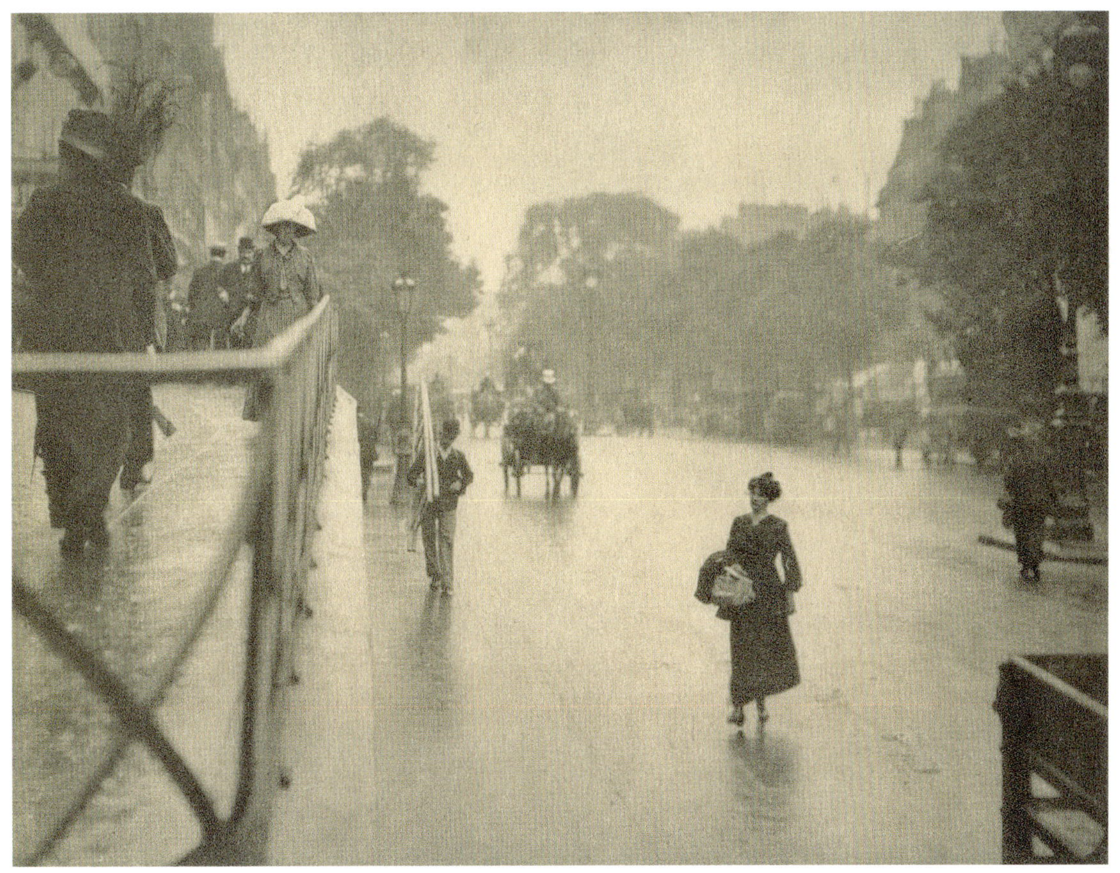

 Paul Strand, *Wall Street, New York*, 1915

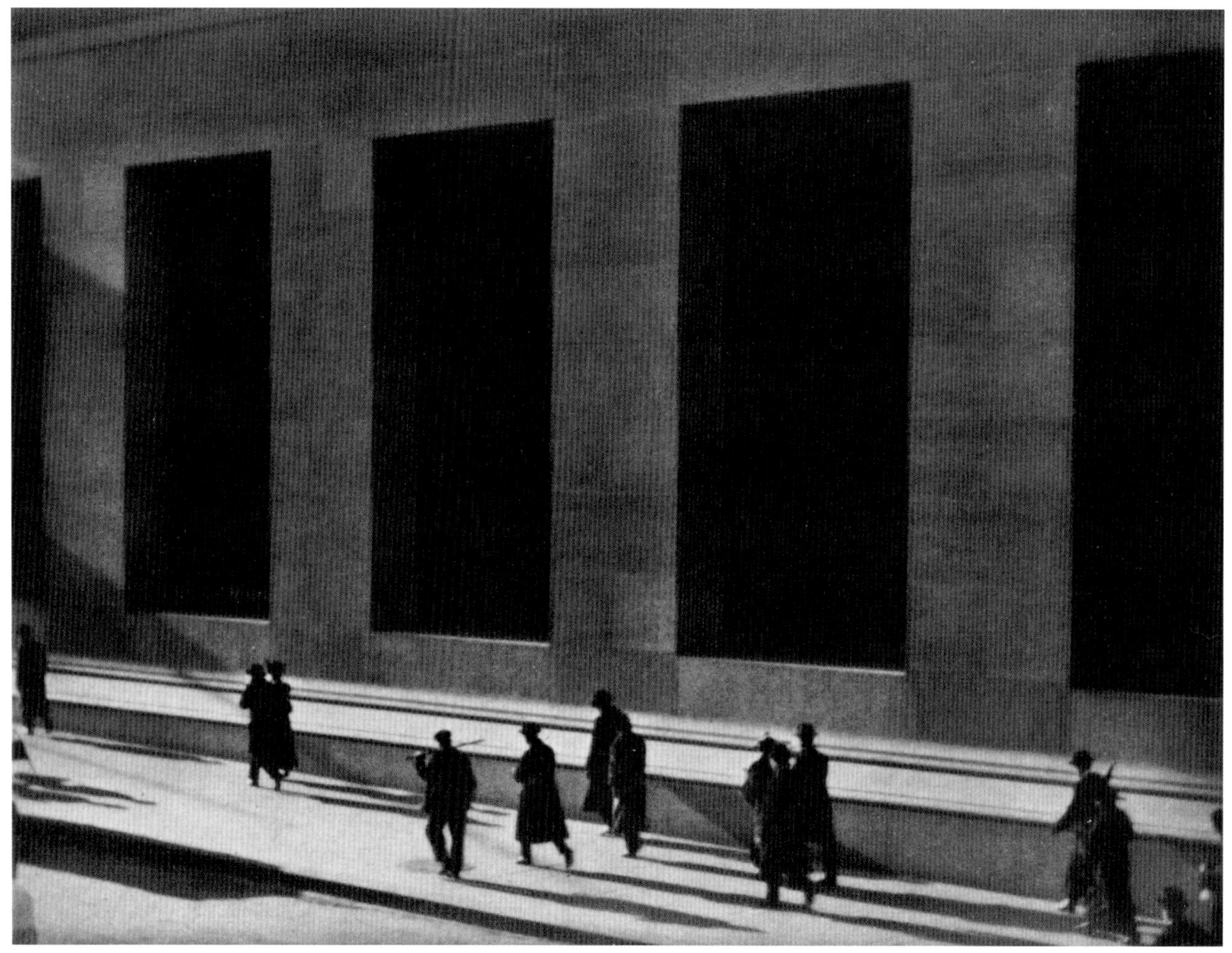

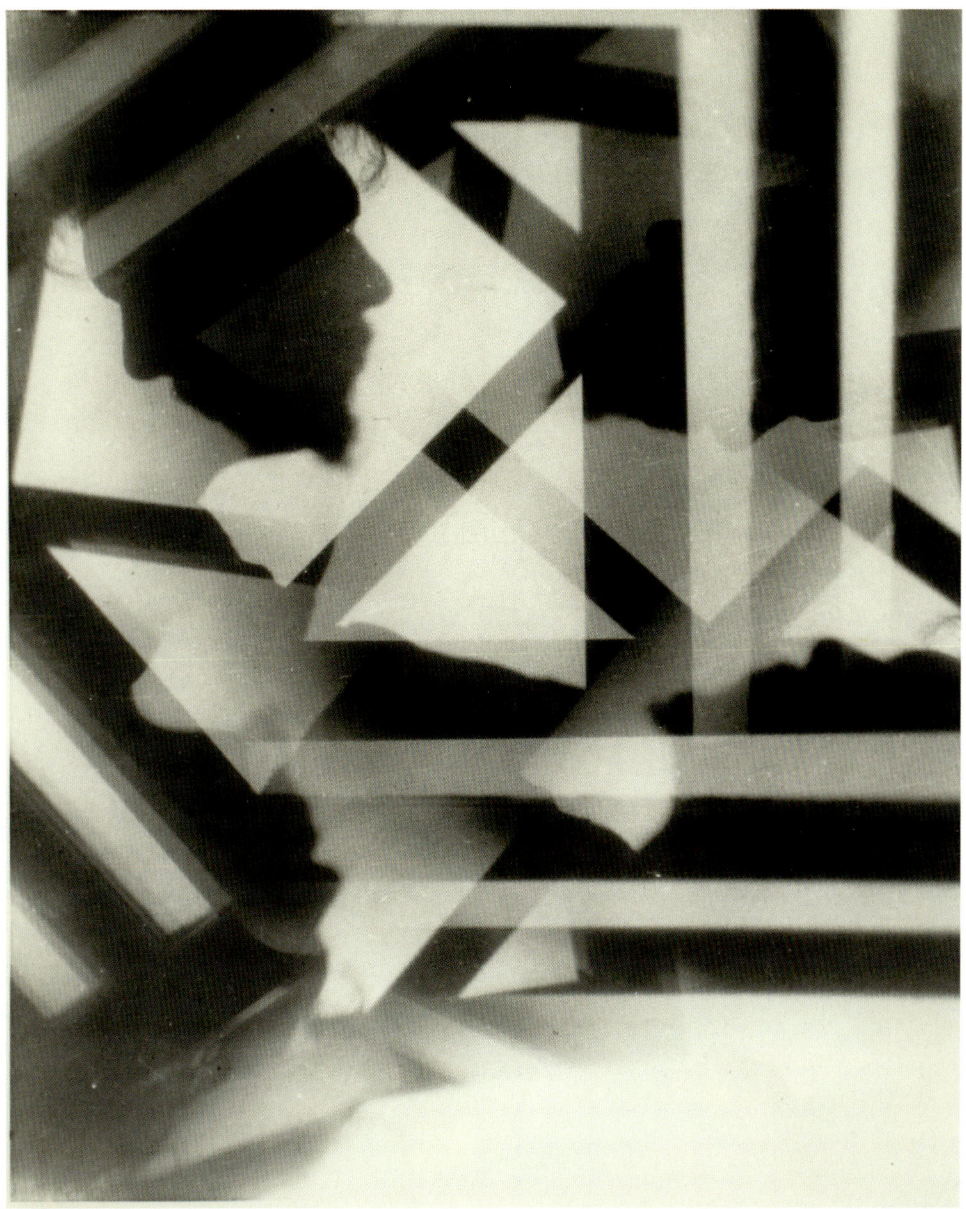

Alvin Langdon Coburn, *Vortograph of Ezra Pound*, c.1917

Baron Adolf de Meyer, *Mannequin, Elizabeth Arden Advertisement,* c.1926

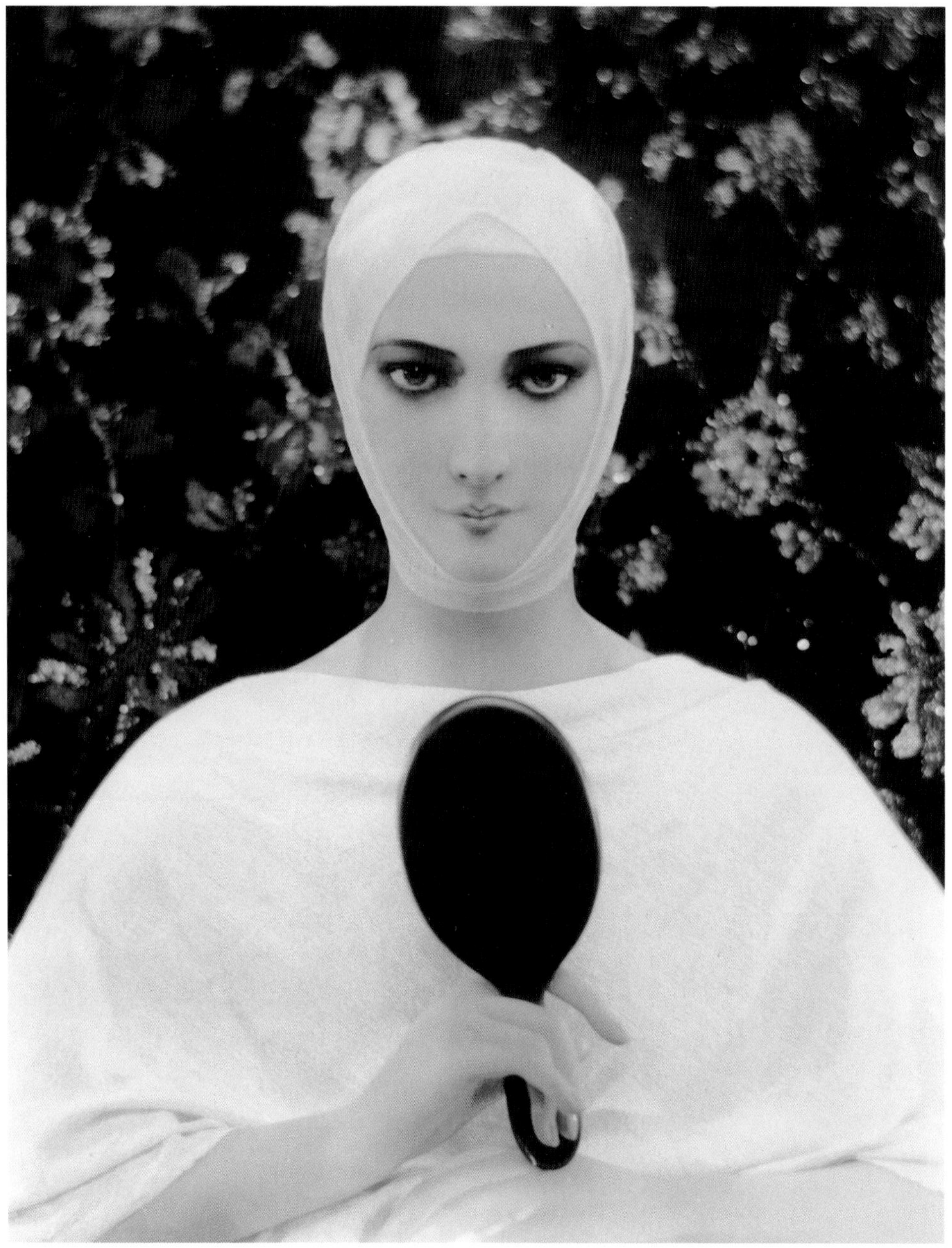

Baron Adolf de Meyer, *Mannequin, Elizabeth Arden Advertisement,* c.1926

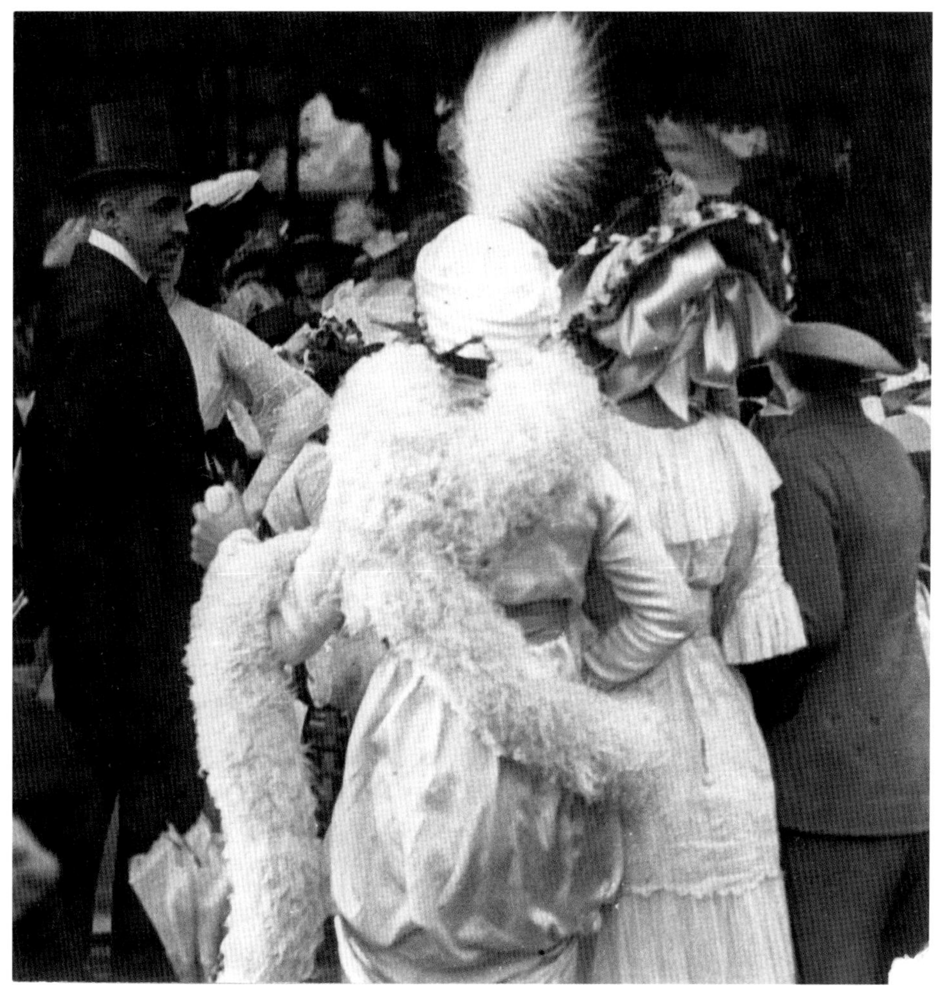

Jacques Henri Lartigue, *Paris, 28 juin 1912* (Paris, 28 June 1912), 1912

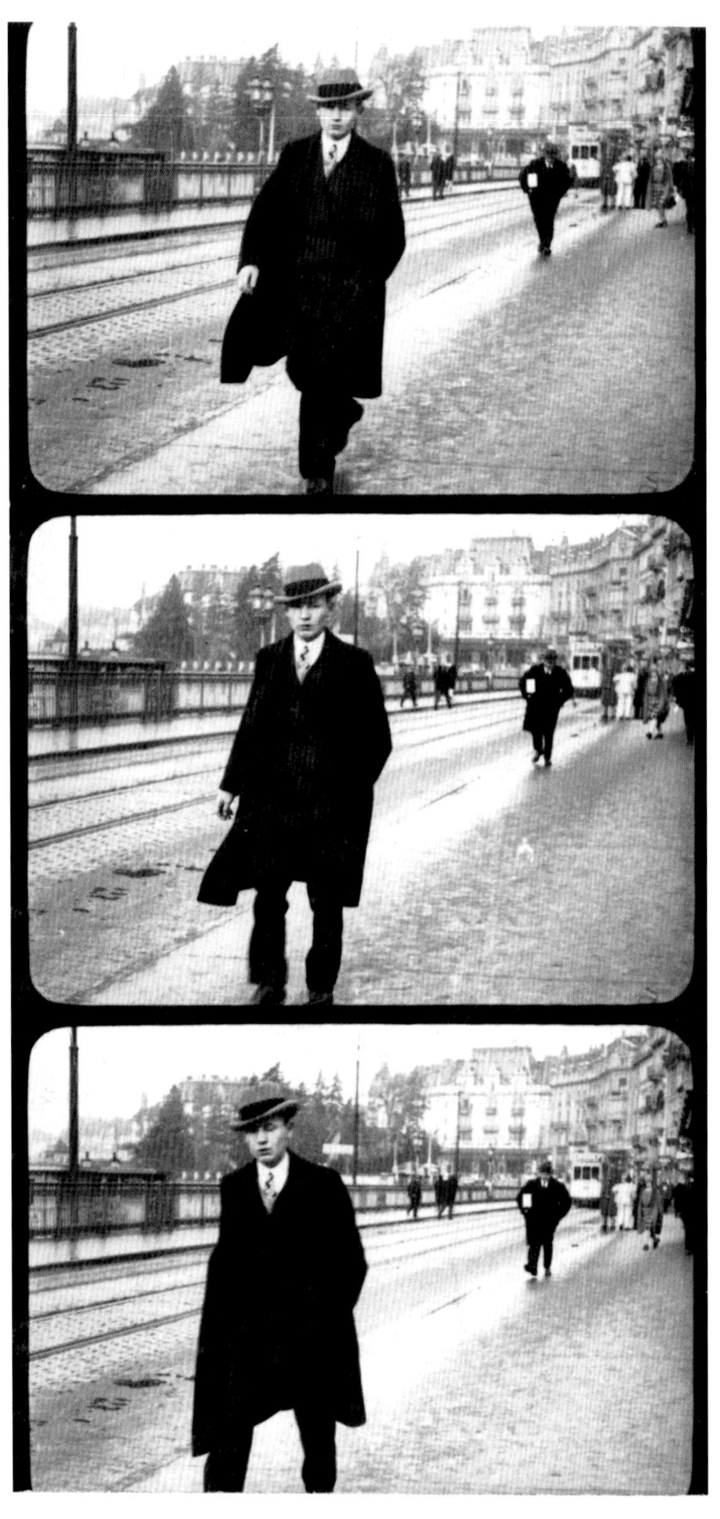

Street Photographer, *'Surprise Photograph'*, c.1925

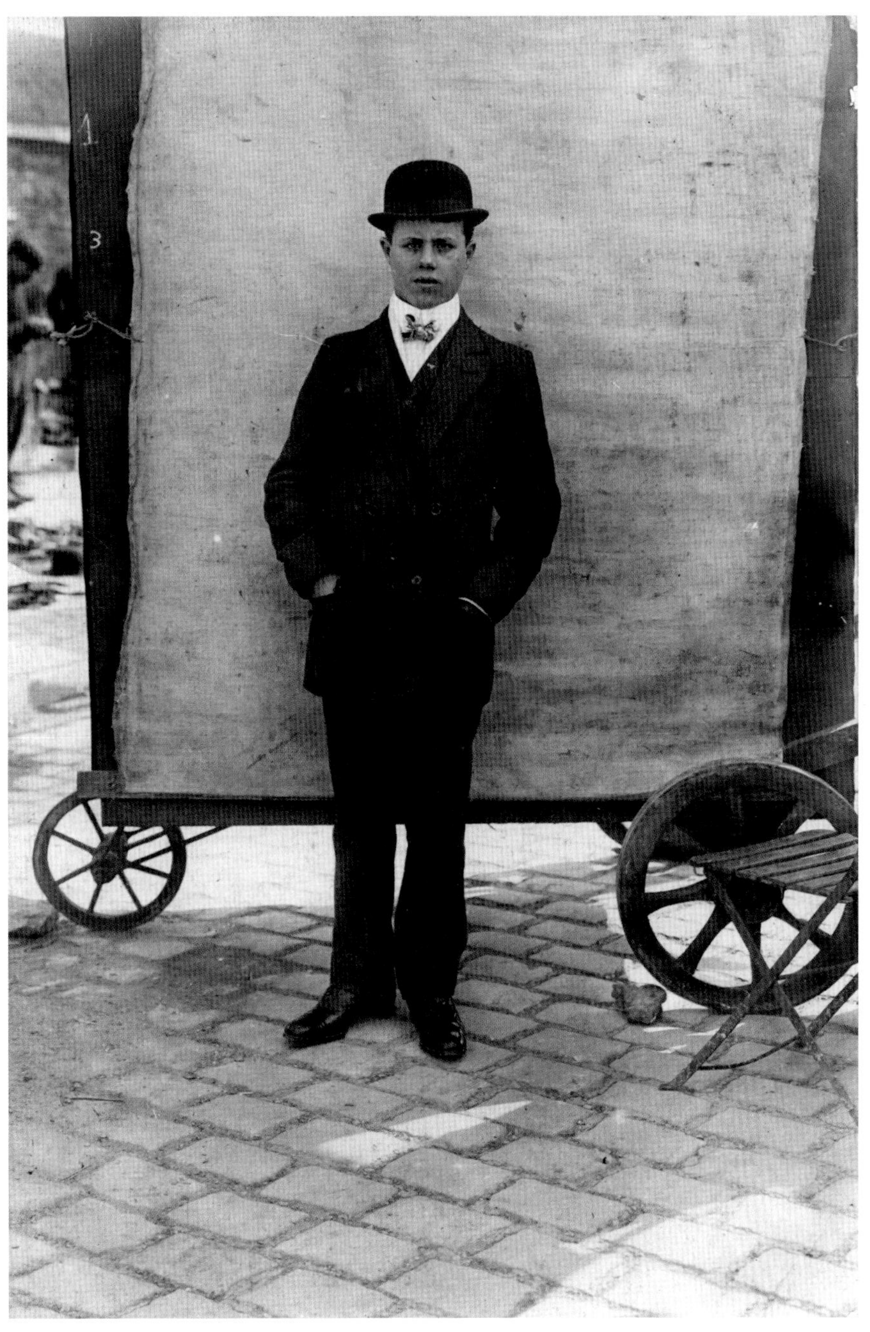

  Lewis Hine, *The Mendicants*, 1910

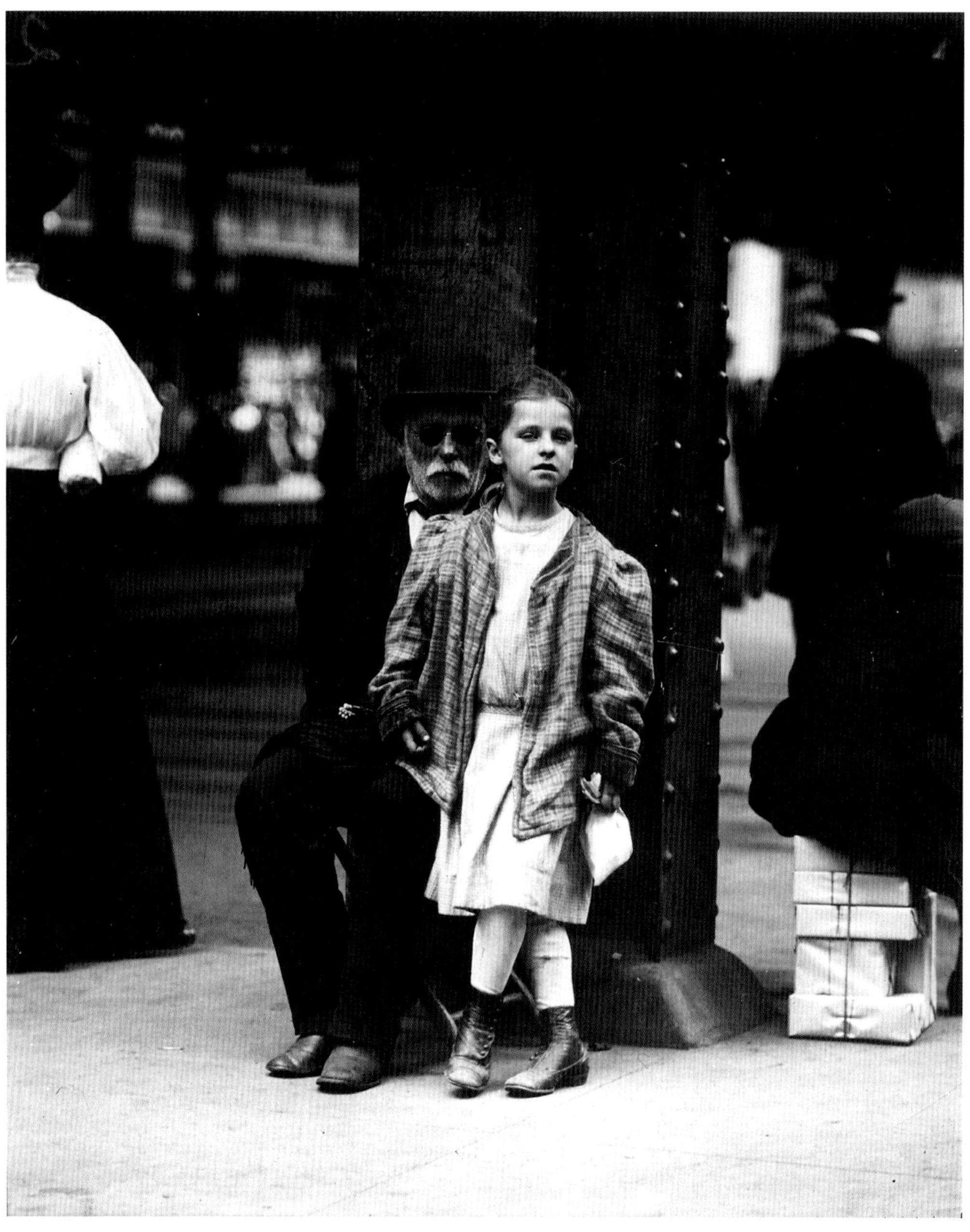

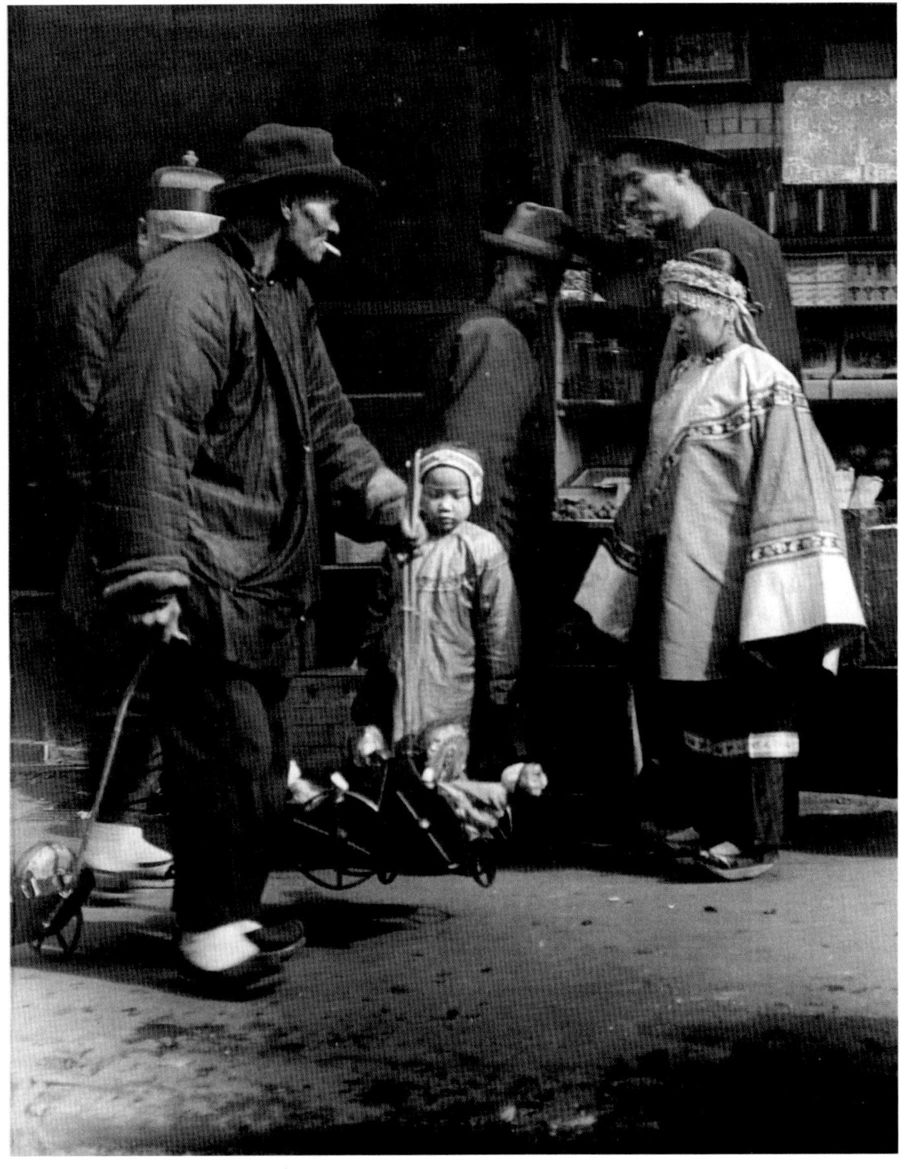

Hugo Erfurth, *Maria Carmi*, 1914

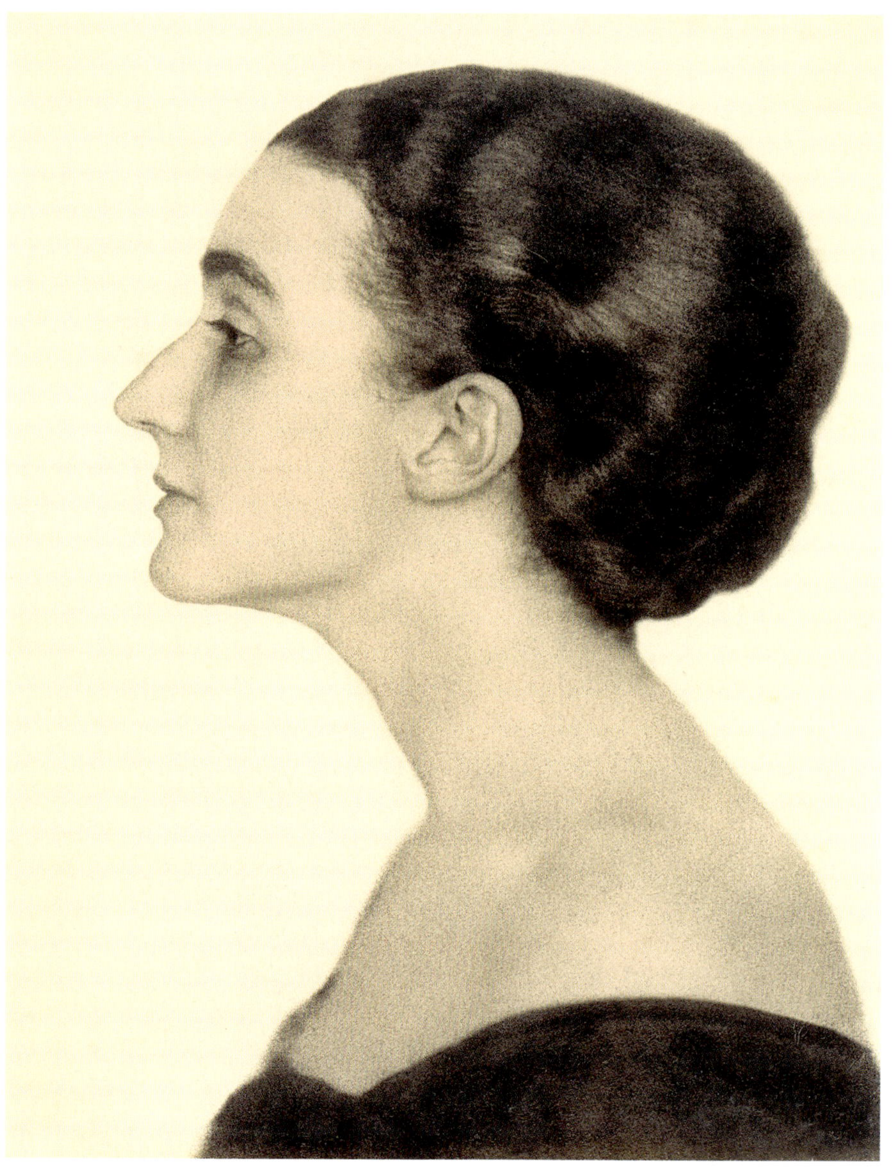

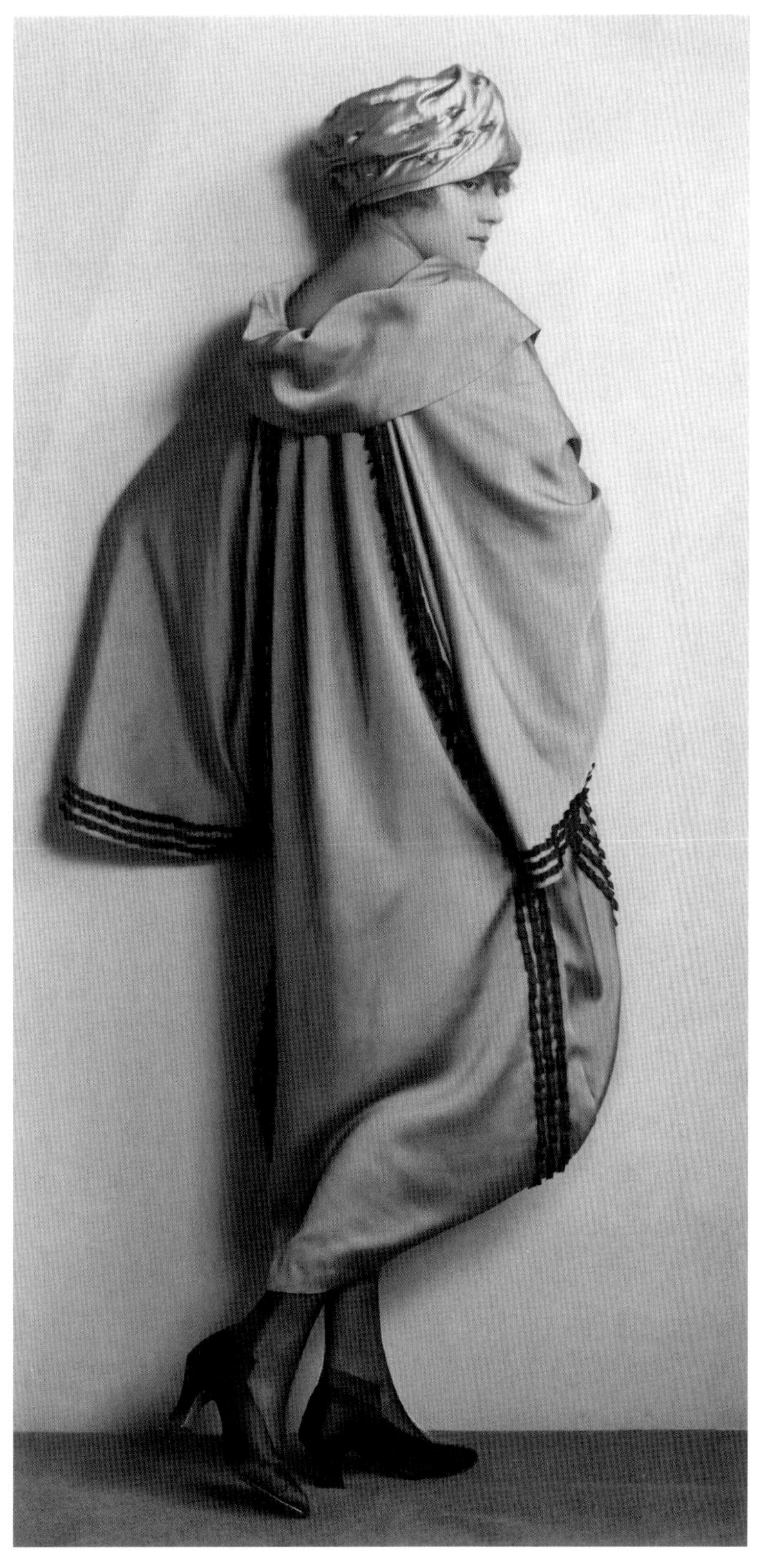

Manuel Álvarez Bravo
Cecil Beaton
Brassaï
Henri Cartier-Bresson
Martín Chambi
Department of Police, Bureau
of Identification, Chicago
Walker Evans
Helmar Lerski
Helen Levitt
Madame Yevonde
Lisette Model
Lee Miller
Cas Oorthuys
Photobooth / Photomaton
August Sander
Friedrich Seidenstücker
Edward Steichen
Umbo
James van der Zee
Weegee
Yva

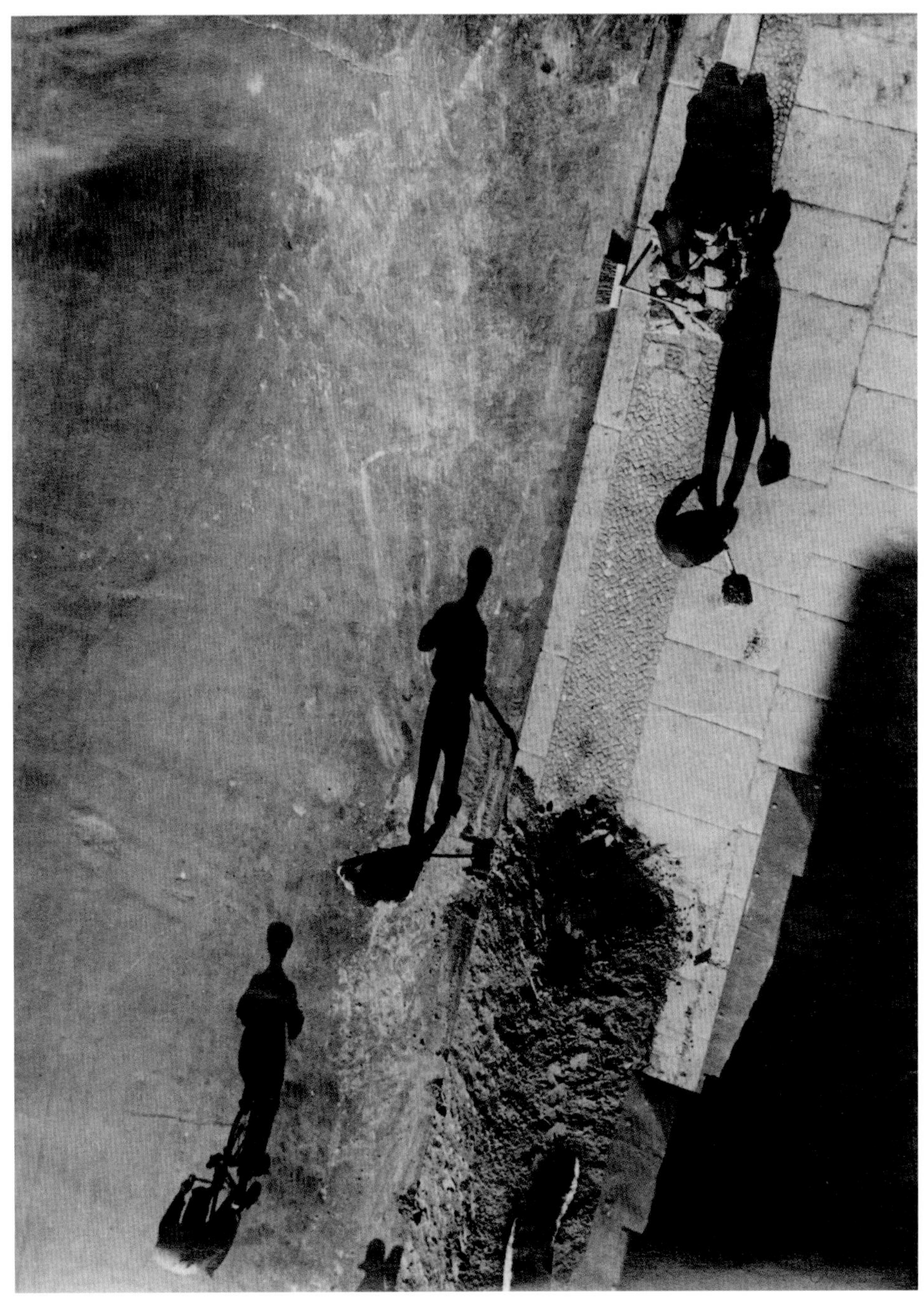

     Yva, *Asta Nielson* and *Max Liebermann*, before August 1930

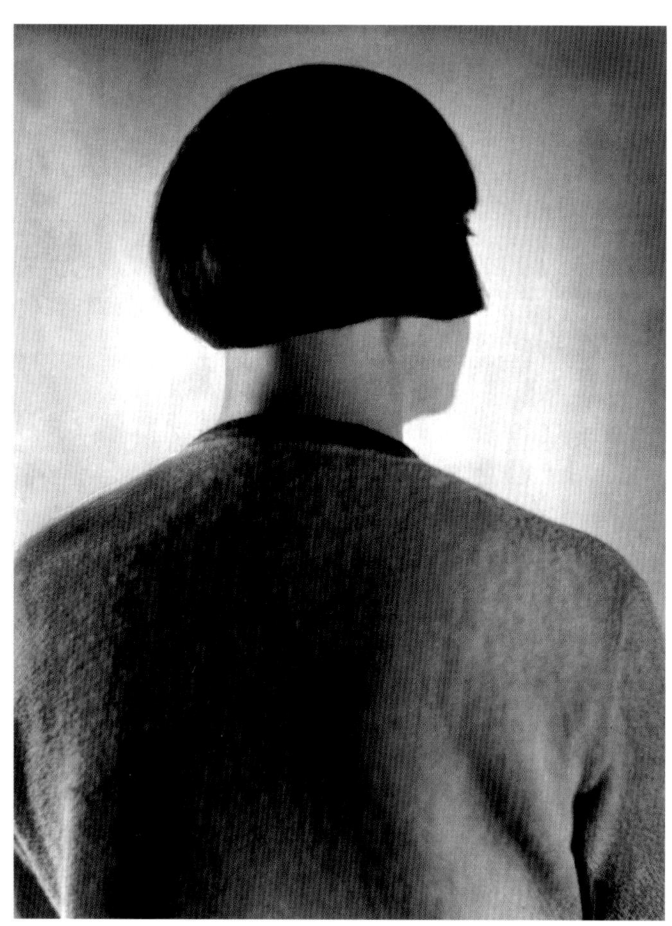
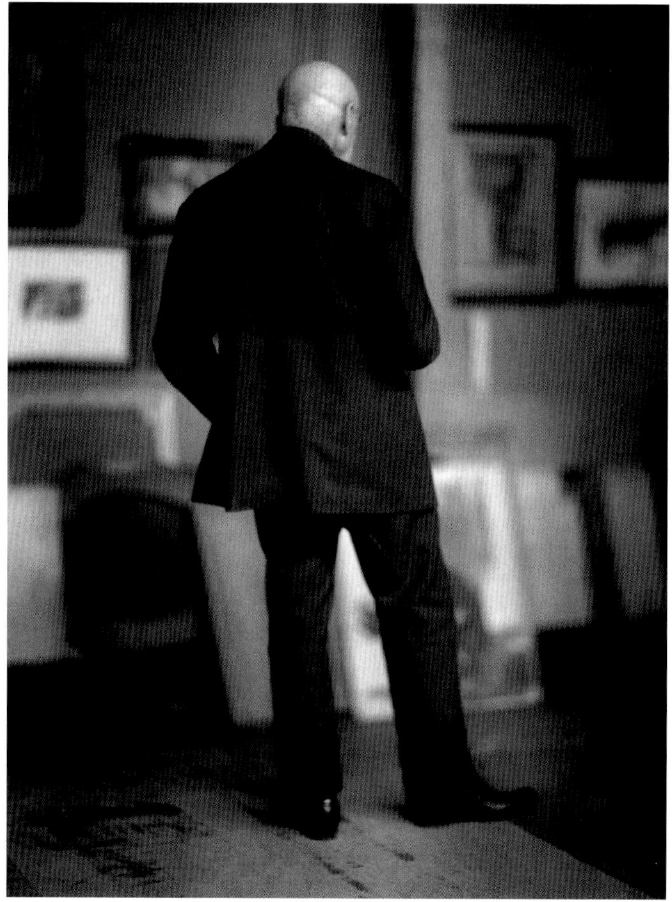

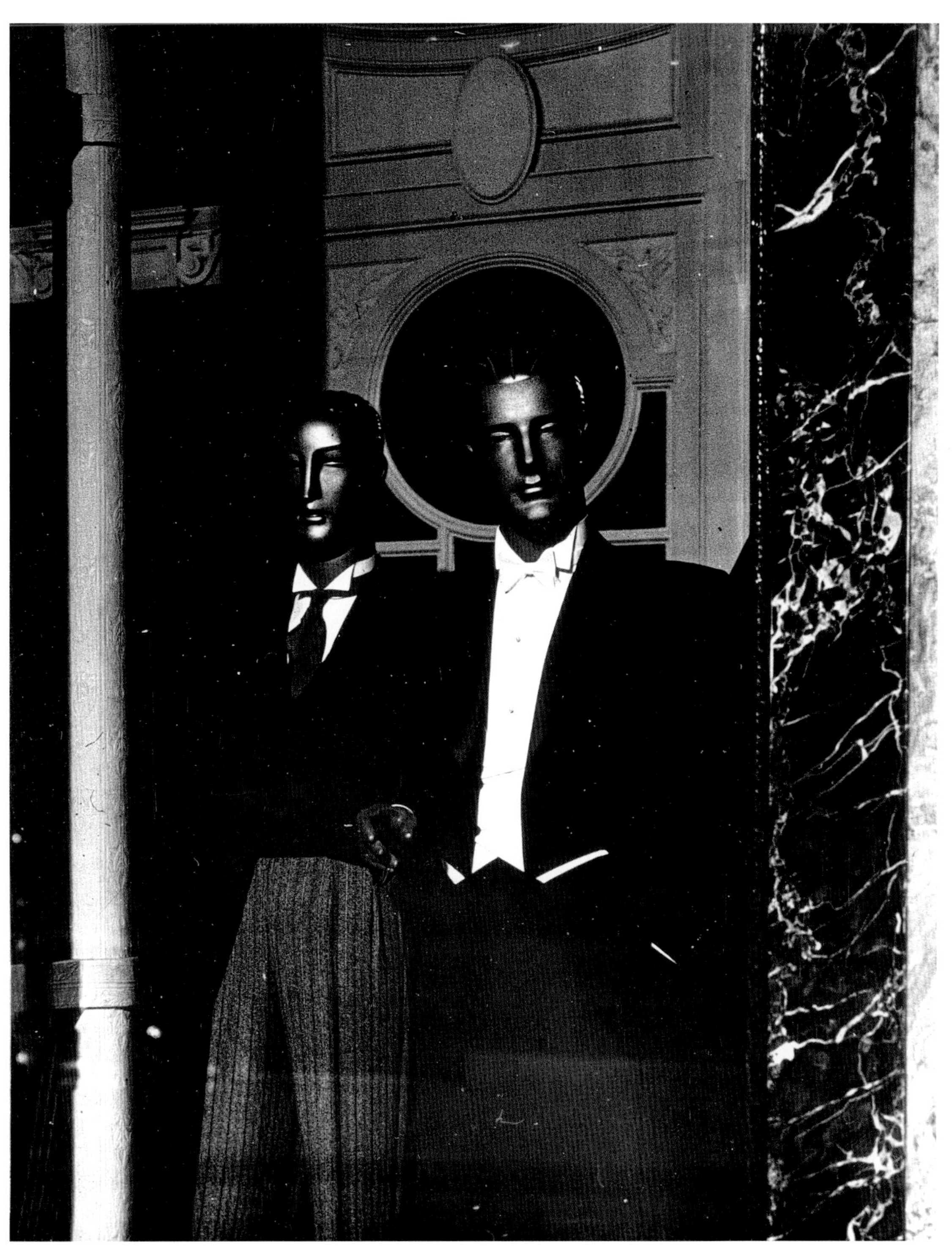

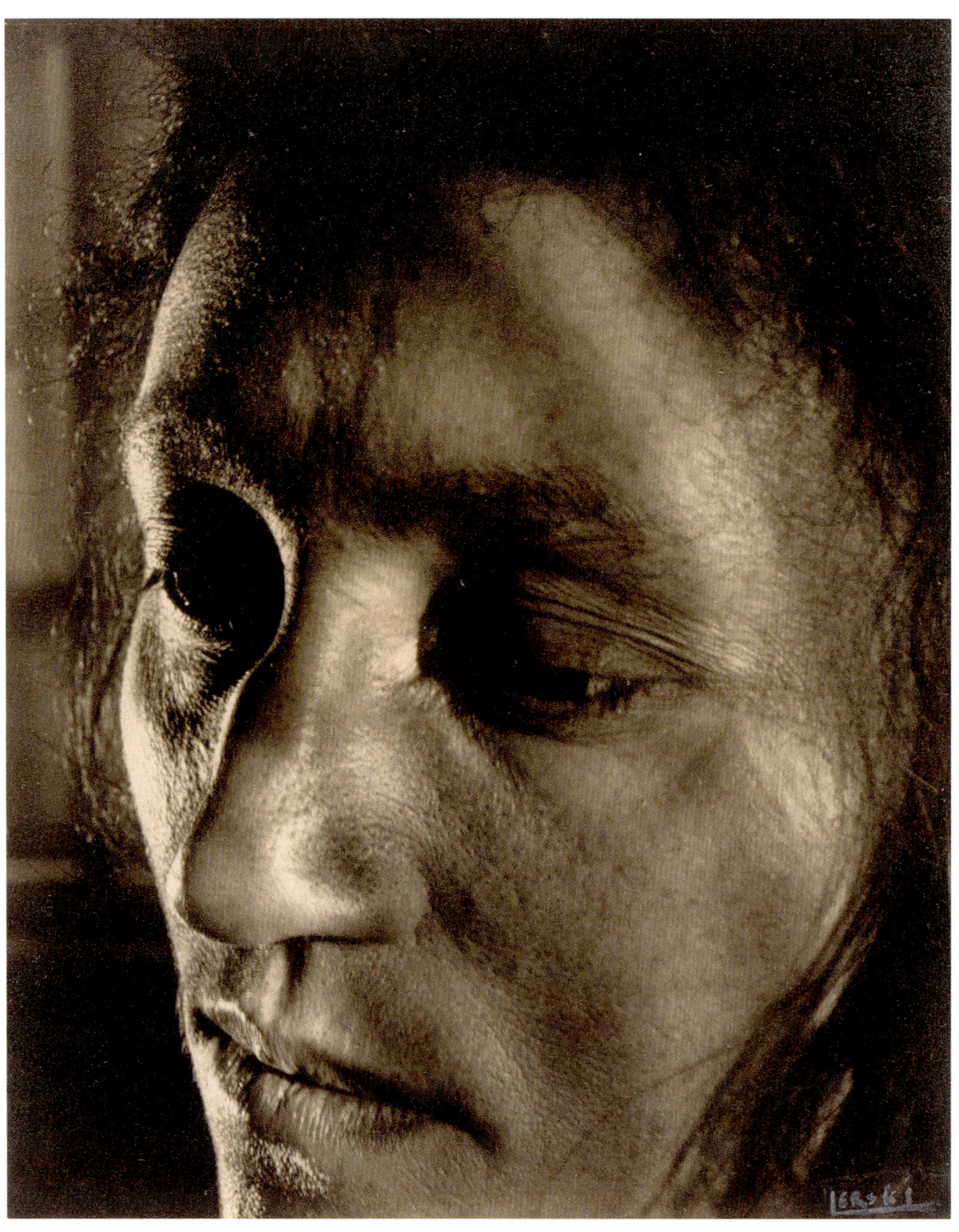

Friedrich Seidenstücker, *Zertrümmerung alter Bordsteine* (Smashing of Kerbstones); *Kokslieferung* (Coke Delivery); *Straßenarbeiter beim Steineschaufeln* (Roadmen Stone Shovelling); *Aufstemmen des betonierten Straßenbelages* (Prying Open Concreted Pavement), 1930s

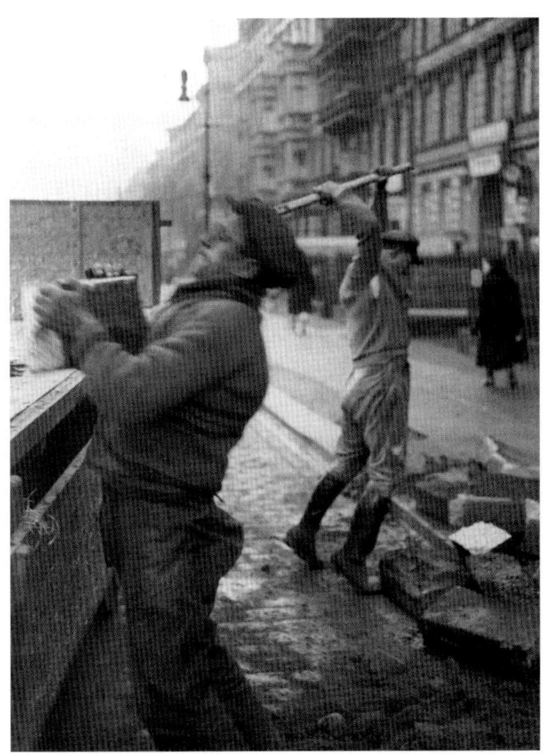

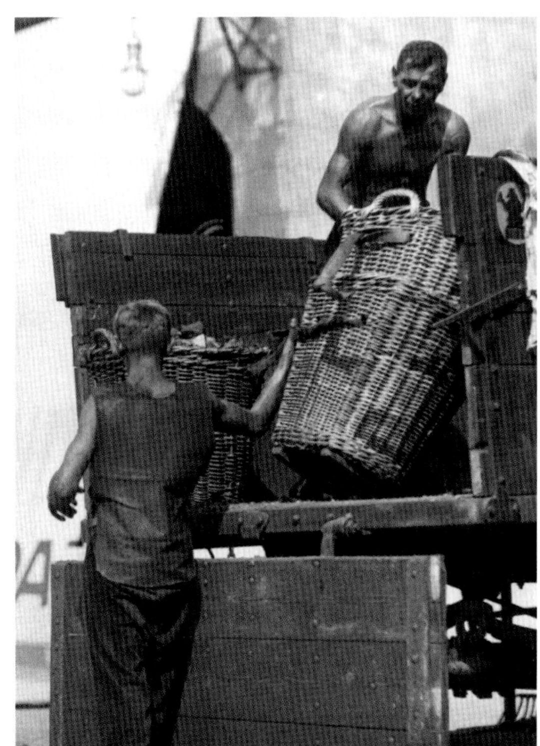

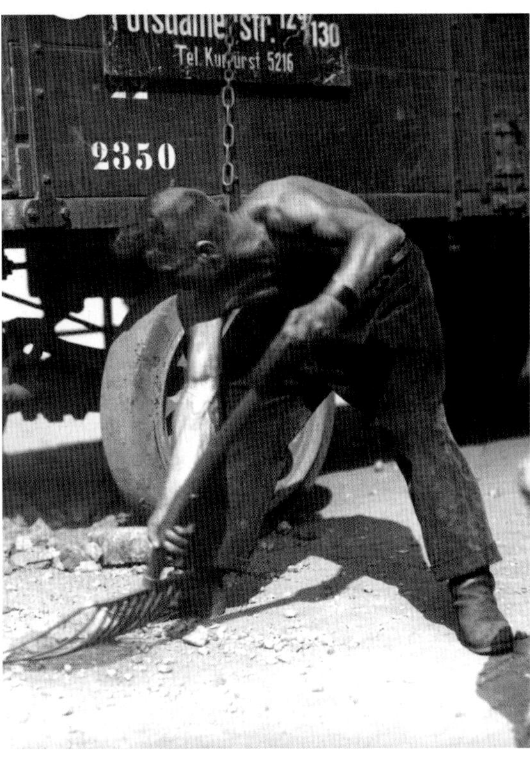

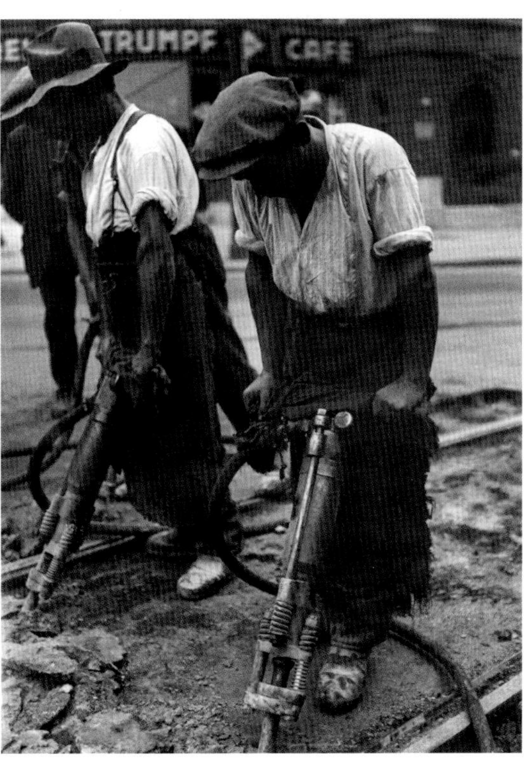

Manuel Álvarez Bravo, *Obrero en huelga asesinado*
(Striking Worker, Assassinated), 1934

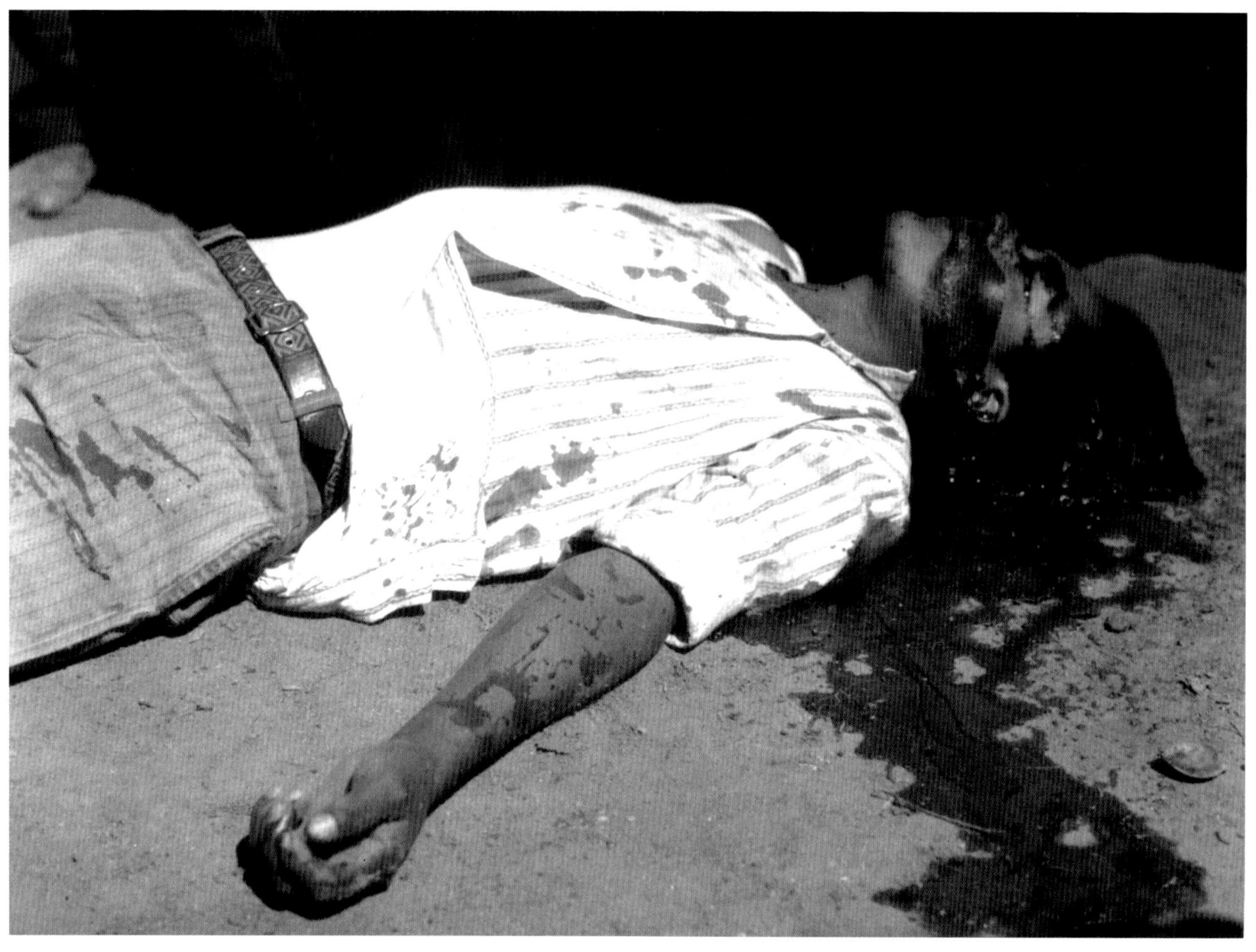

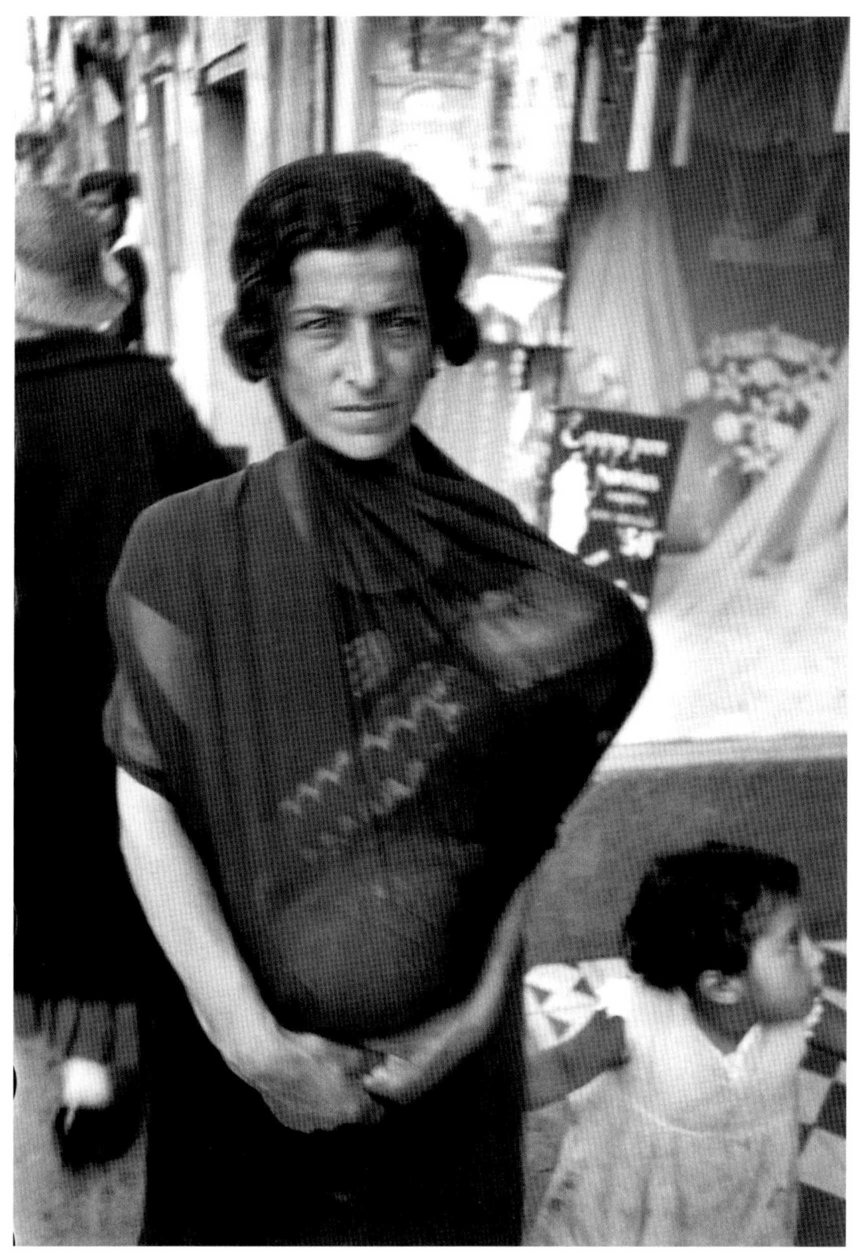

 Martín Chambi, *Señorita en traje de baño* (Girl in Bathing Suit), 1932

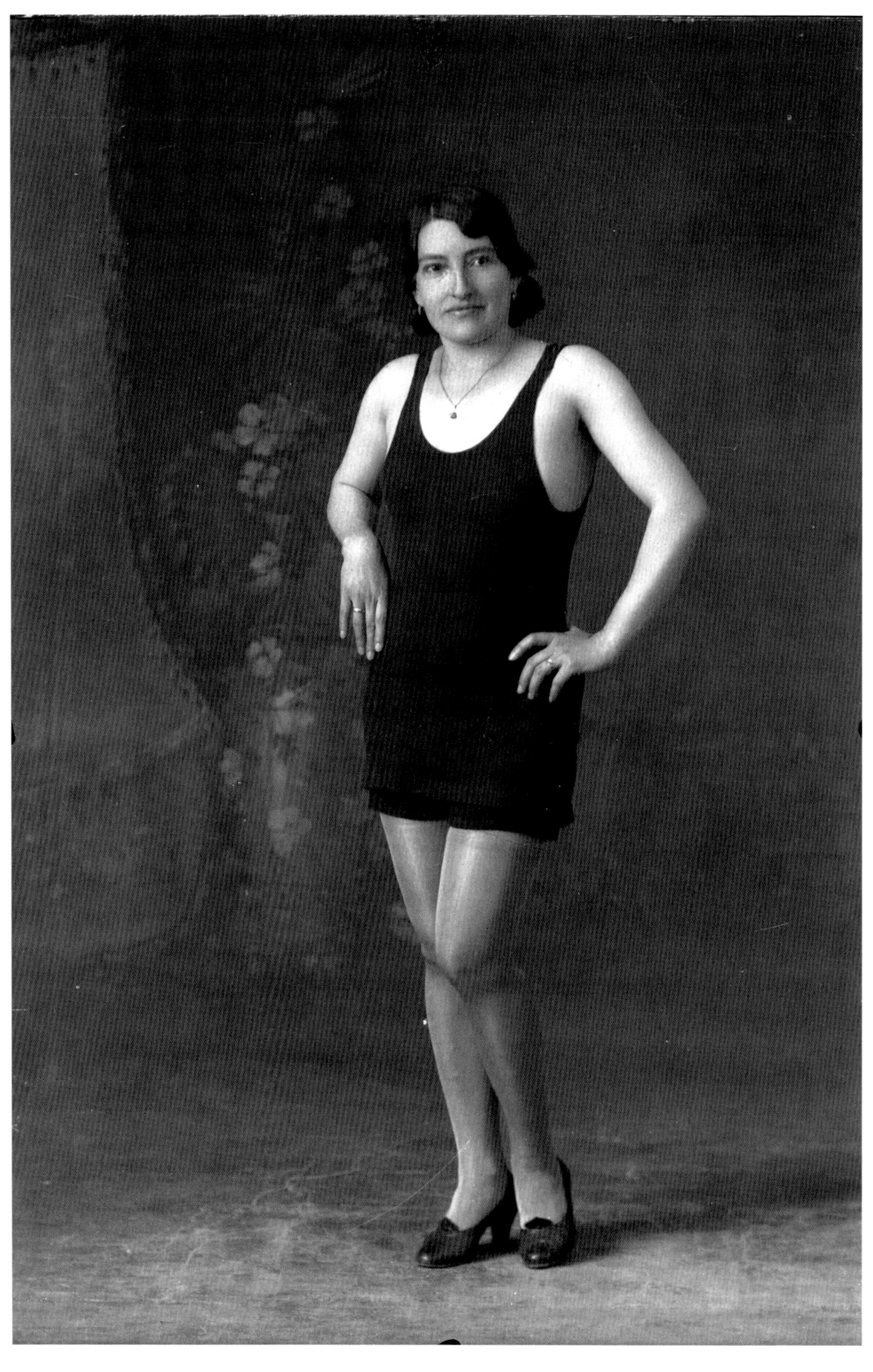

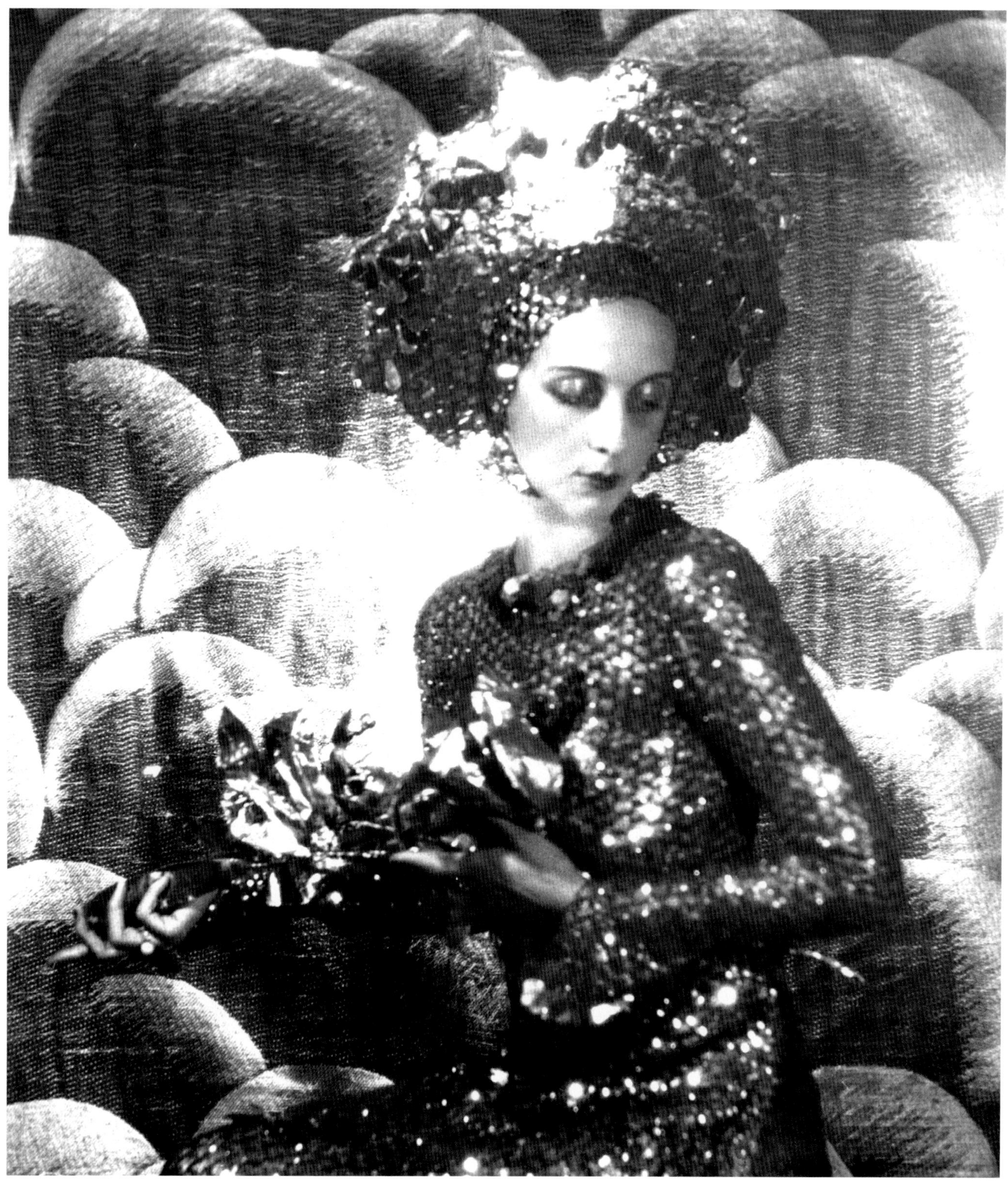

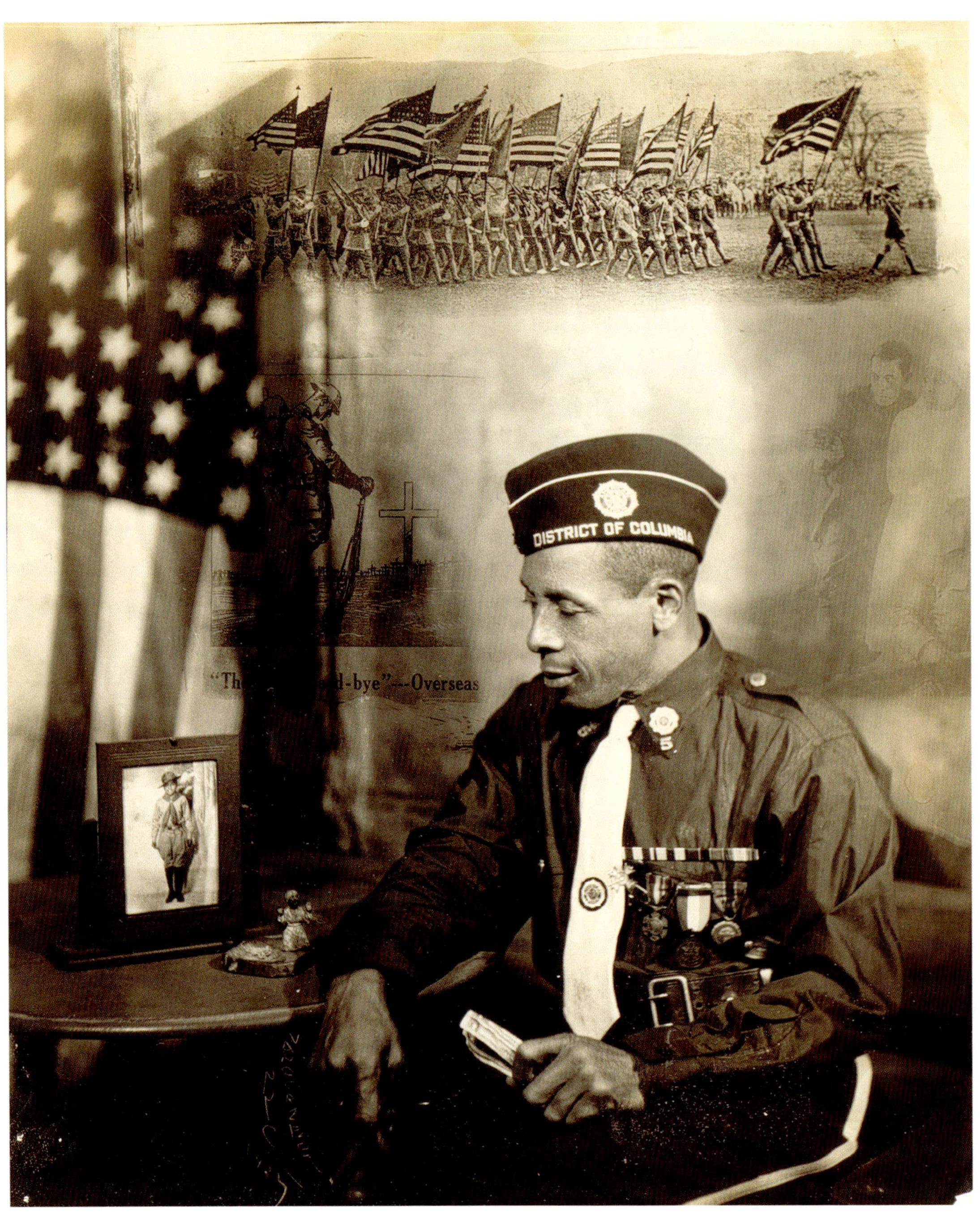
DISTRICT OF COLUMBIA
"The Last Good-bye"---Overseas

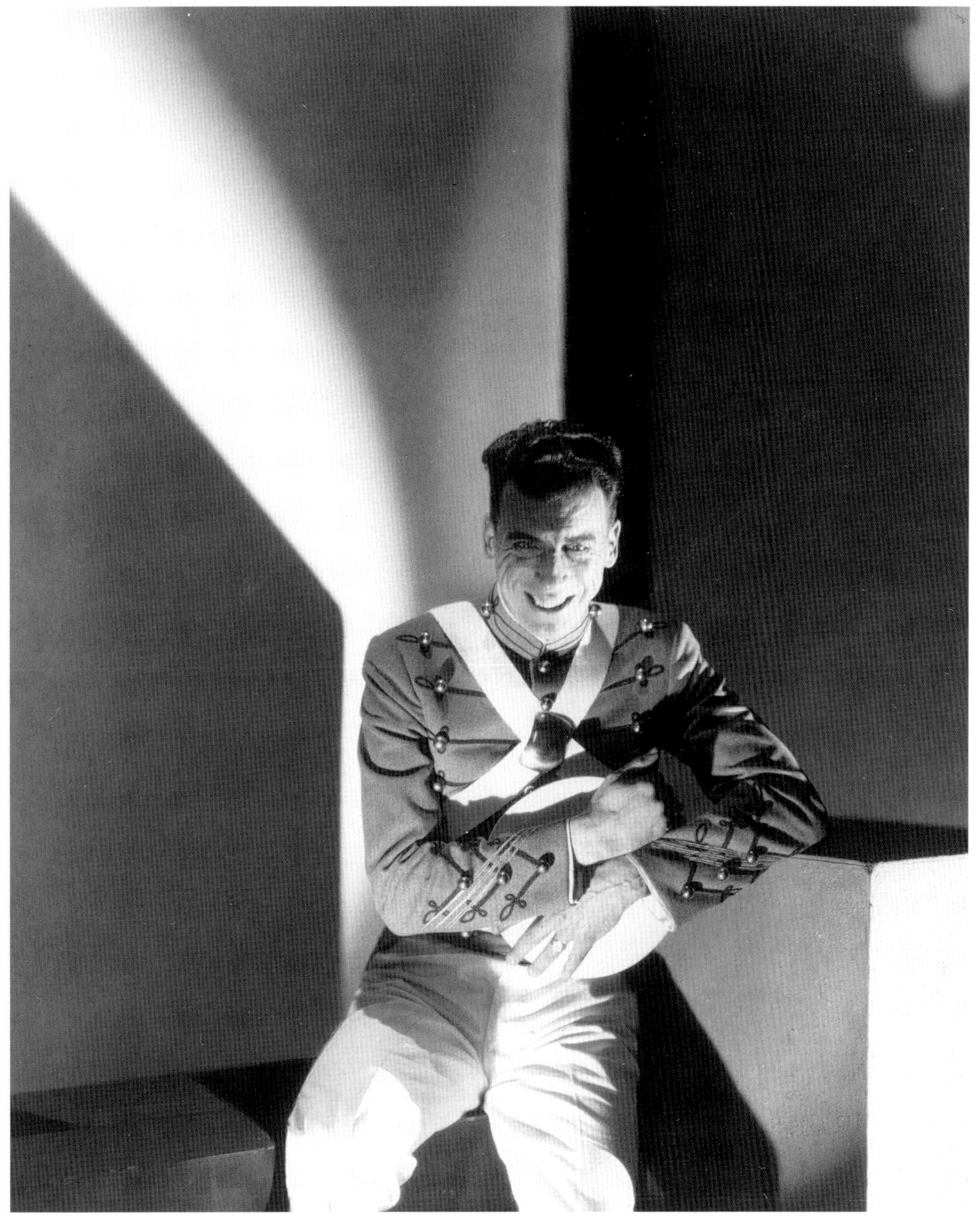

  Walker Evans, *Penny Picture Display, Savannah, Georgia*, 1936

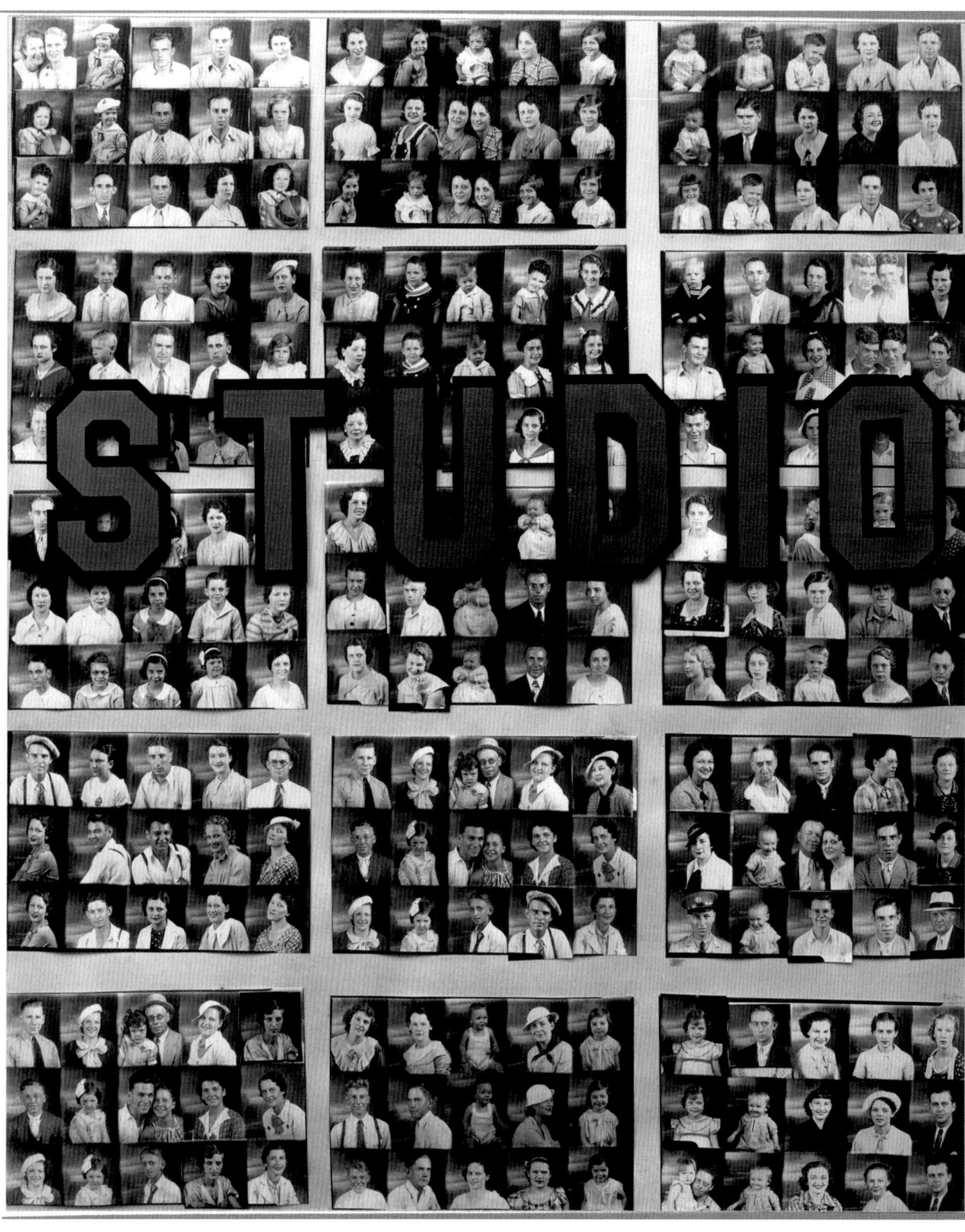

Height	In. 75·1	Head Length	18·2	L. Foot	25·9	Color of Left Eye	Circle Yel	Age 25 Born
Eng. Height	5-9	Head Width	15-4	L. Mid. F	11-7		Periph Bl	Apparent Age
Outside A	In. 78·5	Cheek Width		L. Lit. F	8-7			Nativity Ill
Trunk	89·2	R. Ear	55	Left Fore A. 47·3			Pecul.	Occupation

REMARKS INCIDENT TO MEASUREMENT

DESCRIPTIVE

Forehead		Nose	Profile		R. Ear			
	Inclin.		Ridge				Beard	
	Height		Base ___ Root				Hair	
			DIMENSIONS		Teeth		Complexion	
	Width		Length / Projection / Breadth				Weight 127	
	Pecul		Pecul.		Chin		Build	

BUREAU OF IDENTIFICATION
DEPARTMENT OF POLICE

Description taken _Southern Ill Pen 3 23-26_ 19

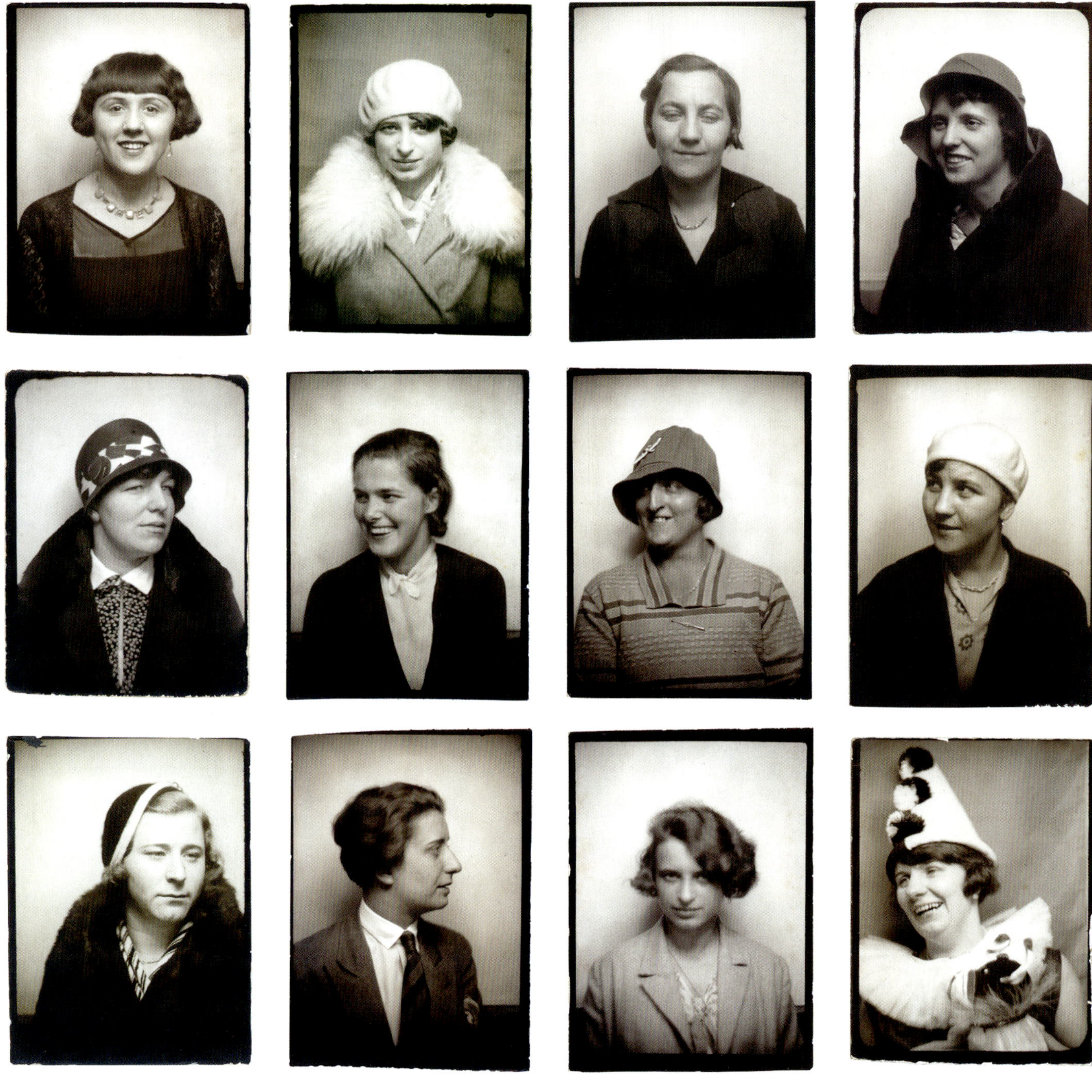

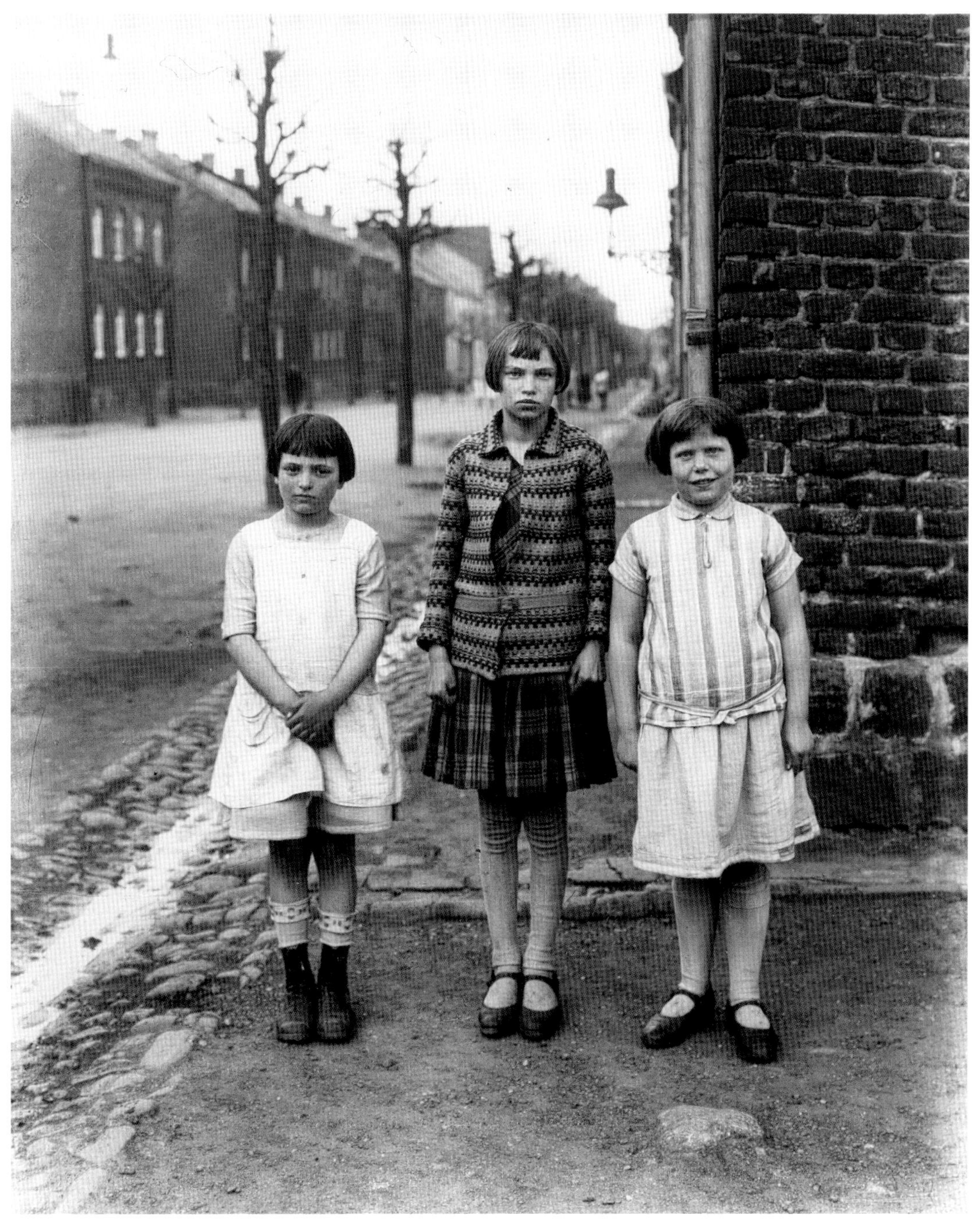

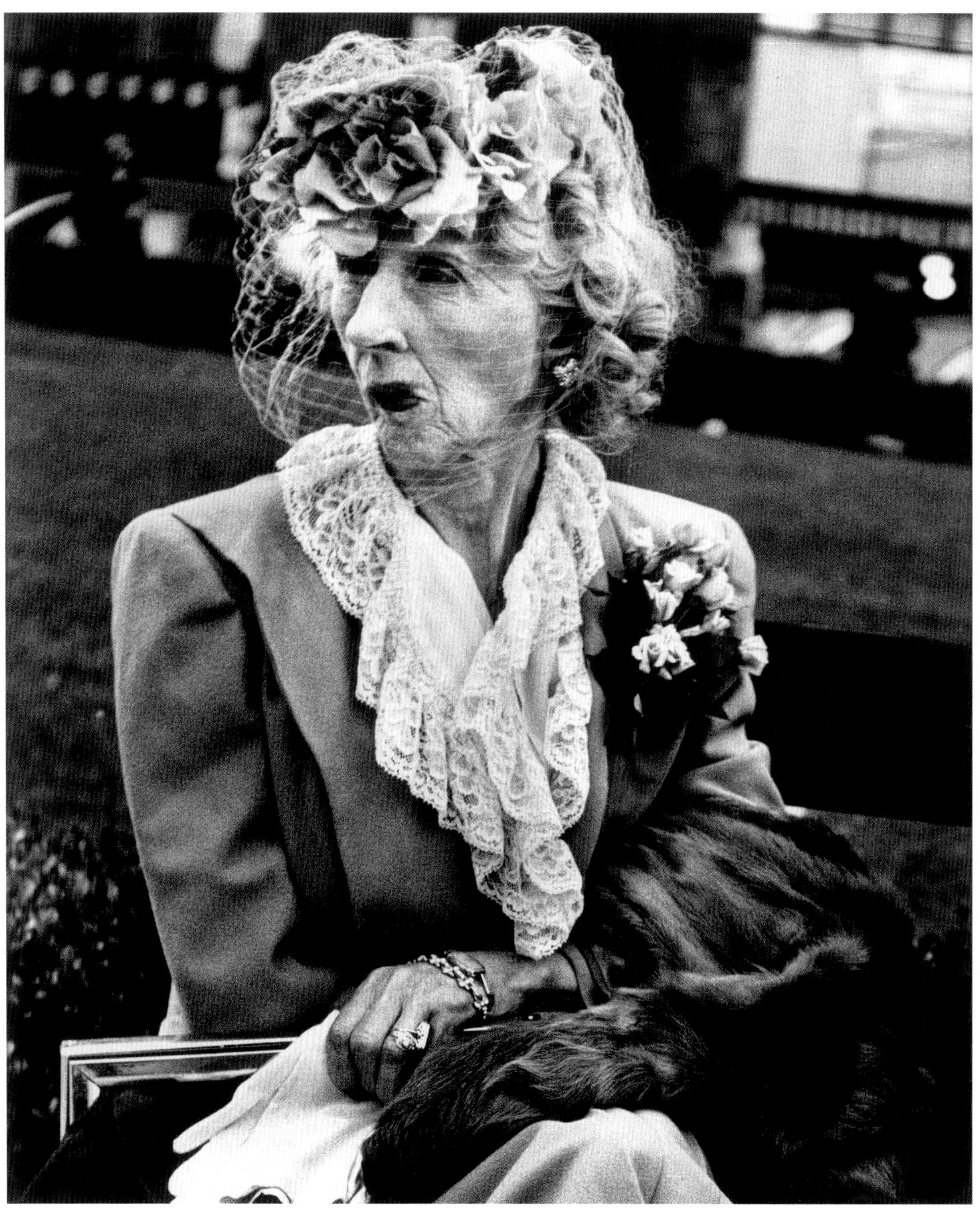

Madame Yevonde, *Lady Bridgett Elizabeth Felicia Henrietta Augusta Poulett Photographed as 'Arethusa'*, 1935

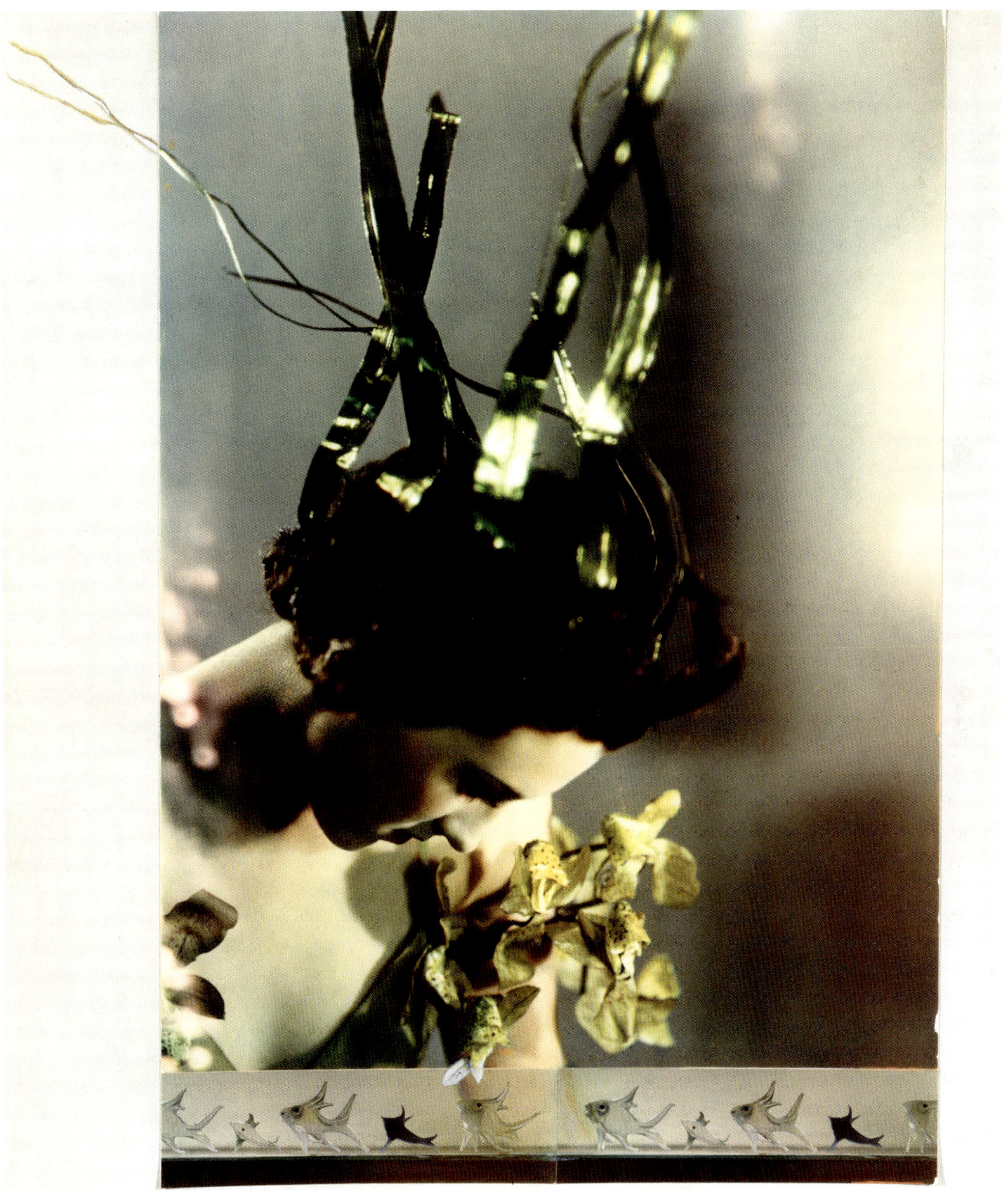

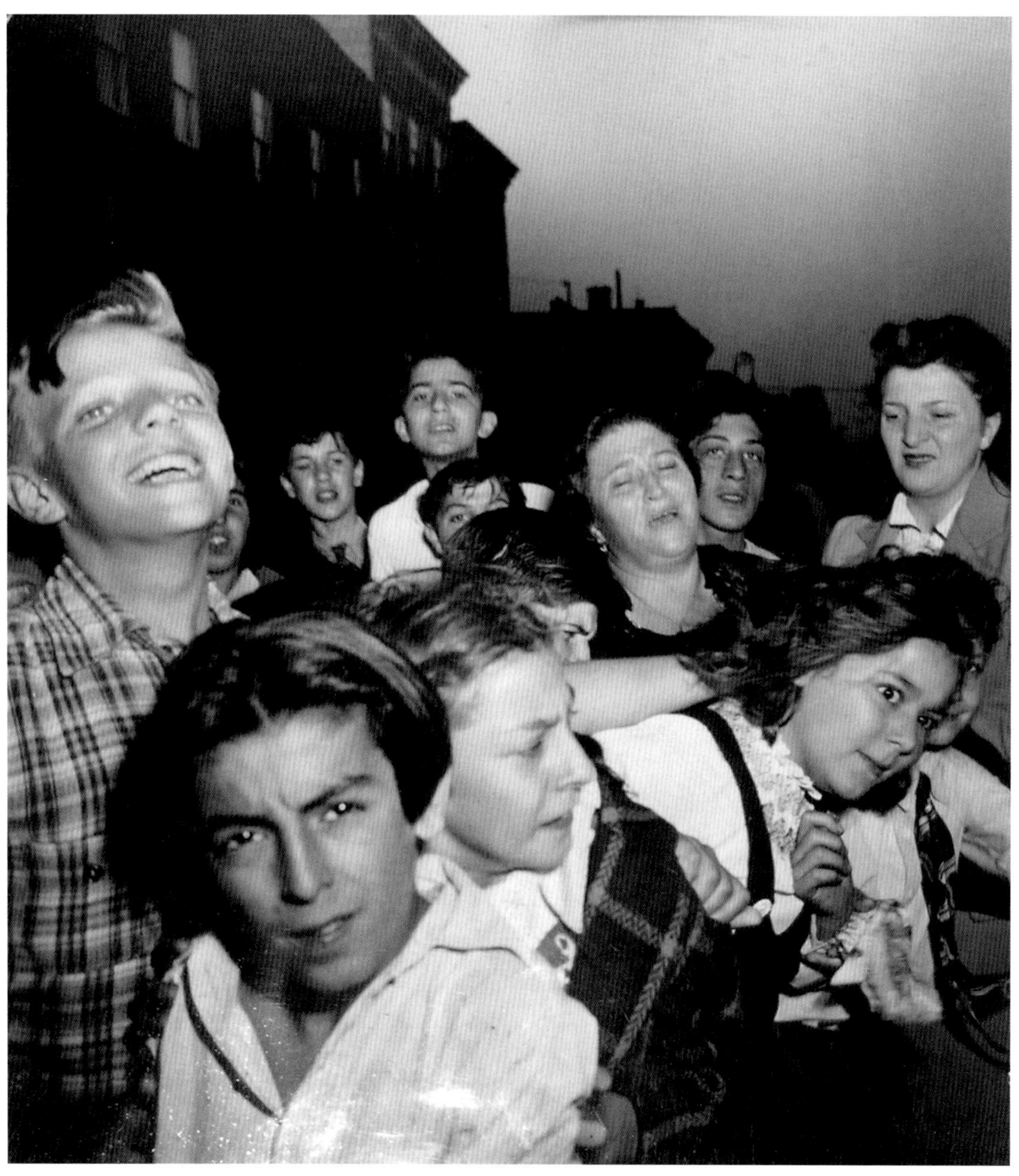

Weegee, *Their First Murder, 9 October 1941*, 1941

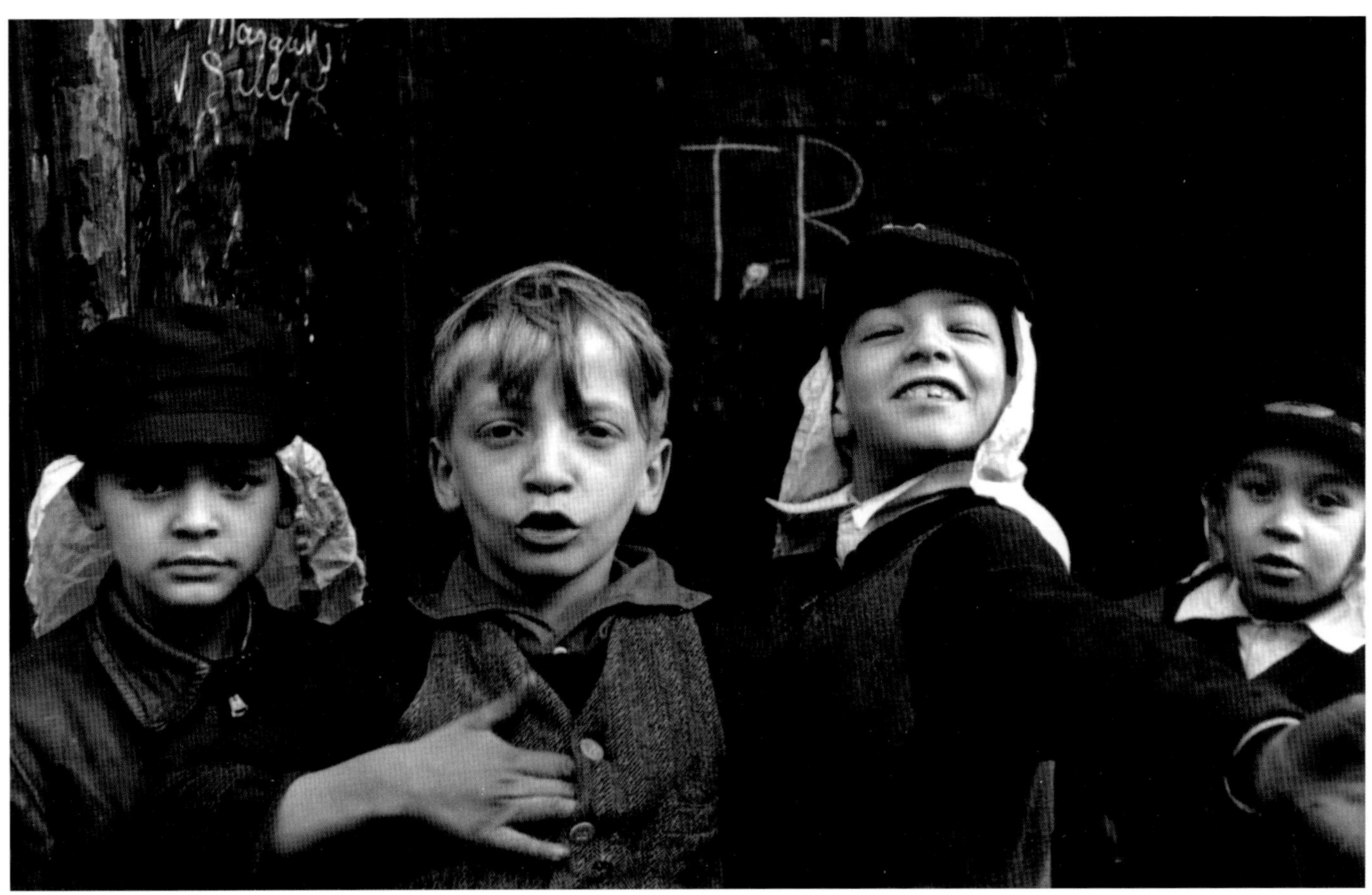

Cas Oorthuys, *Vlaglegging. Weteringplantsoente Amsterdam werd door de illegaliteit een vlag gelegd op plaats waar Nederlanders werden neergeschoten* (The Resistance Lay a Flag on the Weteringsplantsoen in Amsterdam where Dutch People Had Been Killed), March 1945

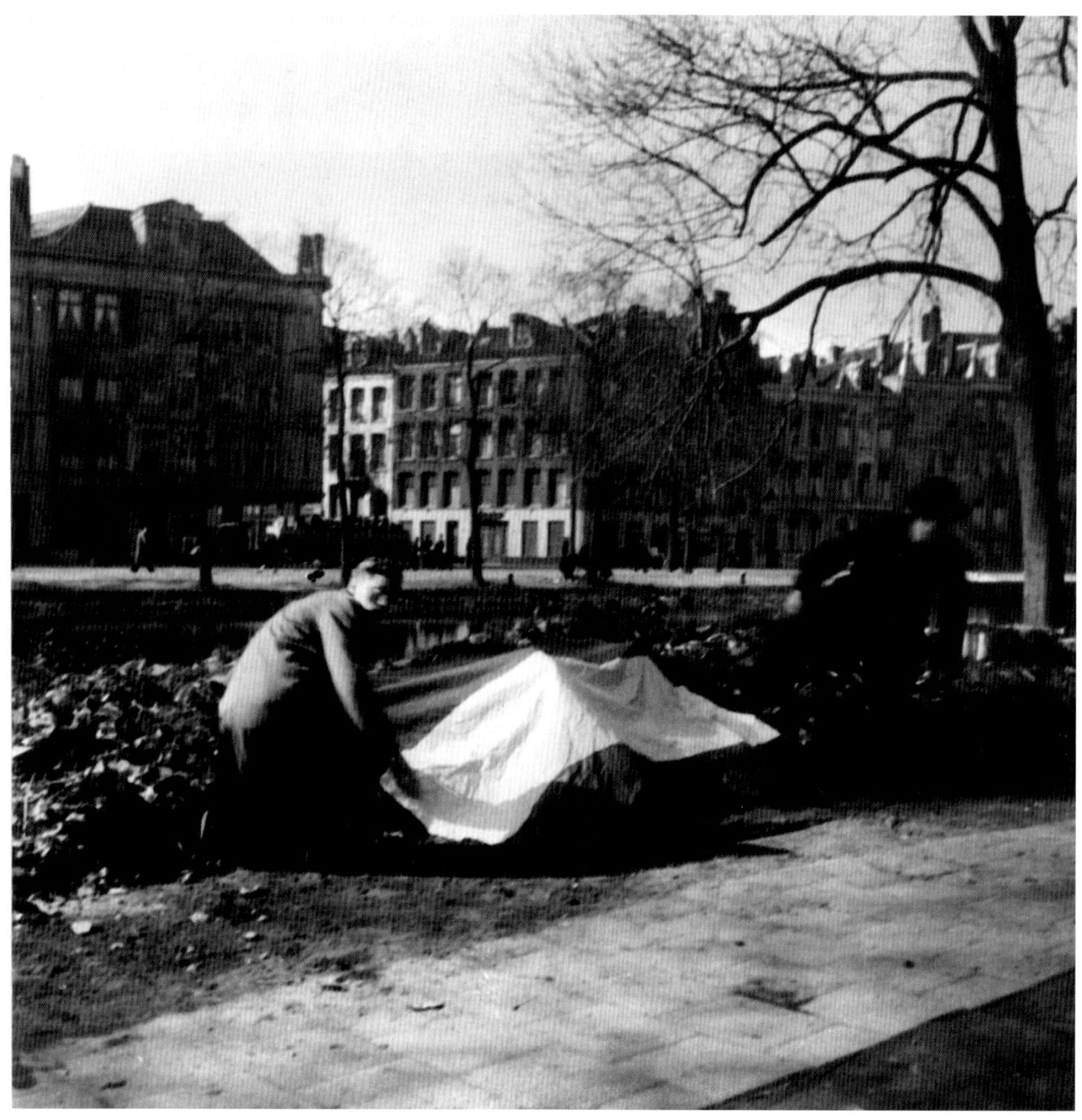

Lee Miller, *Lázló Bardossy, Fascist ex-Prime Minister of Hungary, Facing the Firing Squad, Budapest*, 1946

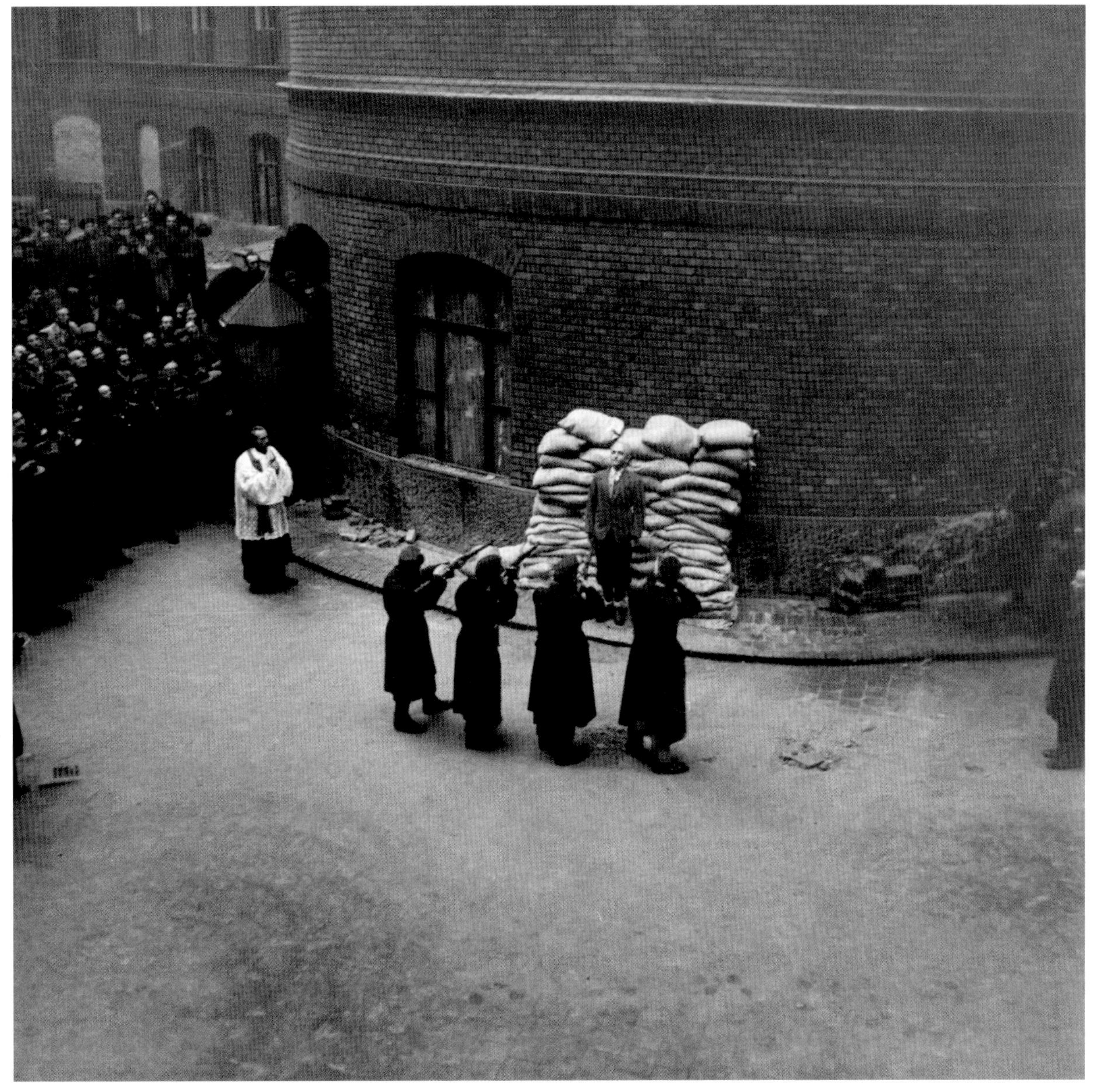

Lee Miller, *Lázló Bardossy, Fascist ex-Prime Minister of Hungary, Facing the Firing Squad, Budapest*, 1946

Erwin Blumenfeld
Joan Colom
Robert Doisneau
Walker Evans
Robert Frank
Arturo Ghergo
David Goldblatt
Philippe Halsman
William Klein
Leon Levinstein
Stefan Moses
Norman Parkinson
Irving Penn
Otto Steinert
Louis Stettner
Tom von Wichert

Walker Evans, from the series *Labor Anonymous, Detroit*, 1946

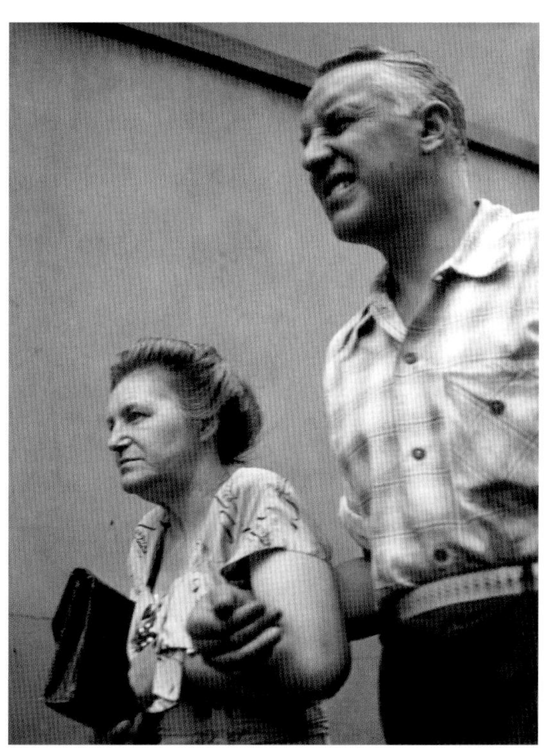
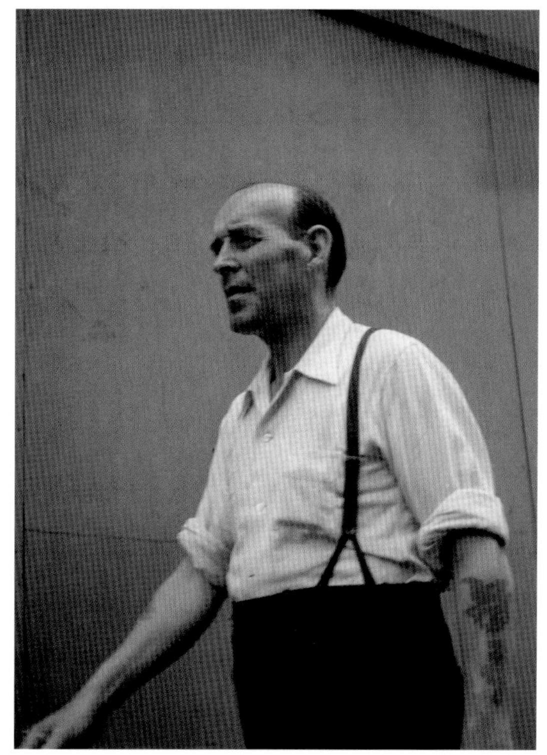
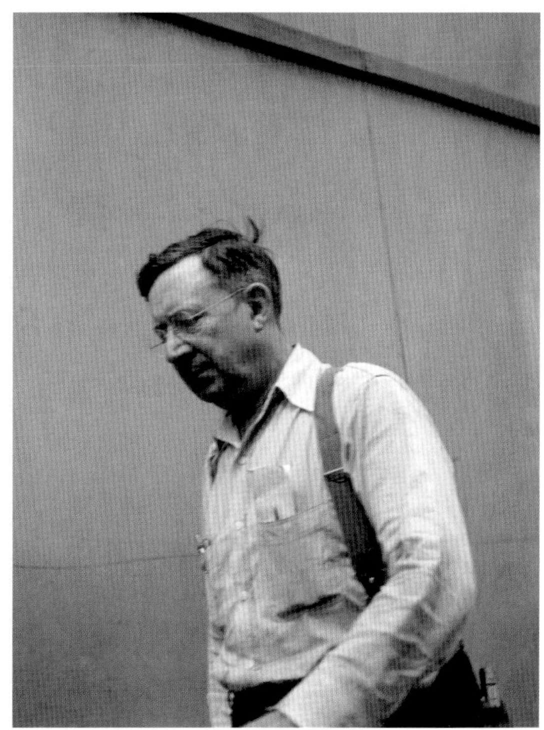
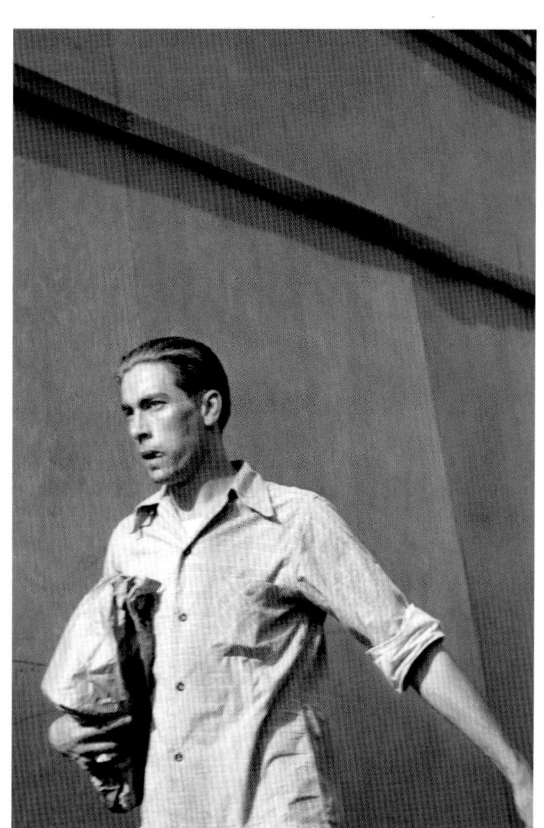

 Leon Levinstein, *Broadway and 42nd Street*, c.1974

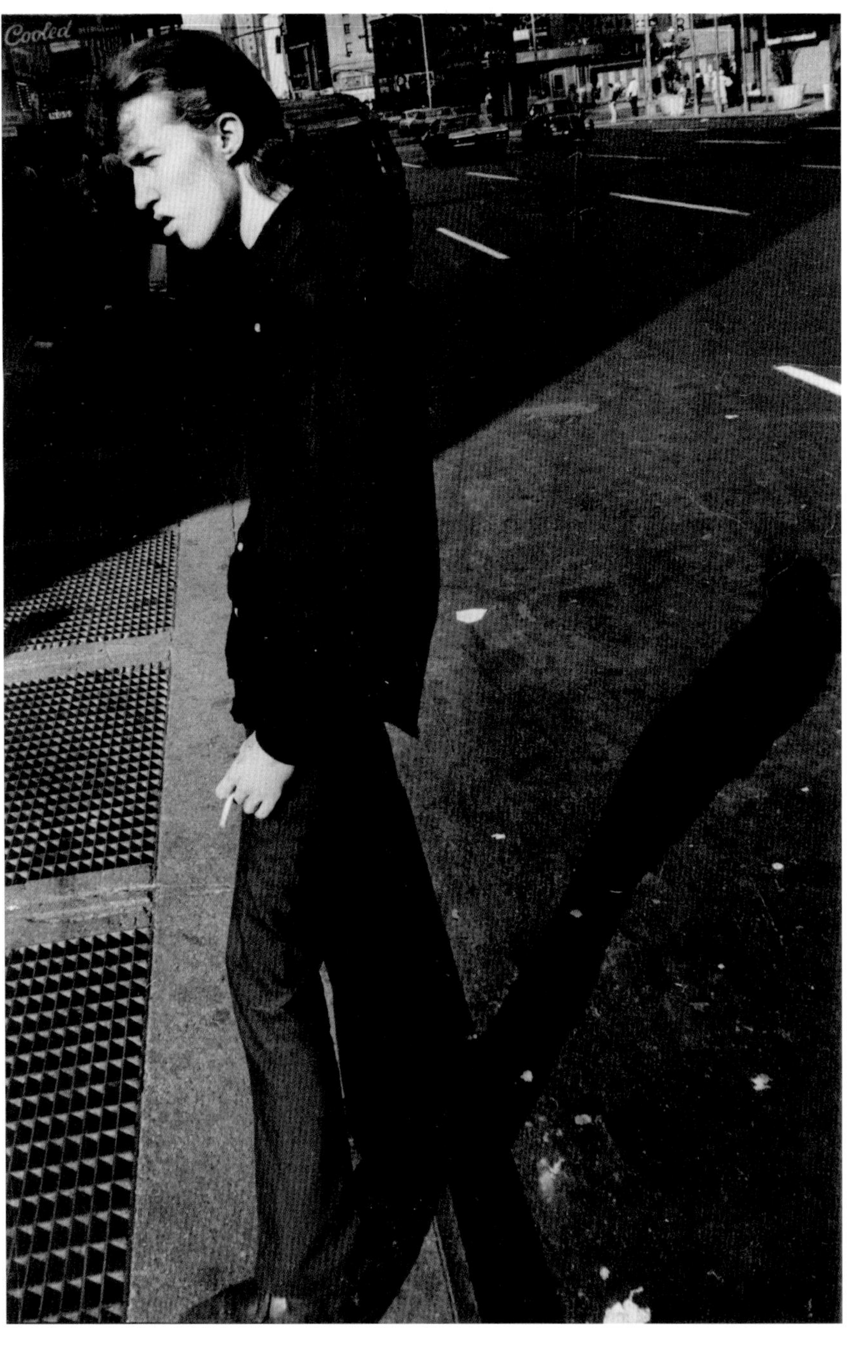

Leon Levinstein, *Broadway and 42nd Street*, c.1974

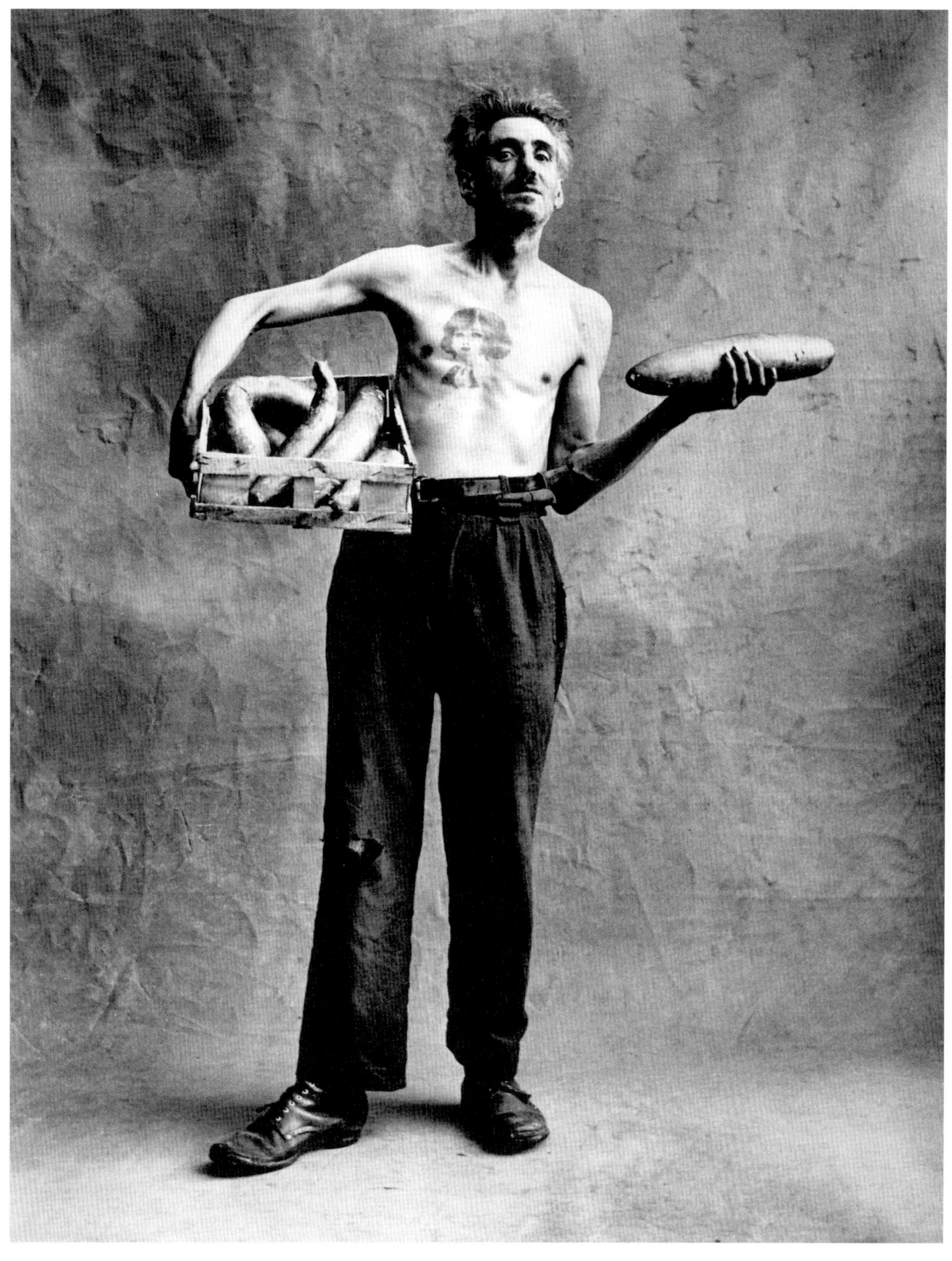

Irving Penn, *Le Marchand de concombres*
(Cucumber Seller), 1950

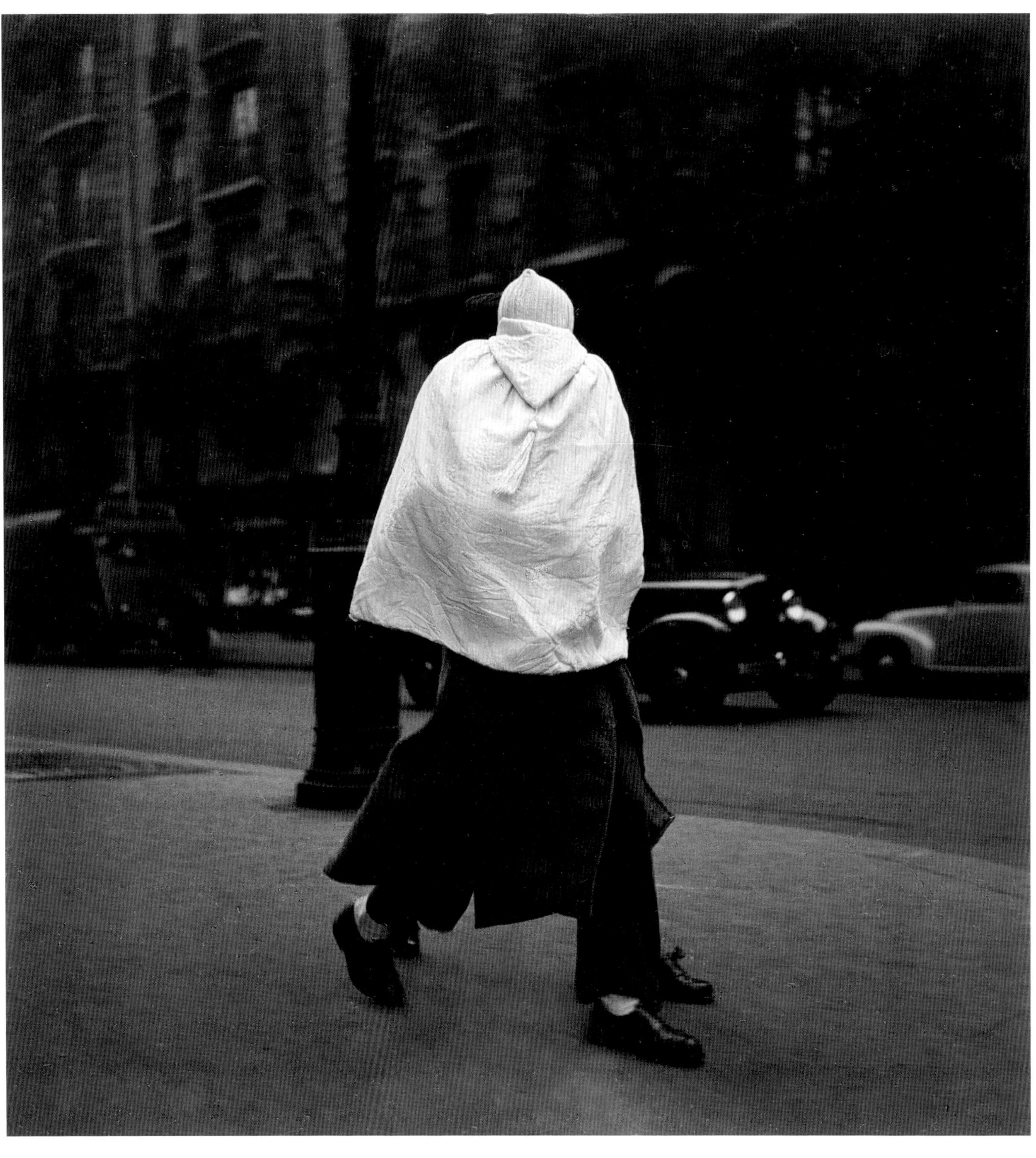

Louis Stettner, *Le Ménage, Paris* (Household, Paris), c.1950

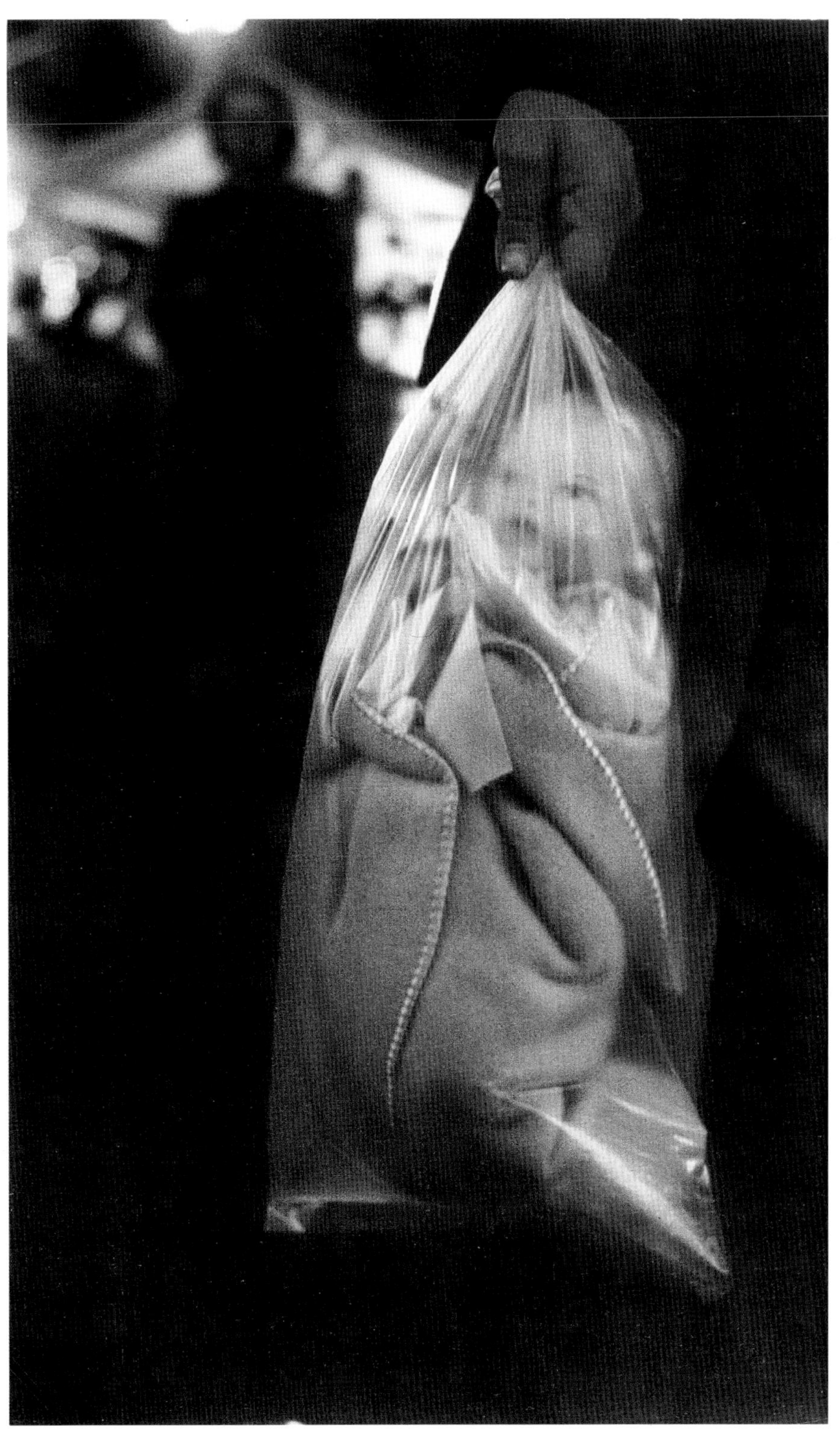

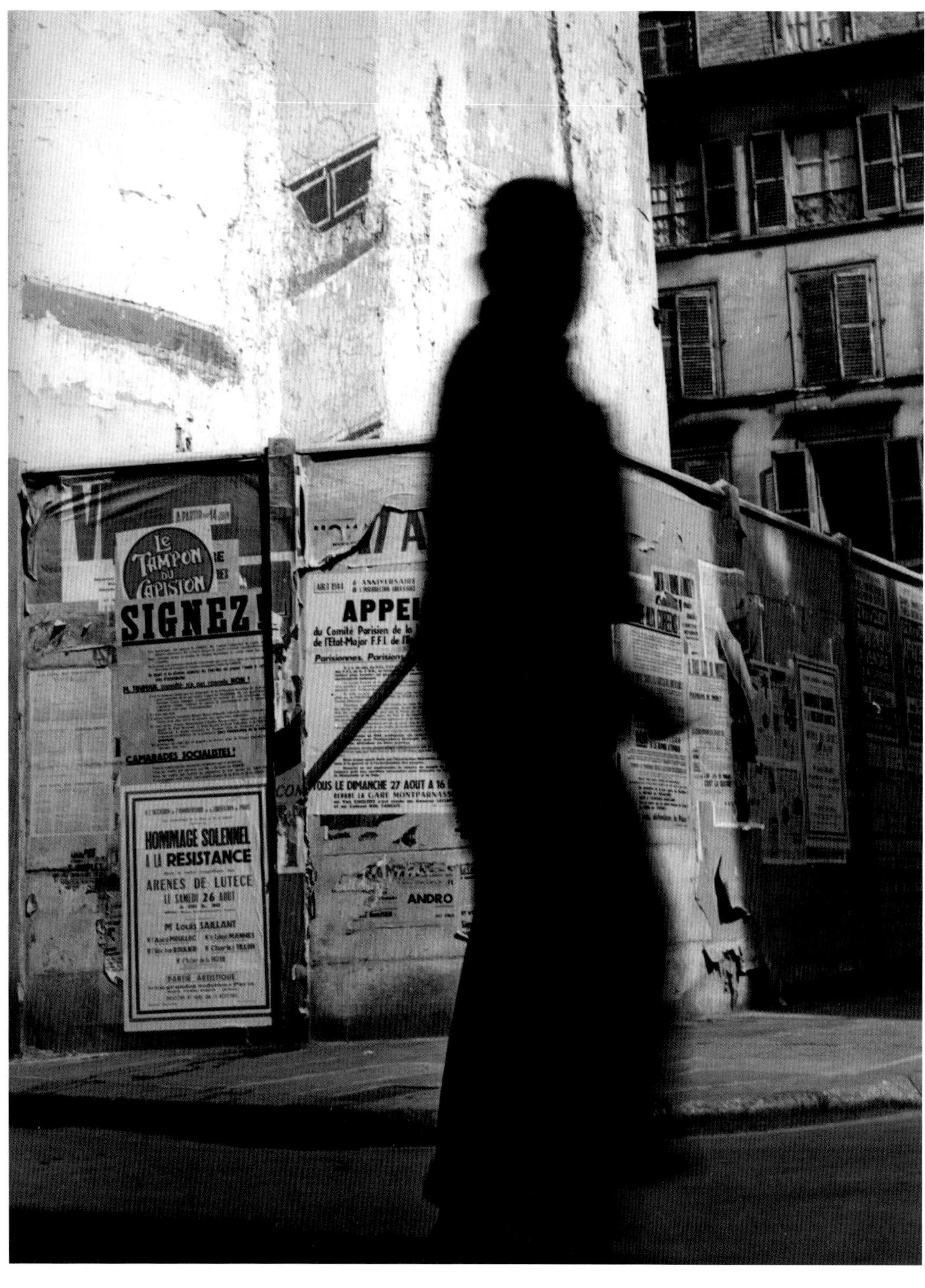

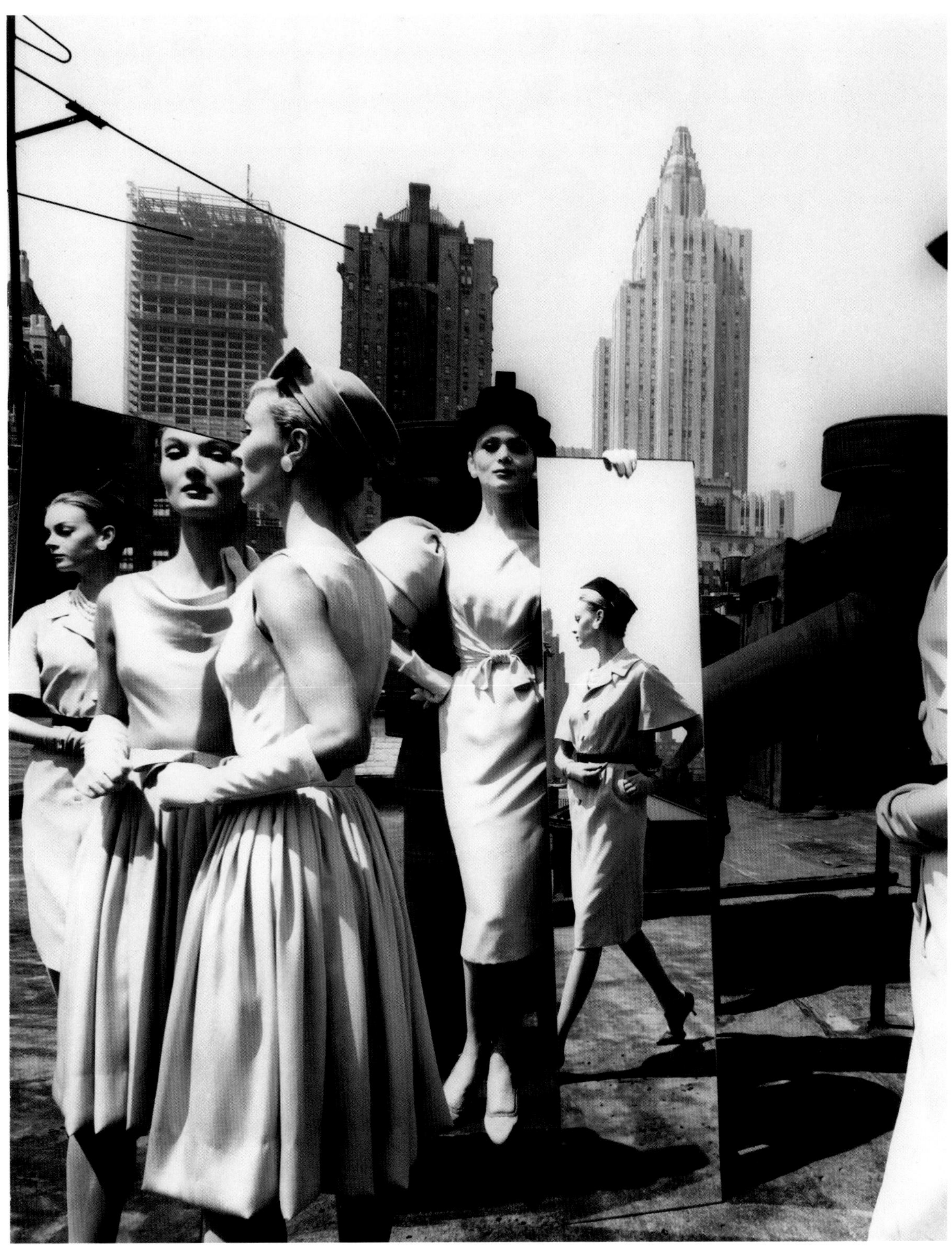

Robert Doisneau, *Les Amoureux du Vert-Galant*
(The Lovers from Vert-Galant), 1950

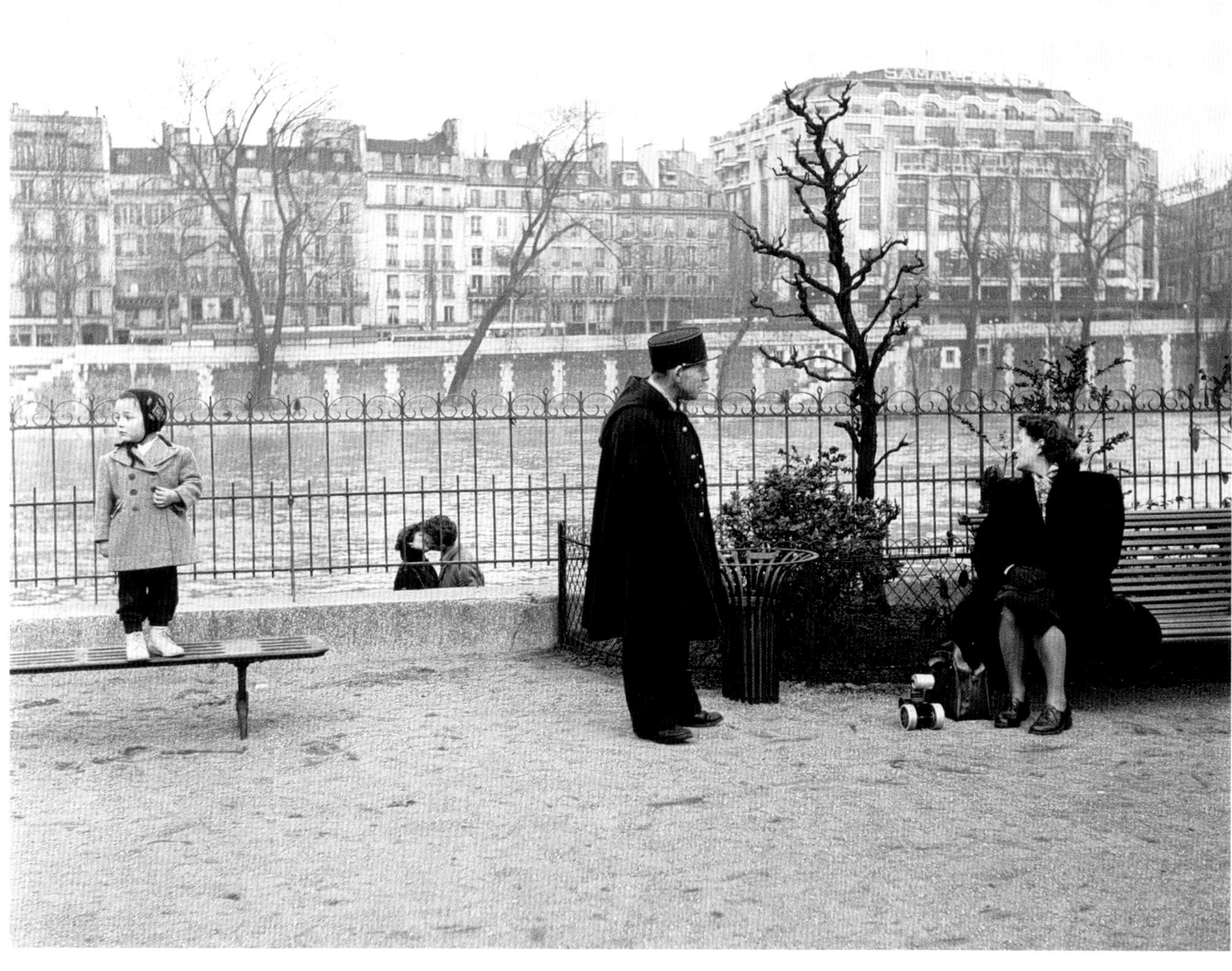

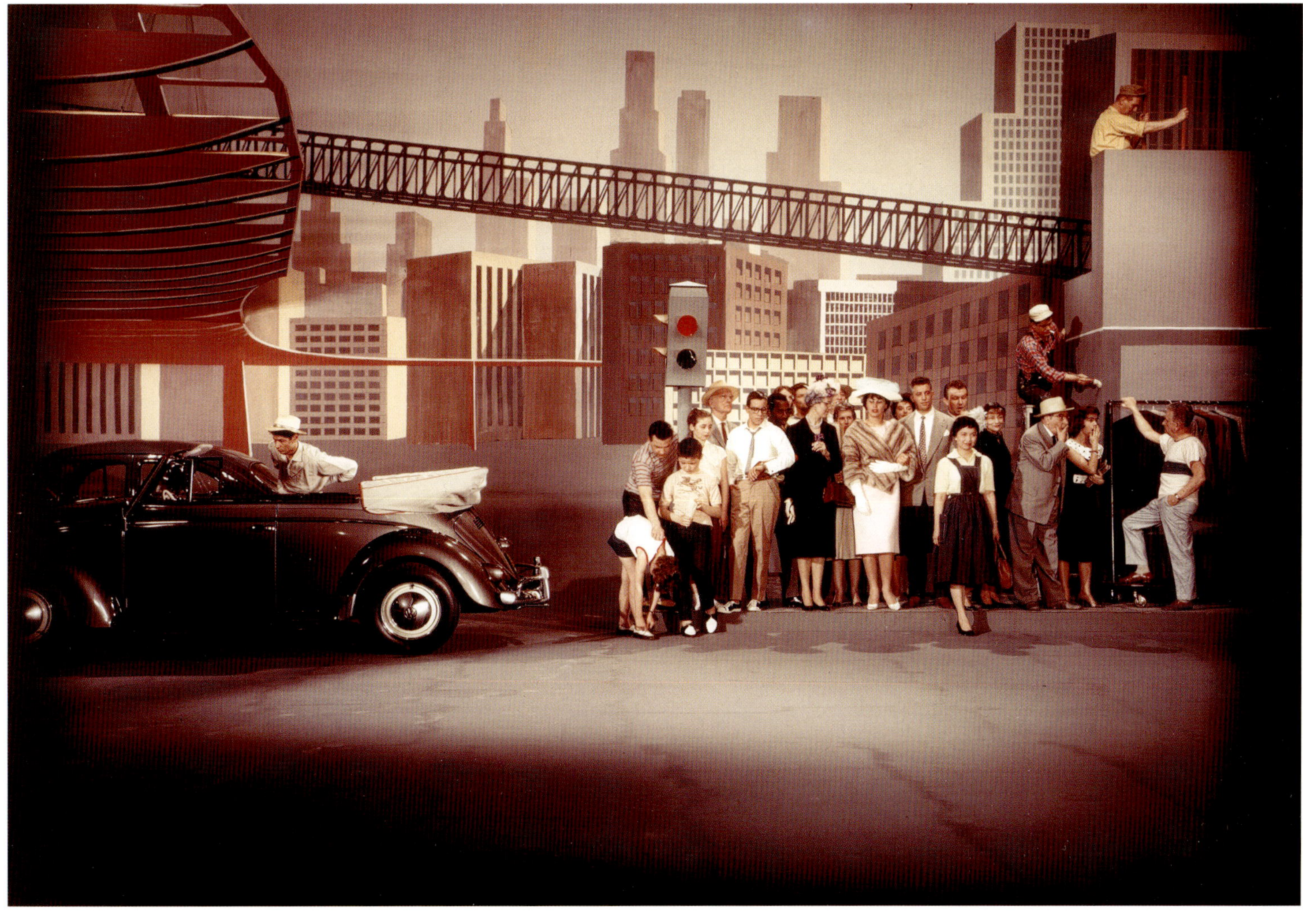

Joan Colom, from the series *Gente del Raval* (People of Raval), 1958–61

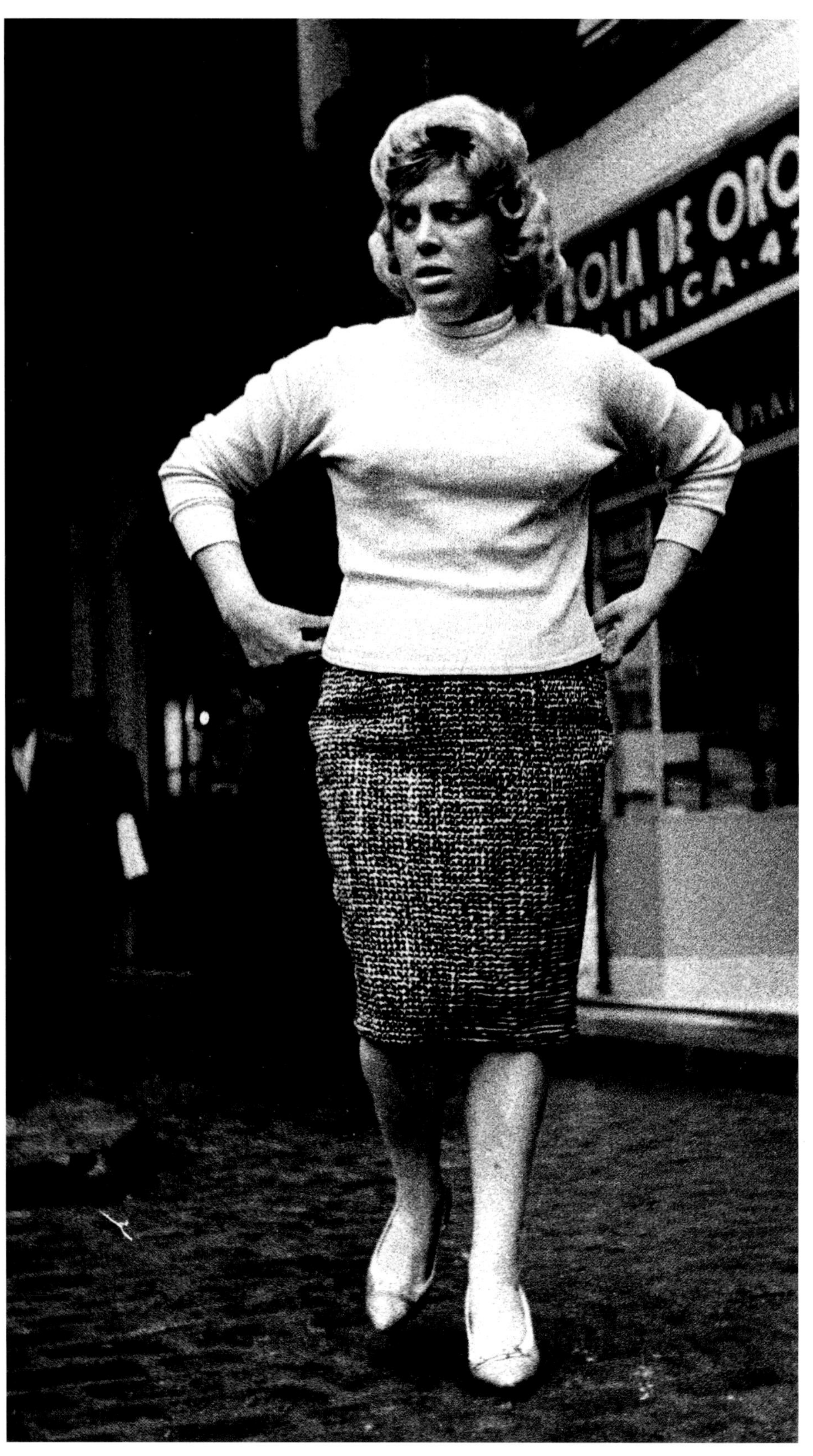

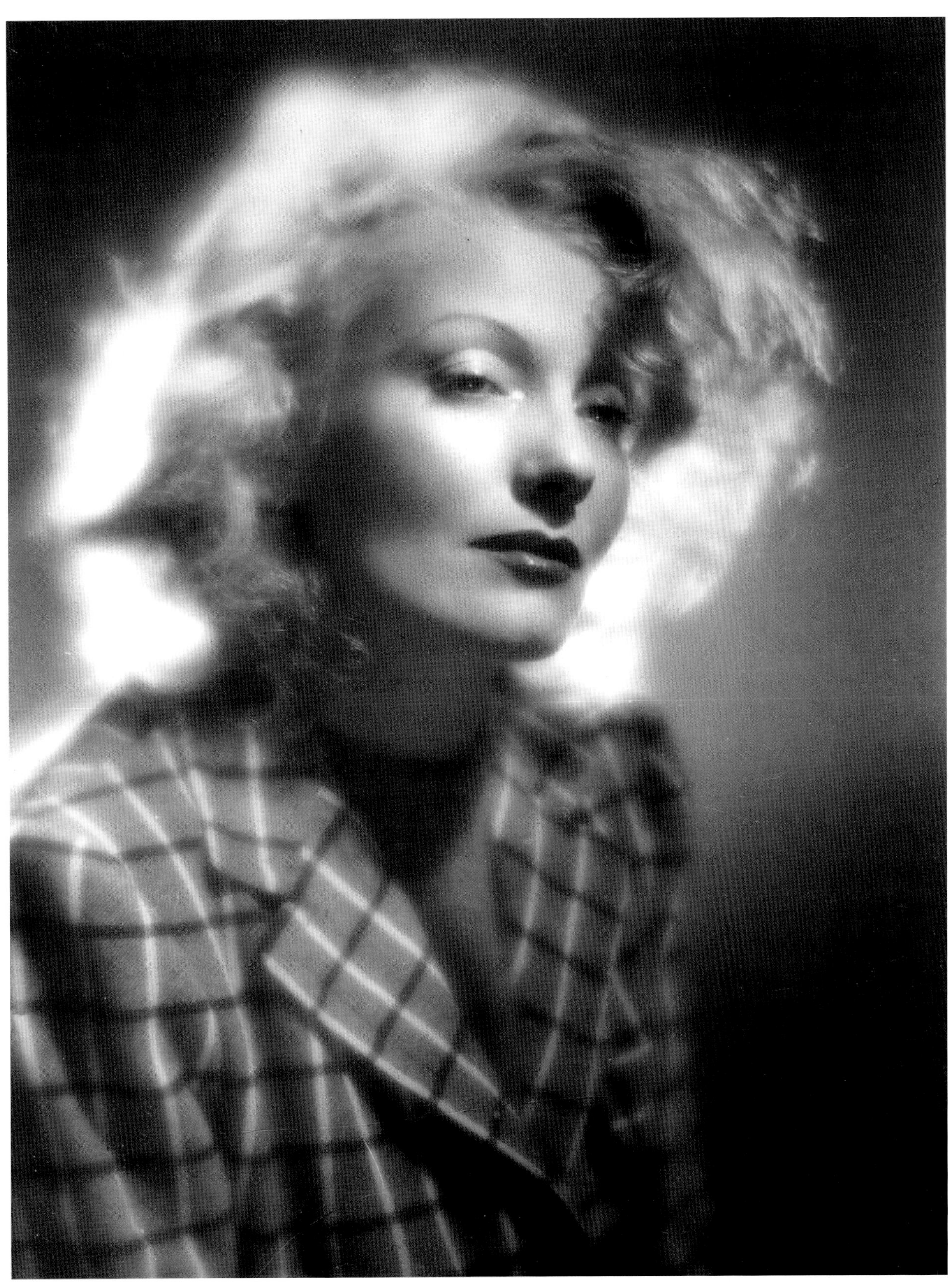

 Erwin Blumenfeld, *City Lights,* 1946

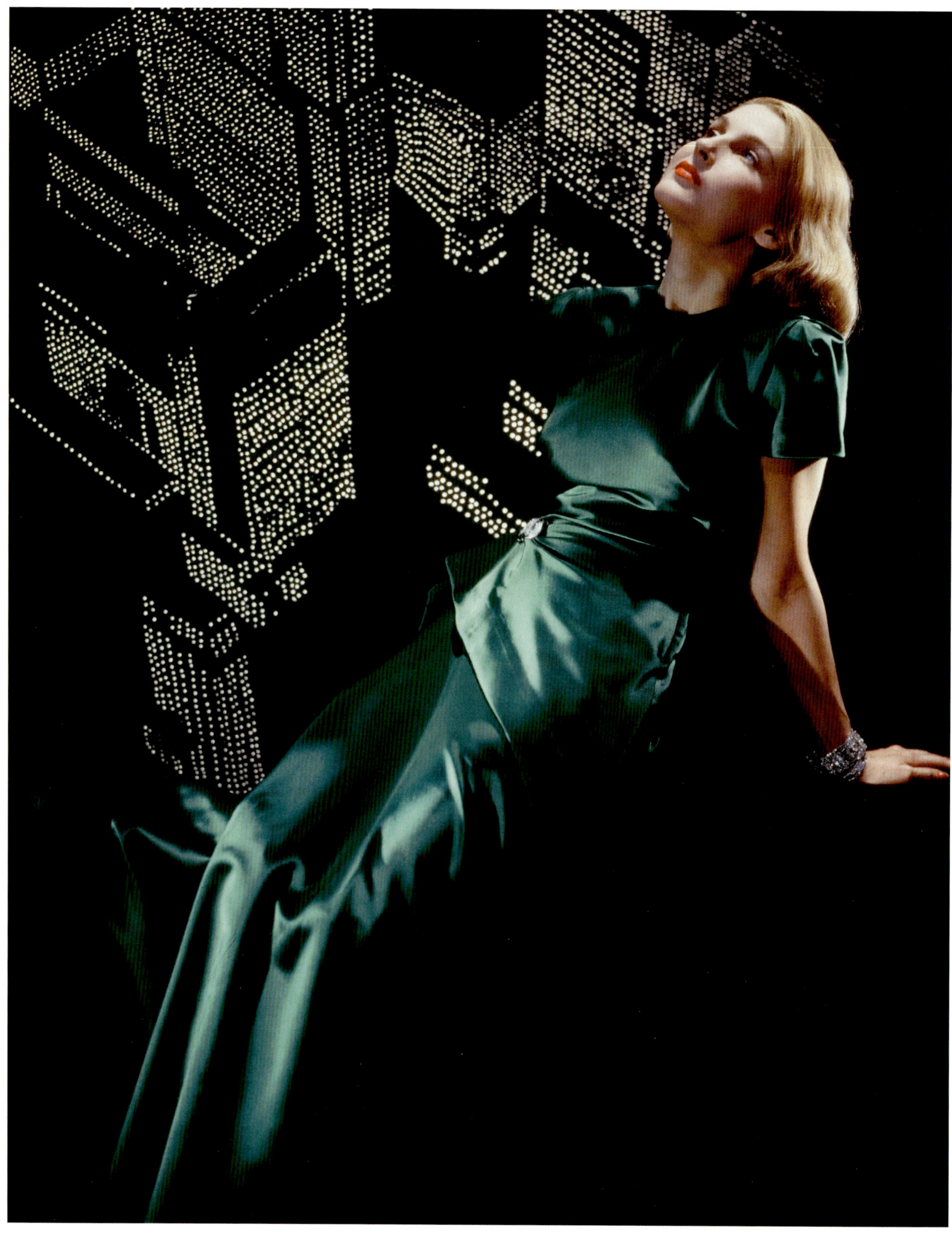

Norman Parkinson, *Wenda, Times Square, NYC, September 1949*, 1949

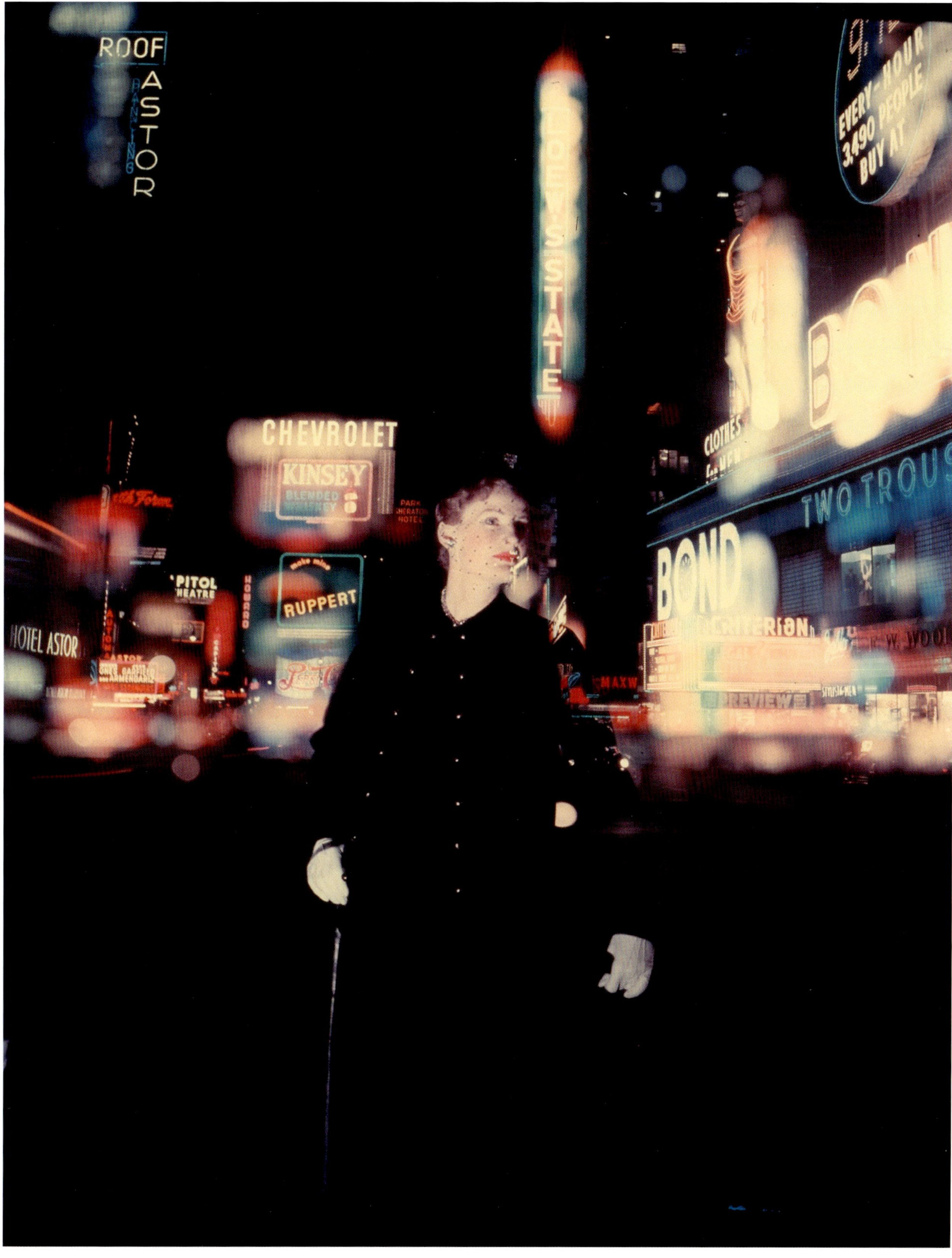

  Philippe Halsman, *Edward Steichen*, 1959

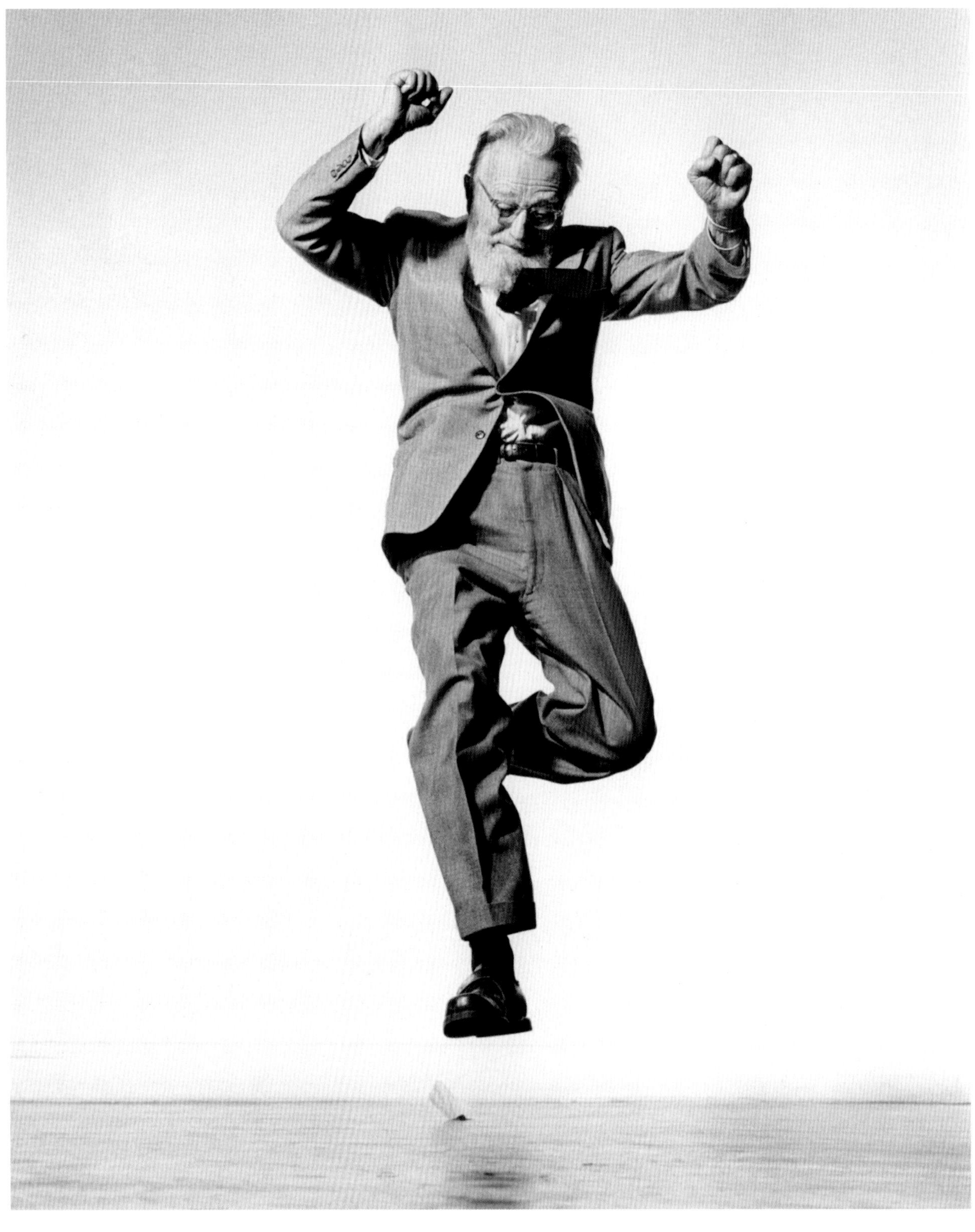

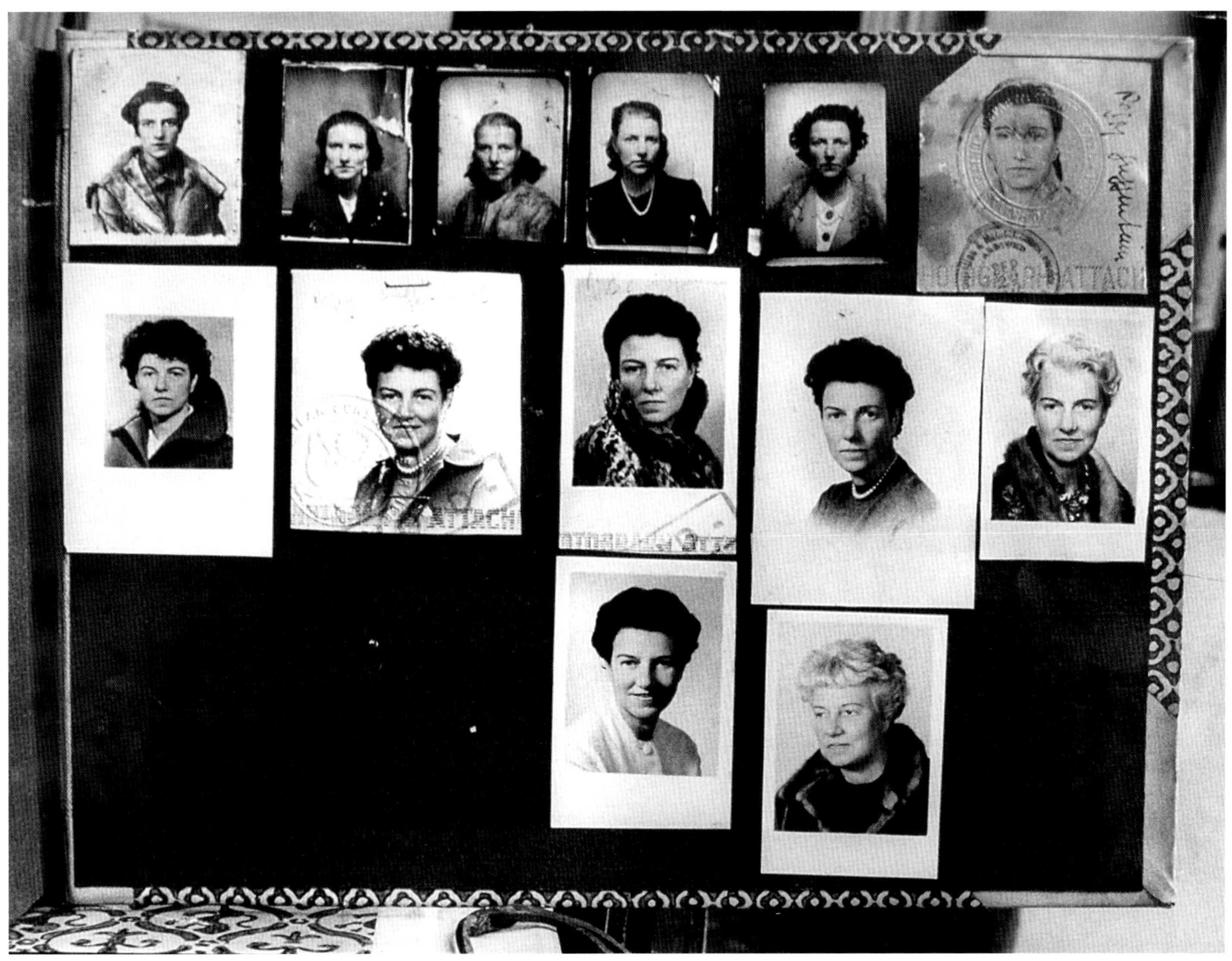

     Robert Frank, from the series *From the Bus, New York*, 1958

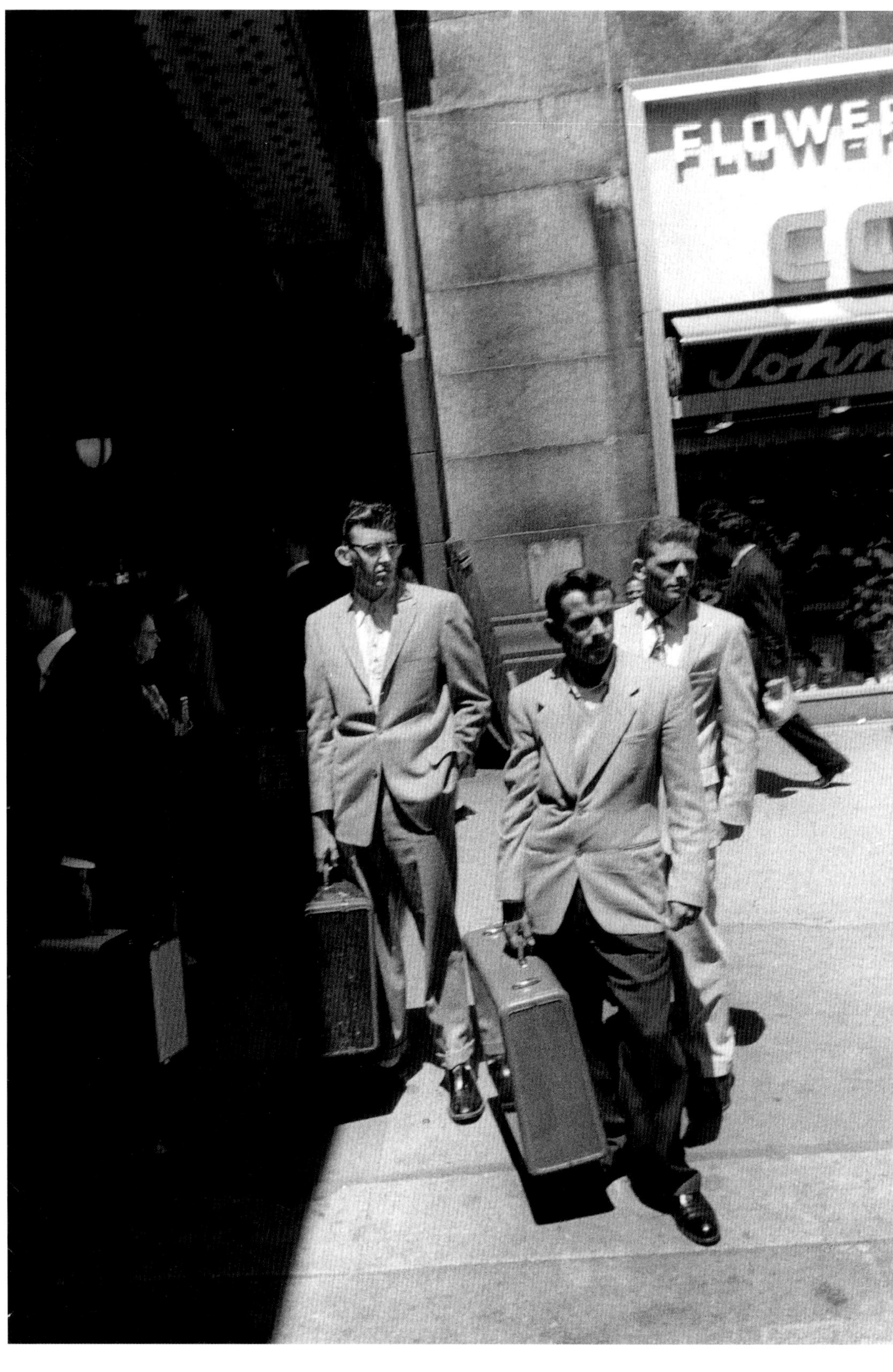

David Goldblatt, from the series *On Eloff Street, Johannesburg, South Africa*, 1966–7

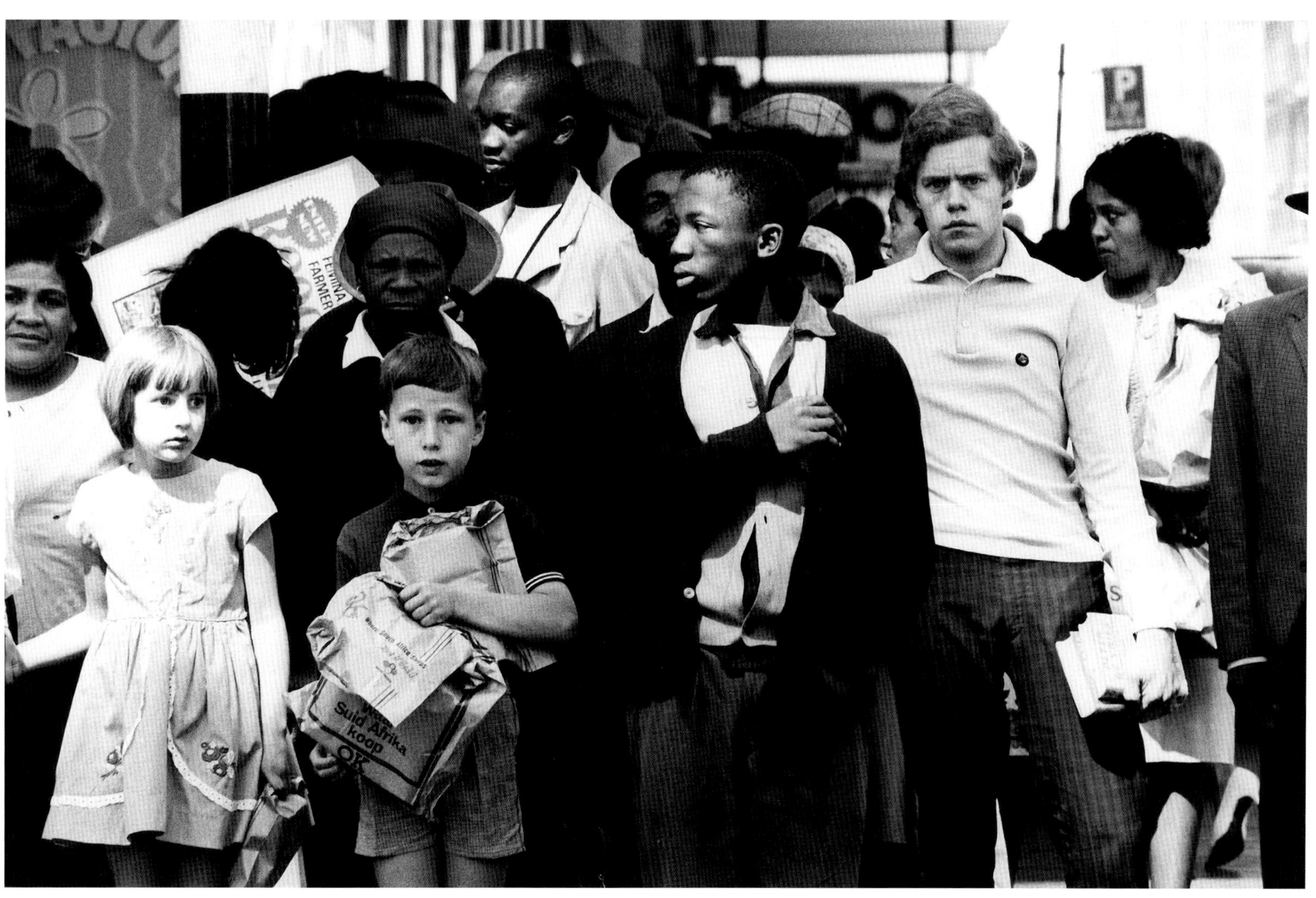

Laurie Anderson
Nobuyoshi Araki
Diane Arbus
Richard Avedon
Samuel Fosso
FotoRamblas
Ron Galella
Peter Hujar
William Klein
Chris Killip
Hashem El Madani
Robert Mapplethorpe
Daido Moriyama
Helmut Newton
Ken Ohara
Richard Prince
Timm Rautert
Thomas Ruff
Cindy Sherman
Malick Sidibé
Bert Stern
Antanas Sutkus
Ed van der Elsken
Garry Winogrand

Bert Stern, *Veruschka von Lehndorff and David Bailey*,
1964

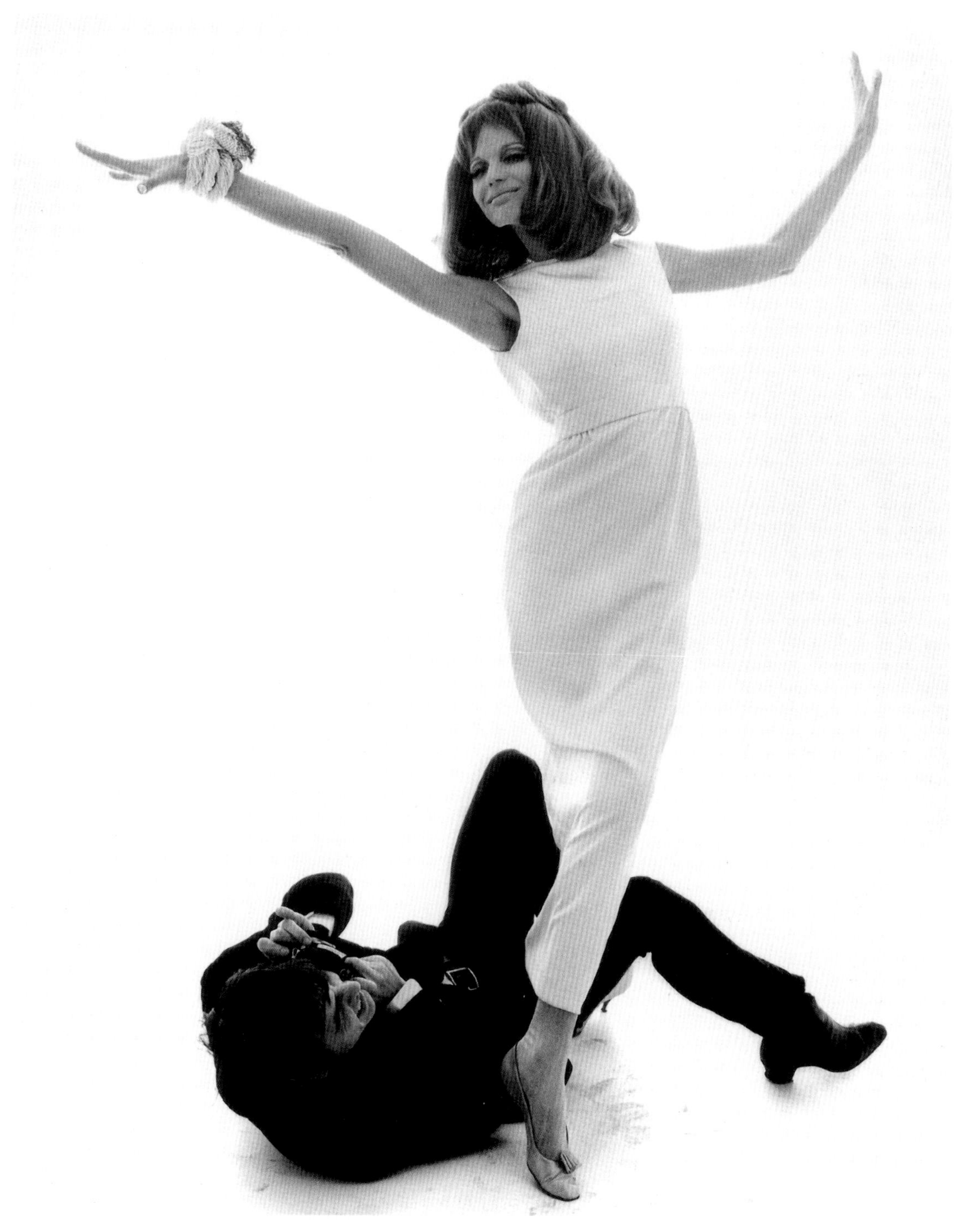

Malick Sidibé, *Monsieur Dembelé agent secret*
(Monsieur Dembelé Secret Agent), 1964

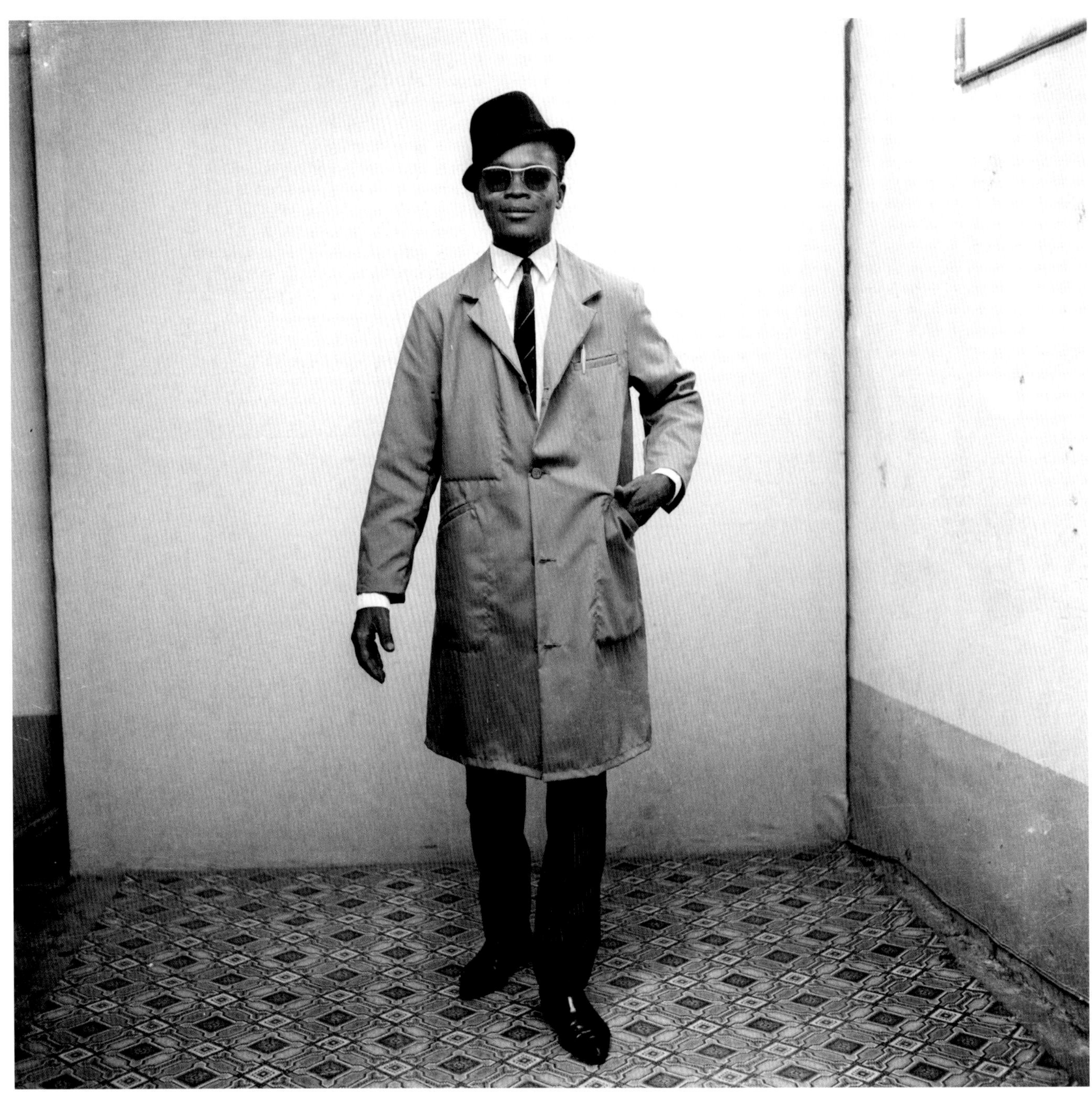

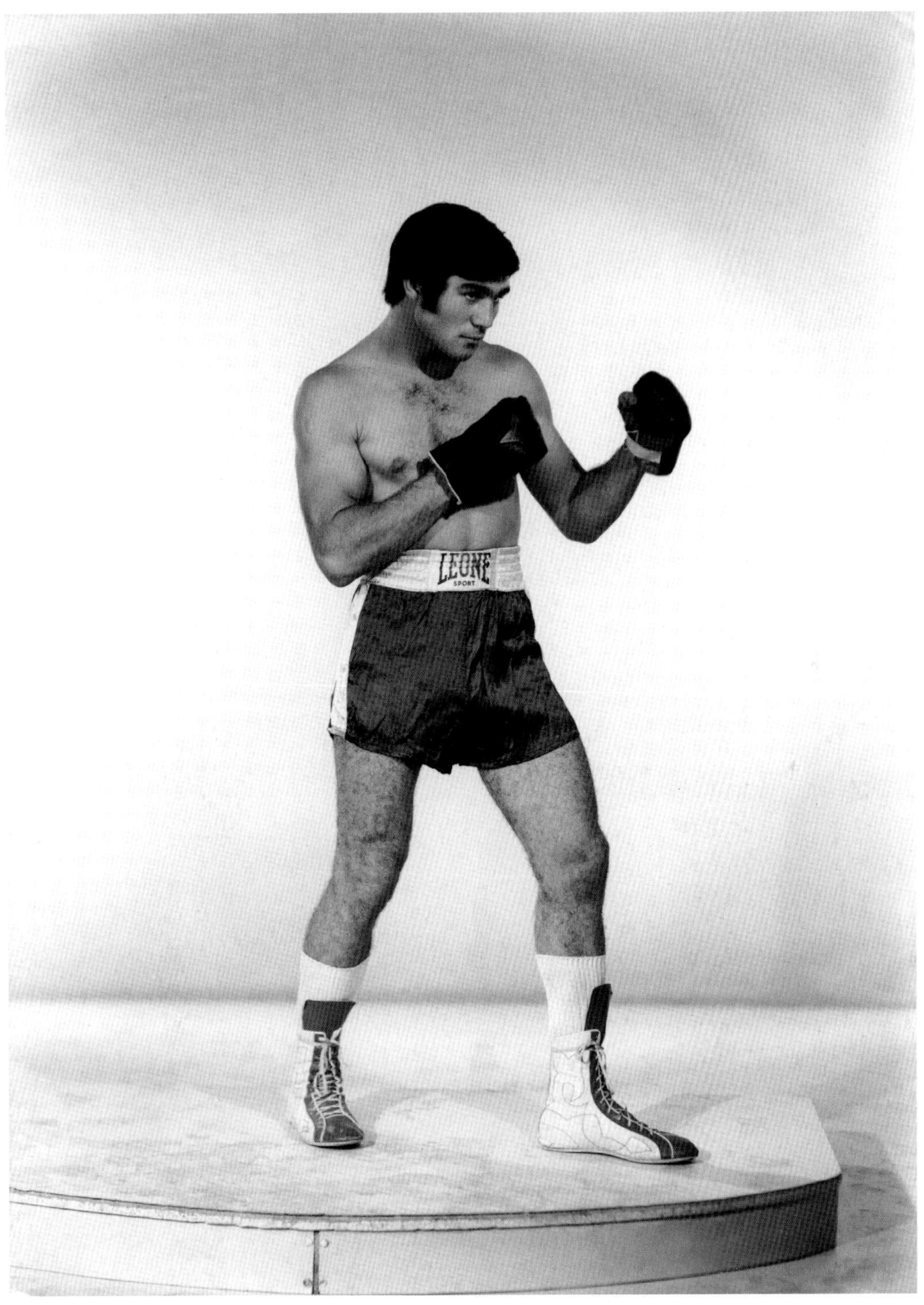

FotoRamblas, from a series of *Boxeadores, lucadores, varietés*
(Boxers, Fighters, Vaudevilles), 1960s

William Klein, *Life Is Good and Good for You in New York: Trance Witness Revels*, 1956; *Rome*,1959; *Moskau* (Moscow), 1964

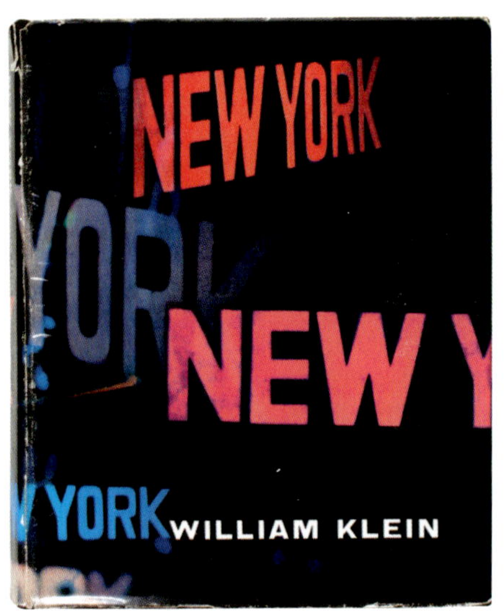

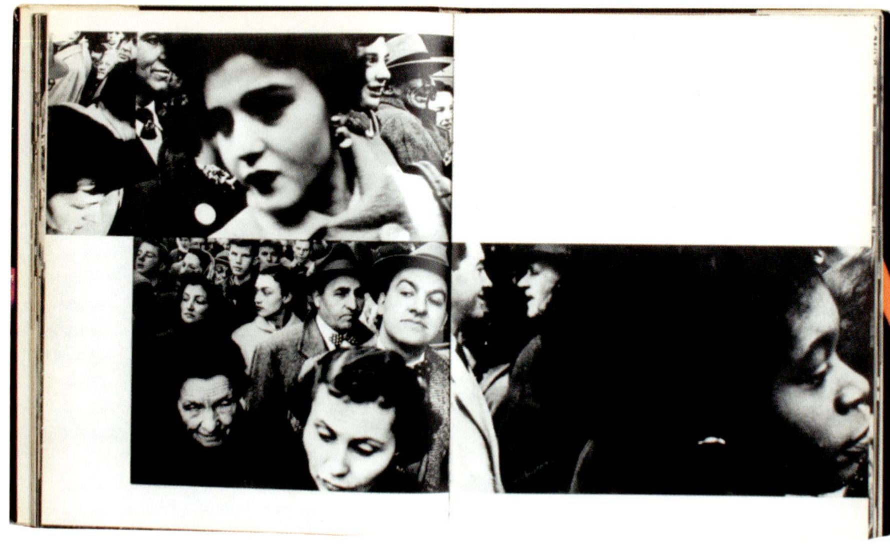

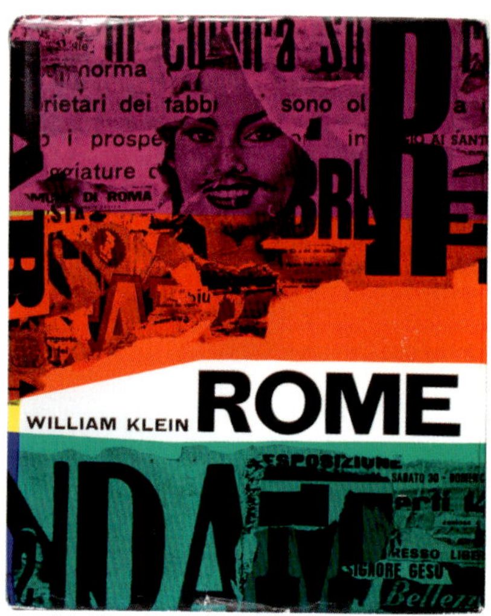

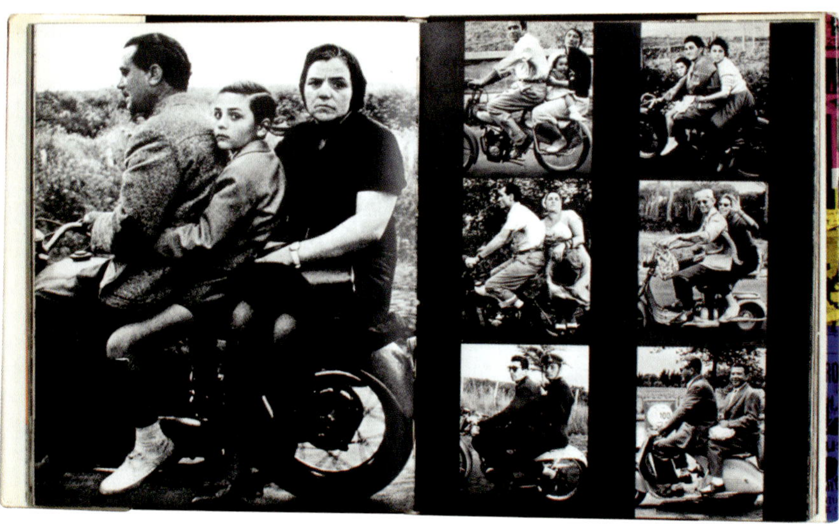

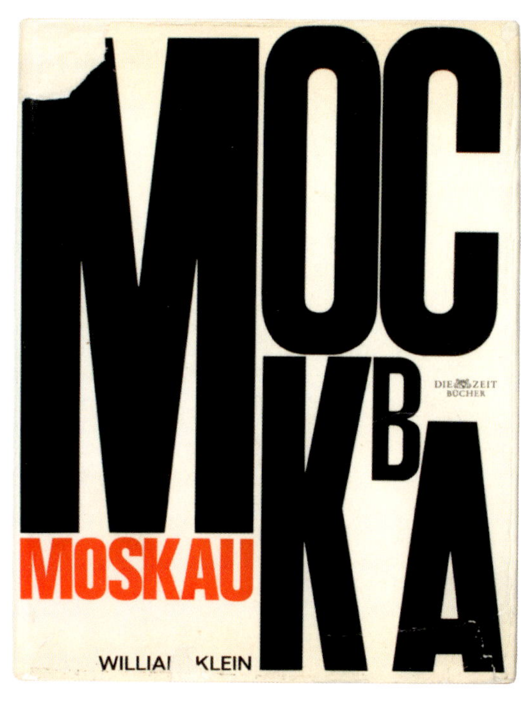

MOCKBA
MOSKAU
DIE ZEIT BÜCHER
WILLIAM KLEIN

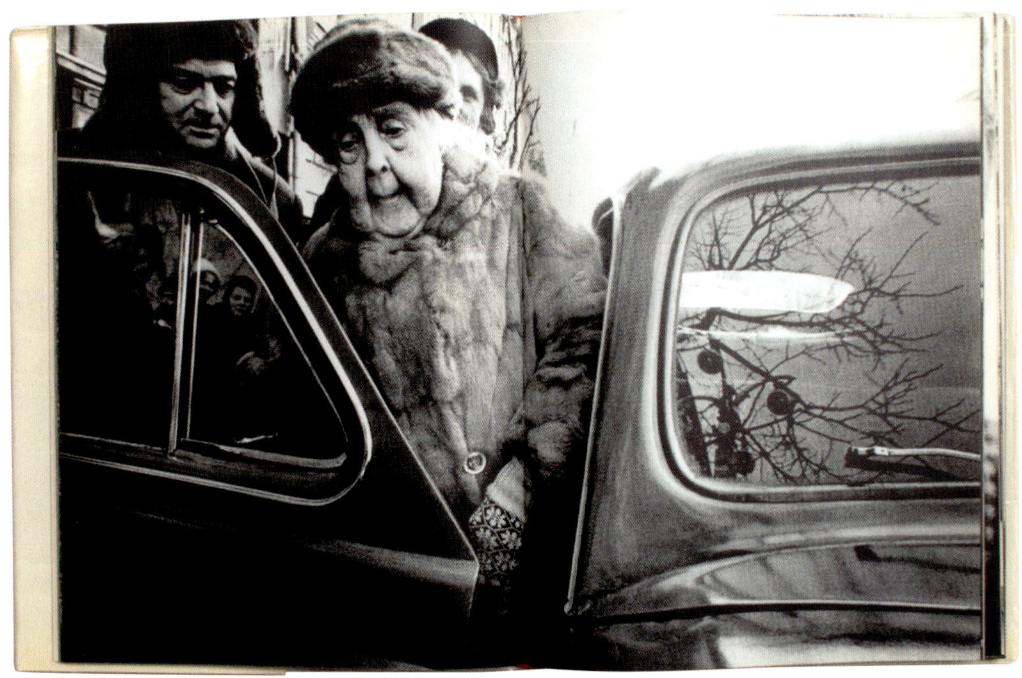

Daido Moriyama, *Nippon Gekijo Shashincho* (Japan: A Photo Theatre), 1968; *Sashin yo Sayonara* (Bye Bye Photography), 1972; *Karyudo (Hunter)*, 1972

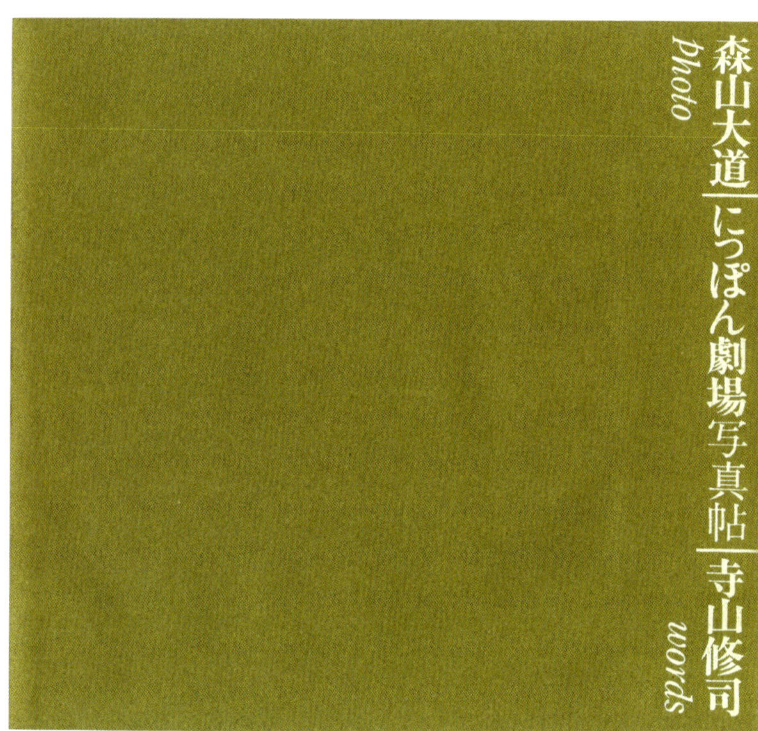

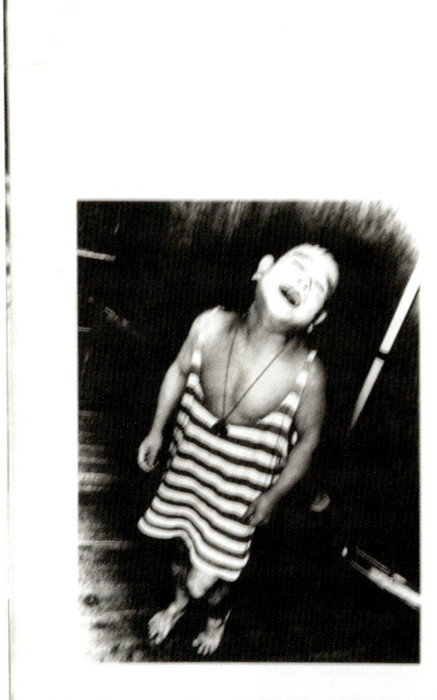

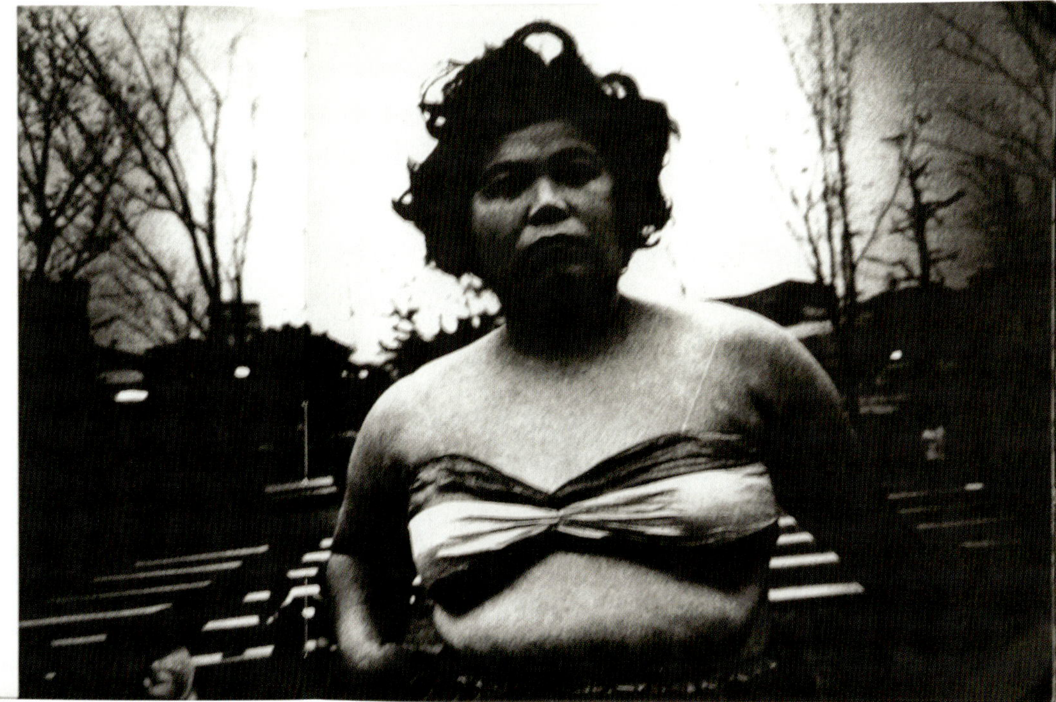

Daido Moriyama, *Nippon Gekijo Shashincho* (Japan: A Photo Theatre), 1968; *Sashin yo Sayonara* (Bye Bye Photography), 1972; *Karyudo (Hunter)*, 1972

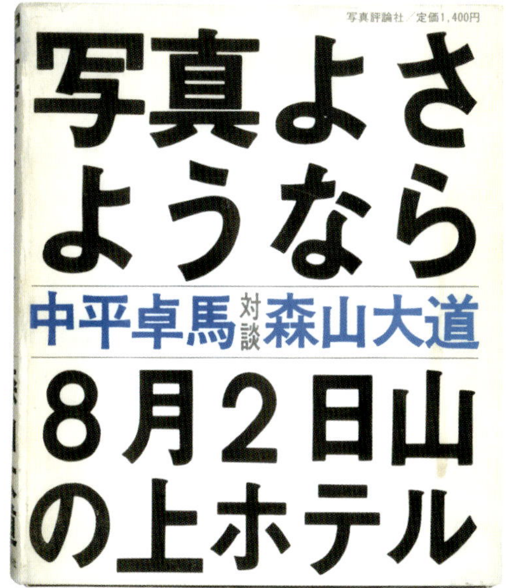

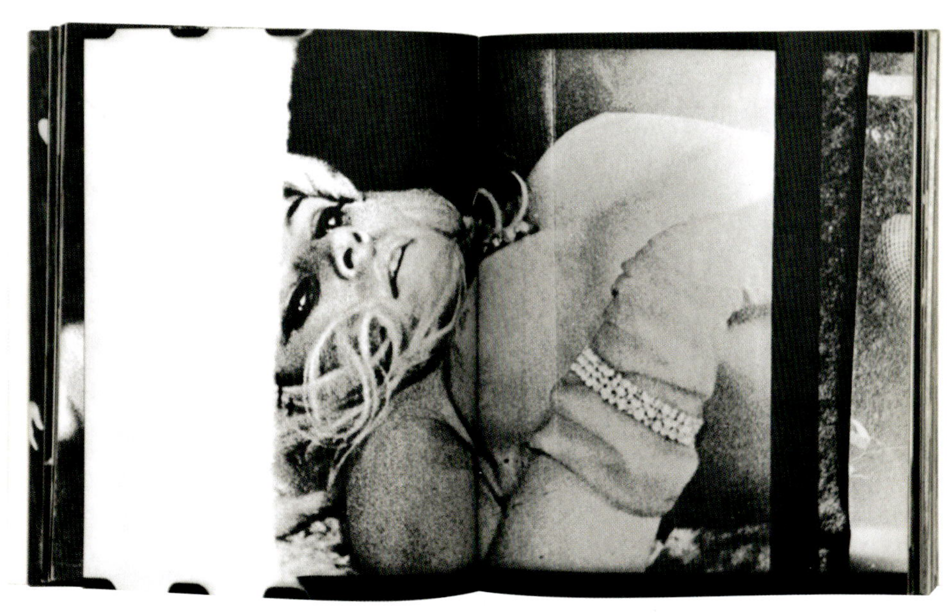

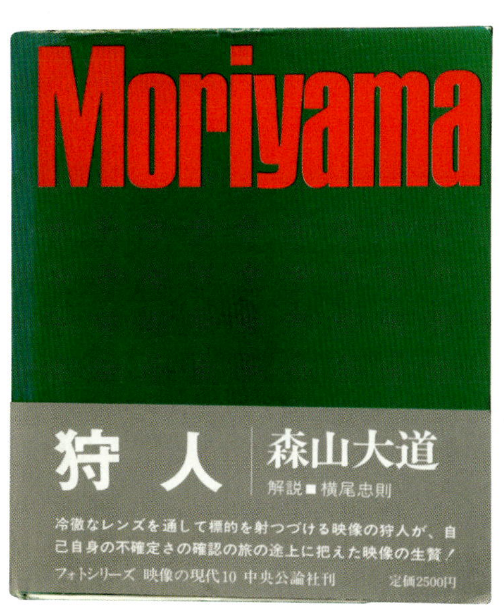

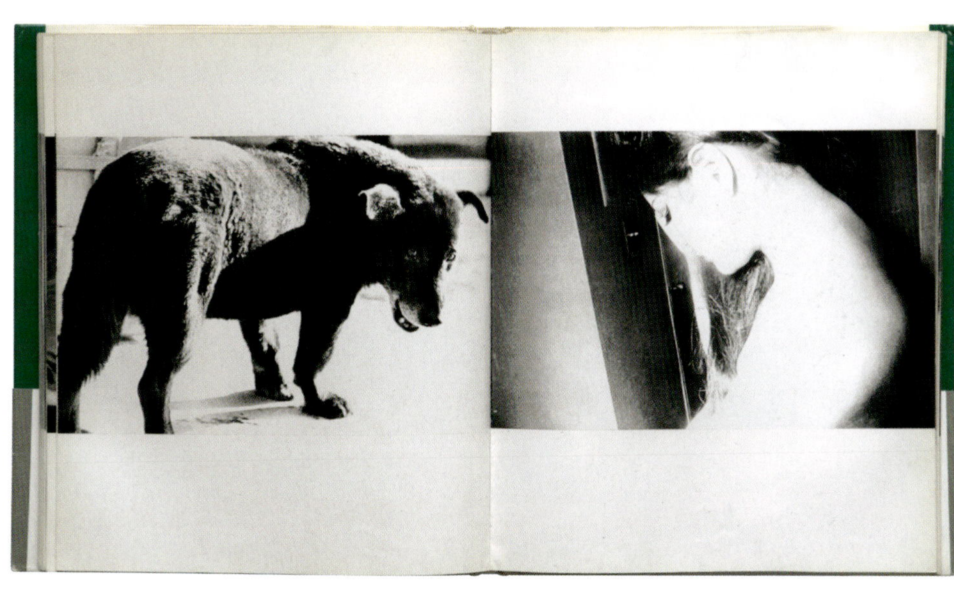

Ken Ohara, *One,* 1970

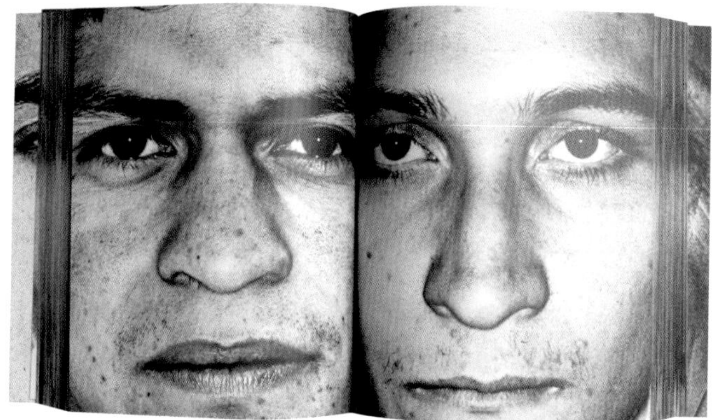

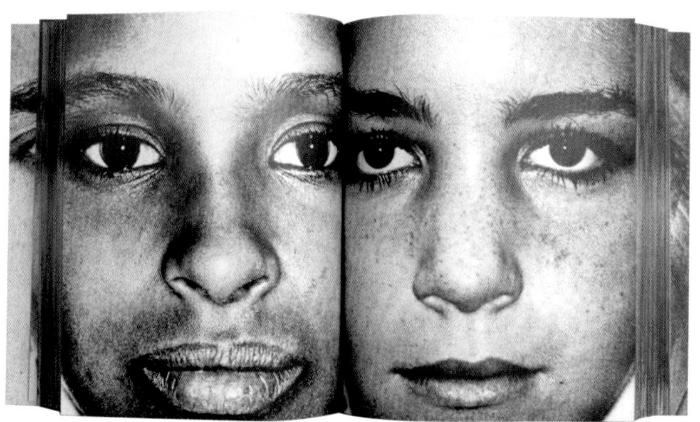

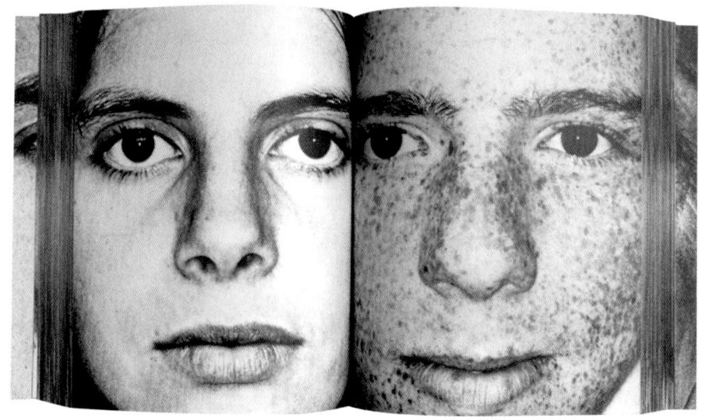

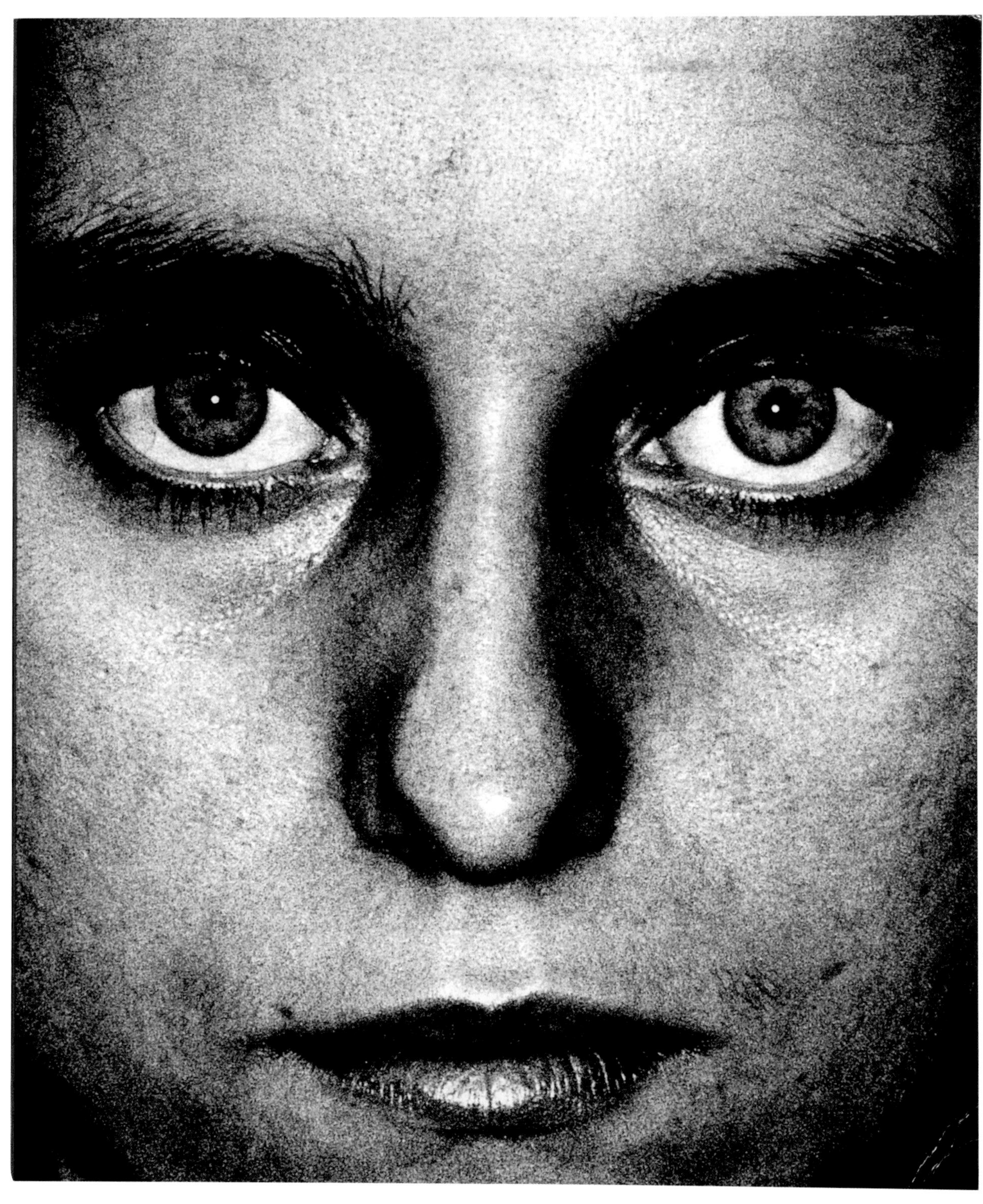

Ron Galella, *Woody Allen / Mia Farrow September 18, 1980 New York City, EXCLUSIVE – Woody Allen and Mia Farrow Heading for Dinner in Greenwich Village*, 1980

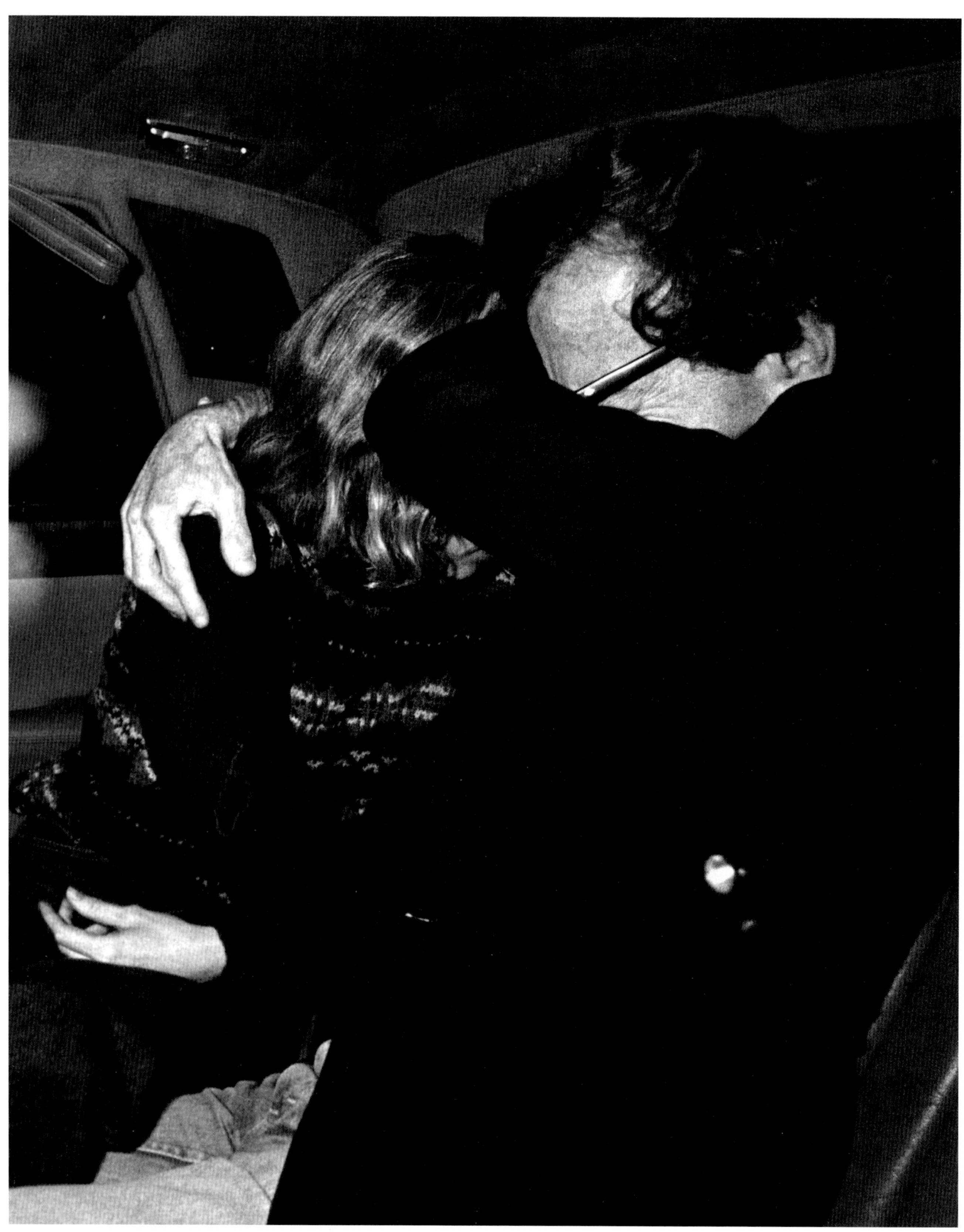

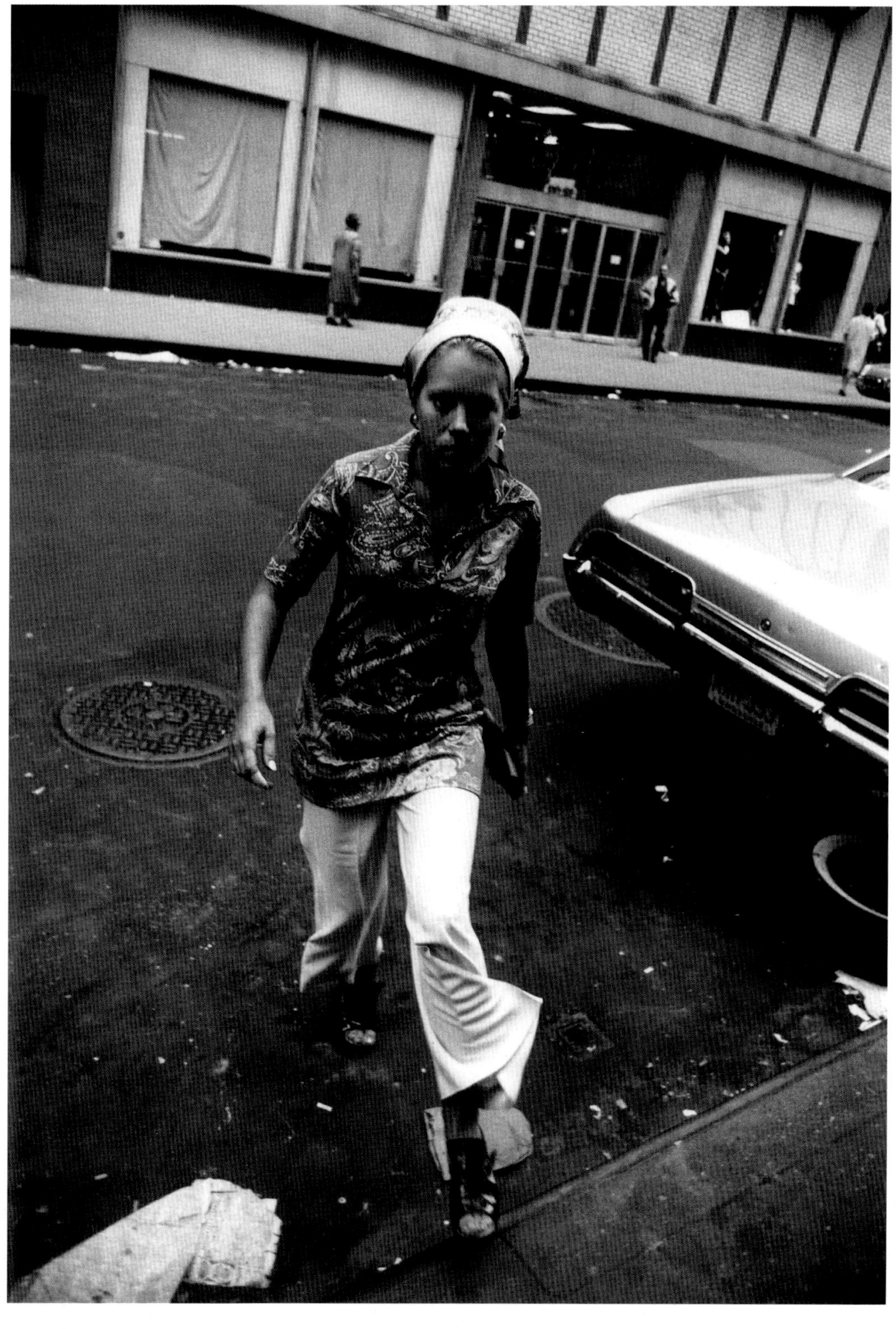

Helmut Newton, *La Mode piégée* (Fashion Caught in a Trap),
Vogue français, October 1971

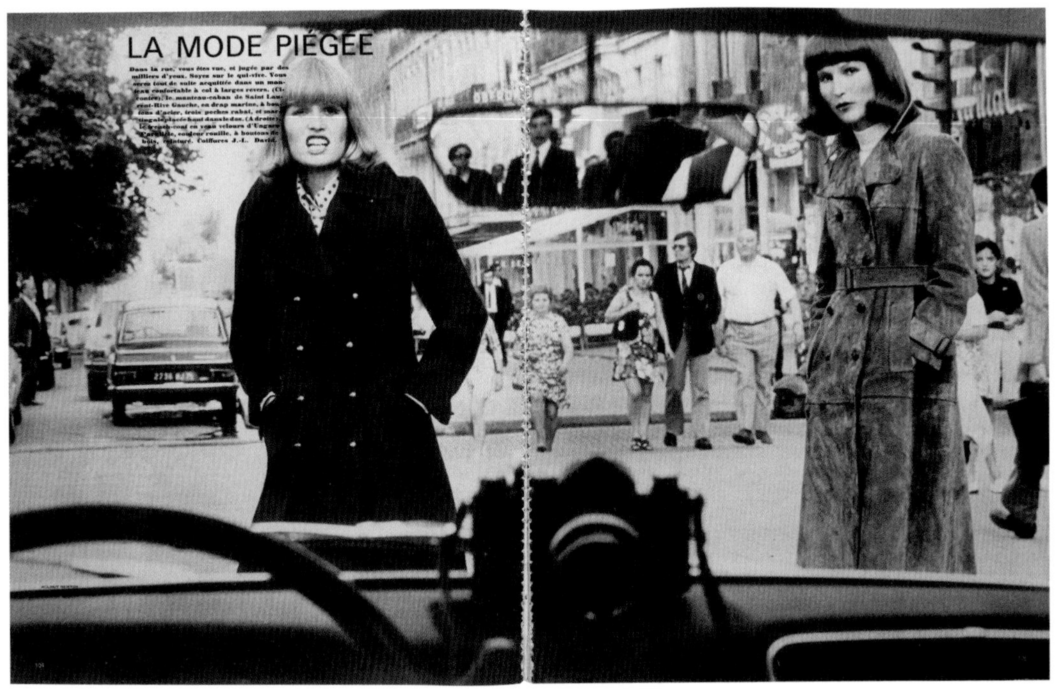

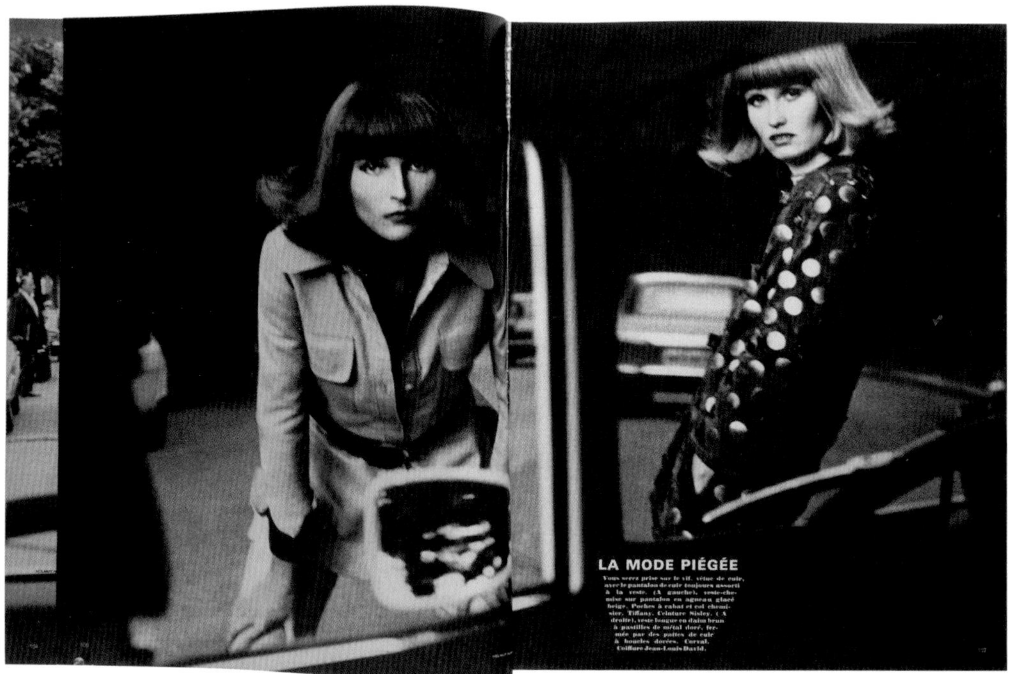

Helmut Newton, *La Mode piégée* (Fashion Caught in a Trap),
Vogue français, October 1971

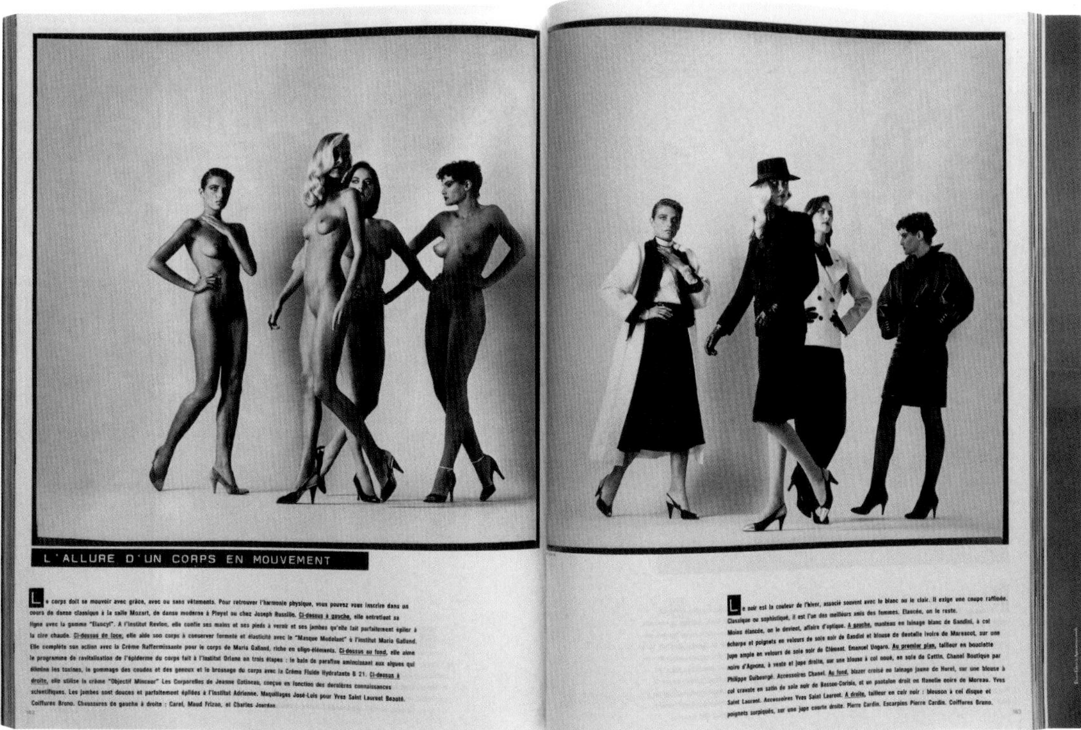

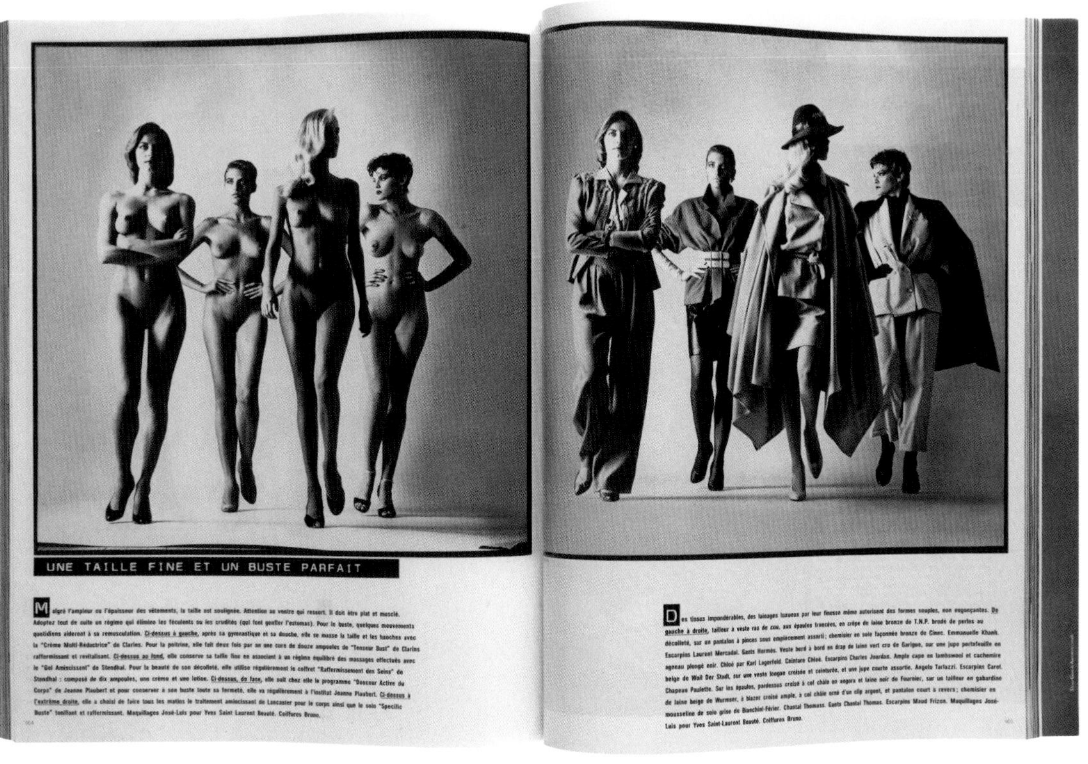

 Diane Arbus, *Woman with a Veil on Fifth Avenue, N.Y.C.*,1968

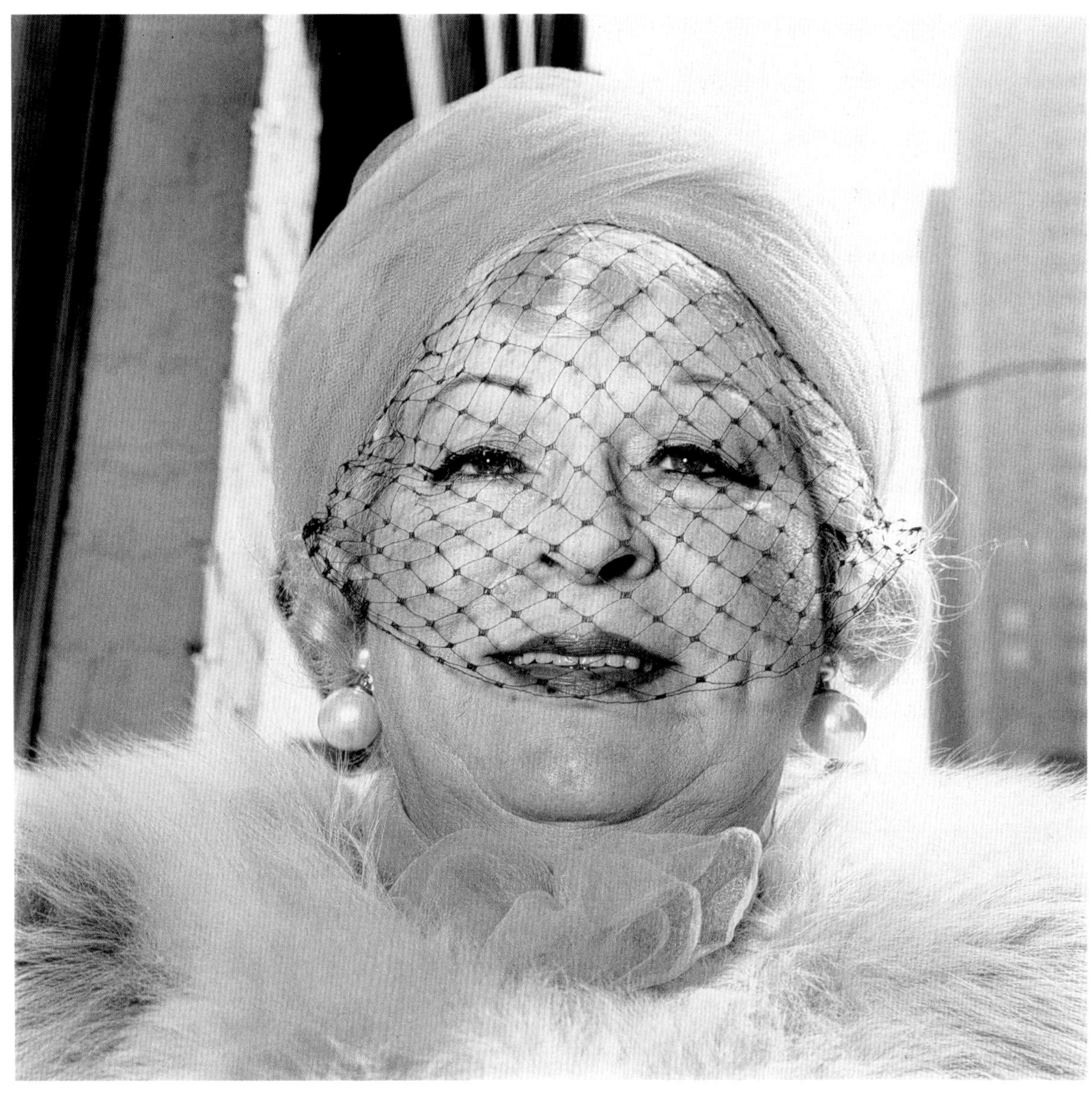

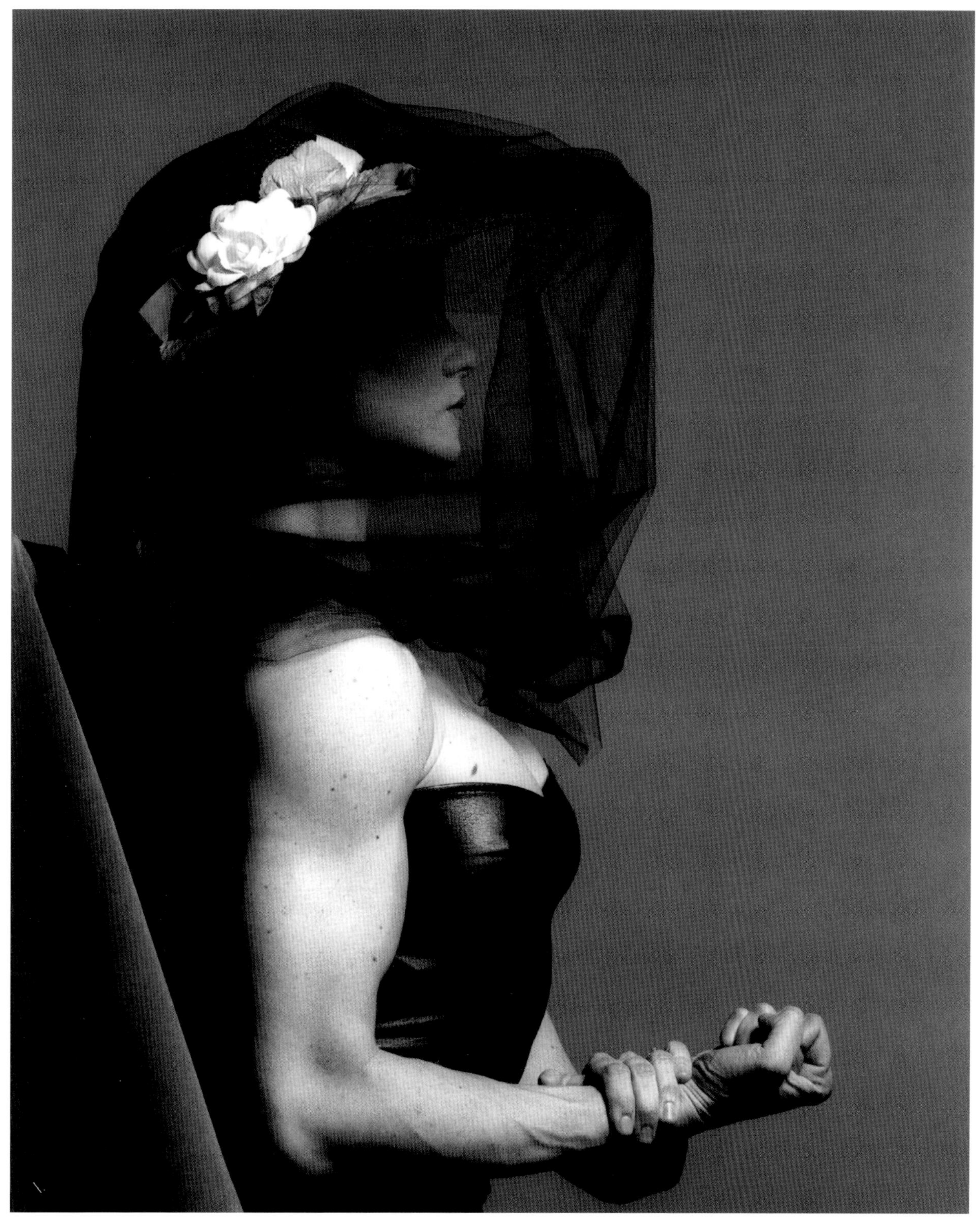

Richard Avedon, *The Chicago Seven: Lee Weiner, John Froines, Abbie Hoffman, Rennie Davis, Jerry Rubin, Tom Hayden, Dave Dellinger, Chicago, September 25, 1969*, 1969

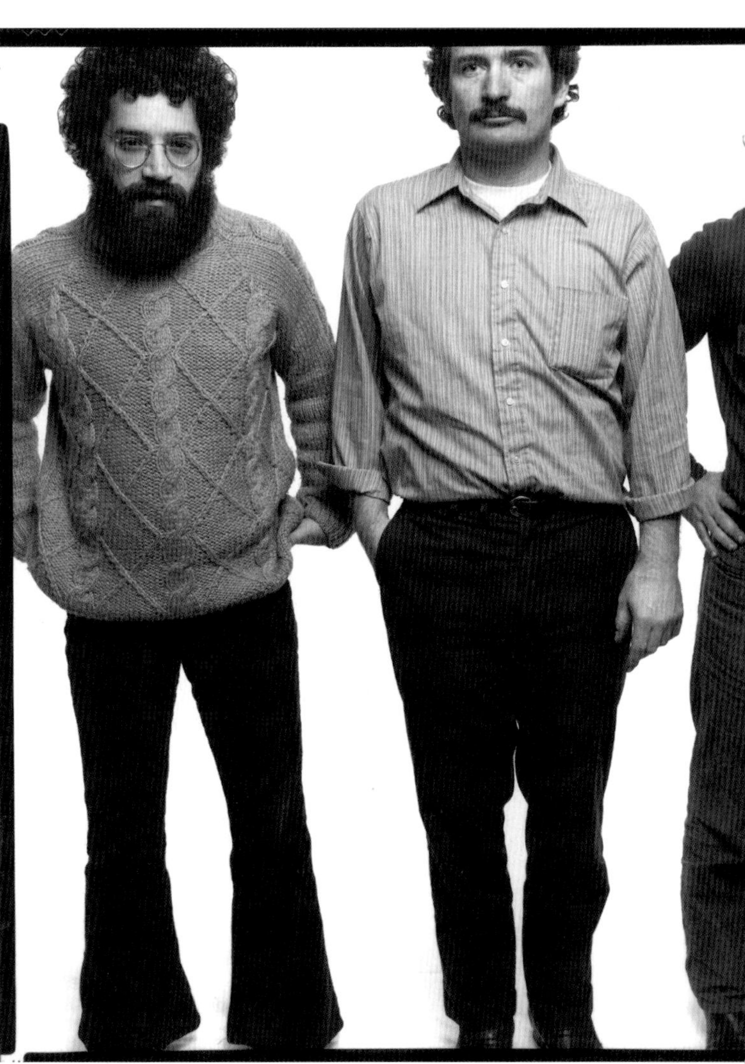

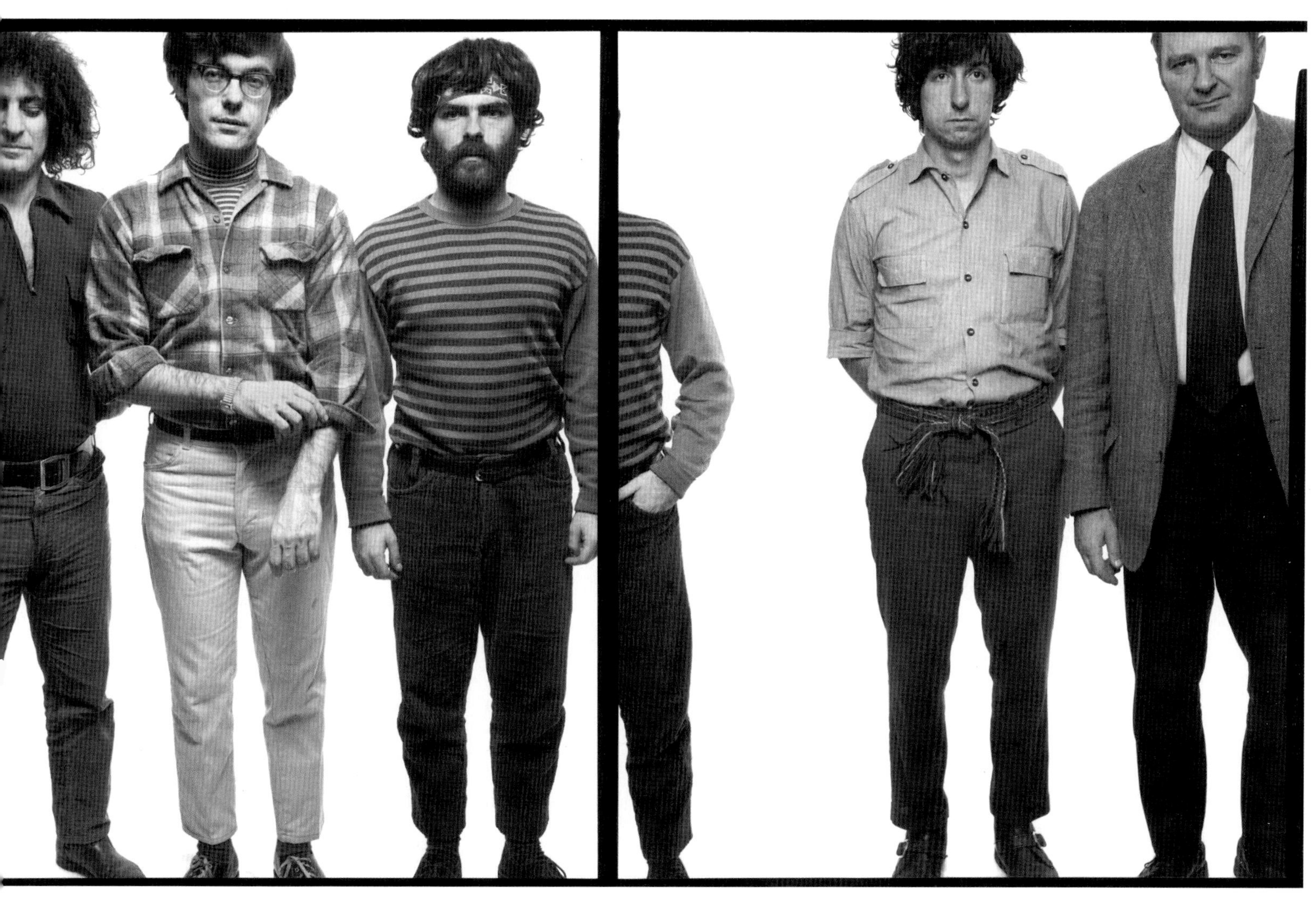

                Nobuyoshi Araki, from the book dummy *Tokyo*, 1973

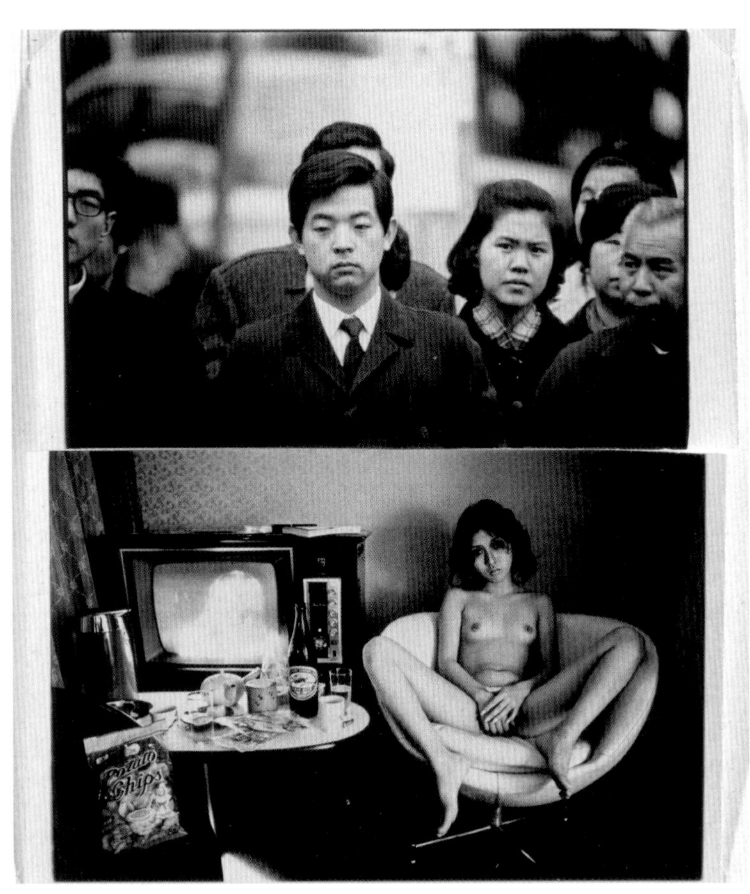

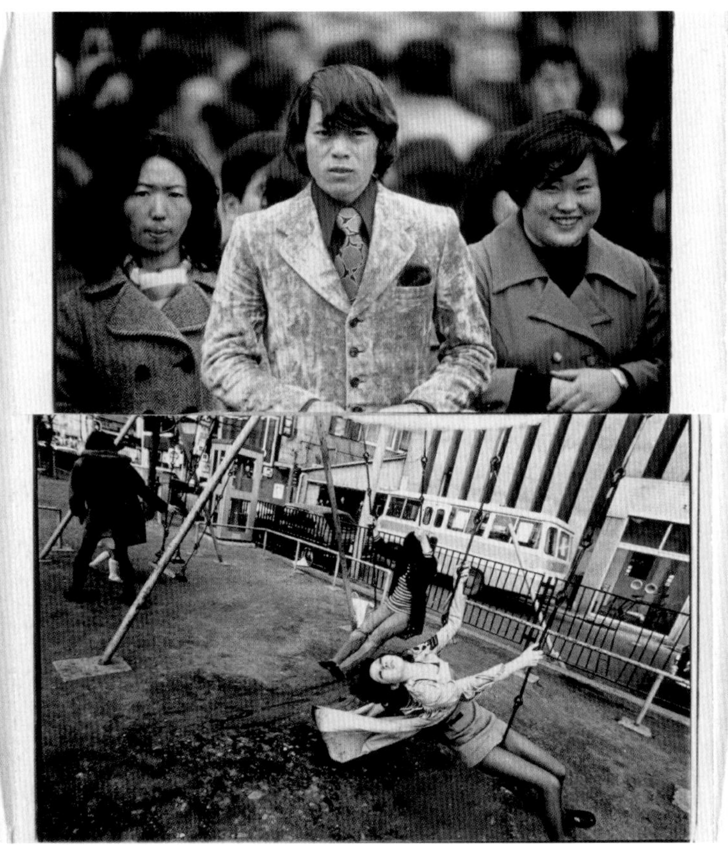

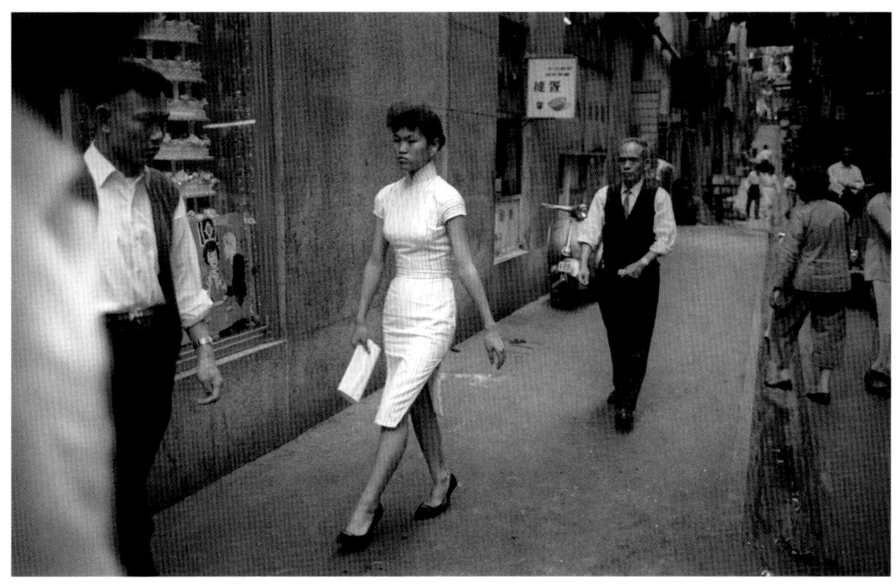

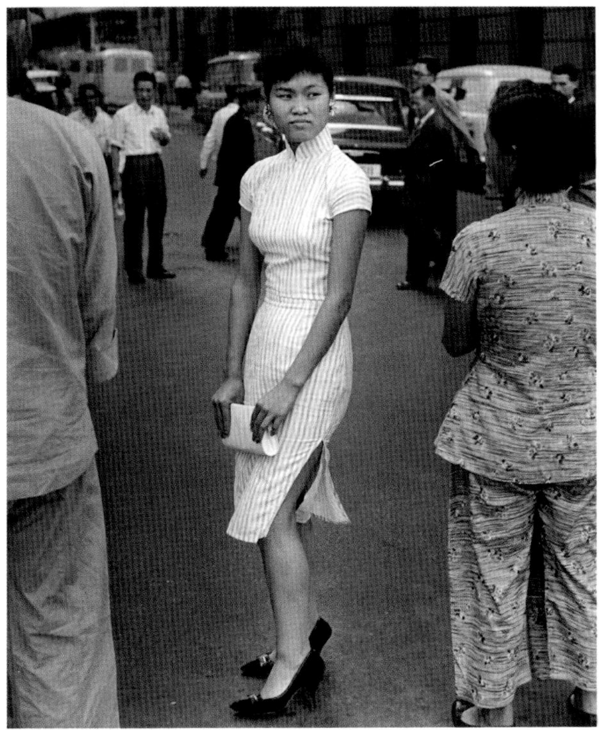

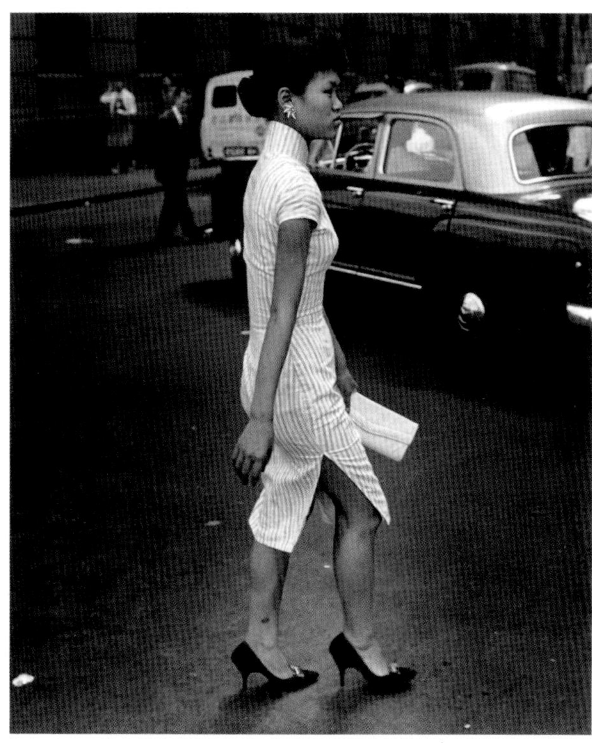

Ed van der Elsken, *Young Woman in Cheong-San Dress, Hong Kong*, 1960

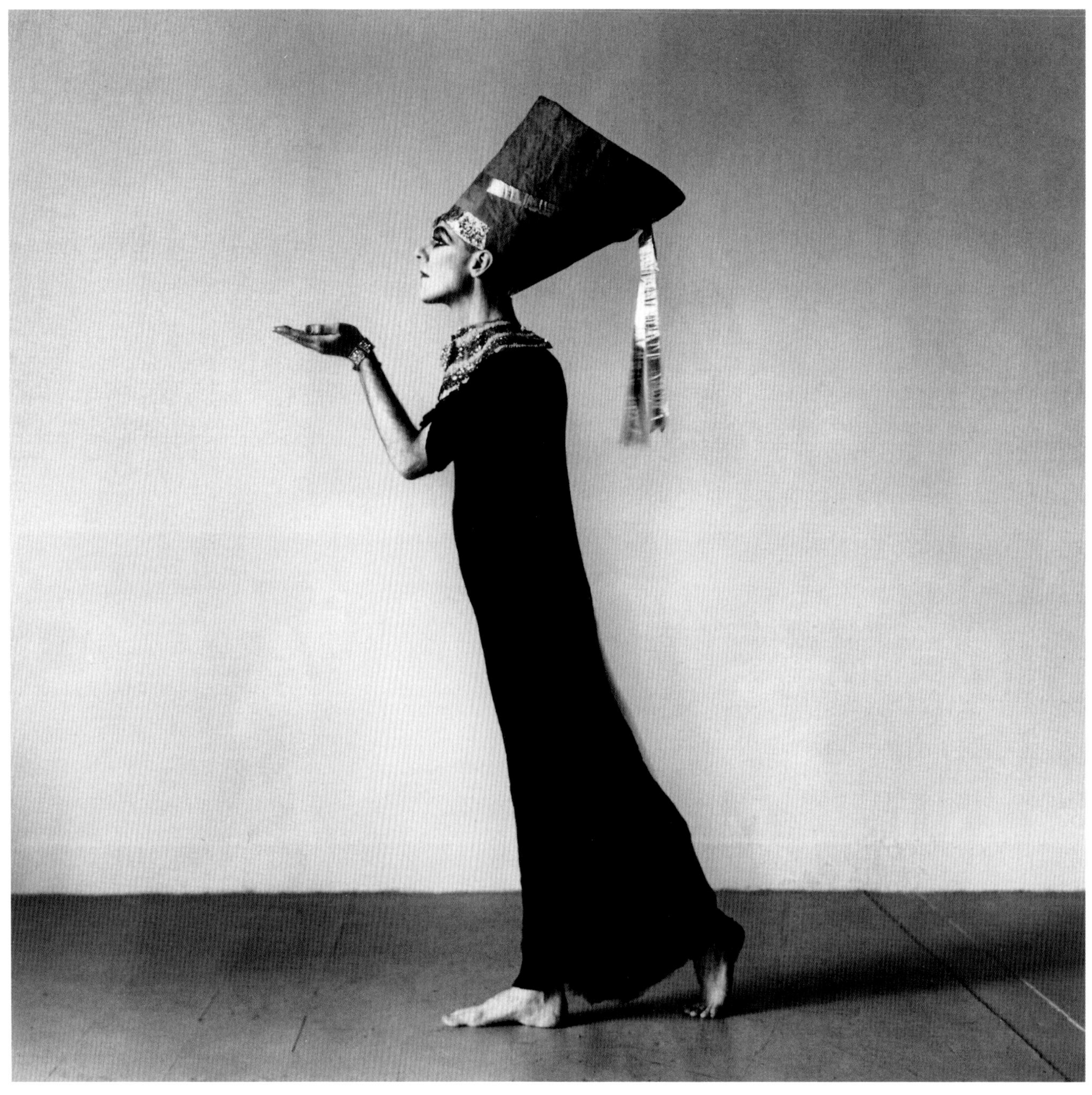

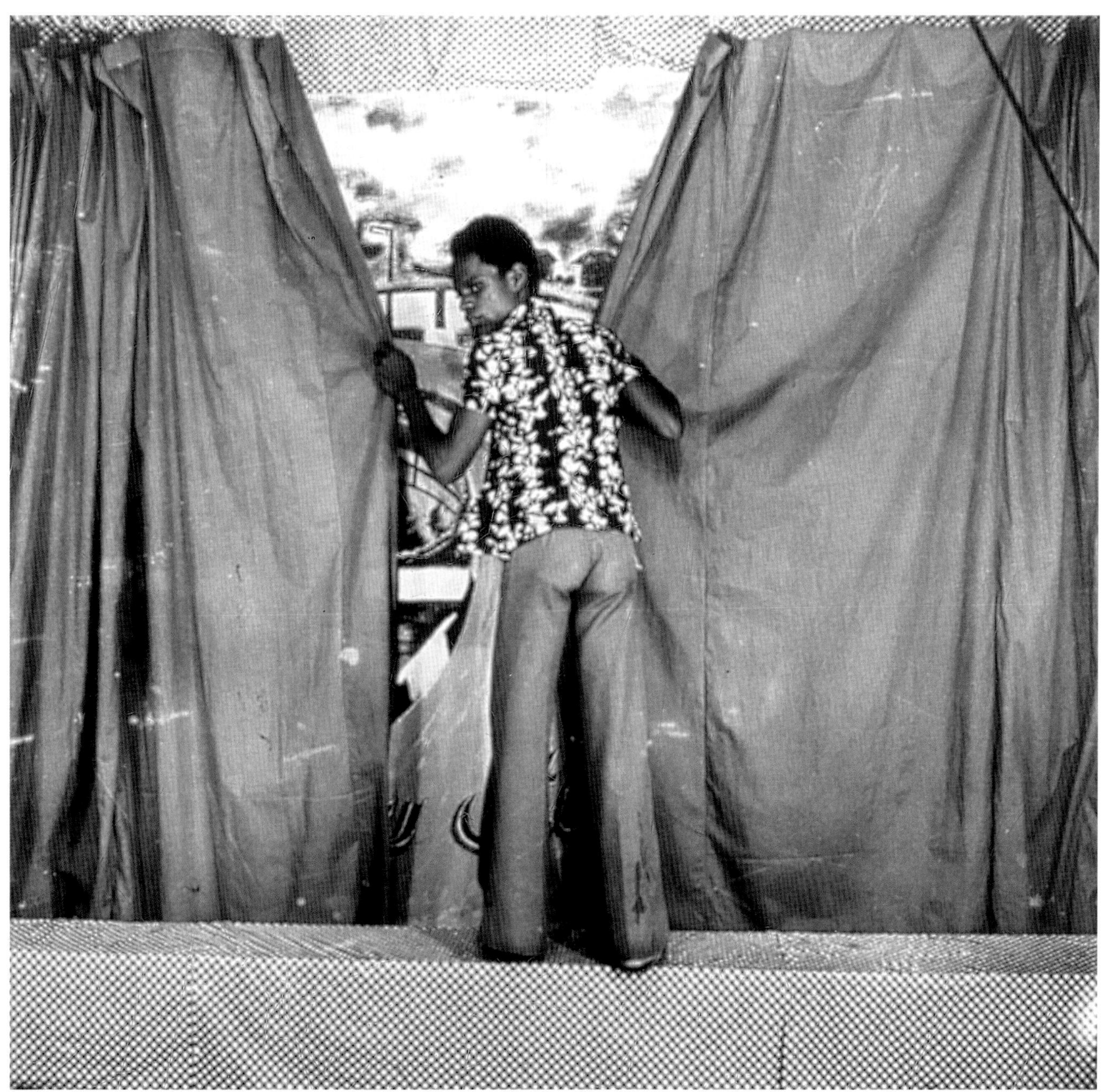

Timm Rautert, *Herr Kurt Bischoff, 29 Jahre, Oberfeldwebel* (Mr Kurt Bischoff, 29 Years Old, First Sergeant); *Fräulein Dorothee Oppermann, 20 Jahre, Schwesternschülerin* (Miss Dorothee Oppermann, 20 Years Old, Nursing Student), 1974

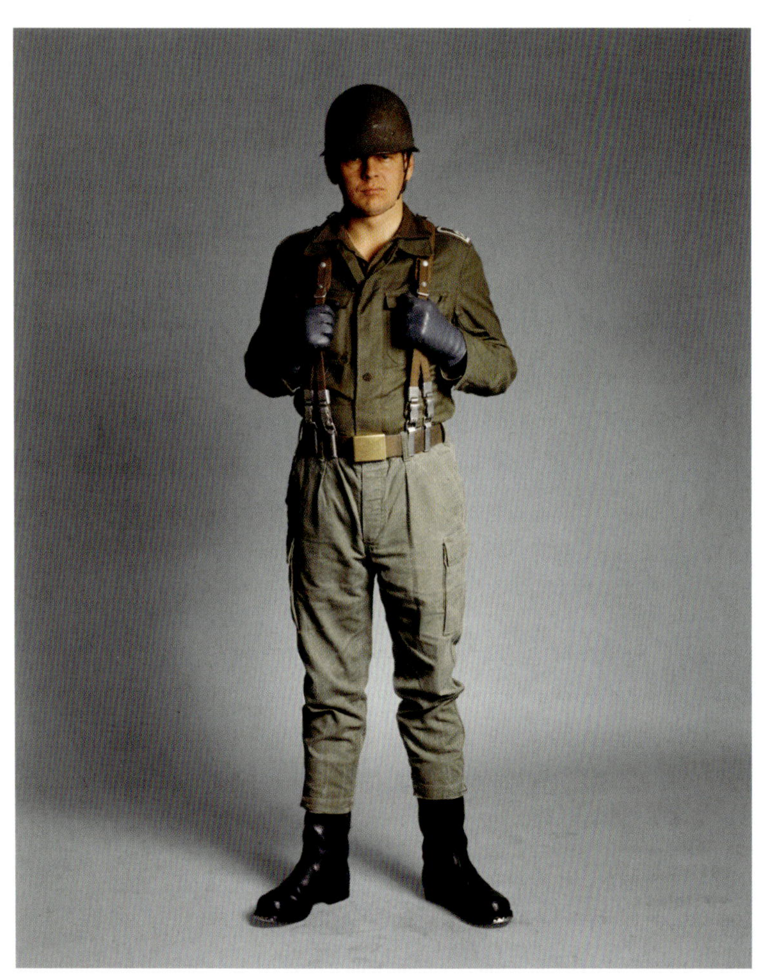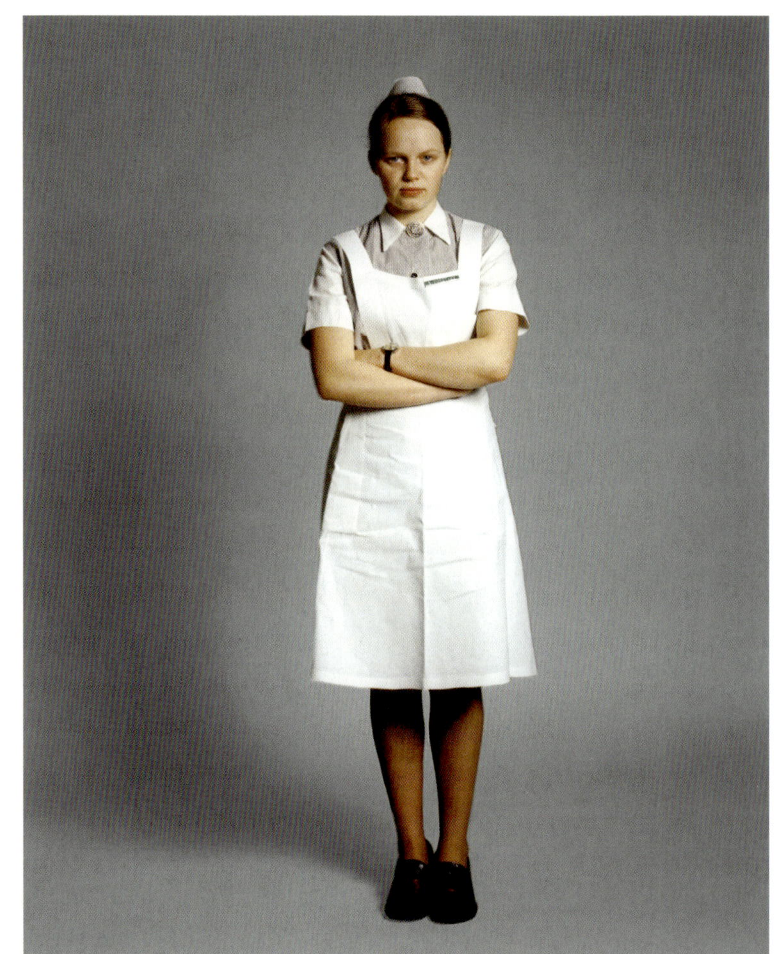

Timm Rautert, *Herr Kurt Bischoff, 29 Jahre, Oberfeldwebel* (Mr Kurt Bischoff, 29 Years Old, First Sergeant); *Fräulein Dorothee Oppermann, 20 Jahre, Schwesternschülerin* (Miss Dorothee Oppermann, 20 Years Old, Nursing Student), 1974

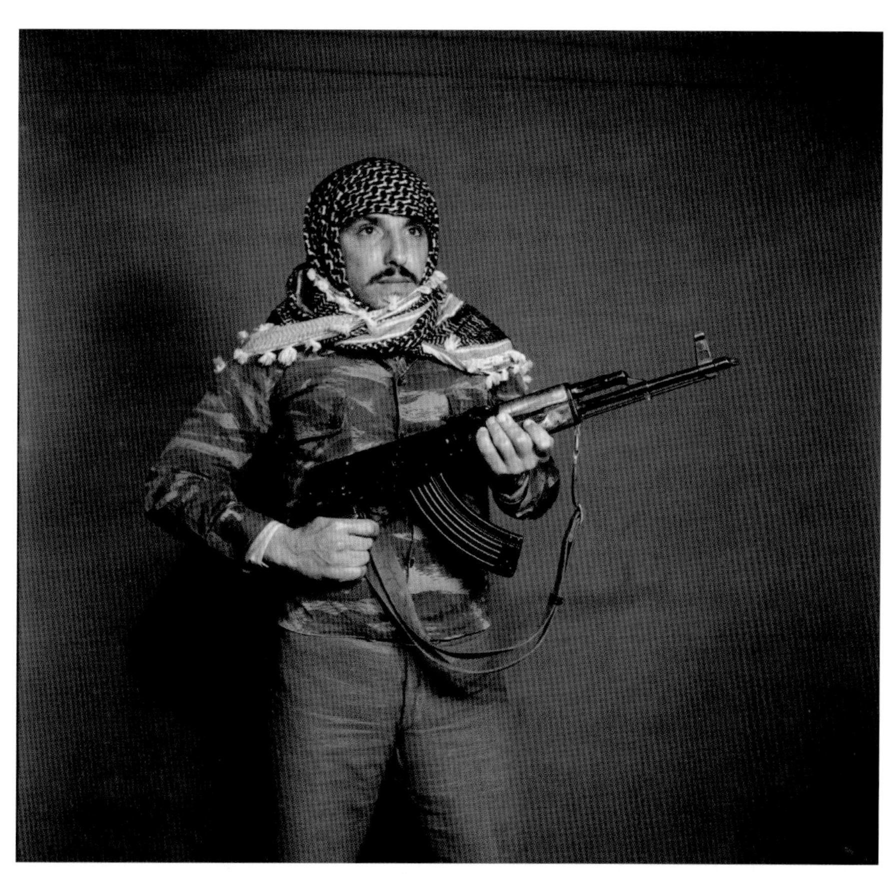

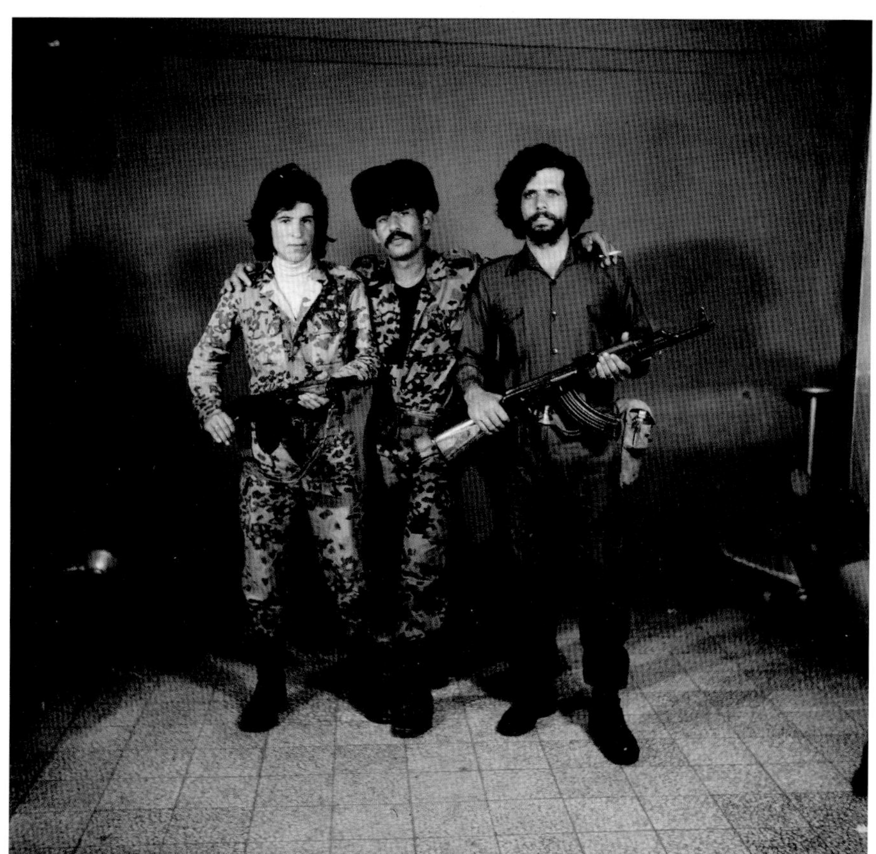

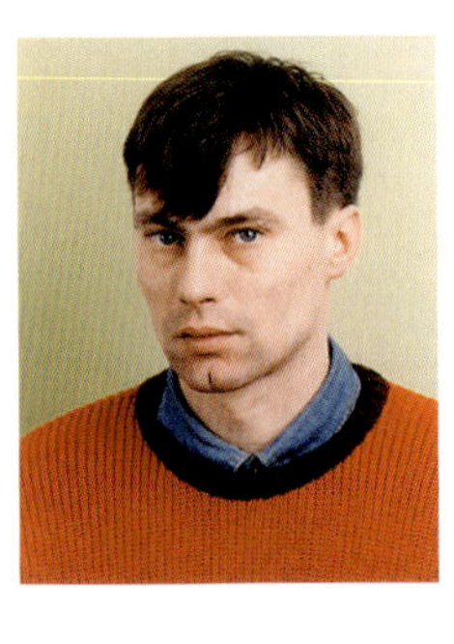 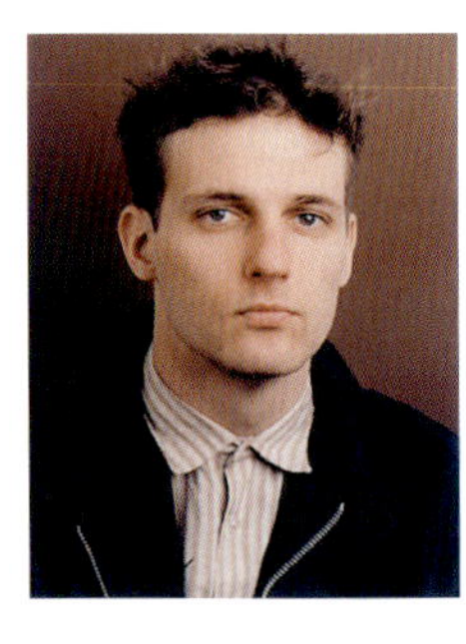 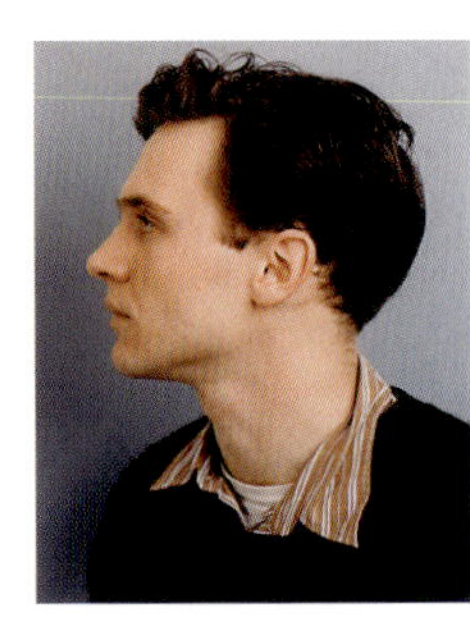 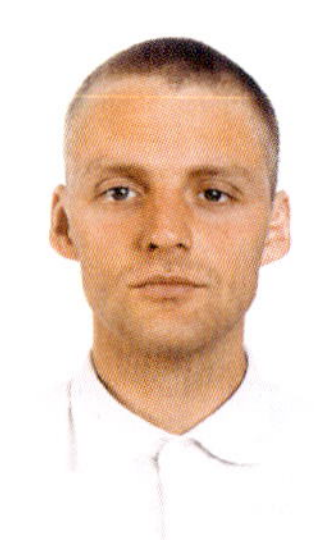 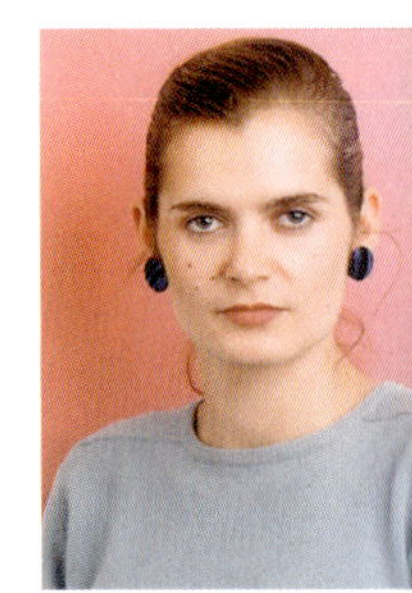
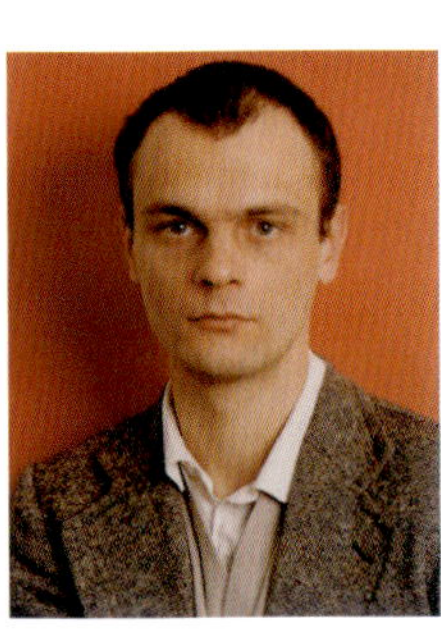 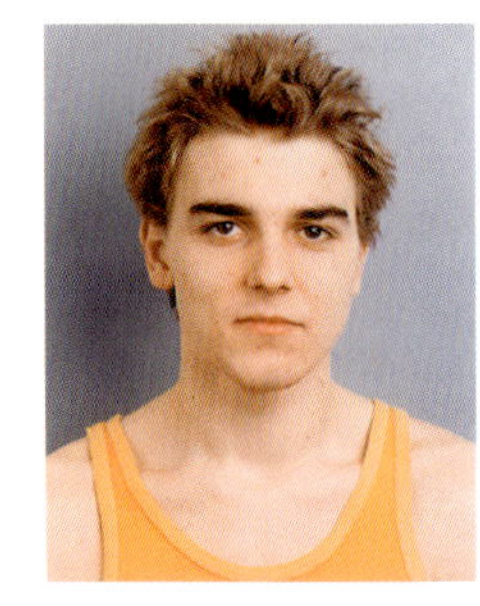 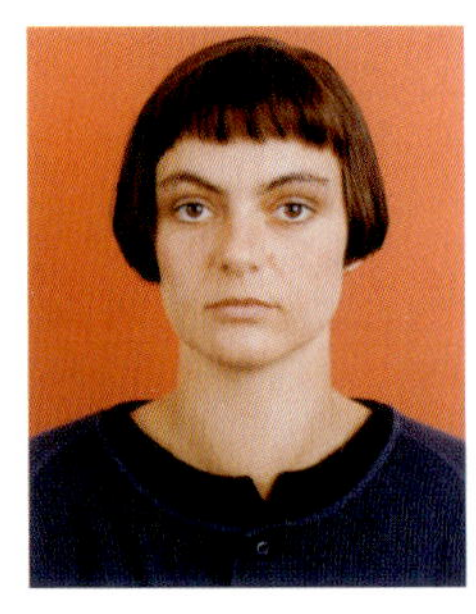 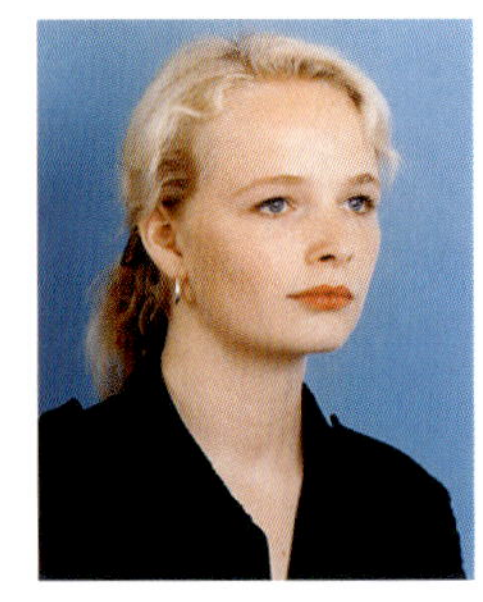 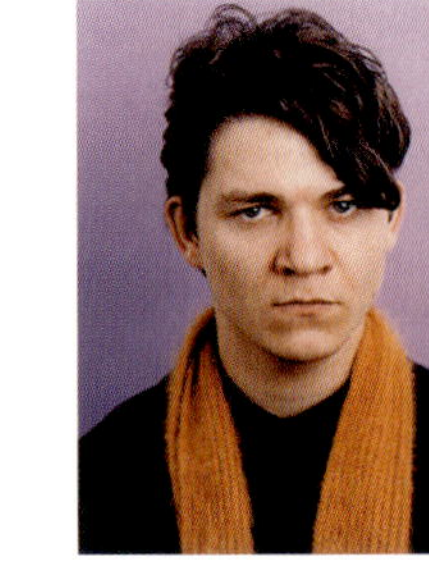
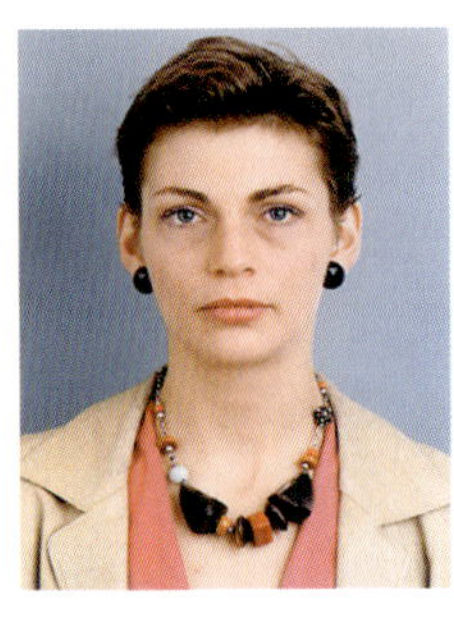 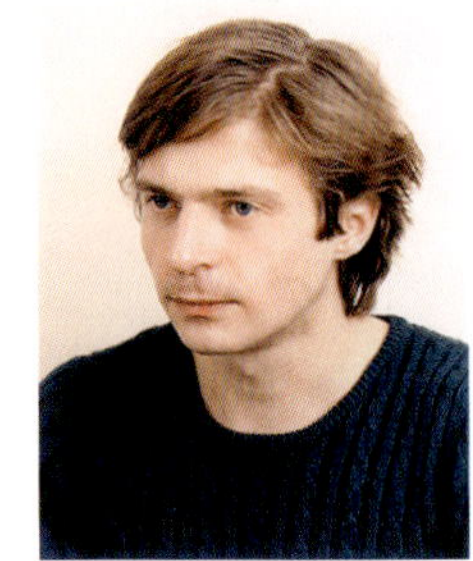 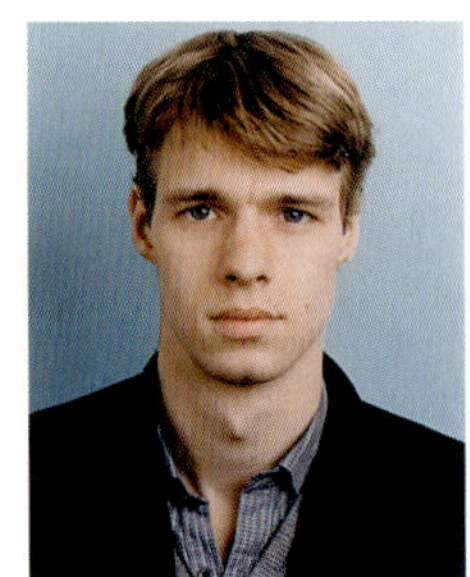 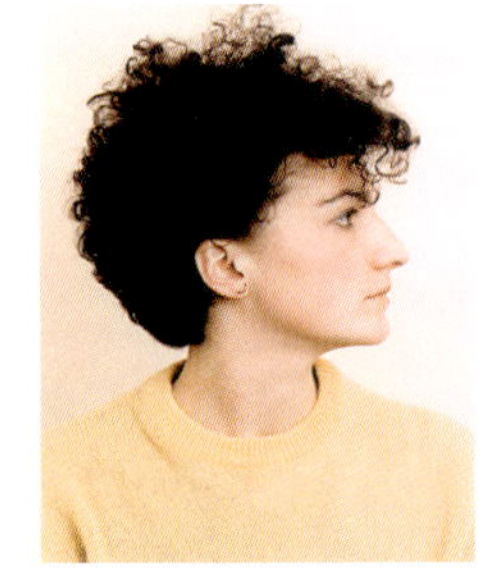 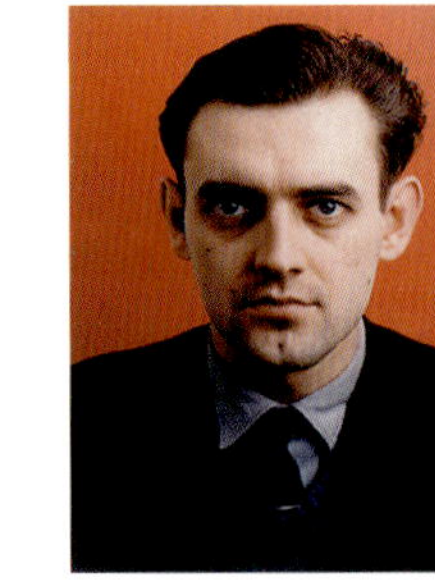
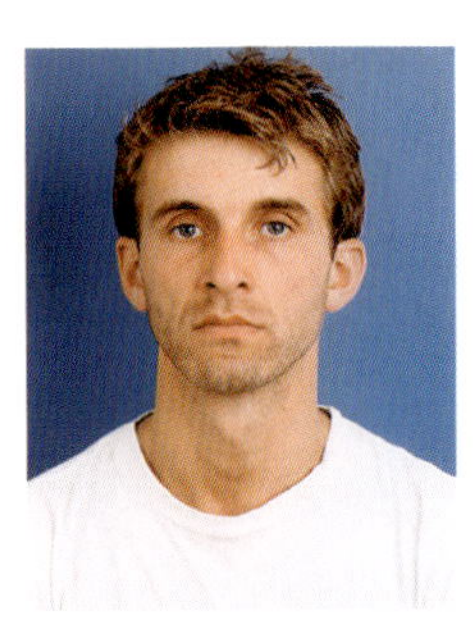 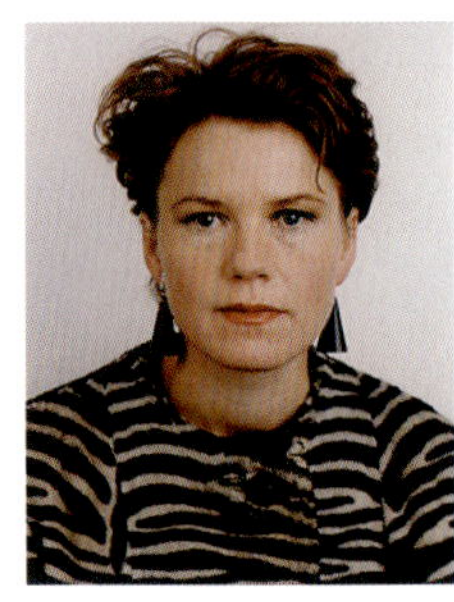 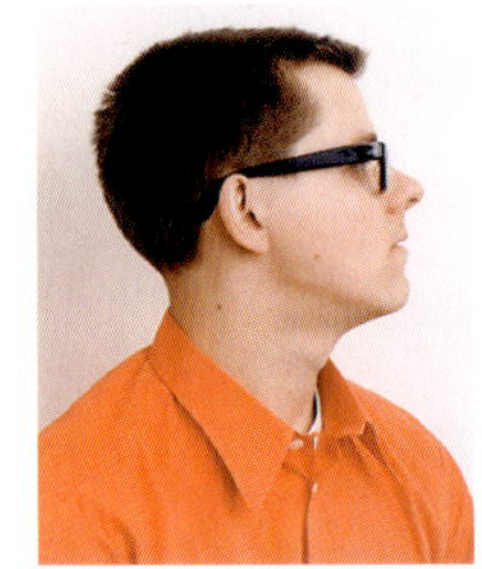 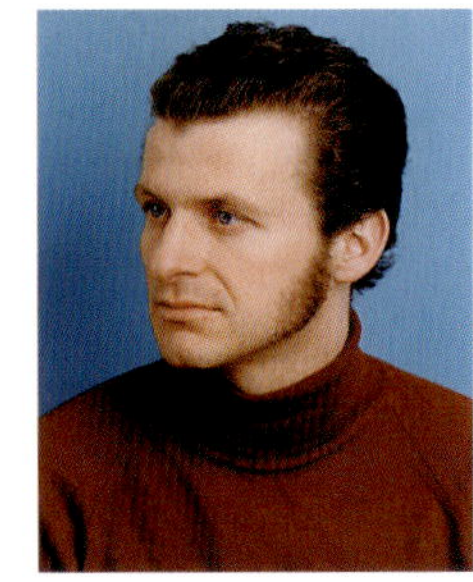 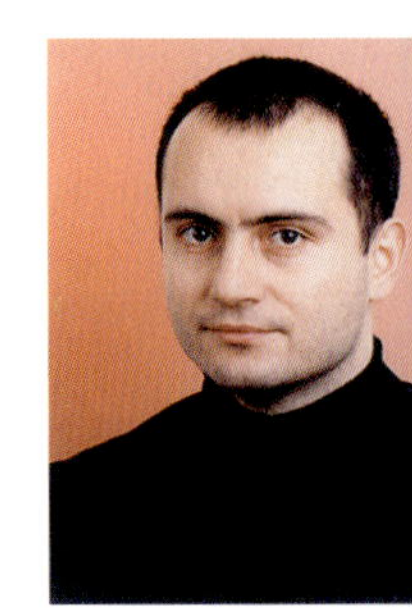

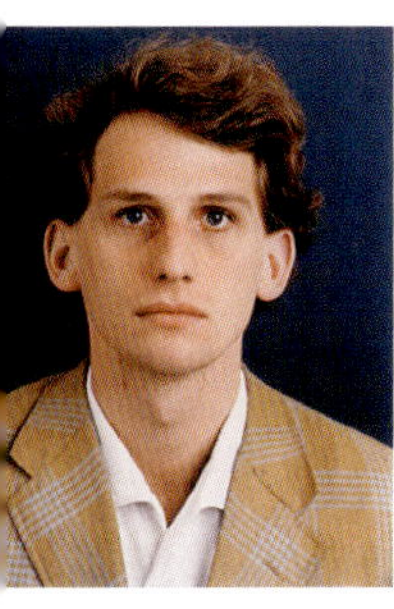 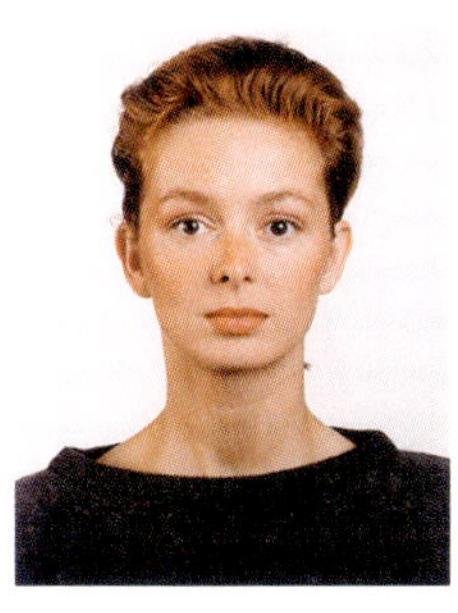 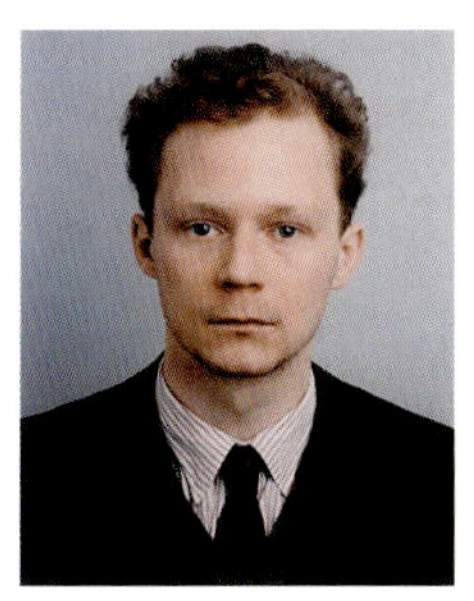 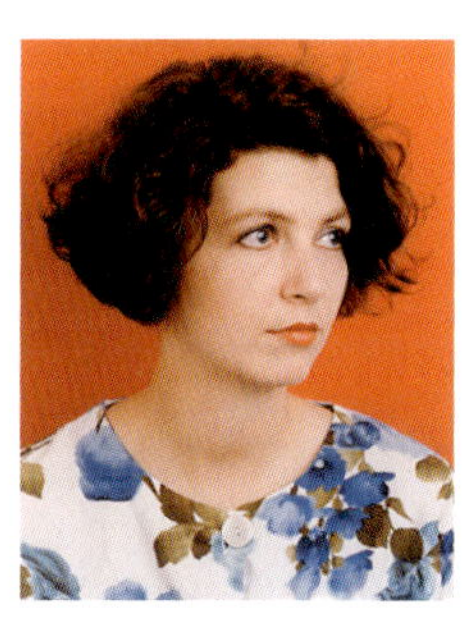 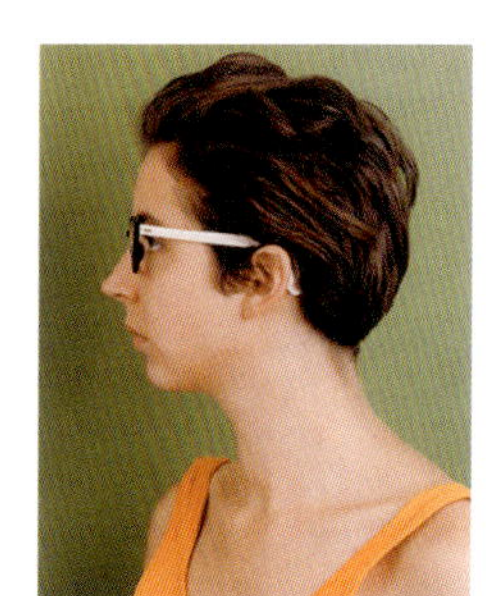

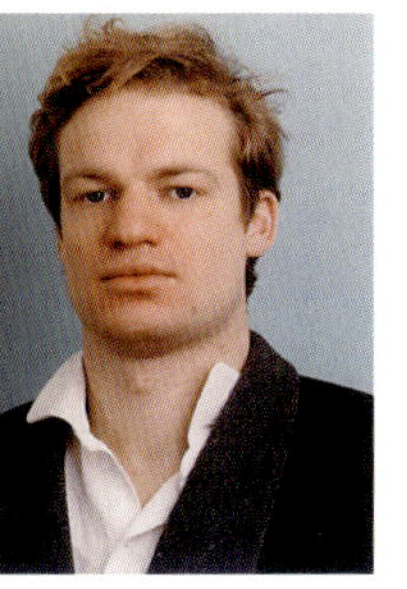 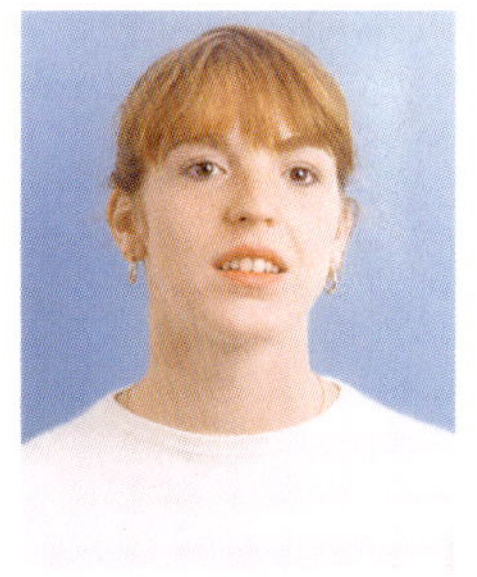 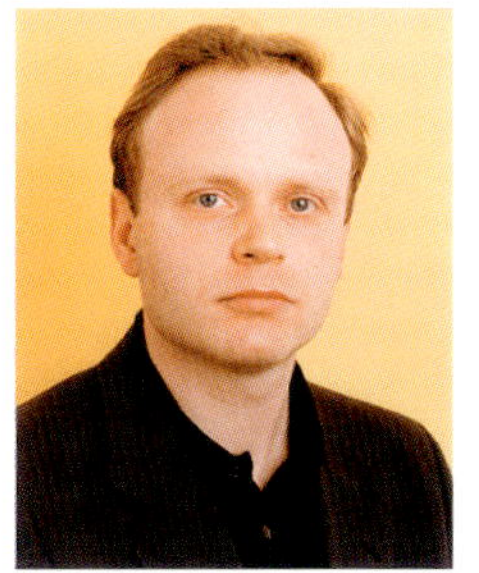 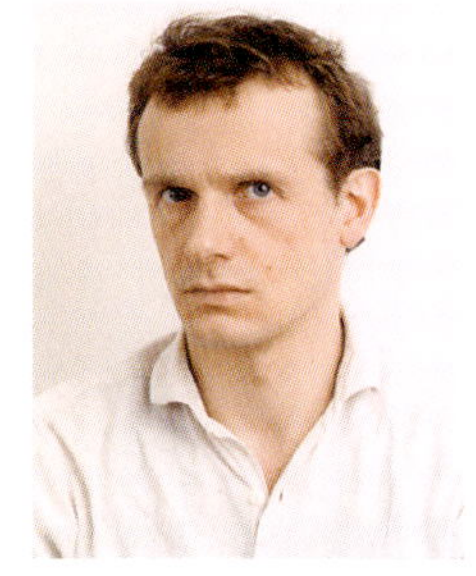 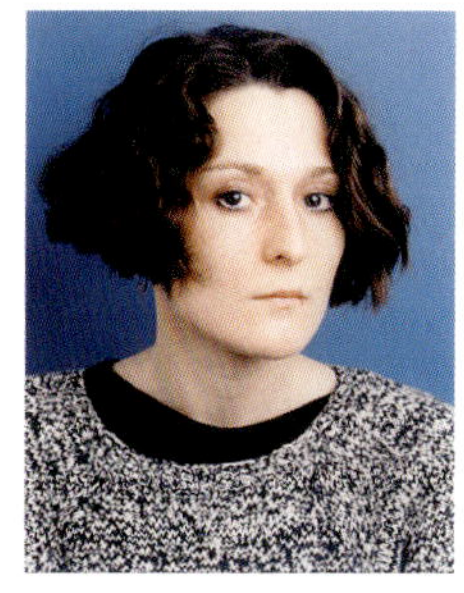

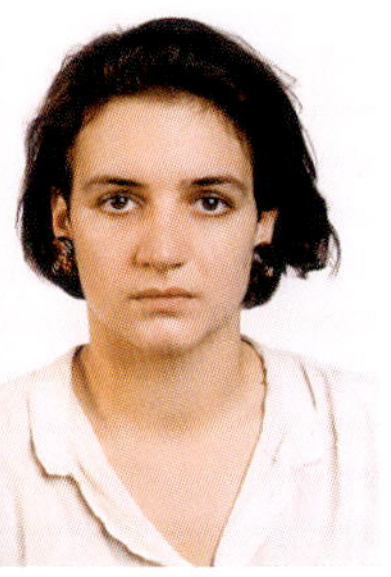 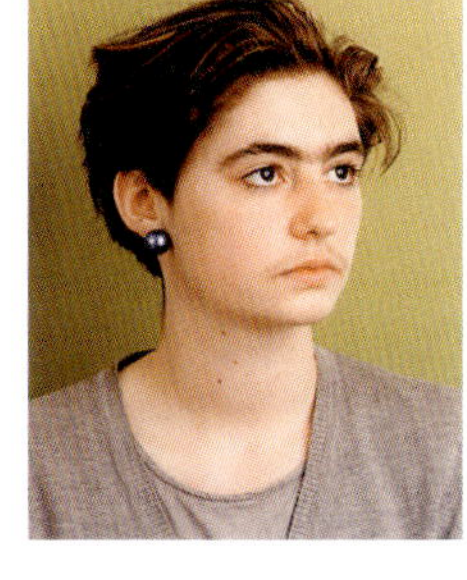 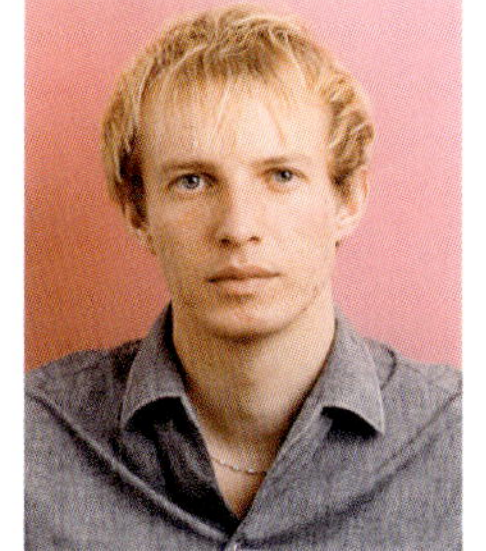 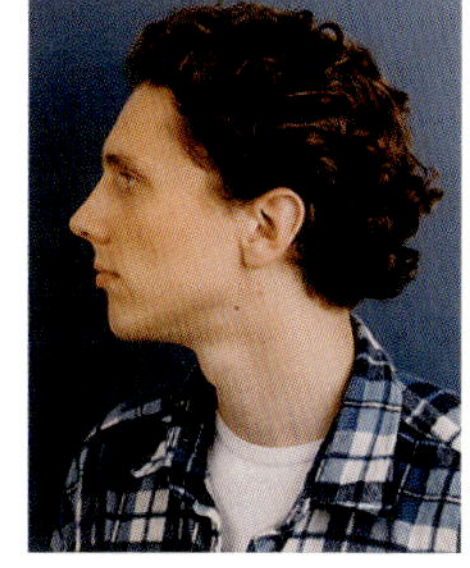 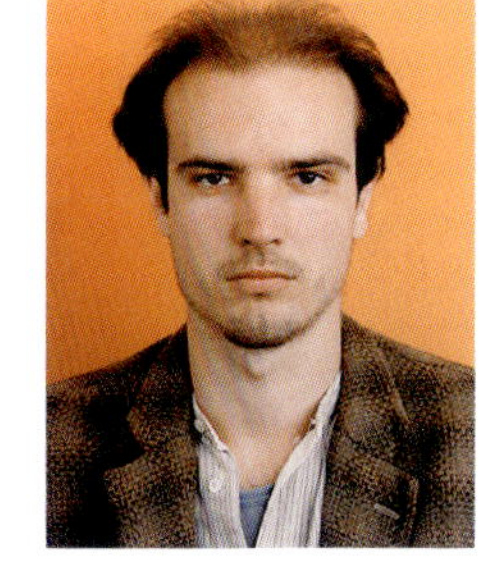

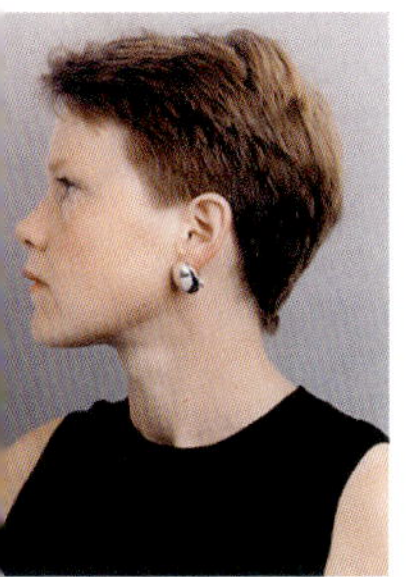 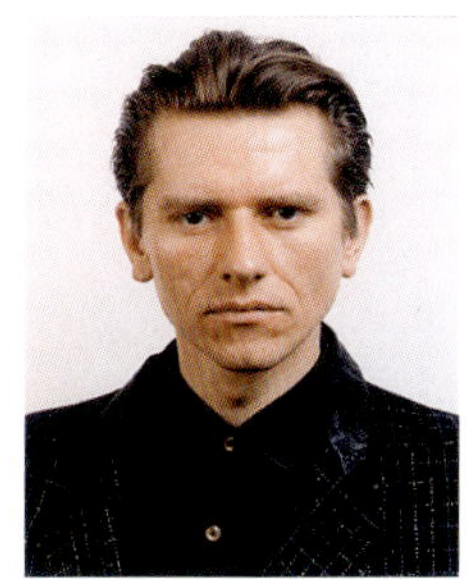 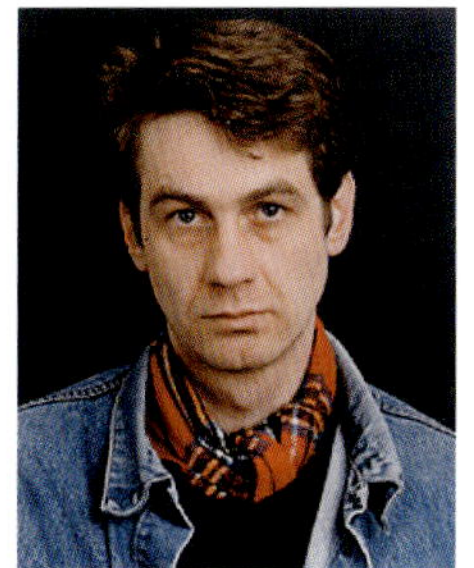 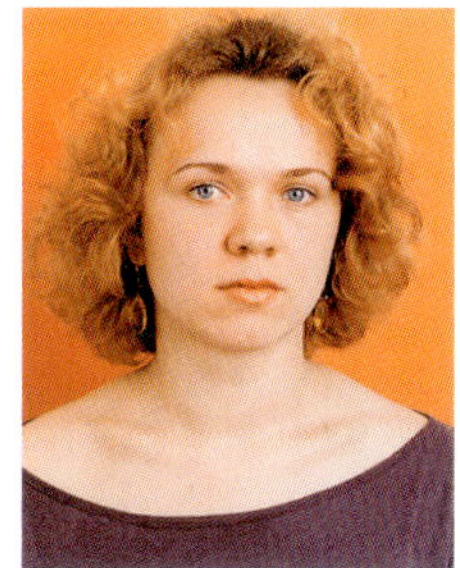 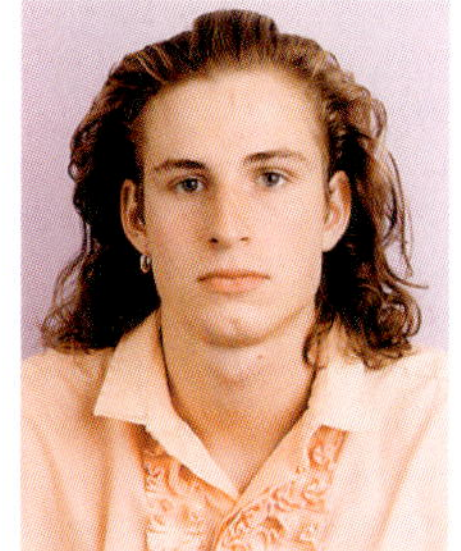

Fully Automated Nikon
1973

In a seafood restaurant in Chincoteague, Virginia, a woman approached me, convinced that I was a soap opera actress -
"the one on 'The Secret Storm' who's in love with the doctor who..."

"No, I'm not her," I said. "I guess I just look like her." This seemed to delight and excite her.

"Of course you deny it!" she said. "You don't want to be recognized!" I smiled. "See! You smile just like her!"

I denied it again but the more I denied it, the more convinced she was. The conversation was slowly turning into an argument and partly to assert myself, I asked if I could take her picture.

As I shot her, I realised that photography is a kind of mugging- a kind of assault.

When I got back to New York, I decided to take pictures of men who made comments as I passed them on the street. I had always resented this invasion of privacy. Now, suddenly I had the means of my revenge.

As I walked through the Lower East Side with my fully automated Nikon, I felt armed, ready.

The standard street technique was: the female passes and the male speaks at the last possible moment, forcing the woman to backtrack if she should dare to object.

My first shot was a man who muttered "Wanna fuck?" just after I passed by. I wheeled around, furious. "DID YOU SAY THAT?" He looked around surprised, then defiant. I raised my Nikon, took aim. His eyes darted back and forth. Undercover cop? Huh? CLICK.

As it turned out, most of the men I shot that day had similar reactions. When I questioned them, they acted innocent -even offended- like some nasty invisible ventriloquist had tricked them into saying dirty words against their will.

By the time I started to shoot, they were posing. They seemed flattered, like taking their pictures was the least I could do.

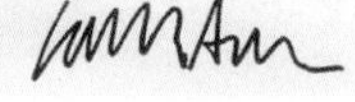

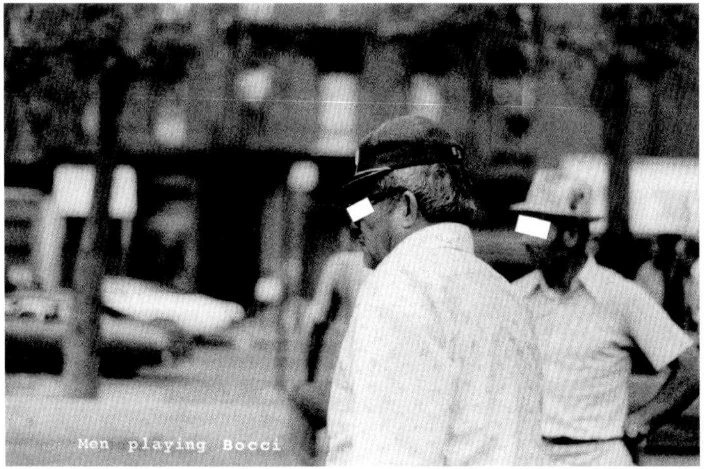

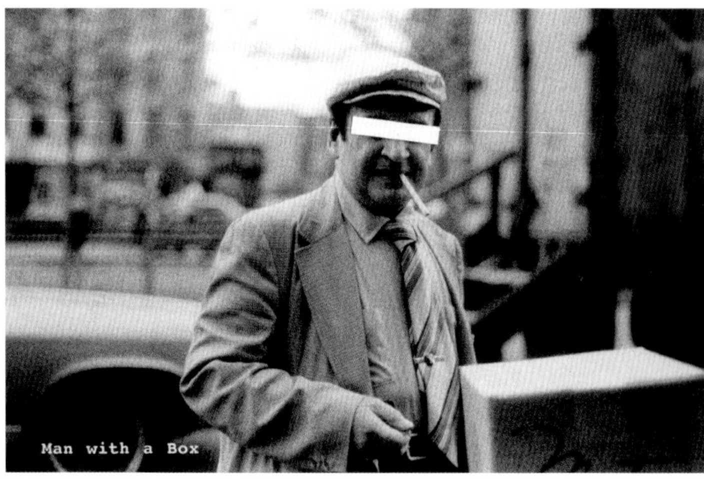

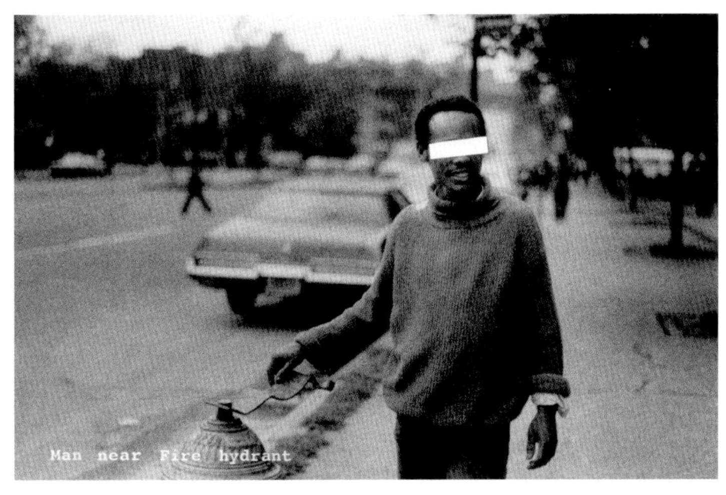
Man near Fire hydrant

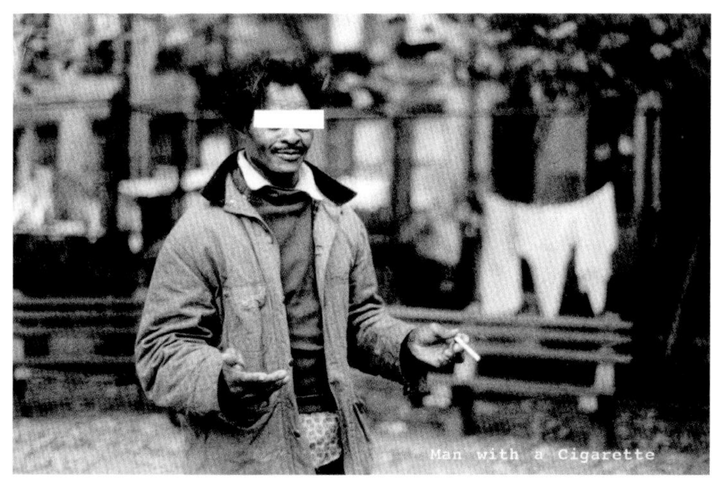
Man with a Cigarette

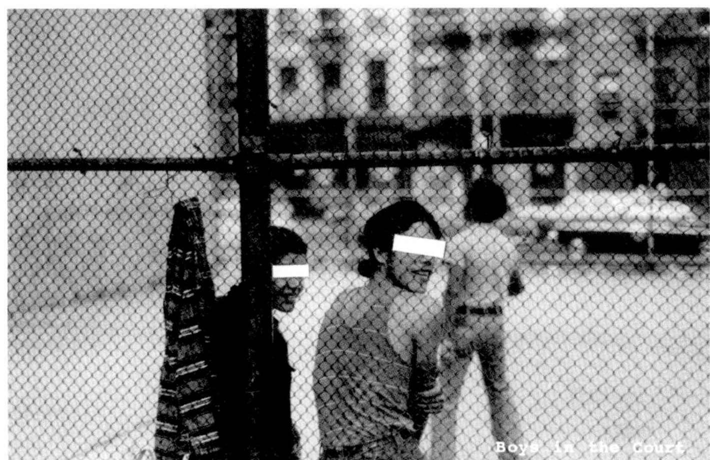
Boys in the Court

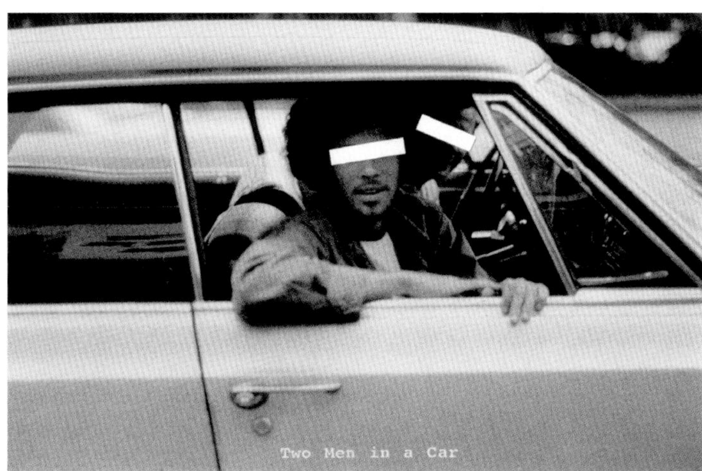
Two Men in a Car

Richard Prince, *Untitled (The Same Man Looking in Different Directions)*, 1978

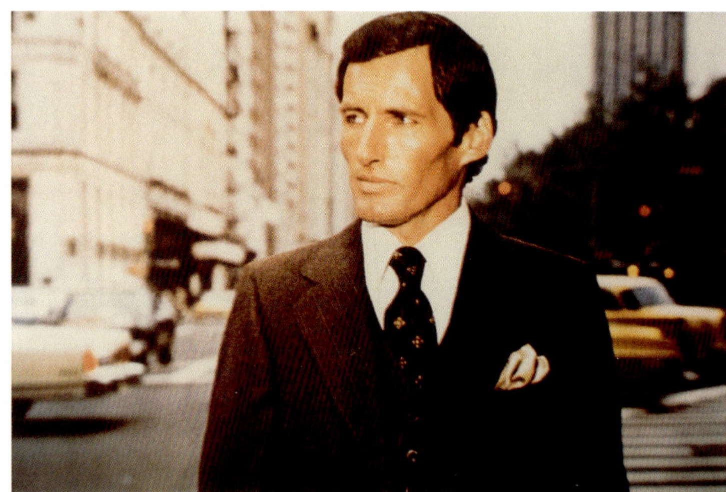
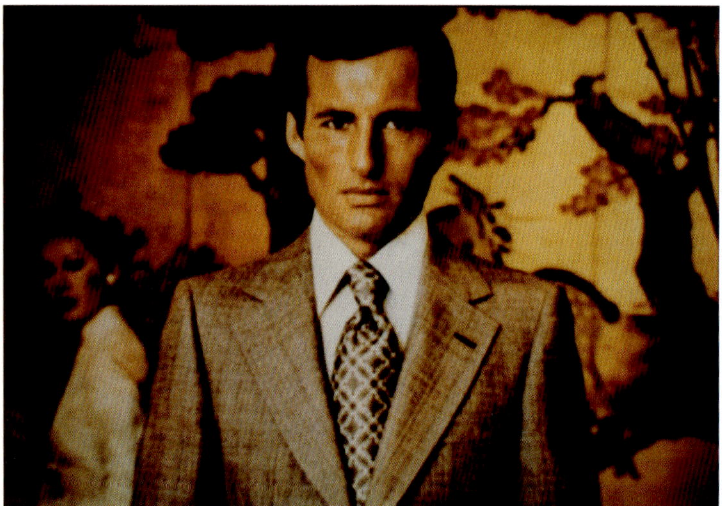
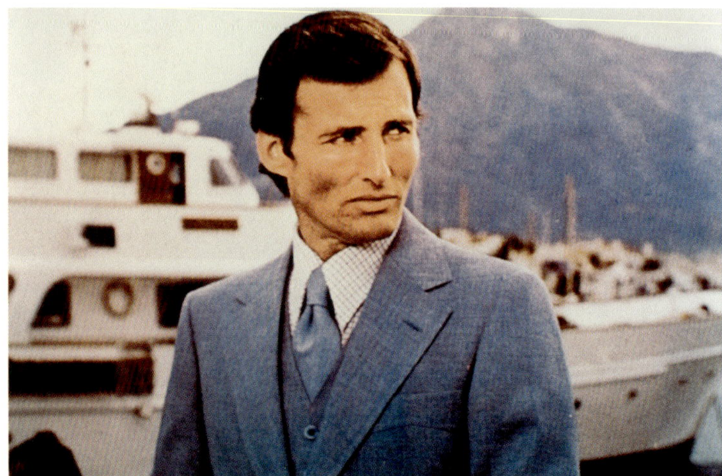

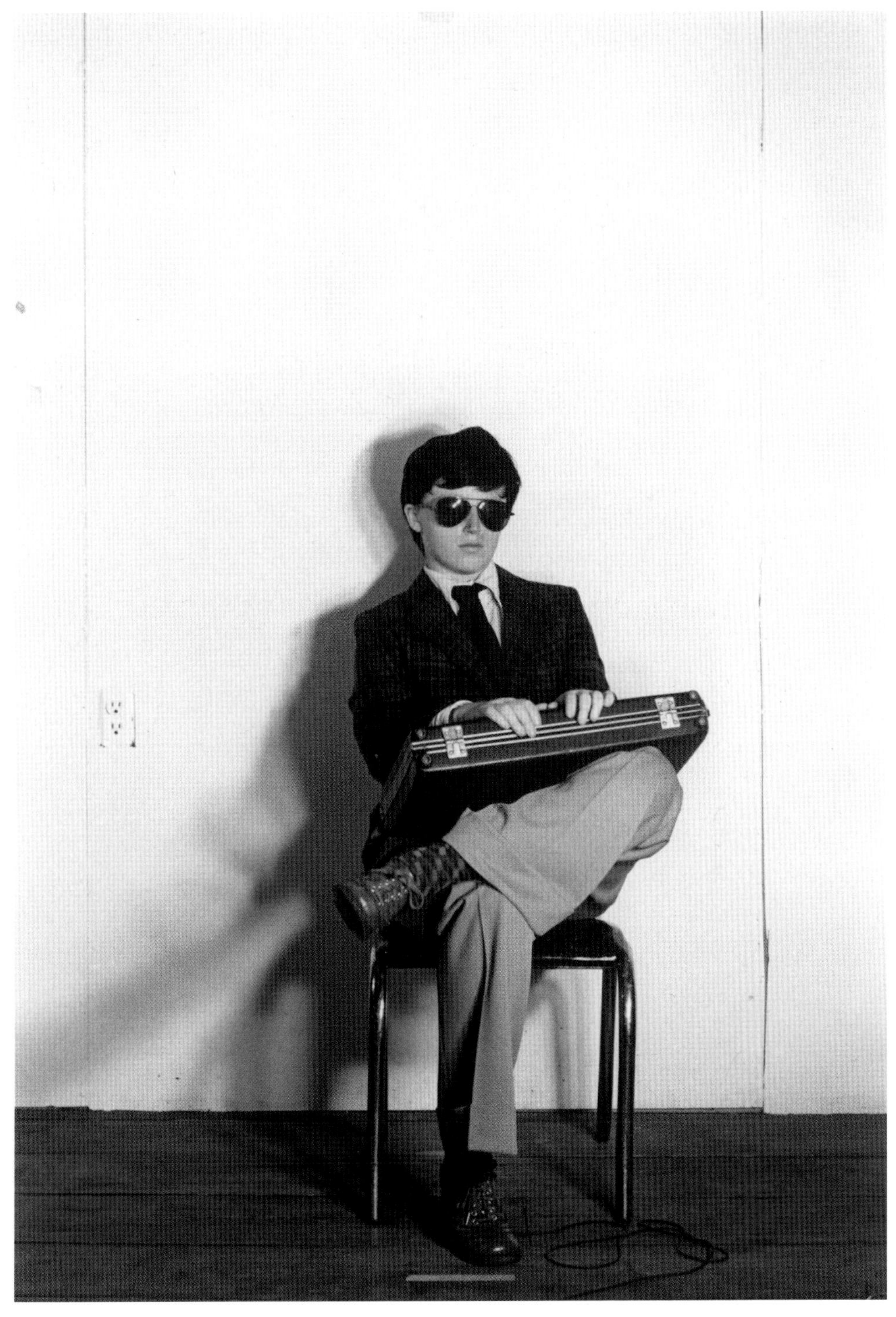

Cindy Sherman, *Untitled*, from the series *Bus Riders*, 1976

     Chris Killip, *Torso, Pelaw, Gateshead, Tyneside*, 1978

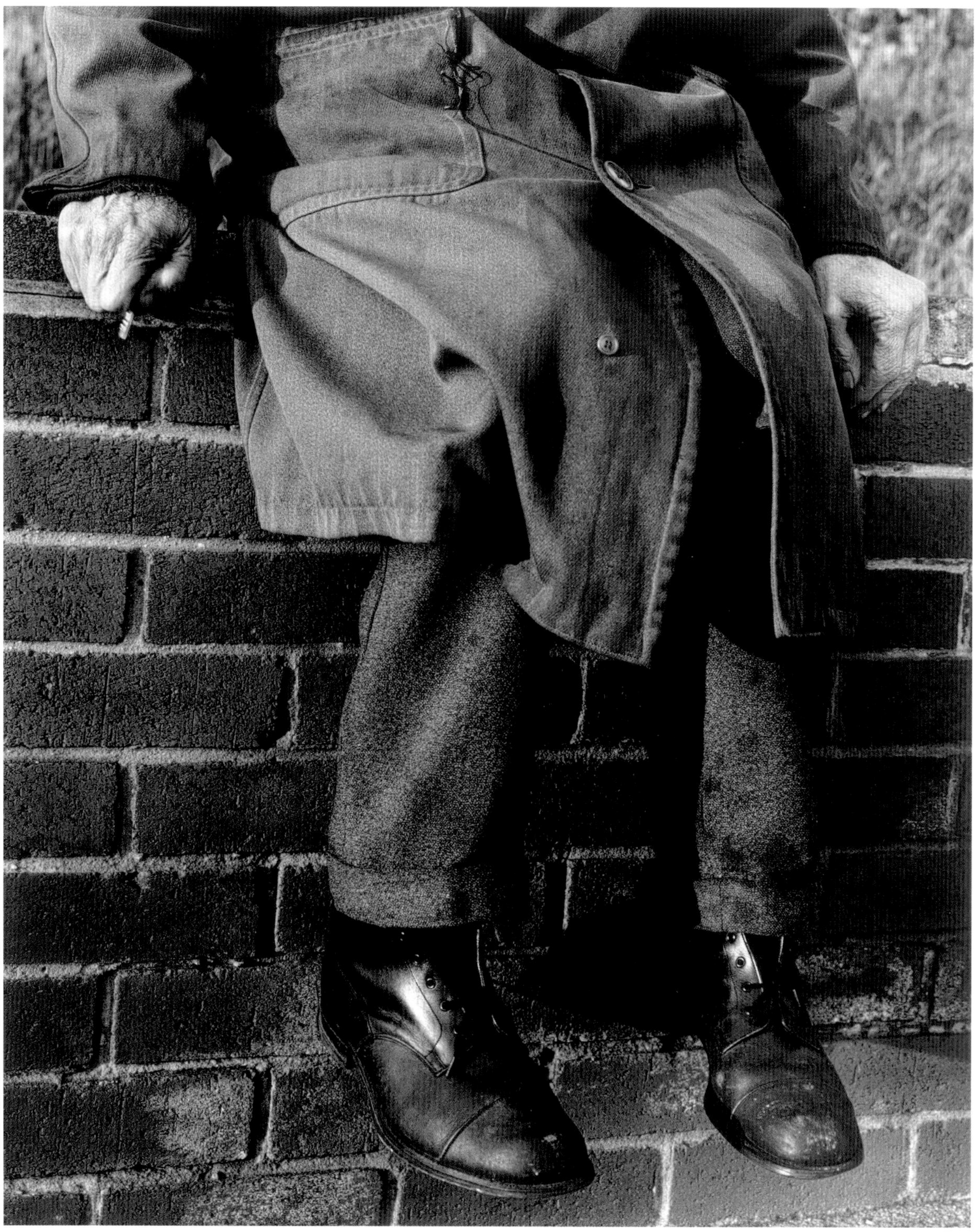

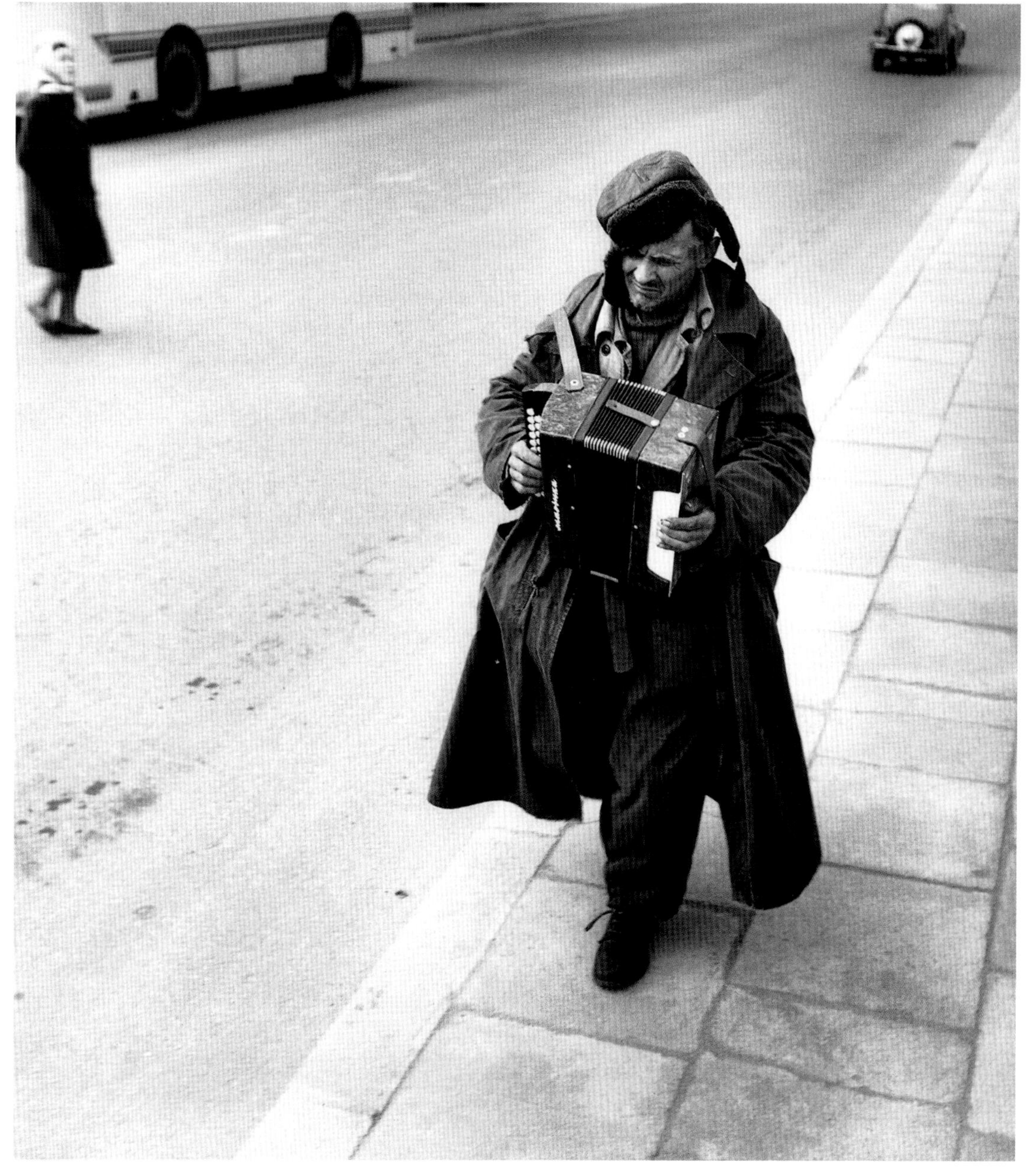

Francis Alÿs
Philip Kwame Apagya
Frank Berger
Kristleifur Björnsson
Philip-Lorca diCorcia
Rineke Dijkstra
Paul Graham
Sunil Gupta
Pieter Hugo
Sarah Jones
Valérie Jouve
Marjaana Kella
Suzanne Lafont
Boris Mikhailov
Adrian Paci
Martin Parr
Bruno Serralongue
Andres Serrano
Joel Sternfeld
Beat Streuli
Mitra Tabrizian
Juergen Teller
Wolfgang Tillmans
Lee To Sang
Jeff Wall
Gillian Wearing

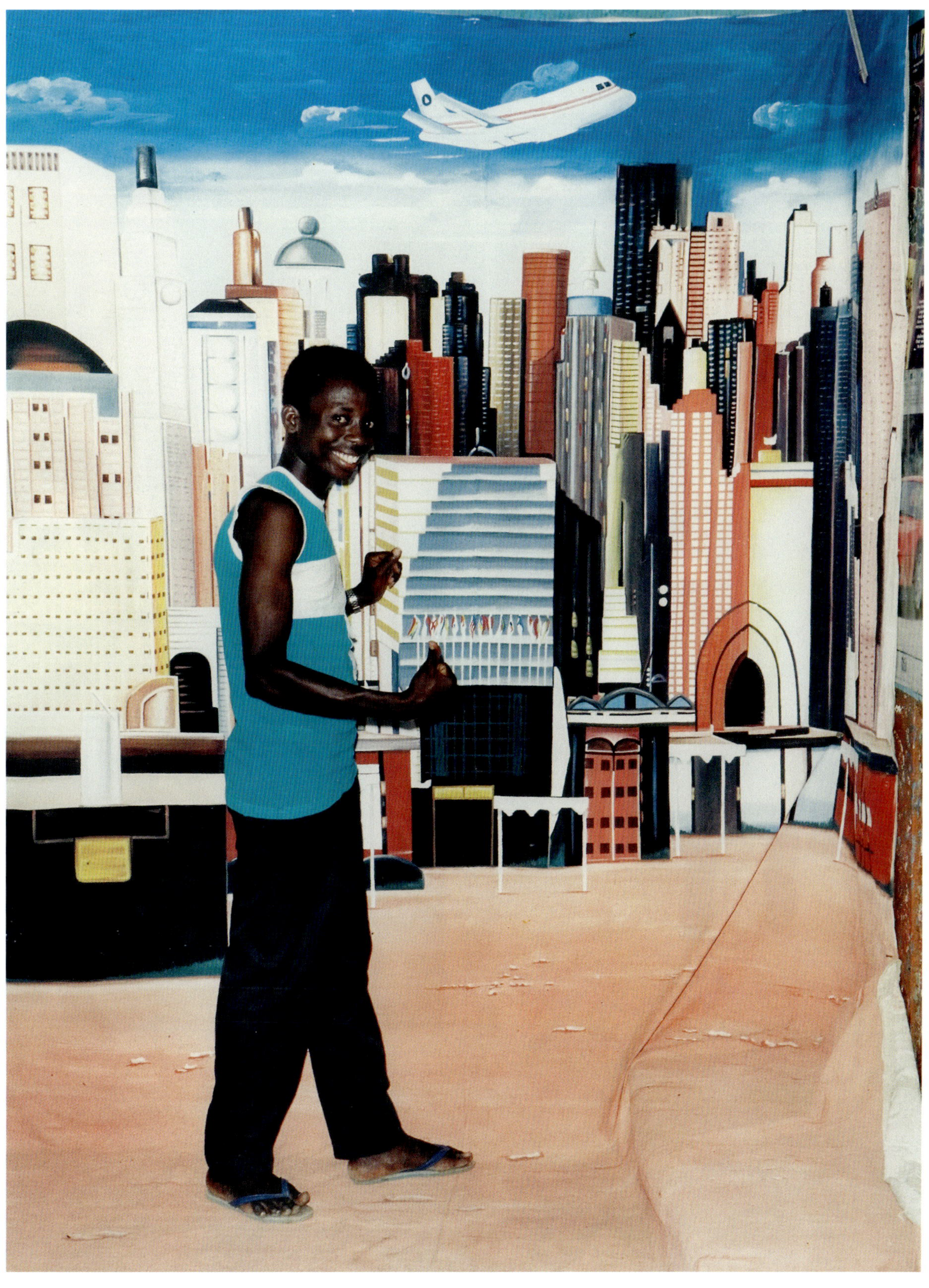

    Boris Mikhailov, from the project *Case History*, 1997–8

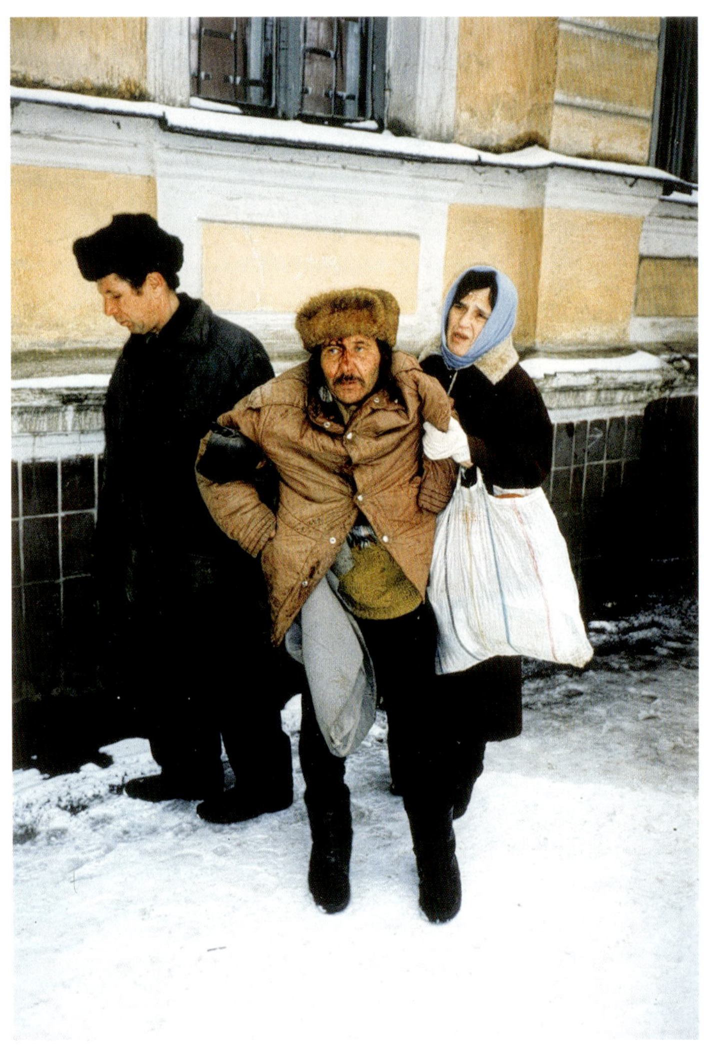
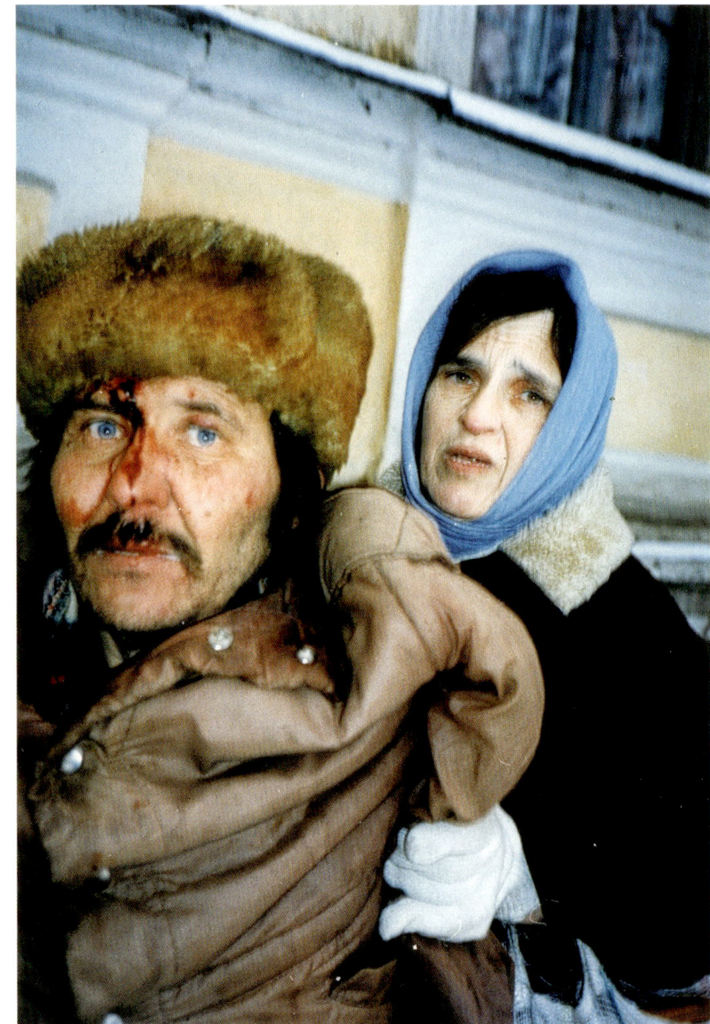

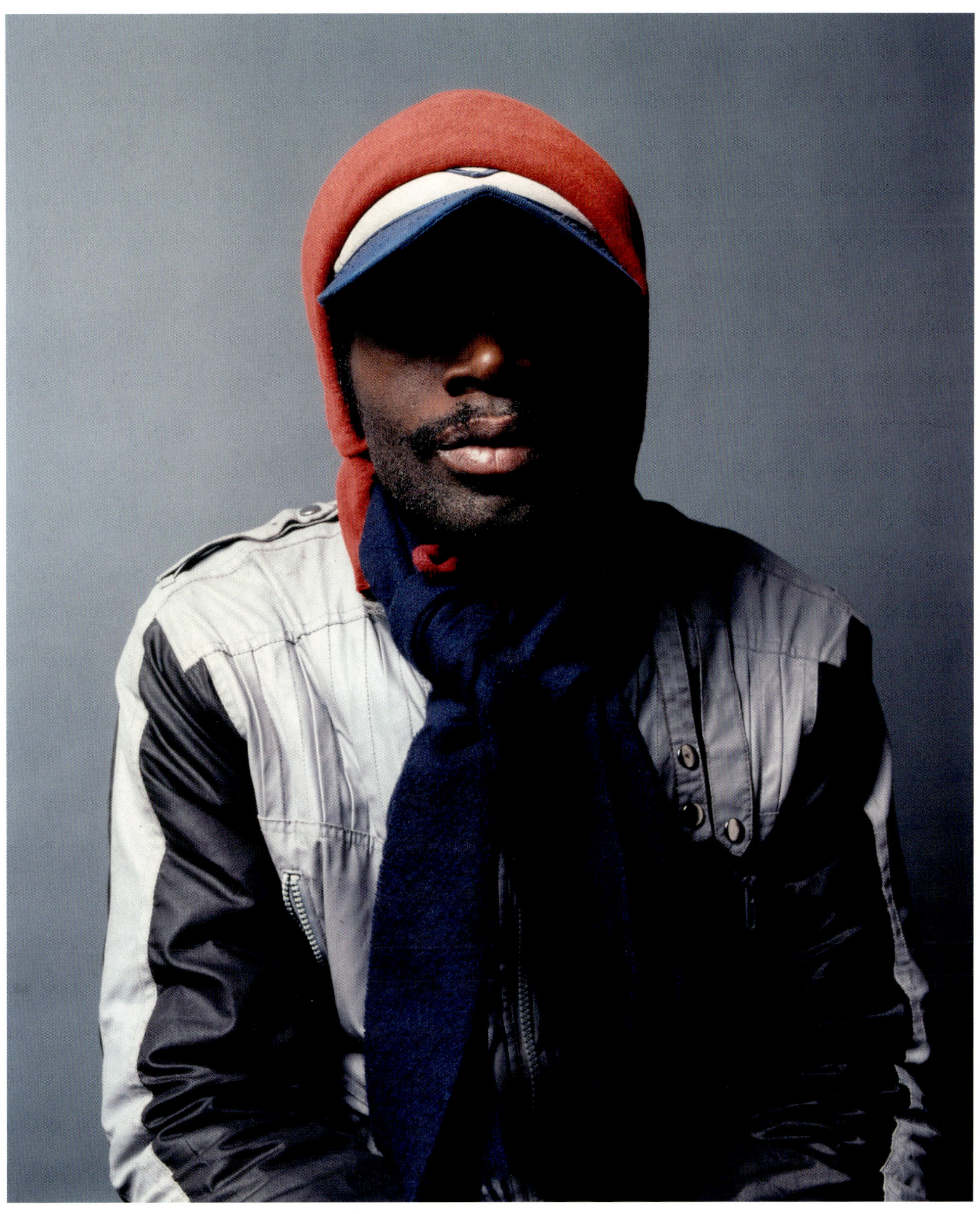

Joel Sternfeld, *A Lawyer with Laundry, Corner Bank and West 41st Street, N.Y.C., October*, 1988

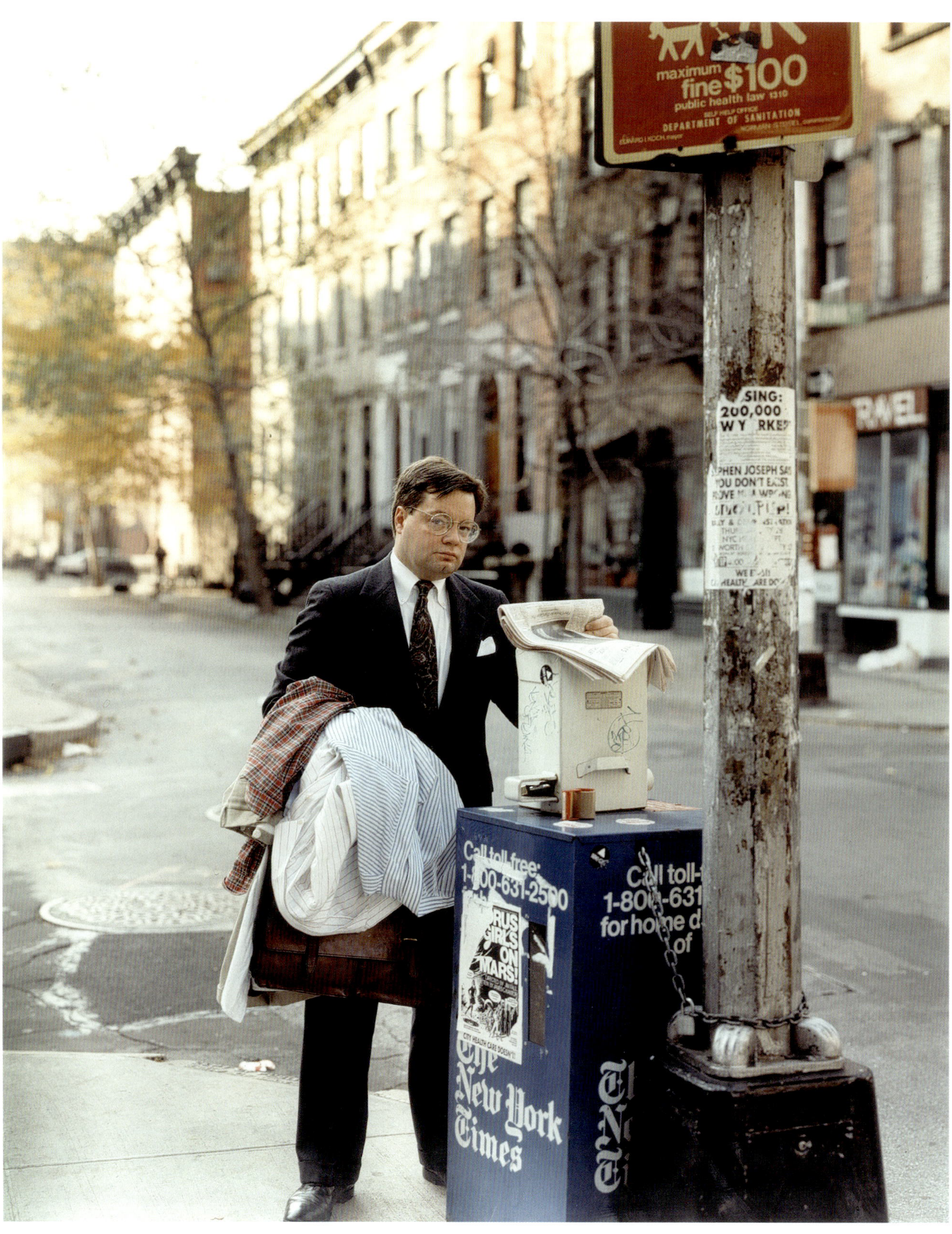

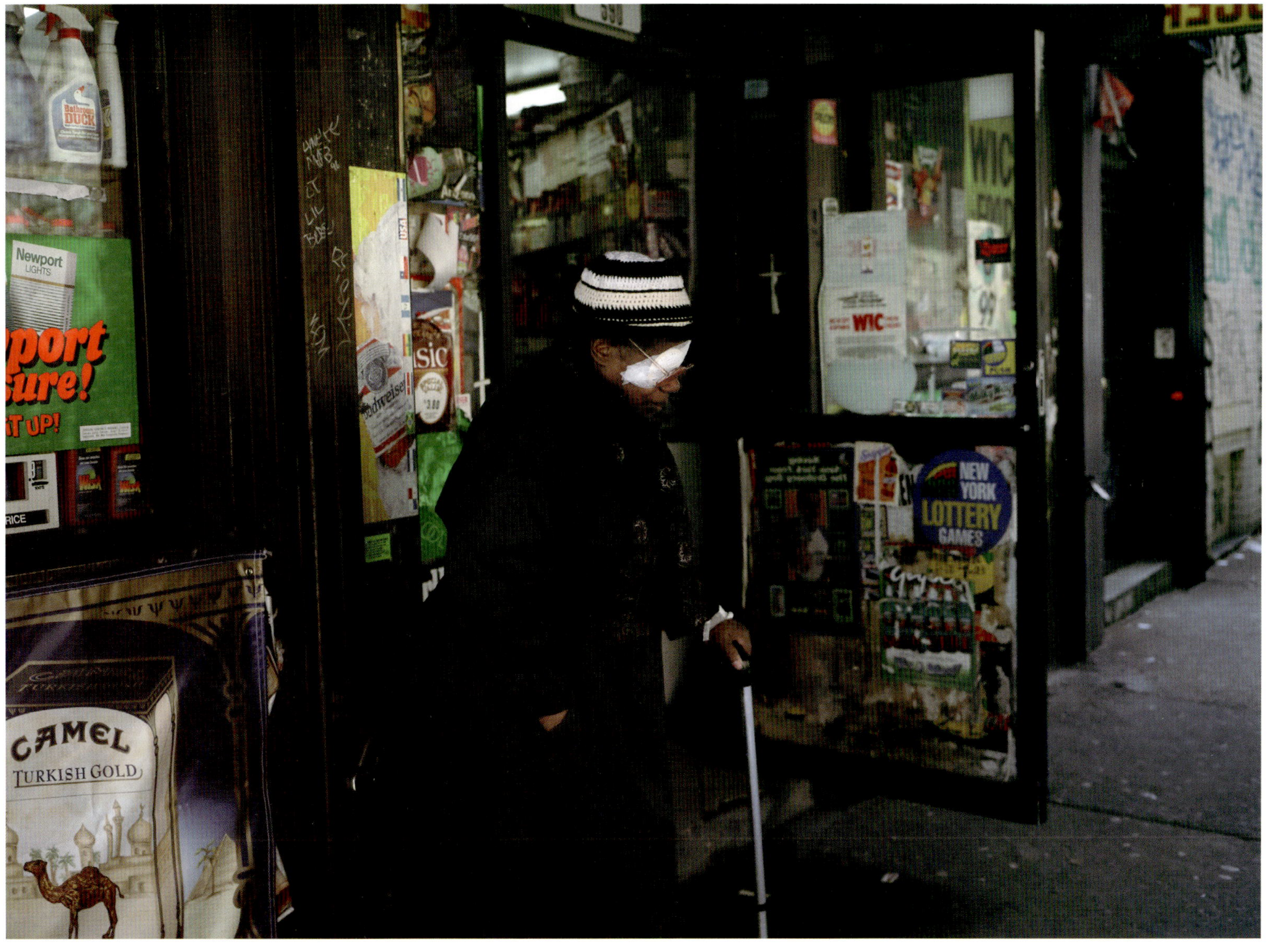

Newport
LIGHTS
port
ure!
T UP!
RICE
CAMEL
TURKISH GOLD
Budweiser
WIC
WIC
99
NEW
YORK
LOTTERY
GAMES

 Philip-Lorca diCorcia, *Head No.8,* 2001

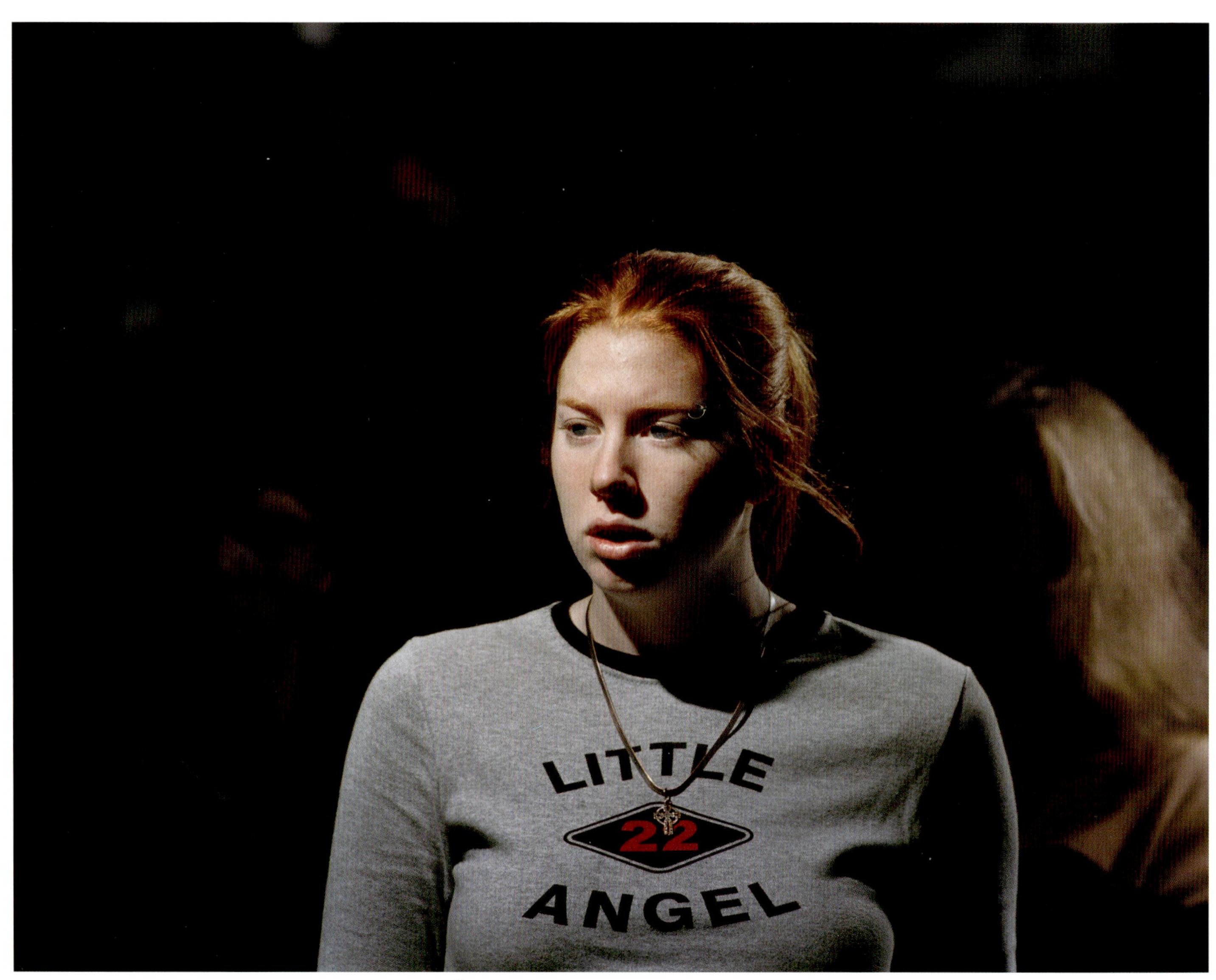

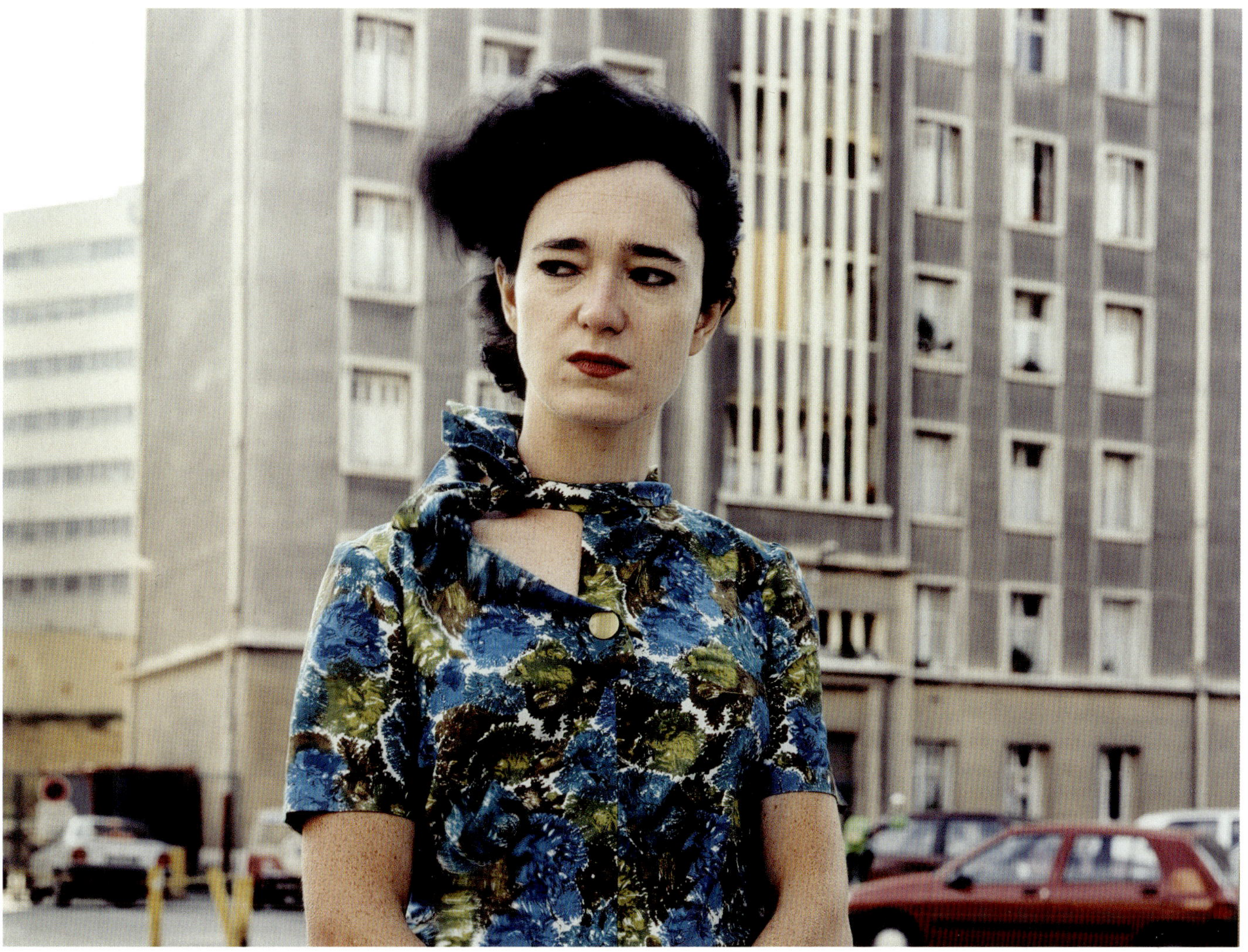

Valérie Jouve, *Sans titre, No.3* (Untitled, No.3), 1994–5

 Marjaana Kella, *Nainen hypnoositilassa* (Hypnotised Woman), 1997

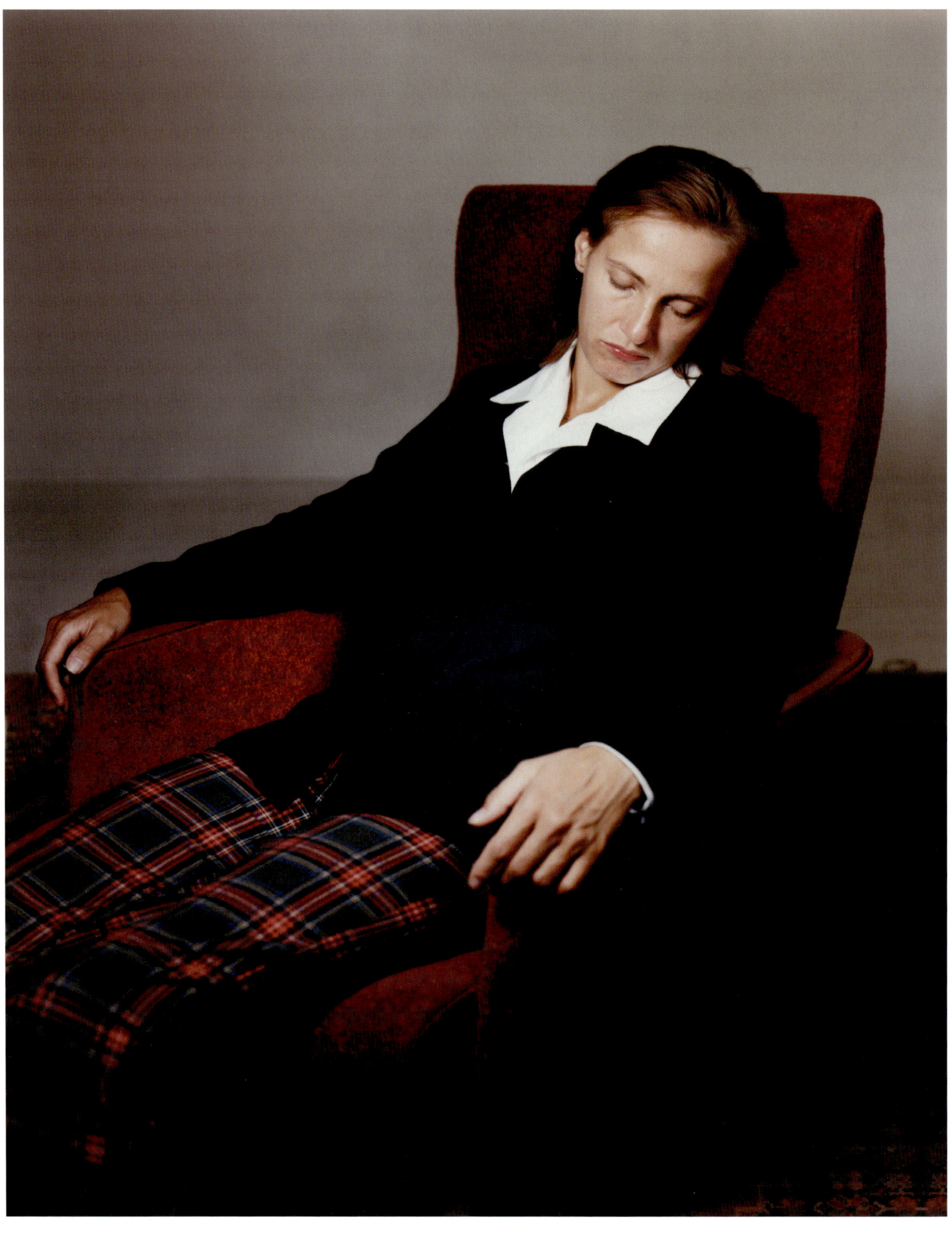

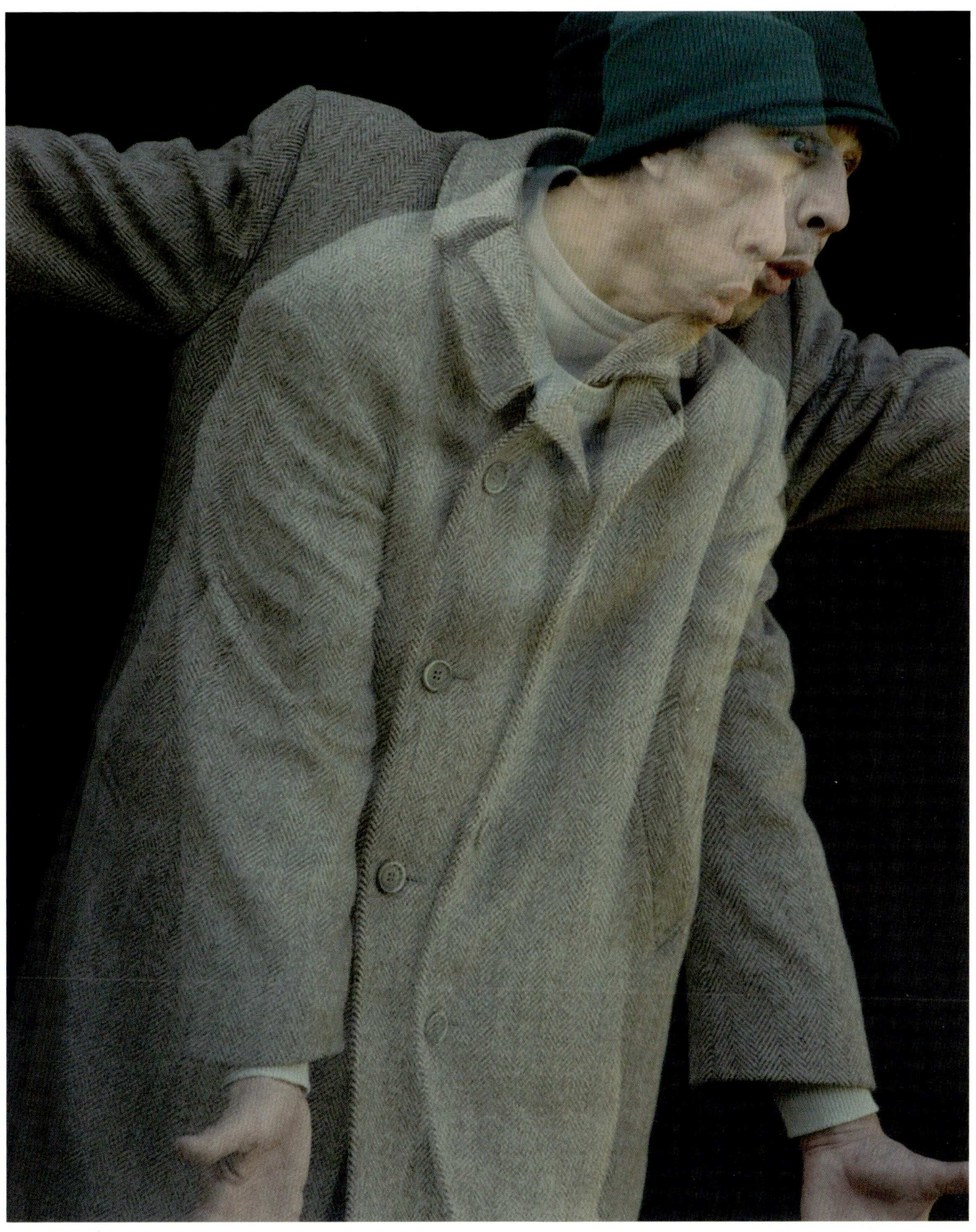

Suzanne Lafont, *Marcheur no.1* (Passer-by No.1), 1995–8

Bruno Serralongue, *Manifestations du collectif des sans-papiers de la Maison des Ensembles, place du Châtelet, Paris* (Demonstrations of the Maison des Ensembles Group of Immigrants, Place du Châtelet, Paris), 2001–3

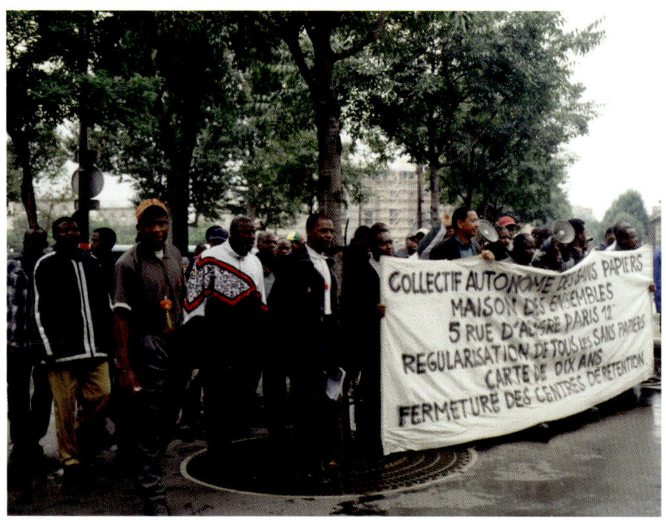

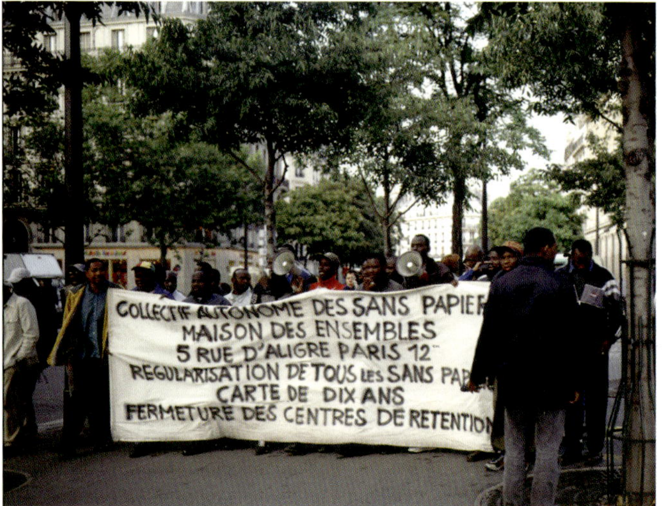

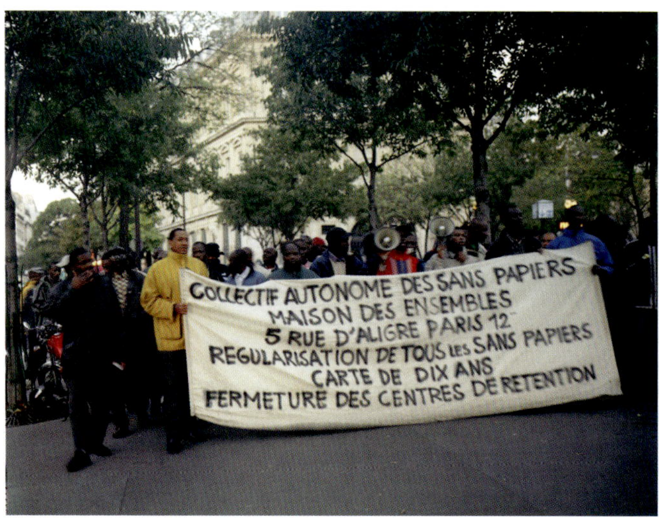

01.	Saturday	08 September	2001
02.	**Thursday**	**20 September**	**2001**
03.	Saturday	22 September	2001
04.	Thursday	27 September	2001
05.	Saturday	29 September	2001
06.	**Thursday**	**04 October**	**2001**
07.	Saturday	06 October	2001
08.	Thursday	11 October	2001
09.	Saturday	13 October	2001
10.	Thursday	18 October	2001
11.	Saturday	20 October	2001
12.	Thursday	25 October	2001
13.	Saturday	27 October	2001
14.	**Saturday**	**03 November**	**2001**
15.	Thursday	13 December	2001

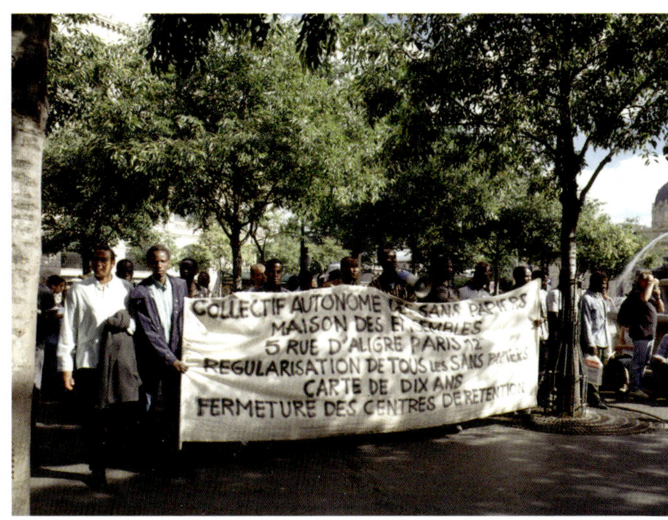

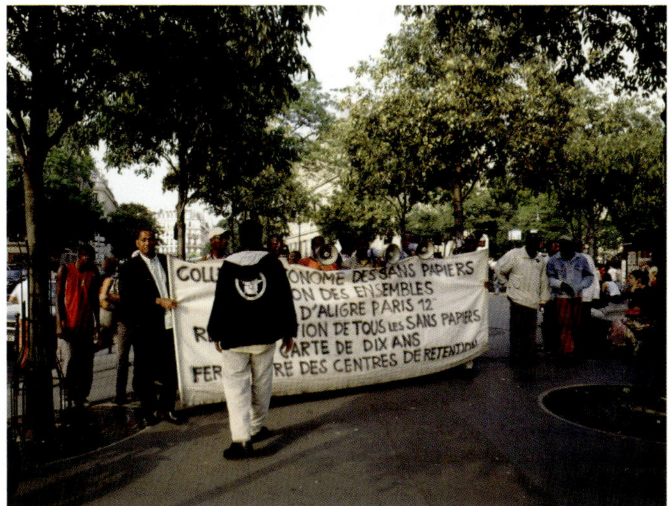

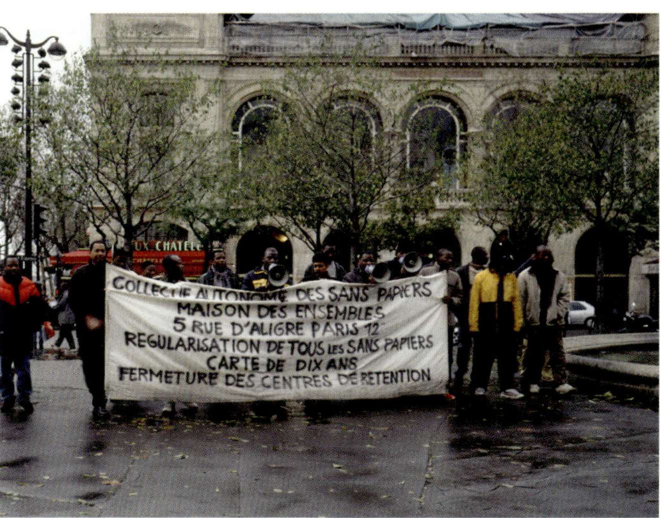

16.	Thursday	20 December	2002
17.	Saturday	12 January	2002
18.	Saturday	19 January	2002
19.	Saturday	26 January	2002
20.	Saturday	02 February	2002
21.	Saturday	16 February	2002
22.	Saturday	09 March	2002
23.	Saturday	23 March	2002
24.	Saturday	30 March	2002
26.	Saturday	06 April	2002
26.	Saturday	04 May	2002
28.	Thursday	01 June	2002
29.	Saturday	15 June	2002
30.	**Saturday**	**22 June**	**2002**
31.	Saturday	29 June	2002
32.	Saturday	13 July	2002
33.	Saturday	20 July	2002
34.	Saturday	27 July	2002
35.	**Saturday**	**14 September**	**2002**
36.	Saturday	21 September	2002
37.	Saturday	28 September	2002
38.	Saturday	12 October	2002
40.	**Thursday**	**09 November**	**2002**
41.	Saturday	30 September	2002
42.	Saturday	14 December	2002
43.	Saturday	21 December	2002
44.	Saturday	28 December	2002
45.	Saturday	11 January	2003

Jeff Wall, *The Arrest*, 1989

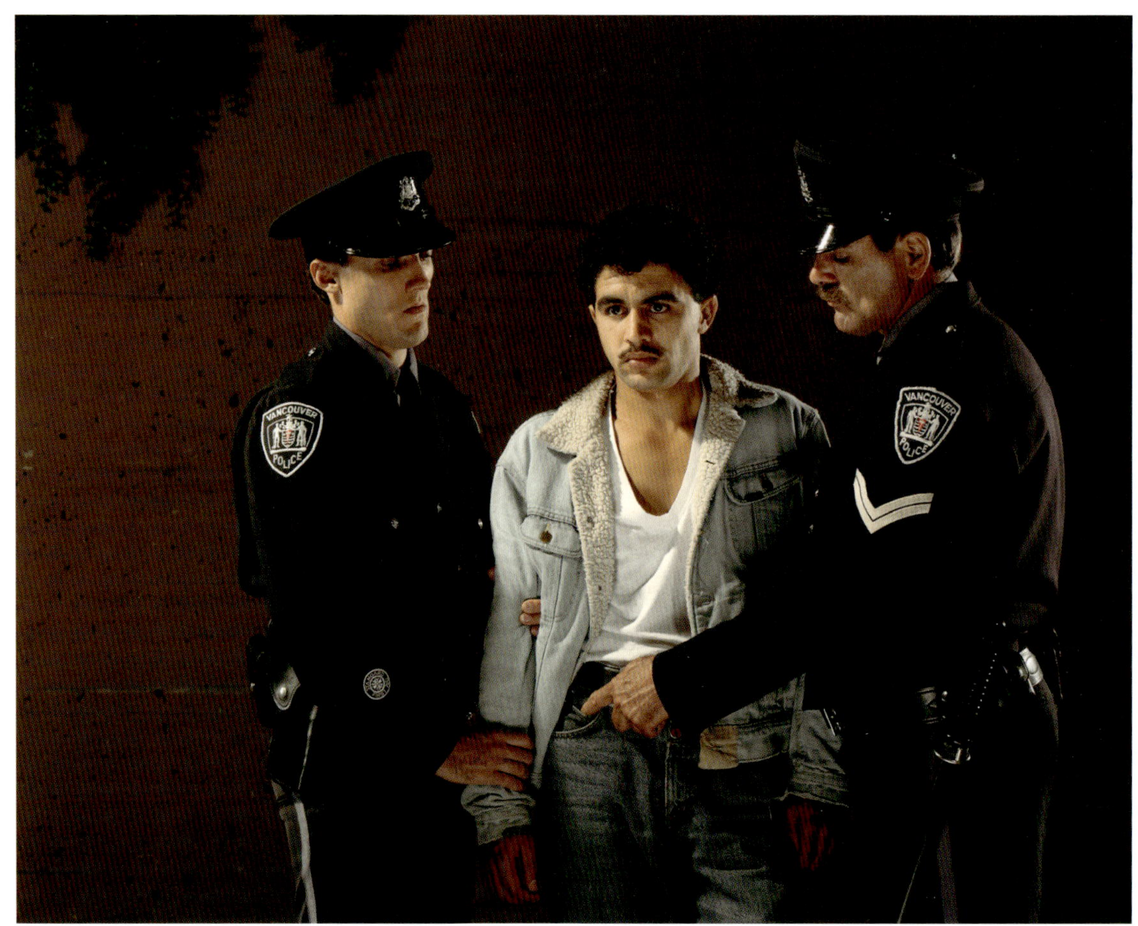

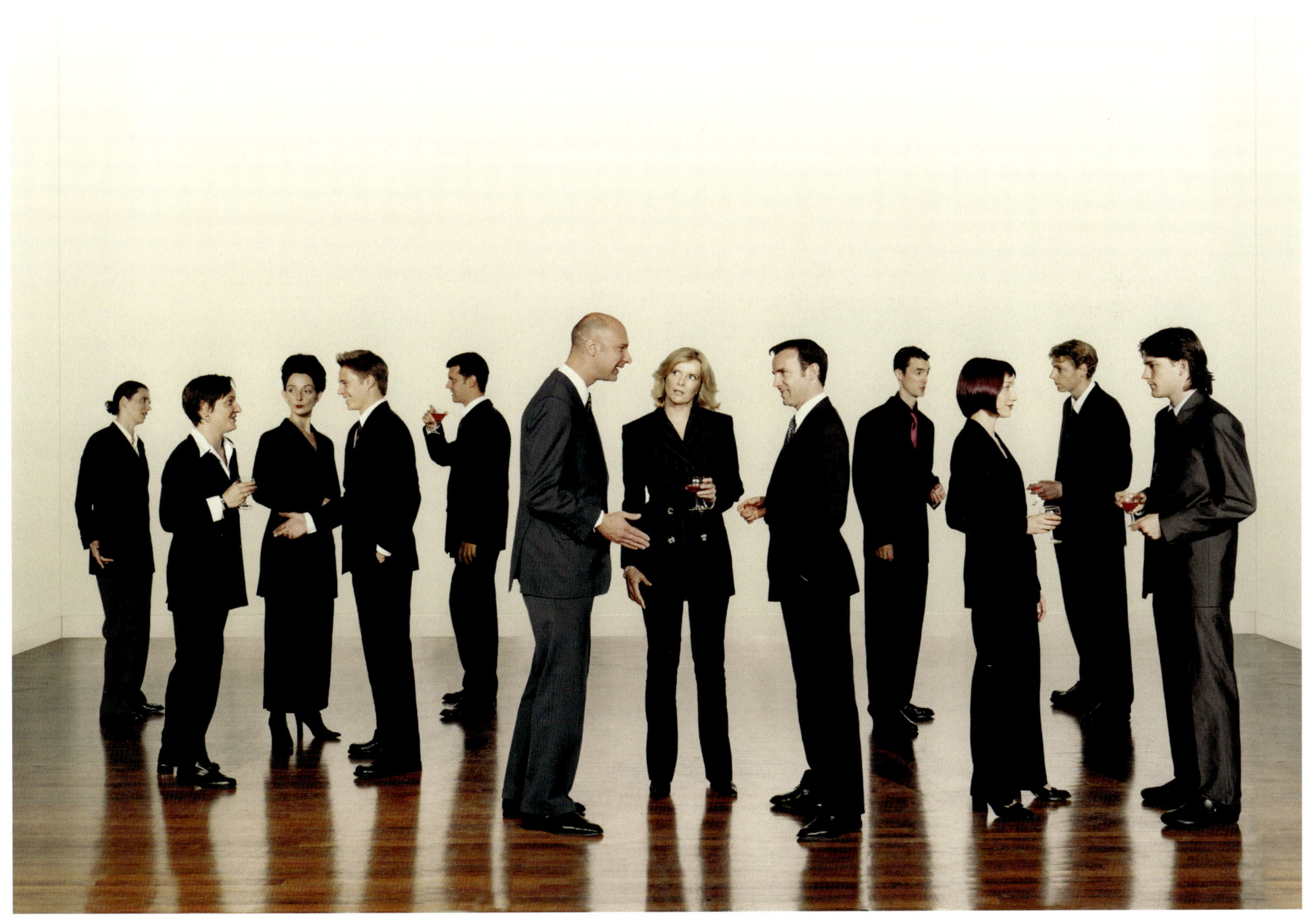

 Sarah Jones, *Actor II*, 1995

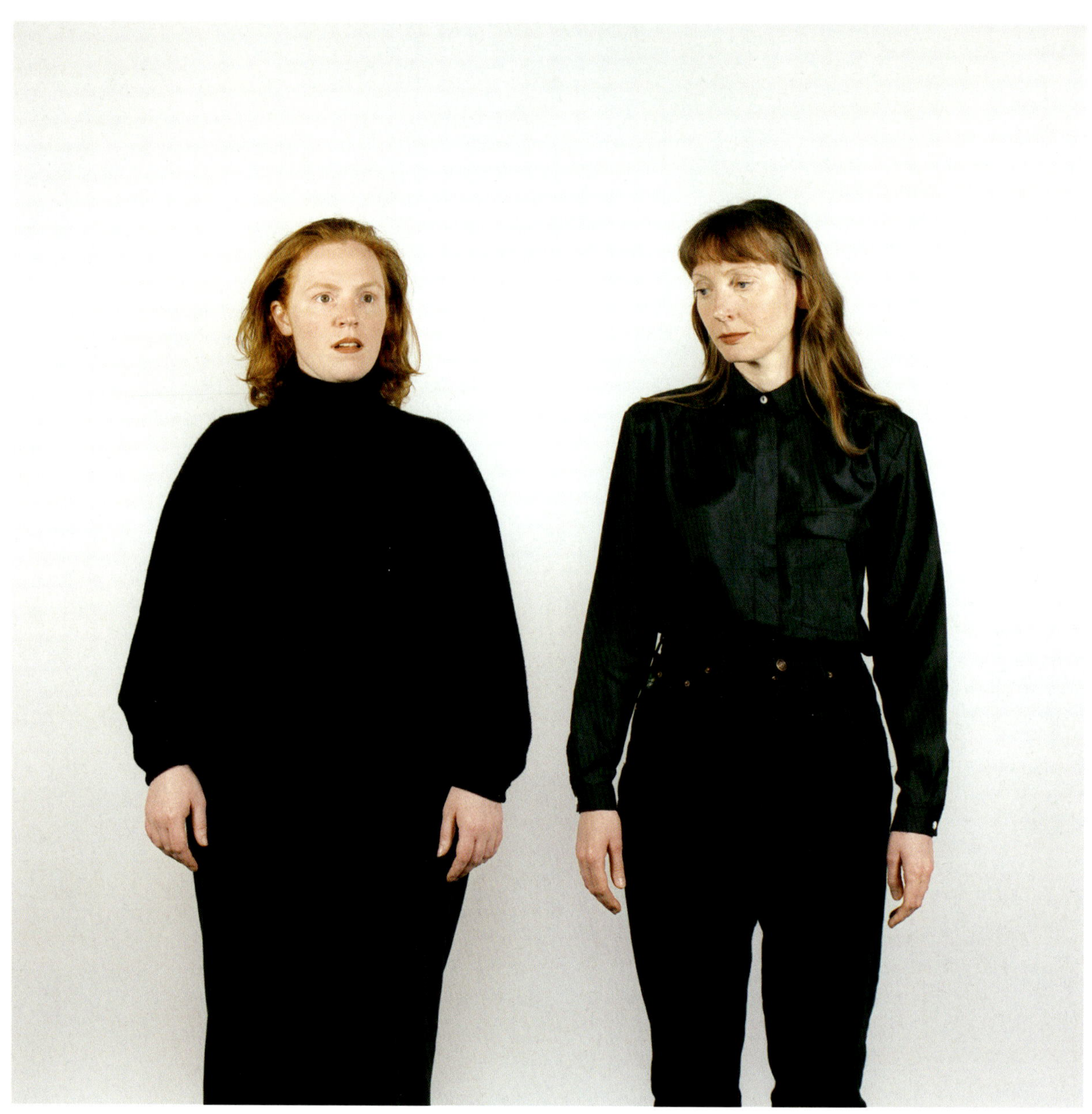

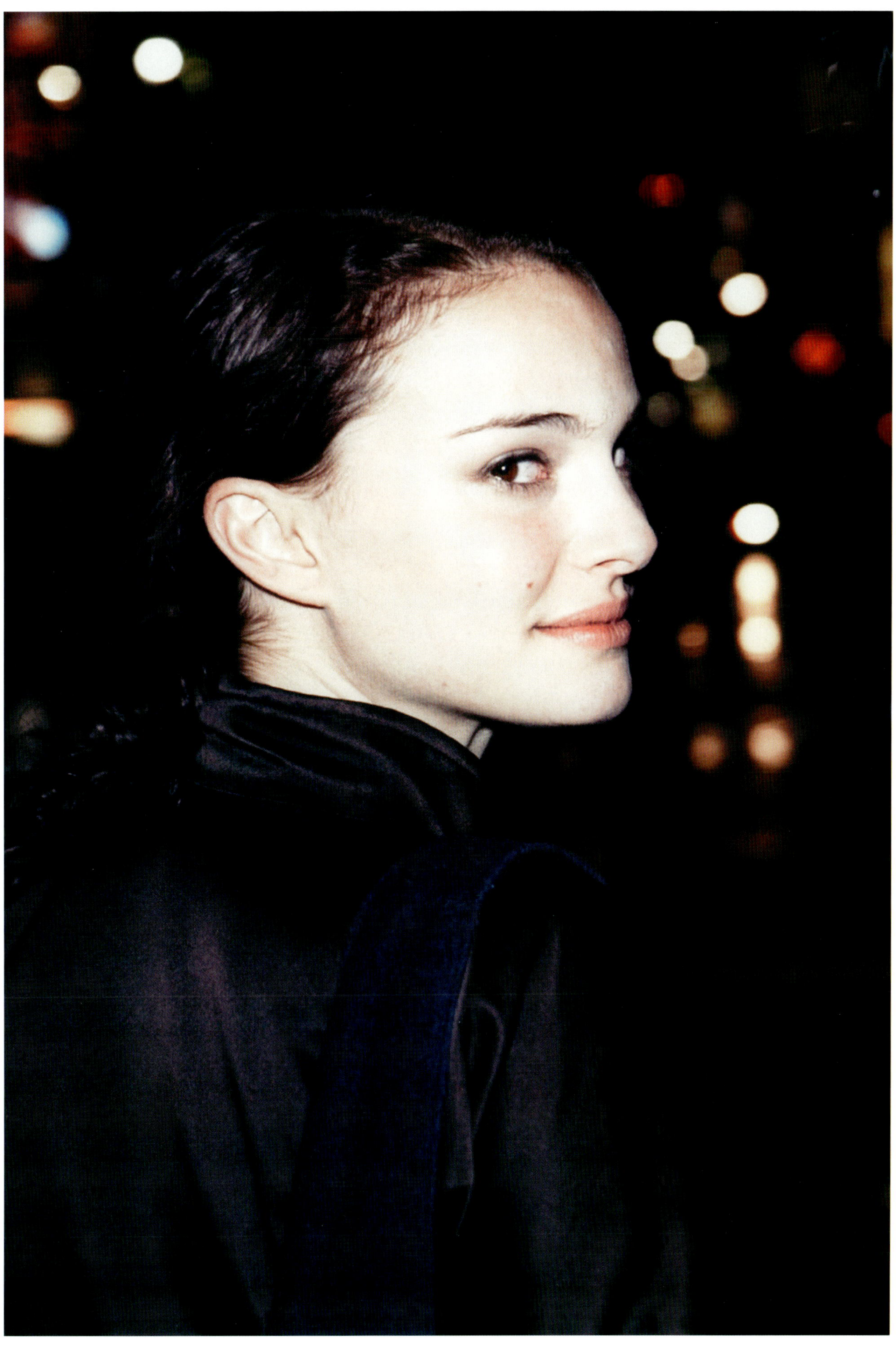

 Adrian Paci, *Back Home 2*, 2001

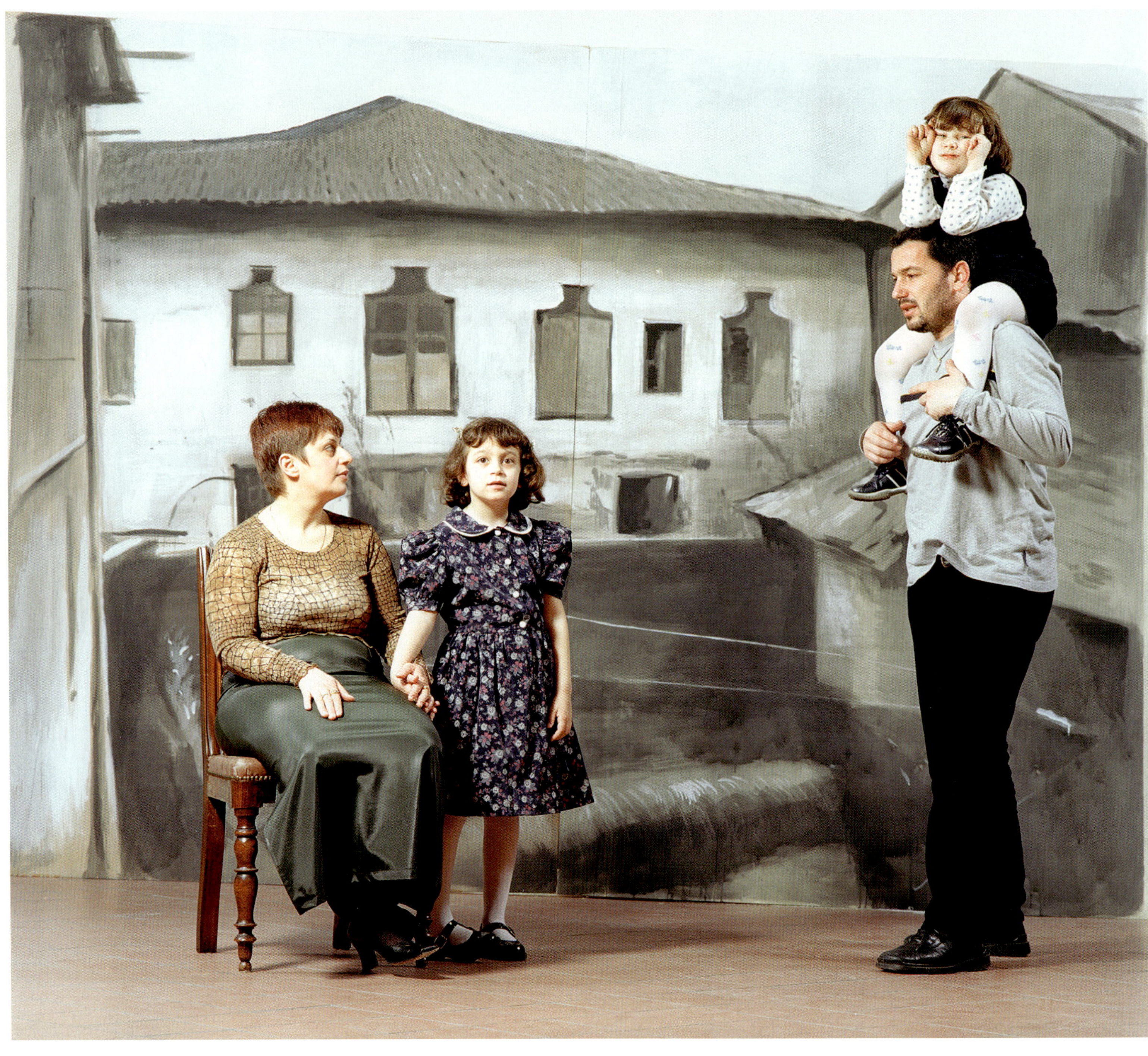

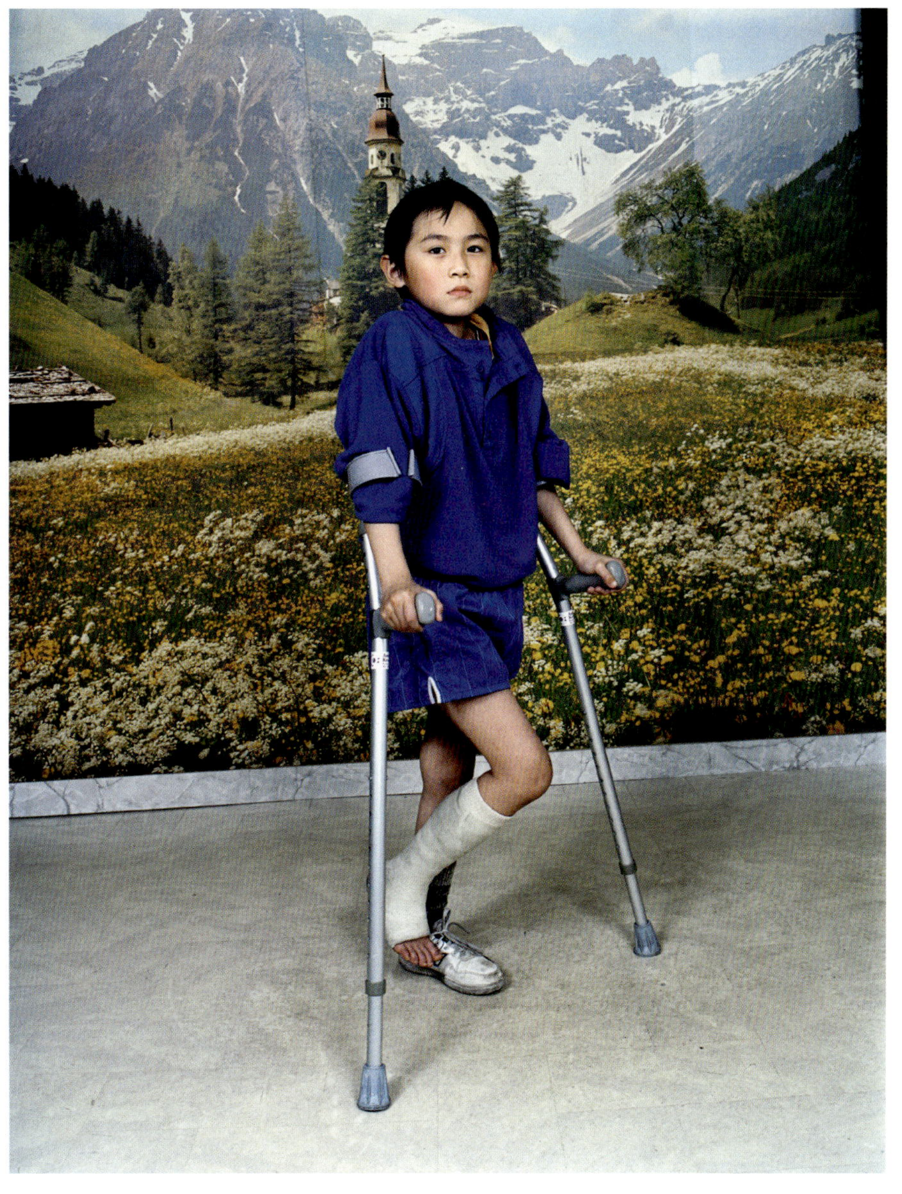

  Martin Parr, from the series *Autoportraits*, 1999–2001

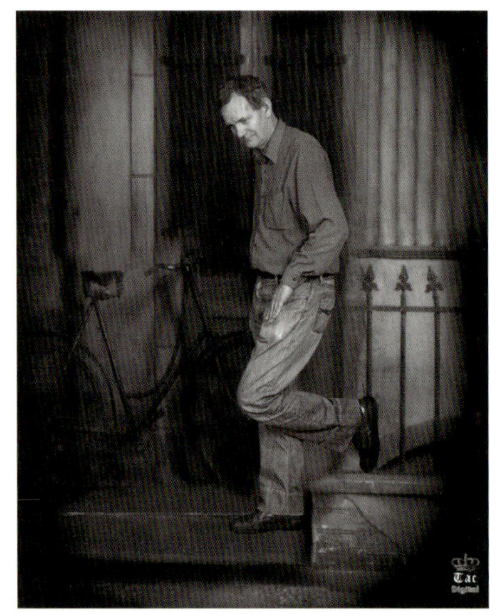

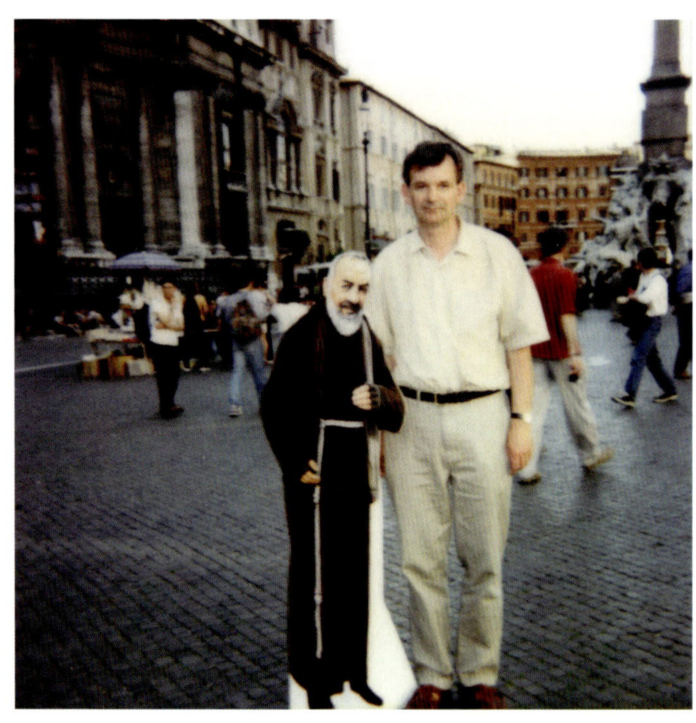

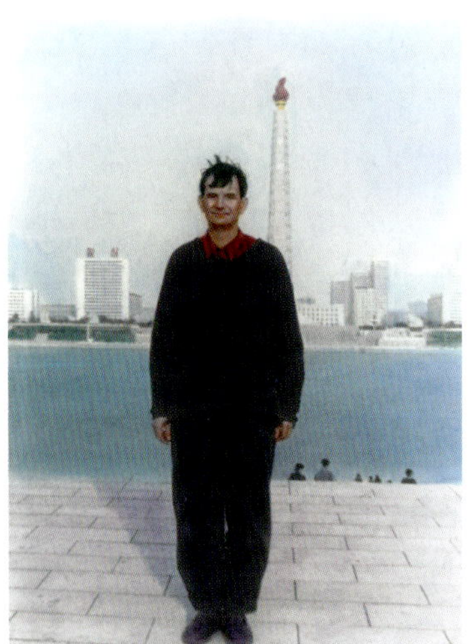

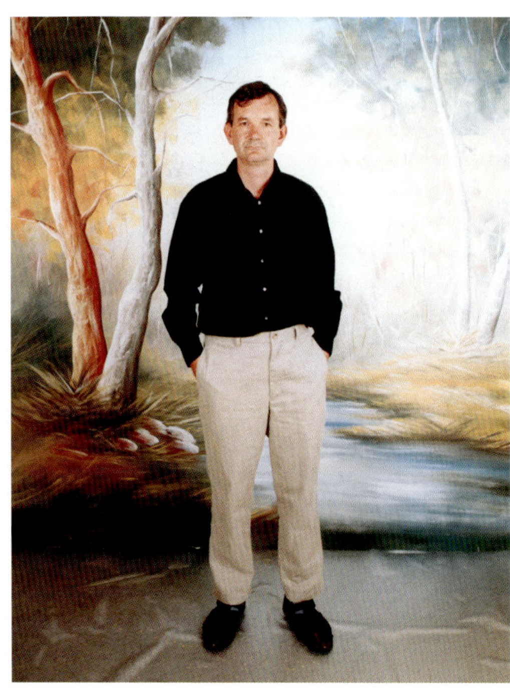

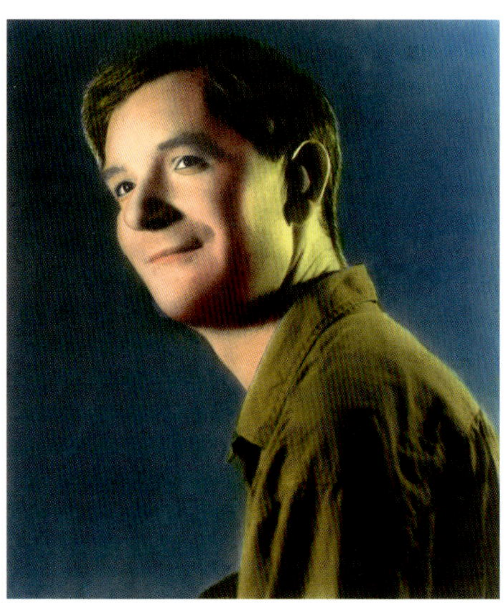

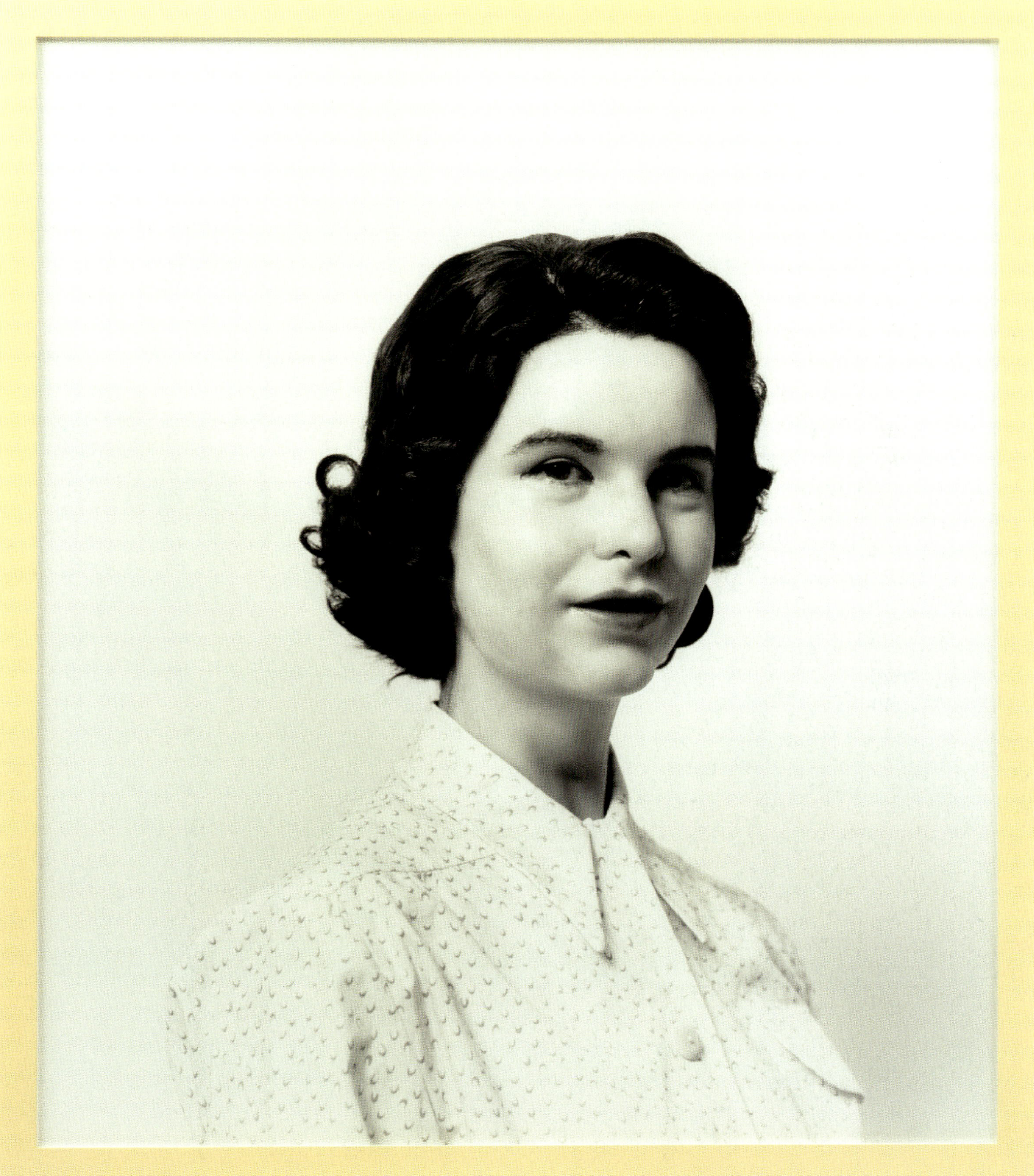

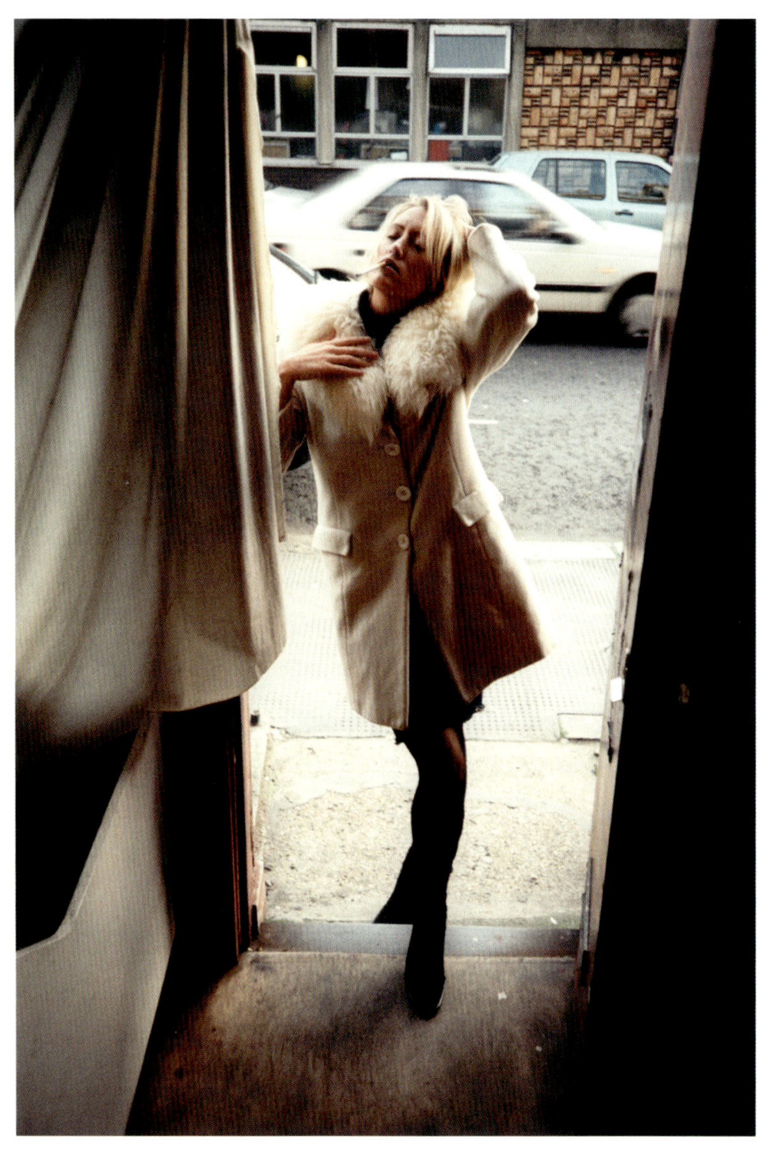
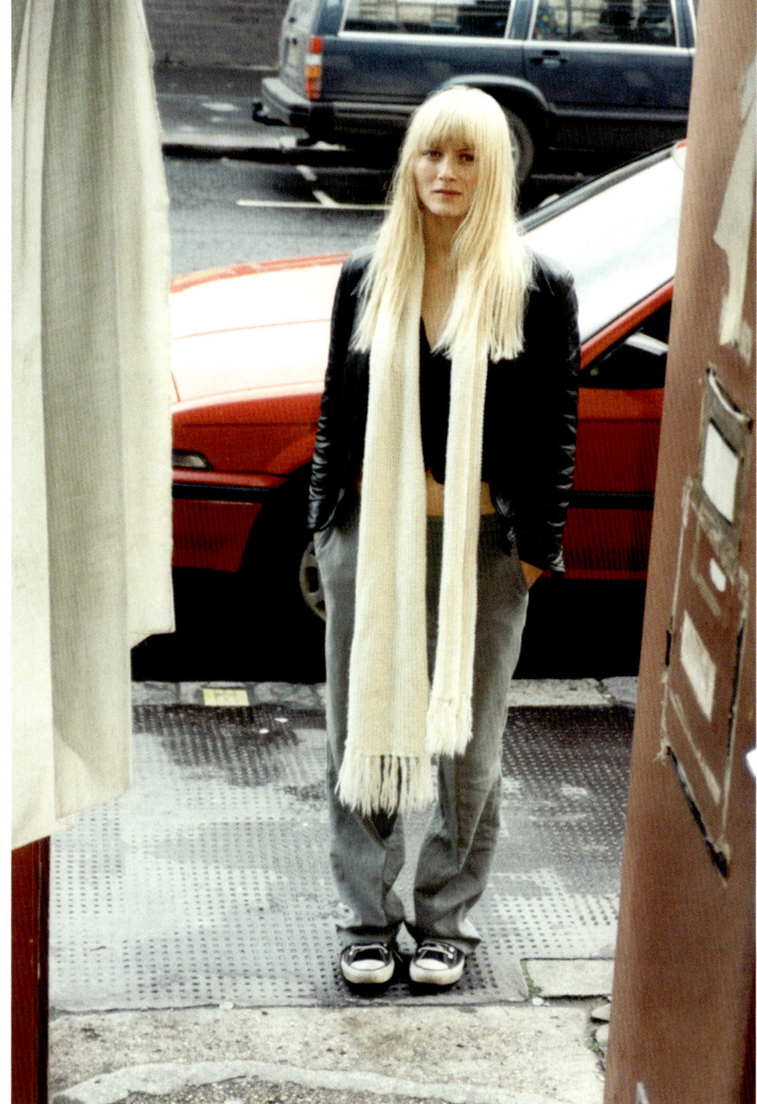

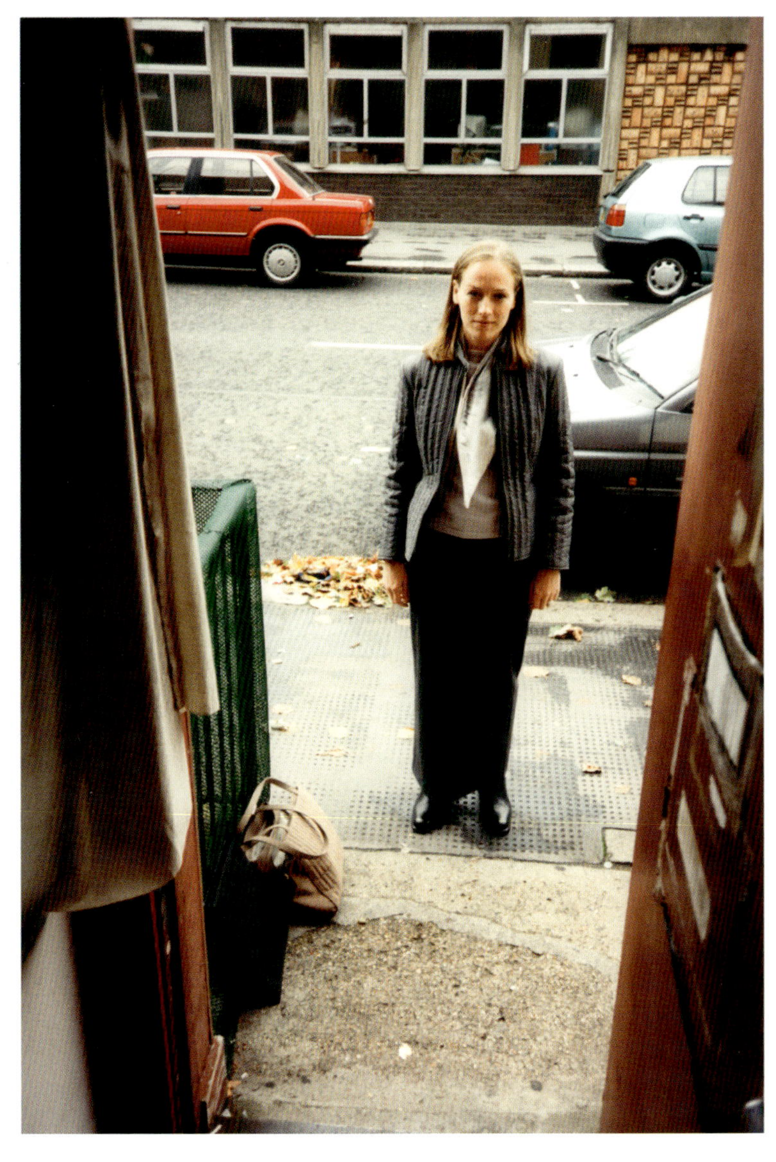

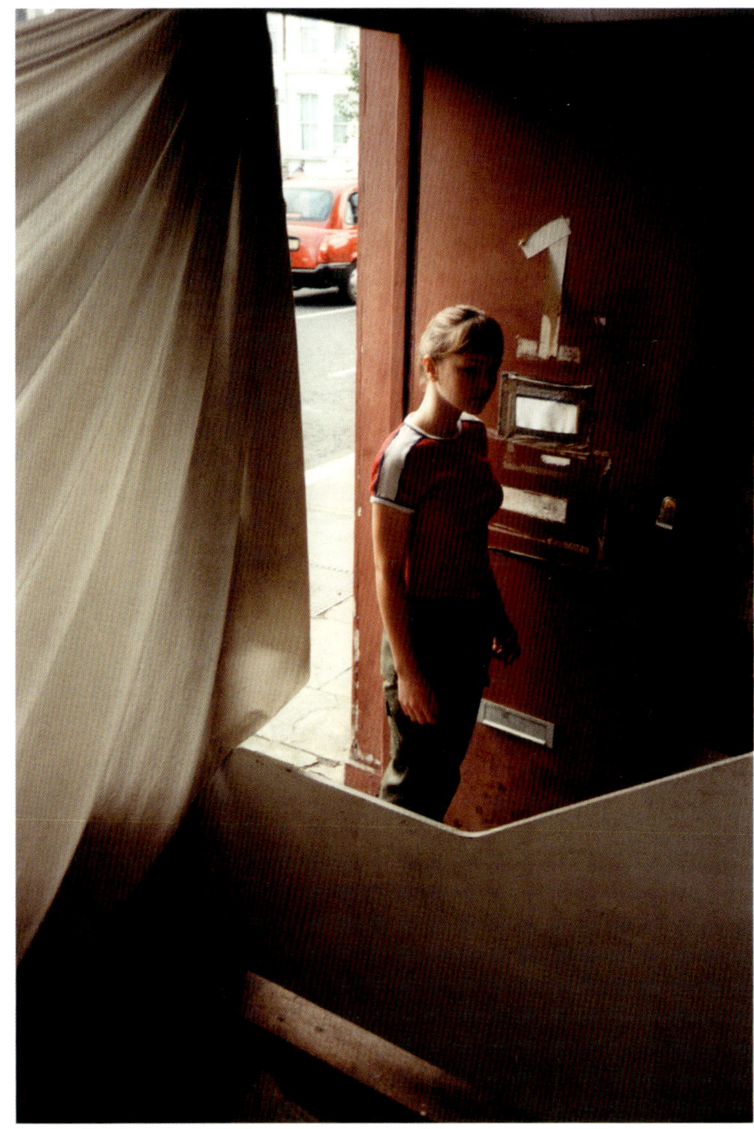

Rineke Dijkstra, *The Buzzclub, Liverpool, UK / Mysteryworld, Zaandam, NL*, 1996–7

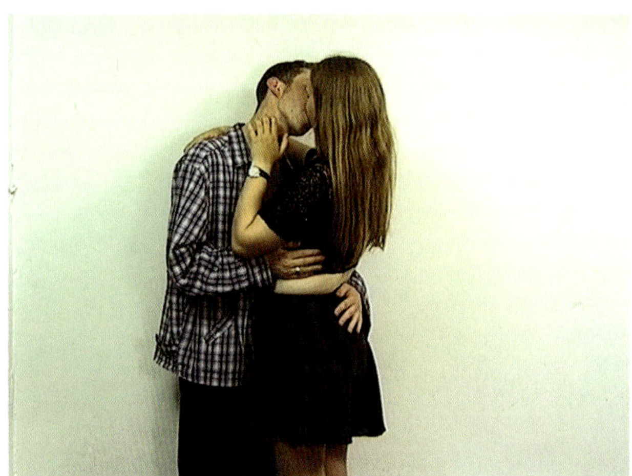
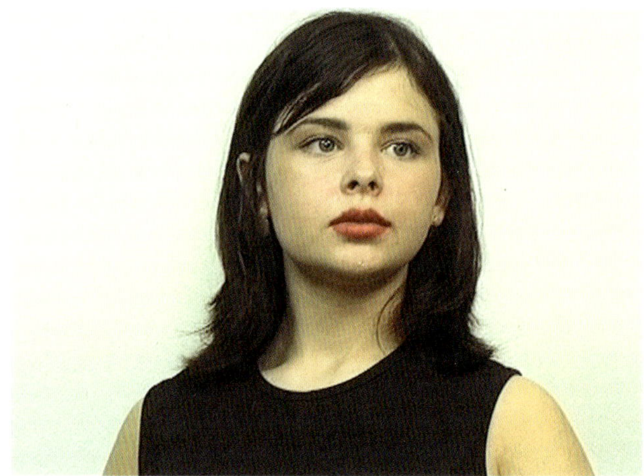
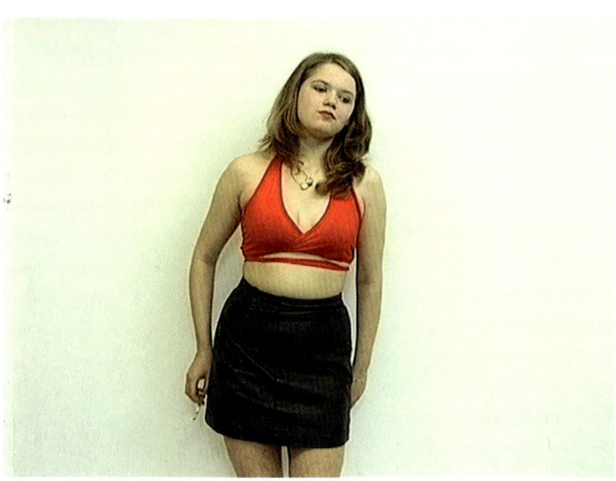
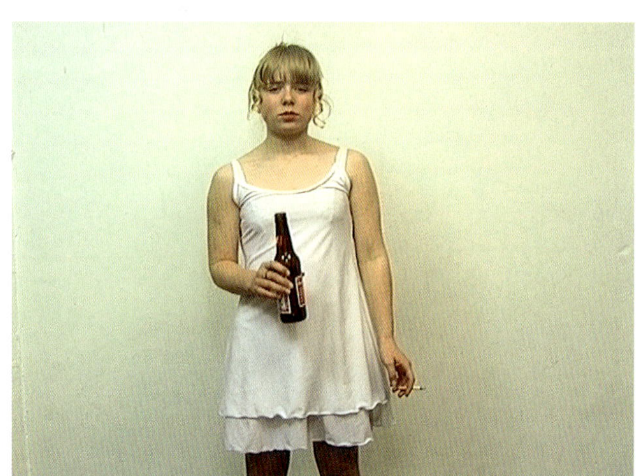
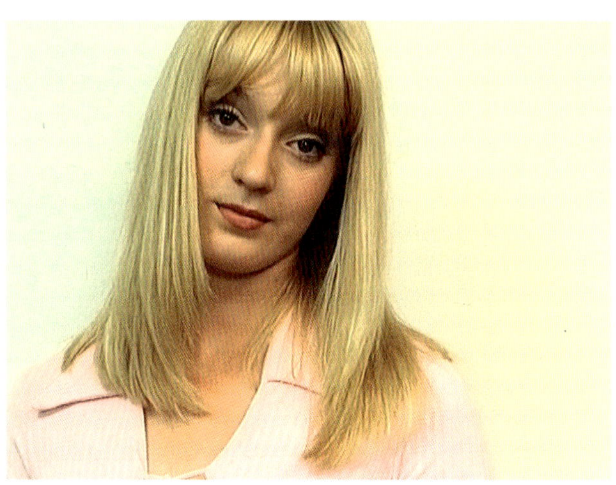
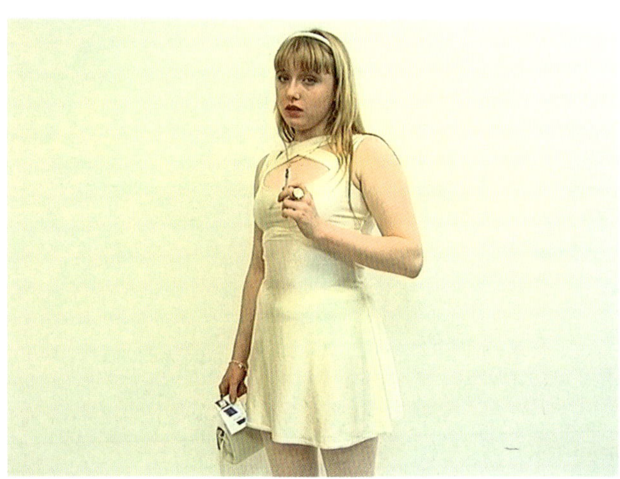

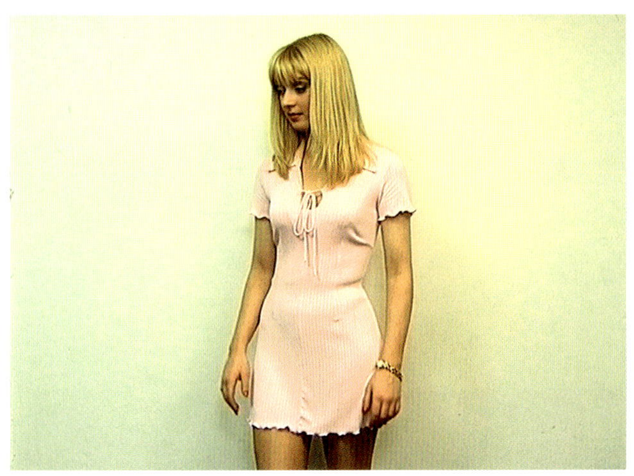
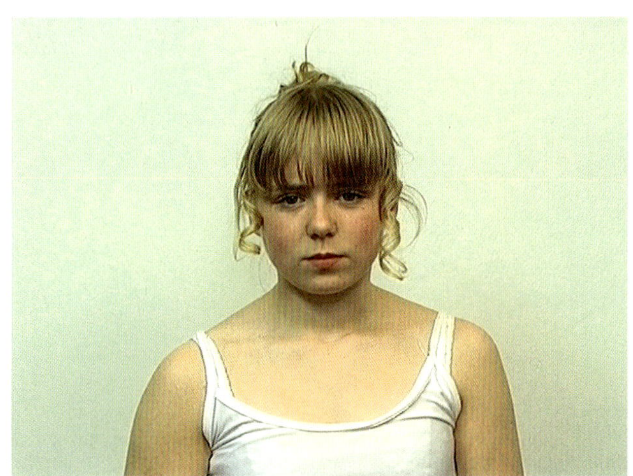
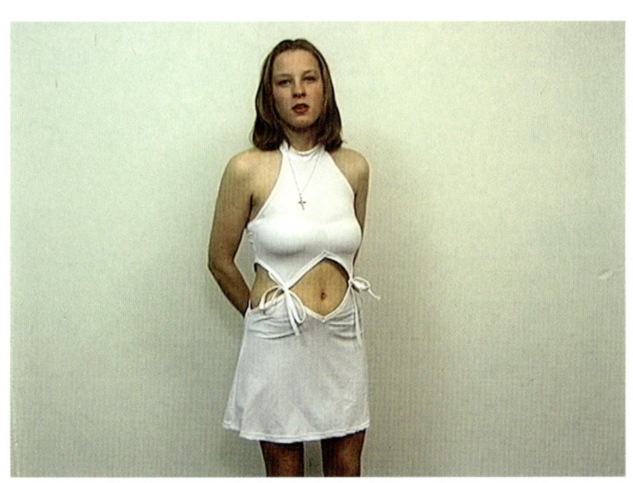
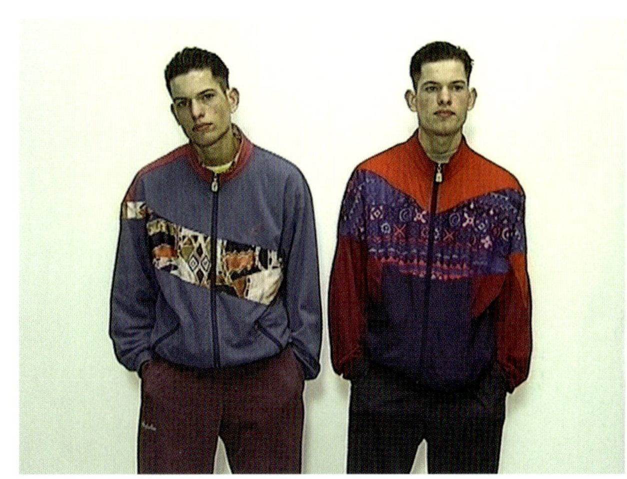
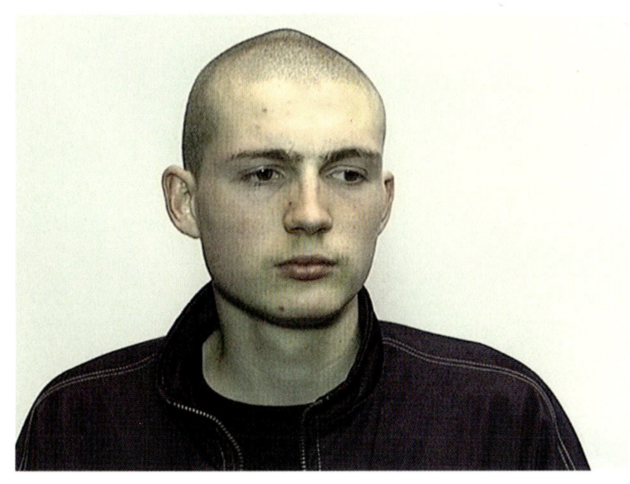
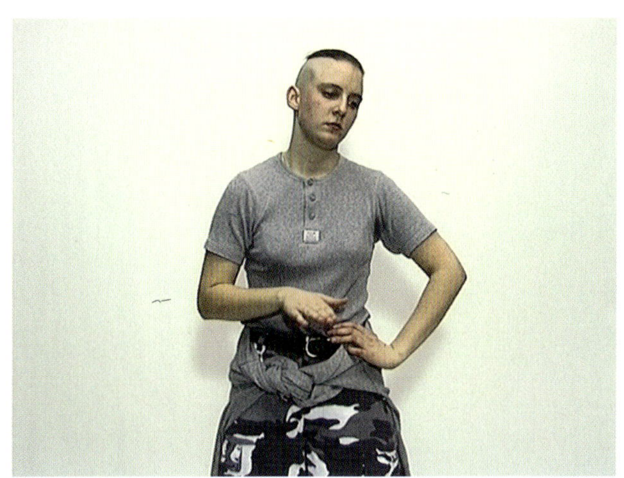

Sunil Gupta, *Pavitr*, from the series *Mr Malhotra's Party*, 2007

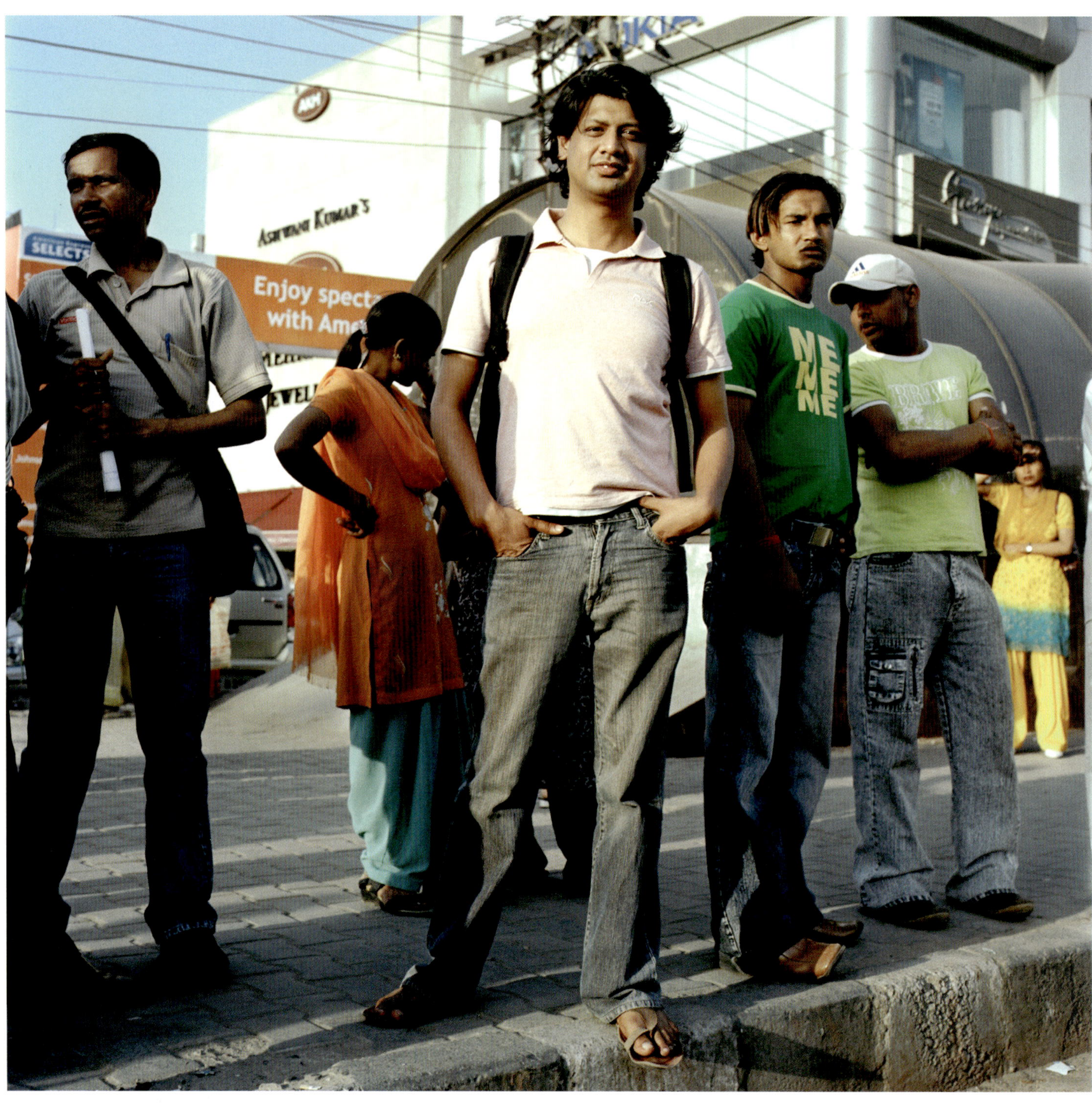

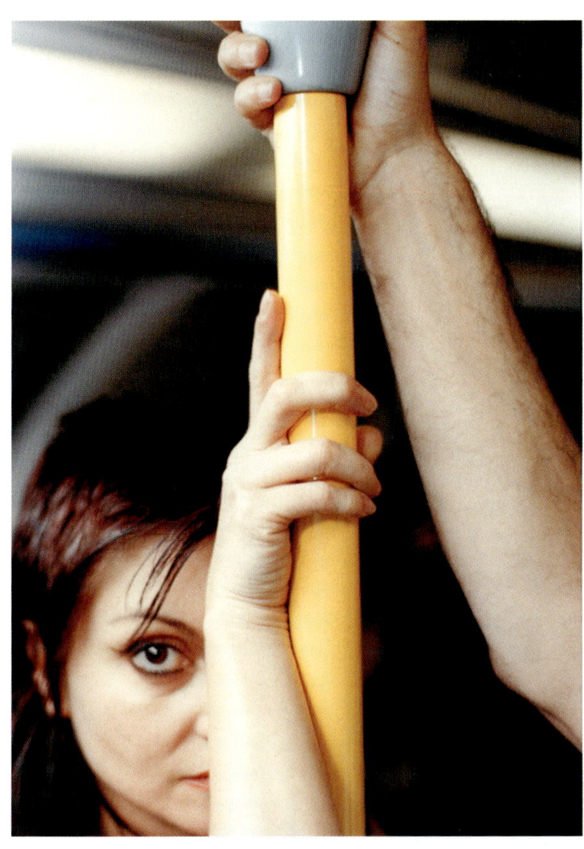
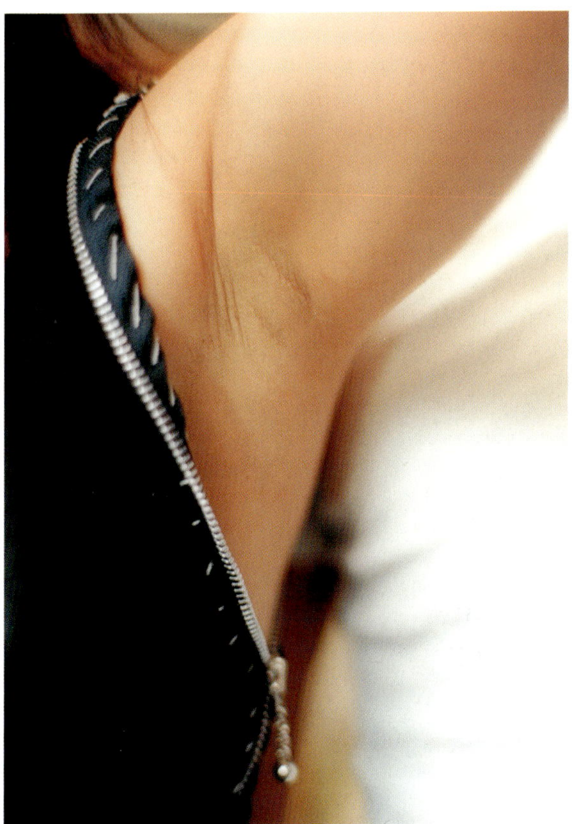
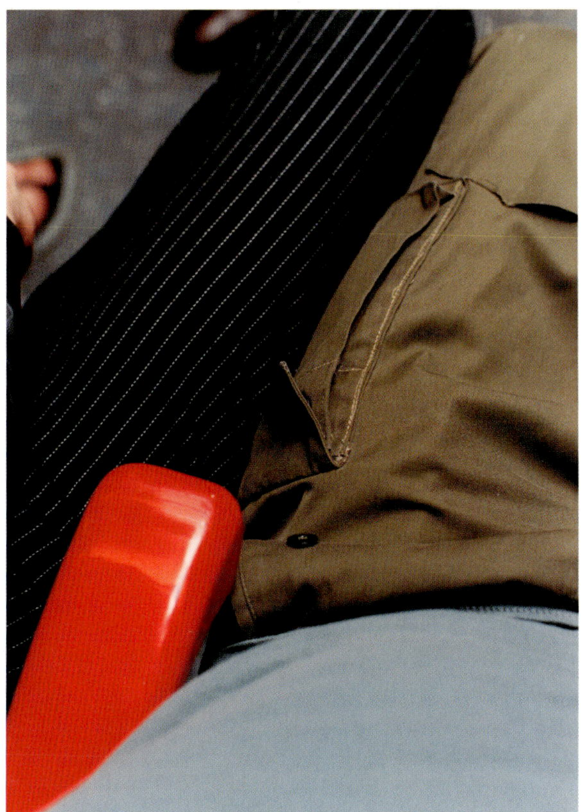
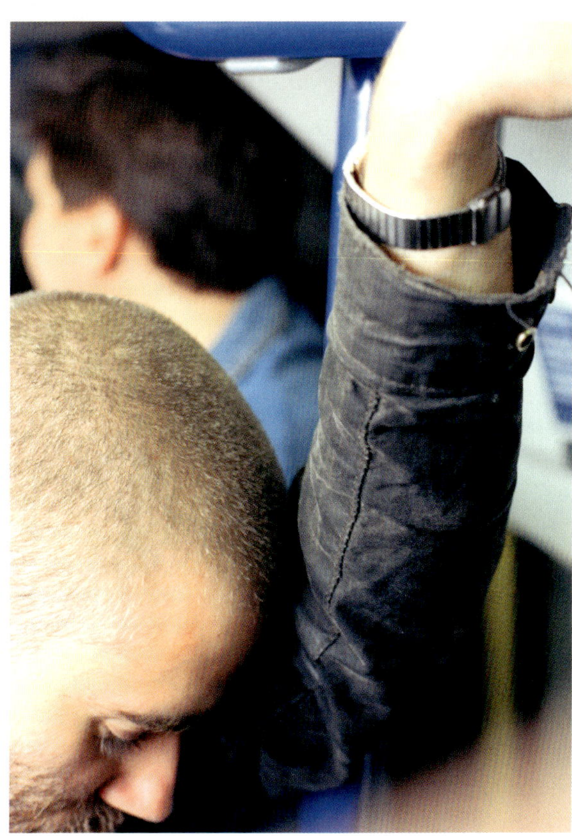

Beat Streuli, *Porte de Ninove, Bruxelles* (Porte de Ninove, Brussels), 2007

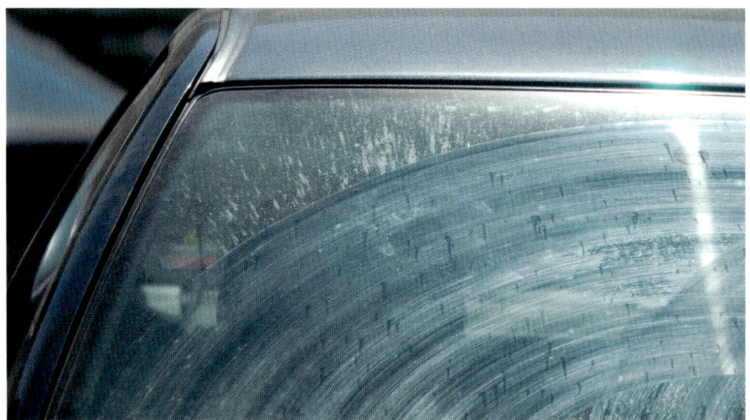
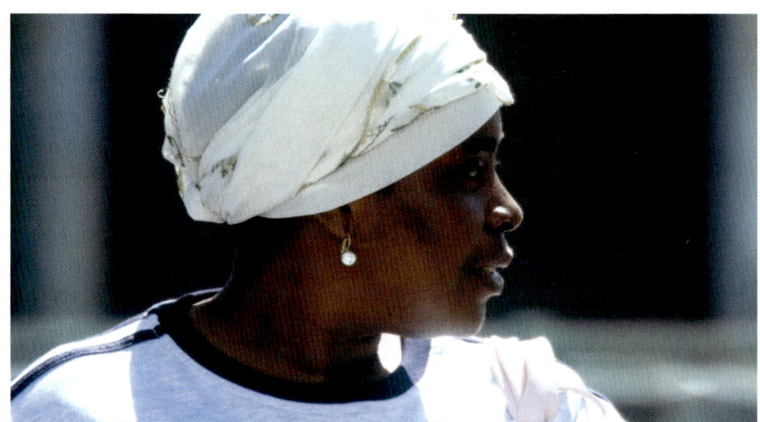
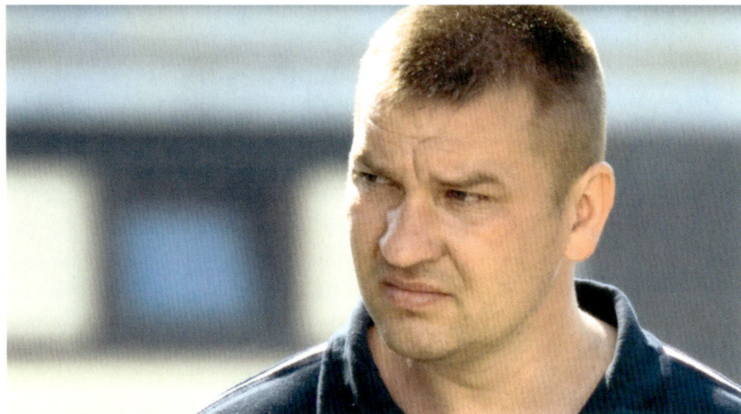
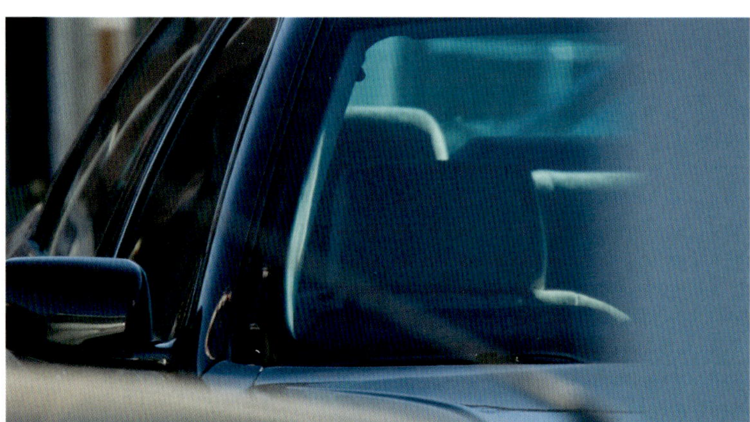

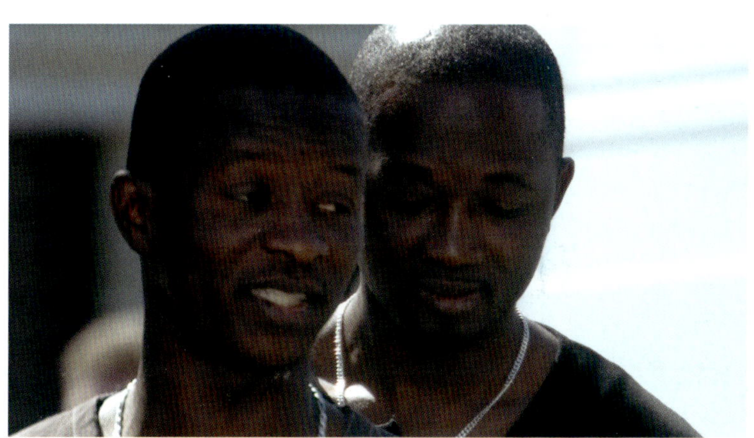

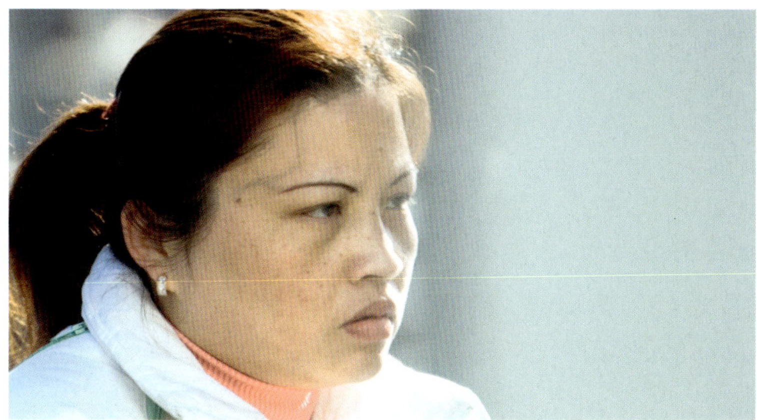

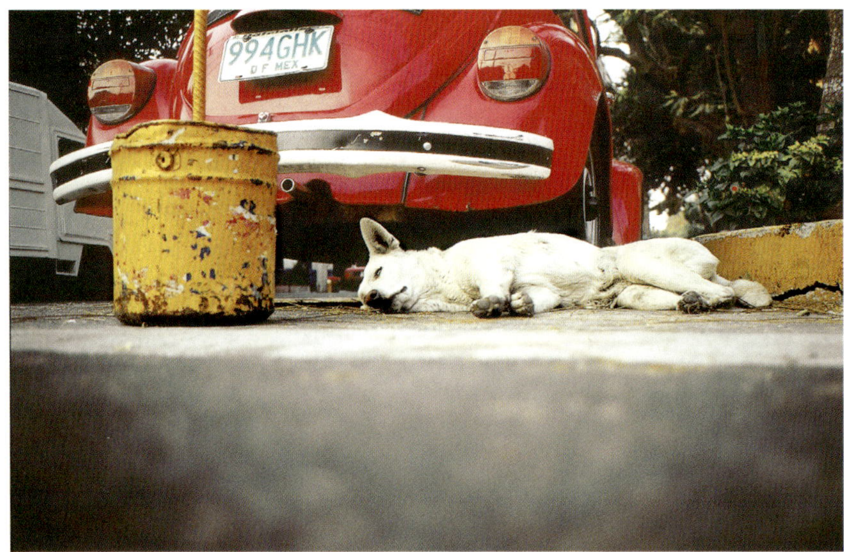

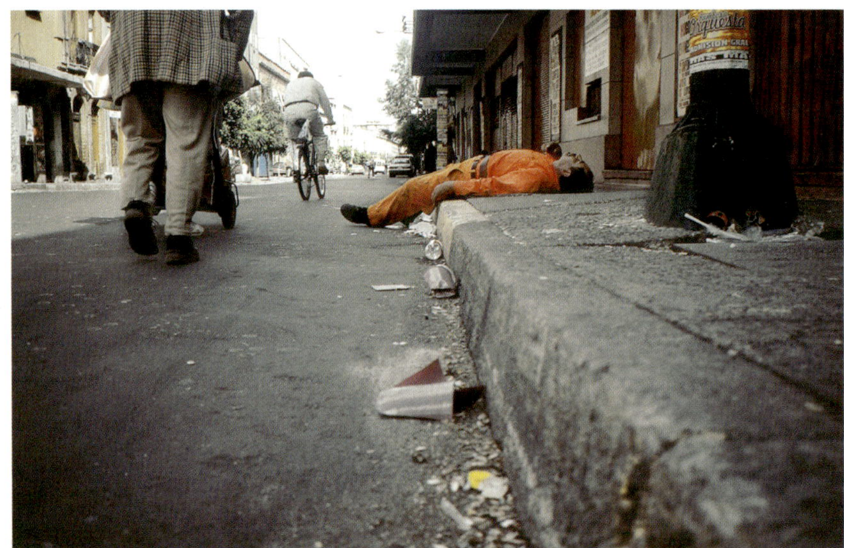

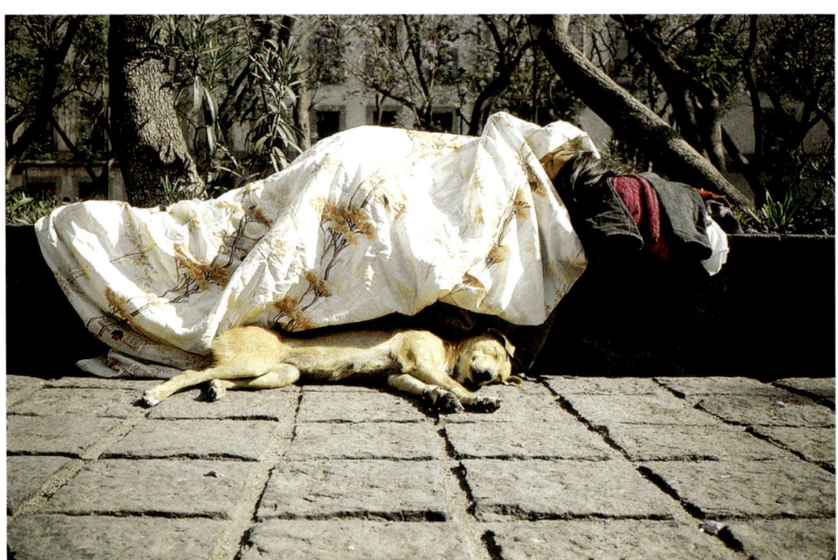

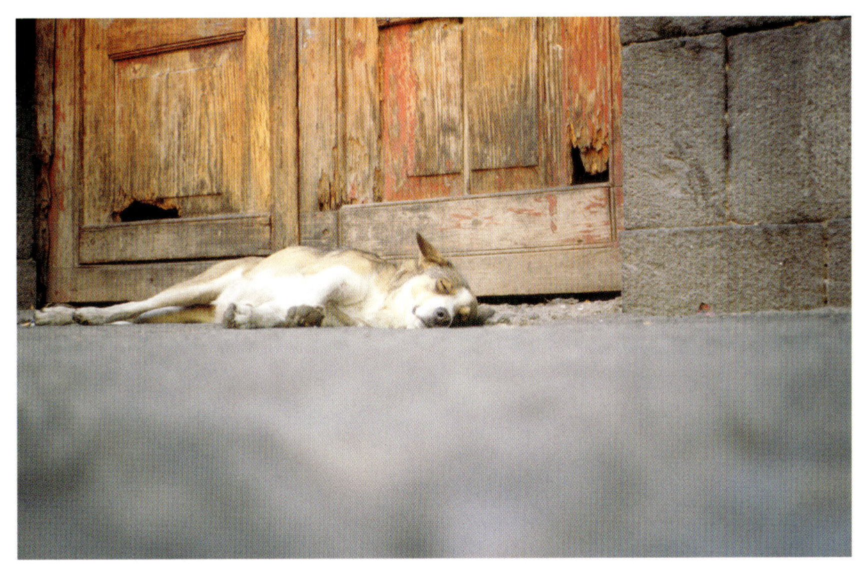

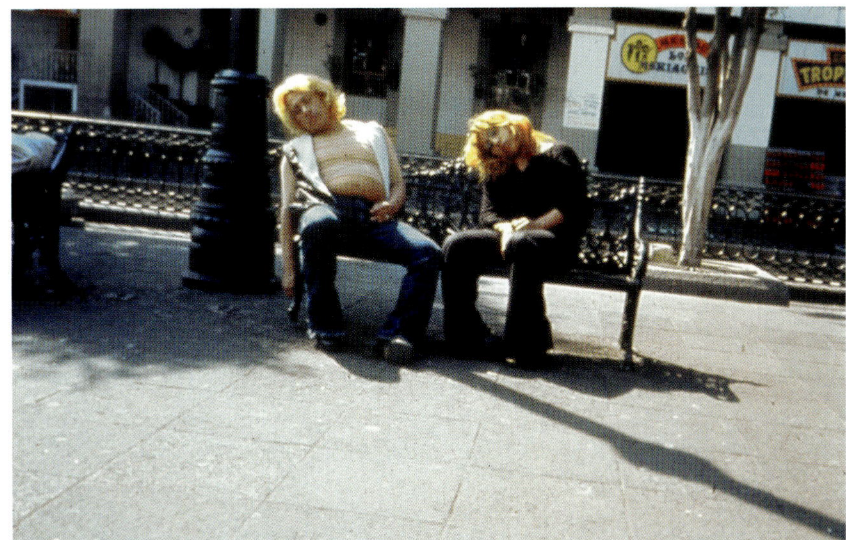

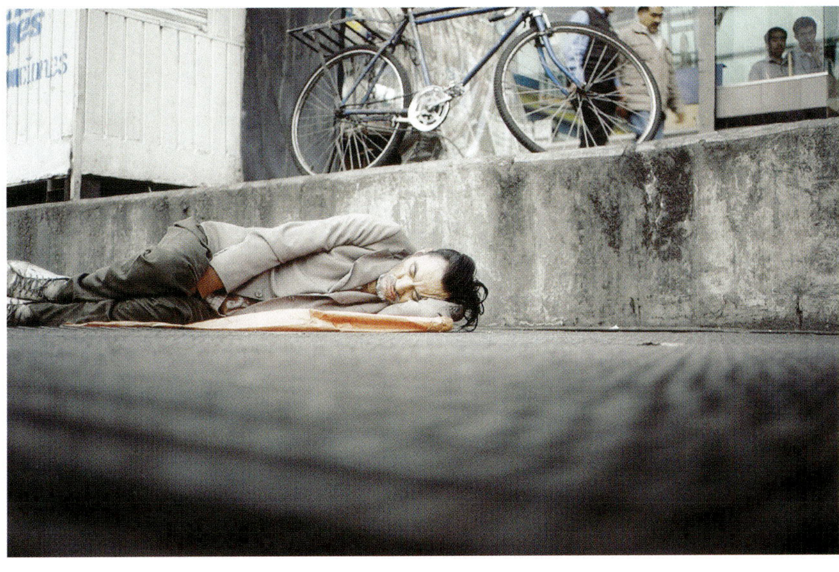

Frank Berger, *Traffic Assistants, Shanghai*, 2007 (detail)

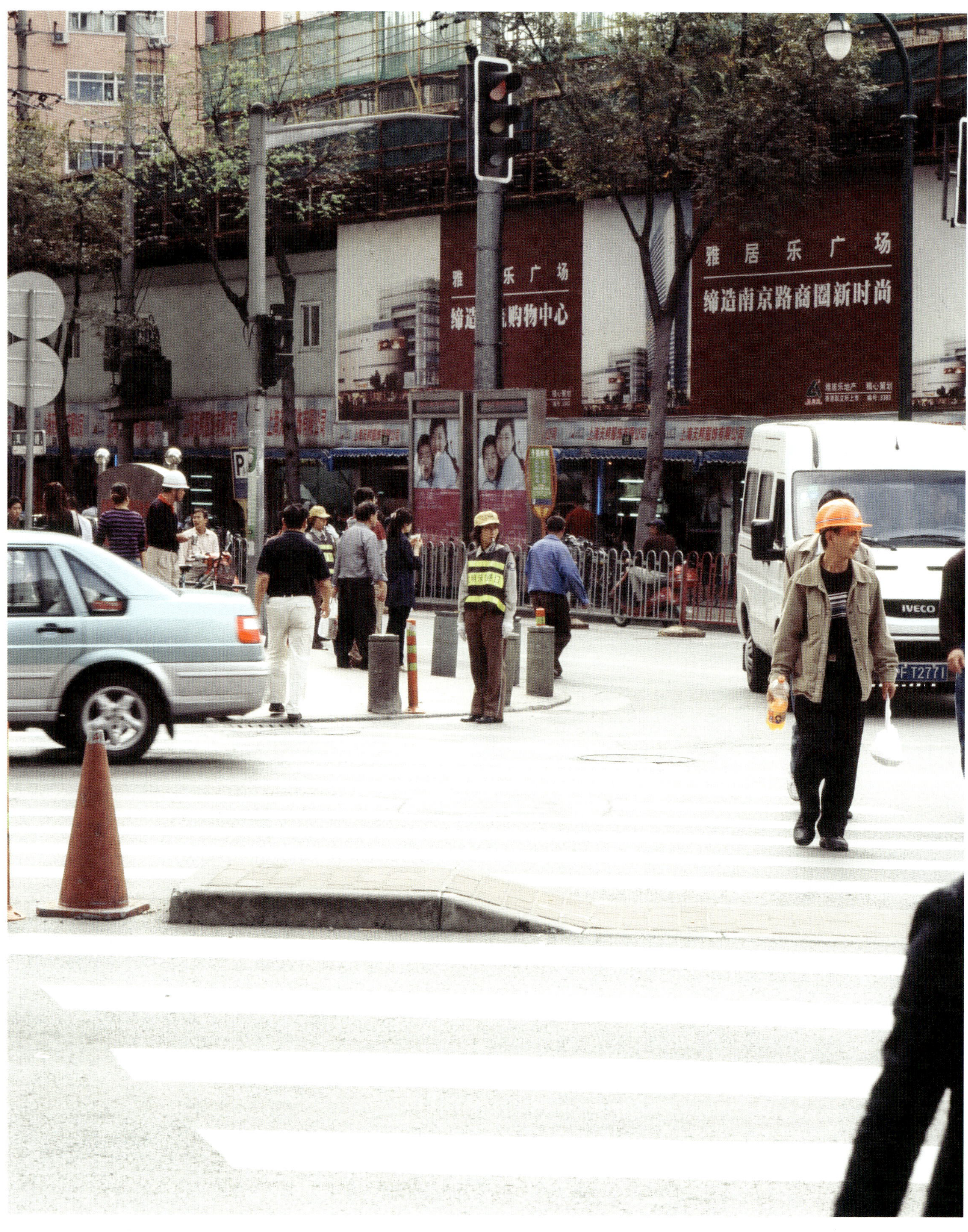

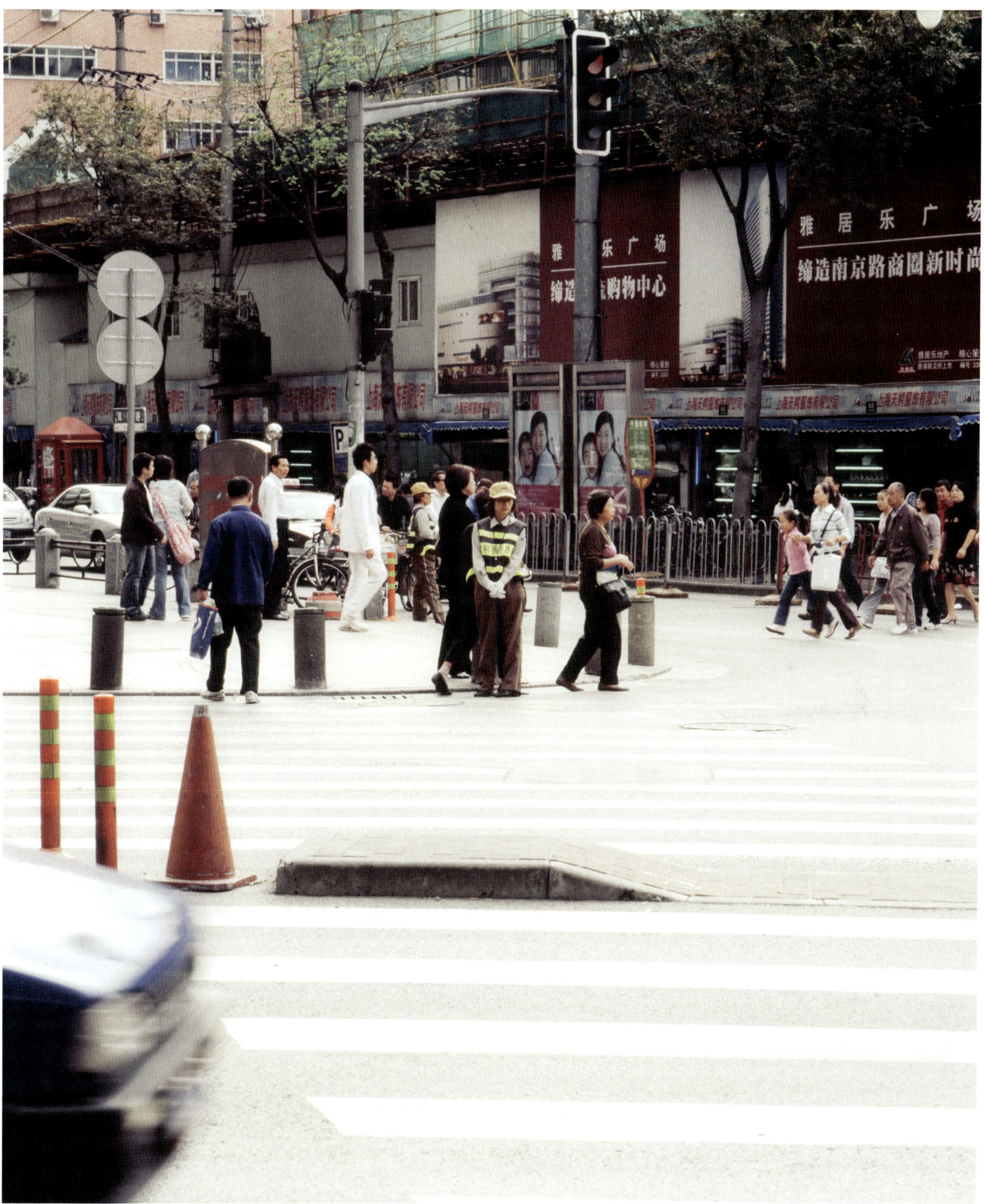
雅居乐广场
缔造南京路商圈新时尚购物中心
雅居乐广场
缔造南京路商圈新时尚

     Pieter Hugo, *Abdullahi Mohammed with Mainasara*, 2007

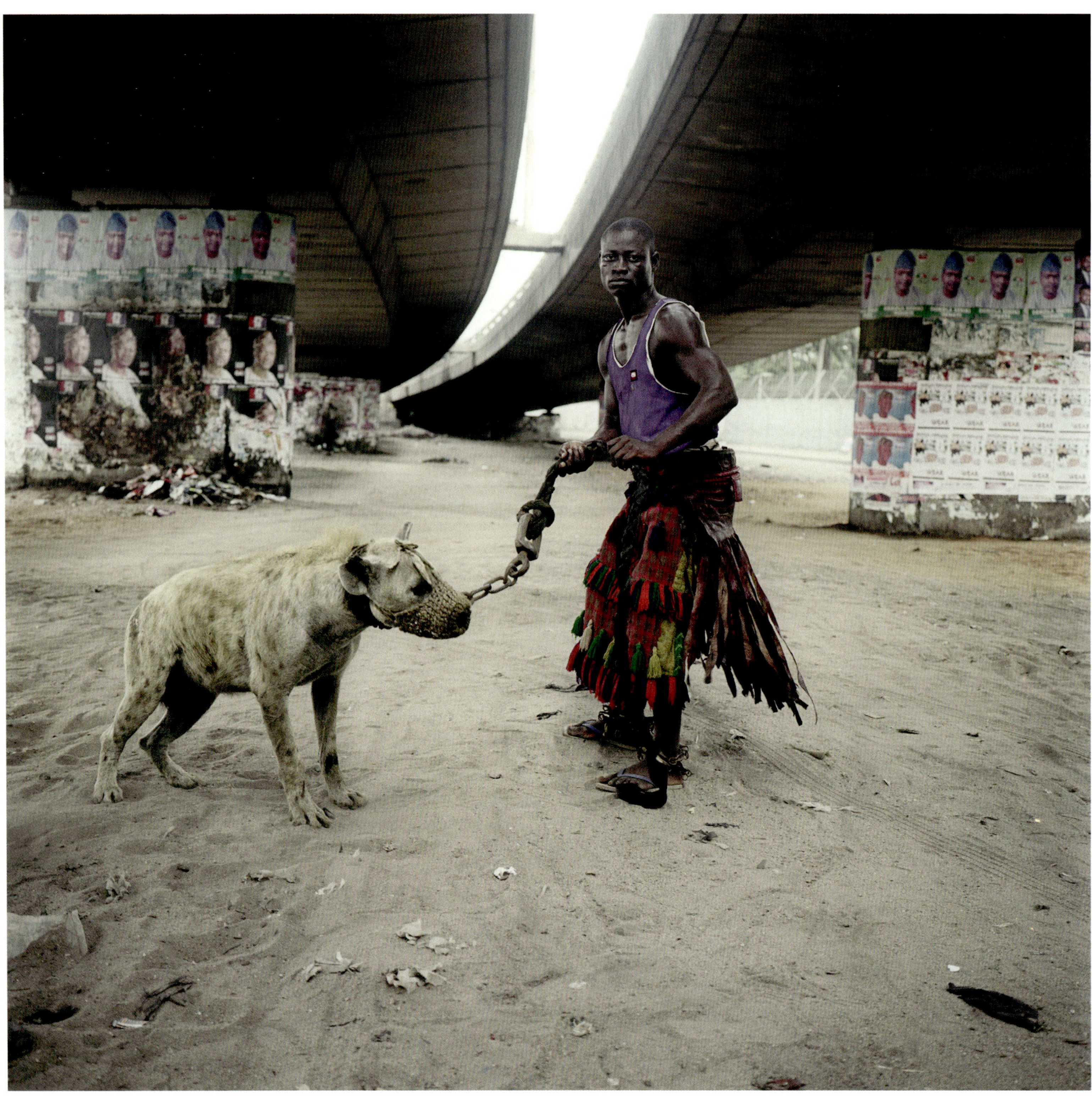

Index to Artists and Works

Compiled by Florian Ebner and Bettina Kaufmann

The following entries combine technical information on the exhibited works with details of the context of their production and publication. This is followed by biographical information on the photographer and bibliographical references to the particular work. If the place of birth and home are identical, the town is only mentioned once. Titles are given in the original language, translations in brackets, and measurements are given in centimetres, height before width. Unless otherwise stated, the photographic prints are on gelatine silver paper, made at the time the photograph was taken (vintage). Page numbers refer to illustrations.

Manuel Álvarez Bravo
1902–2002 Mexico City

Obrero en huelga, asesinado *(Striking Worker, Assassinated)*, 1934, 28 × 35 cm

→ p.44

Victoria & Albert Museum, London

Striking Worker, Assassinated *does not spare the observer. It shows the corpse of a man killed during a sugar-mill strike. The image was taken from a low position, very close to the blood-covered body, to show the brutal result of the events in all their directness and irreversibility. Although this document, published 1939 in the Surrealist magazine* Minotaure, *is one of the most famous images taken by Manuel Álvarez Bravo, it is an exception in his body of work, in which social and political conditions are depicted only indirectly.*

Early in his childhood, Manuel Álvarez Bravo was drawn to photography through his grandfather, a painter, and his father, a teacher and amateur photographer. His career started in post-revolutionary Mexico City, which had emerged early in the twentieth century as an international centre for artistic and intellectual exchange. Having completed his studies in literature, painting and music, Álvarez Bravo began to pursue photography in 1922. His images employ the abstract vision of modernist photography combined with a sensibility that is related to European Surrealism. Examples of these are his photographs of shop windows and public imagery. In 1935 the Julian Levy Gallery in New York organised the exhibition *Documentary and Anti-Graphic Photographs*, where works by Álvarez Bravo, Cartier-Bresson and Evans were shown together.

Susan Kismaric (ed.), *Manuel Álvarez Bravo*, New York 2004; *Manuel Álvarez Bravo: 100 Years, 100 Days*, exh. cat., Instituto Nacional de Bellas Artes, Madrid 2001.

Francis Alÿs
b.1959 Antwerp, lives in Mexico City

Sleepers, 1999–2006, eighty 35mm slides, carousel projection

→ pp.138–9, 209

Courtesy the artist and David Zwirner, New York

Francis Alÿs comments on his photographs of urban characters, which he collected while walking through the streets of Mexico City over the course of some years:

'The style of the documentation series is influenced by August Sander's People of the Twentieth Century *or the eighteenth-century prints* Cries of London*. My method of shooting is always systematic and tries to respond technically to the encountered situations. Sleepers will always have the camera at ground level. Beggars (2002–2004) takes a quasi-hypocritical high viewpoint. Ambulantes (1992–2006) is always shot perpendicularly to the passing subject at a distance of five metres or so. In that sense it is as neutral a register as can be, and it is that which might give it its archival value over time' (Francis Alÿs in conversation with Russell Ferguson, in* Francis Alÿs*, 2007, p.21).*

After completing his studies in engineering and history of architecture during the late 1980s in Belgium, Alÿs was drawn to Mexico in order to help rebuild areas that had been devastated in an earthquake. Shortly afterwards, he settled in Mexico City and began working as an artist. One of his main interests is the city as social landscape and the ways in which people have arranged themselves within it. His continuous walks through the quarters surrounding his studio serve as his inspiration. Alÿs is – to use the title of one of his works – a 'collector' of impressions of the street. In addition to his documentary practice, he also makes interventions and performances focusing on daily street routines. He works with video, takes photographs, often acts as a protagonist in his work, and writes and works conceptually.

Francis Alÿs, exh. cat., Hammer Museum, Los Angeles 2007; Cuauhtémoc Medina, Russell Ferguson, and Jean Fisher, *Francis Alÿs*, London 2007; Francis Alÿs: *Walking Distance from the Studio*, exh. cat., Kunstmuseum Wolfsburg, Ostfildern 2005.

Laurie Anderson
b.1947 Glen Ellyn, Illinois, lives in New York

Fully Automated Nikon *(Object/Objection/Objectivity)*, 1973, new version of the work revised by the artist, six photographs, each 31 × 38 cm, two text panels, each 35 × 22 cm, reprinted 2008

→ pp.104–5

Courtesy the artist and Sean Kelly Gallery, New York

Laurie Anderson's Fully Automated Nikon (Object/Objection/Objectivity) *was taken in New York's Lower East Side and comprises photographs of men and two texts. The men had made insinuating comments to Anderson while she was walking down Houston Street in New York. Anderson photographed them and later reported that they felt flattered by having their portrait taken, although the pictures were actually meant as a kind of defence against their unwelcome advances. The work was first shown in the touring exhibition* C7500 *in 1975, organised by the feminist art critic Lucy Lippard, and represents an important position in feminist art that sarcastically turns a mirror on the gaze of male passers-by and street photographers.*

Laurie Anderson studied art history at the Barnard College in New York, and later sculpture at the University of Columbia, where she realised her first exhibition of sculptures and drawings in 1970. Her first performance *Music* took place in Rochester, New York, in 1972. Her focus increasingly shifted towards performance and music, but she continued to incorporate photographs, films and texts within these live events. Today, she is equally known as a musician and a multi-media artist.

Roselee Goldberg, *Laurie Anderson*, New York 2000; *Laurie Anderson: Works from 1969 to 1983*, exh. cat., Institute for Contemporary Art, Philadelphia 1983.

Philip Kwame Apagya
b.1958 Sekondi, Ghana, lives in Georgia, USA

Francis in Manhattan, 1996, C-print 69.5 × 49 cm, printed 2000

→ p.111

Fifty One Fine Art Photography, Antwerp

Francis in Manhattan *shows a boy in front of a painted background that represents the impressive skyline of a metropolis. Self-confidently, he has turned towards it and casts a smiling glance back at the observer as if he is about to disappear into the image at any moment. Unlike European studio photographers, Philip Kwame Apagya tries less to compose a representative portrait of his clients – in the sense of their actual social identity – than to transfer them onto another imaginative level, the realm of their desires and dreams. In his painted dream factory, cultural imprints and fetishes of the consumer society merge. '[A] picture is a silent talker – but if you know how to look at a picture, you will always see what is hidden deep inside.' (Philip Kwame Apagya in* Snap me one, *1998, p.52)*

Before Philip Kwame Apagya studied photography at the Ghana Institute of Journalism in Acra, he learned the photographic craft in his father's studio. In 1982 he set up his own studio, P.K.'s Normal Photo Studio, in Shama (Ghana). In reaction to the widespread colour and mini-labs at the end of the 1980s and the consequent declining interest in the classical studio portrait, Apagya began working with bright and colourful backdrops. He designed these himself, but had them realised by painters in the advertising industry. The backdrops show diverse aspects of the modernisation of Ghana: urban life, stagings of lifestyle and fanciful depictions of houses and parks.

FLASH Afrique: Fotografie aus Westafrika, exh. cat., Kunsthalle Wien, Göttingen 2001; Tobias Wendl and Heike Behrend (eds.), *Snap me one. Studiofotografen in Afrika*, Munich 1998.

Nobuyoshi Araki
b.1940, lives in Tokyo

From the book dummy ***Tokyo***, twenty-eight plates, 1973

→ p.96

Montages, each with two photographs on cardboard, 50 × 40 cm

*Plates **1**, 4, 5, 6, 7, 10* (London only)
Plates 9, 11, 12, 14, 17, 20 (Essen only)

Pinakothek der Moderne, Bayerische Staatsgemäldesammlung, Munich

The twelve plates are part of the layout of the slim, vertical-format book Tokyo, *one of the early volumes by Nobuyoshi Araki and the first that he dedicated to his city through its title. The twenty-eight-part sequence consists of mounted pairs of images in which pictures of passers-by in the street, taken with a zoom lens, are contrasted with erotically staged photographs of a young woman. In this juxtaposition of public space and sexual fantasy – a relationship that pervades Araki's photographic oeuvre – the street becomes an expanded eroticised zone.*

Araki studied photography and film at Chiba University in Tokyo from 1959 to 1963. Between 1963 and 1972 he was employed as a commercial photographer in an advertising agency. Since then, he has worked for magazines, often men's or porn publications. In 1971 he married Yoko Aoki and dedicated a book to their wedding; later, he devoted another to her death.

Araki is a prolific, even manic photographer, and a great erotomaniac. Through his vision, the world is transformed into a theatre of sex and death, no matter whether he is depicting cityscapes, plants or young naked women, explicitly displayed and often bound. For him, the city of Tokyo is not just a visual screen, it is *the* place of the unconscious. His photography articulates itself in countless books whose production, often through photocopying, started in the 1970s and by November 2006, according to Araki, had reached 357.

Nobuyoshi Araki: Self, Life, Death, exh. cat., Barbican Art Gallery, London 2005; *Nobuyoshi Araki: Akt-Tokyo, 1971–1991*, exh. cat., Forum Stadtpark, Graz 1992.

Diane Arbus (Diane Nemerov)
1923 – 1971 New York

Woman with a Veil on Fifth Avenue, N.Y.C., 1968, 37.6 × 37.2 cm

→ p.92

Fotografische Sammlung, Museum Folkwang, Essen

A Woman with Pearl Necklace and Earrings, N.Y.C., 1967, 40.6 × 50.8 cm

Child with a Toy Hand Grenade in Central Park, N.Y.C., 1962, 30.2 × 29.5 cm

A Child Crying, N.J., 1967, 50.8 × 40.6 cm

Olbricht Collection

In 1967 the New York photographer Diane Arbus wrote to her friend Carlotta Marshall: 'The pictures are getting bigger. Some are life-size or more' (Revelations, 2003, p.185). This remark might refer to the close-ups of faces that became more prominent in her photographs at this time: along with the adipose babies in Diaper Derbies, toddlers and young women in parks, she also photographed elderly middle-class ladies, self-confidently endowed with the symbols of their wealth. The precision of Arbus's medium-format camera, as well as its strobe attachment, isolate and single out her subjects, like the Woman with a Veil on Fifth Avenue, from the urban context. They are part of a multi-faceted American panopticon.

Diane Nemerov grew up in New York. Aged fourteen, she met Allan Arbus, whom she married four years later. Together, they opened a studio and supplied magazines with fashion photography. In 1959 Arbus studied under Lisette Model, an important incentive for her artistic career. She received Guggenheim Fellowship grants in 1963 and in 1966. In her work, she sheds light on the marginal phenomena of society, 'freaks' and eccentric people, representatives of the most diverse milieus, but also exponents of consumer society, the upper class and patriotic America. She was to become one of the central figures of the new socio-critical documentary photography of the twentieth century. In 1971 she took her own life.

Anthony W. Lee and John Pultz (eds.), *Diane Arbus: Family Albums*, New Haven 2003; *Diane Arbus: Revelations*, San Francisco 2003.

Richard Avedon
1923 New York – 2004
San Antonio, Texas

The Chicago Seven: Lee Weiner, John Froines, Abbie Hoffman, Rennie Davis, Jerry Rubin, Tom Hayden, Dave Dellinger, Chicago, September 25, 1969, 1969, 25.4 × 53.3 cm

→ pp.94–5

Andy Warhol and members of The Factory: Paul Morrissey, director; Joe Dallesandro, actor; Candy Darling, actor; Eric Emerson, actor; Jay Johnson, actor; Tom Hempertz, actor; Gerard Malanga, poet; Viva, actor; Paul Morrissey; Taylor Mead, actor; Brigid Polk, actor; Joe Dallesandro; Andy Warhol, artist, New York, October 30, 1969, 1969, 20.3 × 76.2cm

Courtesy The Avedon Foundation, New York, and Fraenkel Gallery, San Francisco

Renée, Model, Suit by Dior, Place de la Concorde, Paris, August 1947, 1947, from the portfolio *Avedon Paris*, 1978, 44.9 × 35.8 cm

Haus der Photographie / Sammlung F.C. Gundlach, Hamburg

During their ongoing court case, Richard Avedon photographed seven anti-Vietnam war activists, the so-called 'Chicago Seven', who were accused of instigating a demonstration on the occasion of the Democrat party convention in 1969 that had ended in violence. The trial had attracted wide public attention. Avedon used his preferred white, 'empty' background, thus focusing entirely on the seven men, whom he considered part of his portrait of America, in this case representing the Civil Rights movement. Through his established style, the demonstrators take on the aura of pop stars.

The nineteen-year-old Richard Avedon came into contact with photography through working in the photography department of the US Merchant Marines, where his job was to take ID photos. His studies at the New School for Social Research in New York, and especially the formative influence of his teacher Alexey Brodovitch, led him to become a widely acclaimed fashion photographer for *Harper's Bazaar* in 1945 and later for *Vogue*. In his early fashion photographs he staged scenes from everyday life, either on the street or in the studio with film lights. In 1963 he began to portray people from civil rights and anti-war movements. Increasingly, he took the challenge of working with only a white background and a static large-format camera in order to focus on the person and the formal tension created on the image plane. His series of pictures of the working class *In the American West* was taken under these conditions.

Richard Avedon 1946–2004, exh. cat., Louisana, Humlebaek 2007; *Richard Avedon, The Sixties*, Munich 1999; Richard Avedon, *Evidence 1944–1994: Richard Avedon*, Munich 1994.

Cecil Beaton
1904 – 1980 London

Margot Asquith, Lady Oxford, 1927, 26.7 × 14.5 cm

Victoria & Albert Museum, London

Untitled (The Soapsuds on the Living Posters Ball; Baba Beaton, Wanda Baillie-Hamilton and Lady Bridget Poulett), 1928, pub. 1930, 43.1 × 33.5 cm

Miss Tilly Losch, c.1930, 29.9 × 25.3 cm

Paula Gellibrand, The Marquise de Casa Maury, 1928, 28.1 × 23.6cm

→ p.47

Haus der Photographie / Sammlung F.C. Gundlach, Hamburg

Miss Nancy Beaton as a Shooting Star, 1928, 30.4 × 23 cm

Courtesy of the Cecil Beaton Studio Archive at Sotheby's

Fourteen photographic portraits of Paula Gellibrand, wife of the 1st Marquise de Casa Maury, are known to have been produced by Cecil Beaton in 1928. Among them are several images that show the young woman wearing a glittering, chainmail-like dress and helmet. With this extravagant fish skin, Beaton turns her into a mixture of modern nymph and glamorous siren, seated as half-length figure or standing in front of different painted and sparkling backgrounds. Beaton's cool, staged elegance is imbued with the spirit of the 1920s. According to the society magazine The Sphere, his clientele, which it called the 'Photocracy', comprised 'posh bohemians and the beau-monde … It was a complex, social mixture of rich heiresses, celebrated artists, important theatre personalities and descendants of the Patricians – idle, rich citizens of a new world which had been created by the mechanisms of publicity' (Cecil Beaton, 1994, p.12).

Cecil Beaton received his first camera on his ninth birthday. In 1922 he began his studies at St John's College, Cambridge, and became involved in amateur theatre. An exhibition in London helped launch his career as a 'society' photographer, leading to a contract with British *Vogue*; later on he also worked for Condé Nast. In contrast to Edward Steichen's modernist staging of light, Beaton developed a playful, even eccentric, aestheticism that made him one of the most famous portraitists of his age, and later photographer to the Royal family. In addition to his photographic career, he created countless stage designs and theatre costumes. In the 1940s he produced portraits of members of the war cabinet and documented the devastation caused by the war.

Philippe Garner and David Alan Mellor, *Cecil Beaton*, London 1994; *Cecil Beaton*, exh. cat., Barbican Art Gallery, London 1986; *Beaton's Photographs*, exh. cat., National Portrait Gallery, London 1968.

Frank Berger
b.1972, lives in Leipzig

Traffic Assistants, Shanghai, 2007, projection, eighty slides 6 × 7 cm

→ pp.140–1 (detail)

The Artist

Traffic Assistants, produced at an intersection in Shanghai in the autumn of 2007, is the most recent inclusion in a body of work by Frank Berger uniting several large-scale slide projections. Like his previous works on urban space, Traffic Assistants has a sequential structure, always retaining the same framing of the subject within an urban setting. A recurrent theme in his work is the single figure, here the traffic assistants, remaining a fixed constant amidst the ever-changing street life, thus being isolated from the stream of passers-by.

Frank Berger studied photography at the Academy of Visual Arts in Leipzig, where he passed both his diploma and his masterclass exam with distinction. Since the late 1990s he has continuously presented his photographic series in the form of slide projections with an abundance of detail and visual depth.

Frank Berger, National Poatait Gallery, exh. cat., C/O Berlin and Goethe-Institut New York, Leipzig 2006; *Vor aller Augen. Fotografie aus Leipzig*, exh. cat., Goethe-Institut Paris, Leipzig 2005.

Kristleifur Björnsson
b.1973 Reykjavik, lives in Berlin

– From the series ***Mindi*** –

my indian flower, 0803_observer3_lg, August 2005, 246 × 177 cm

– From the series *My girlfriend Natalie* –
THE_PLAY_3_30_03_4_HI, June 2003,
290 × 196 cm

→ p.25

Montages of inkjet prints
Kristleifur Björnsson / Stalke Gallery Denmark

For his project My Girls, *Kristleifur Björnsson uses photographs of actresses such as Natalie Portman or Parminder Nagra that he finds on the internet. He translates these small images – the titles refer to the name of the digital file – into montages of A4-sized prints that are as big as a wall in his studio. Through these found images, taken either by professionals in a studio or by fans in public, Björnsson evokes the imaginative relationship that a fan develops with his famous 'girlfriend'.*

Björnsson studied photography at the Academy of Visual Arts in Leipzig, graduating with distinction in 2003. In addition to these projects using appropriated image material, other works examine the phenomena of longing and desire. He has also produced extensive photographic series on the Icelandic landscape, as well as three-dimensional works made with Lego blocks.

Forschen und Erfinden/Research and Invention, *exh. cat., Fotomuseum Winterthur, Zurich 2007; Walter Schoppmann,* Silver & Gold. Klasse Rautert/Fotografie, *Cologne 2003.*

Erwin Blumenfeld
1897 Berlin – 1969 Rome

Red Cross, 1945
City Lights, 1946

→ p.72

C-prints, each 40 × 30 cm, printed 2007
© The Estate of Erwin Blumenfeld

The fashion photograph City Lights, *which was probably commissioned by Harper's Baazar, shows the subtle humour that is recurrent in Blumenfeld's photographs. The visual narrative of the image conveys the idea of an elegant lady, posing classically in front of a panorama window on the twenty-first floor of a modernist skyscraper. The nocturnal skyline in the background is not real, but an imaginative visualisation. In order to create a background that suggests sparkling skyscrapers against a night sky, Blumenfeld either placed twinkling glass on black velvet or employed finely perforated black cardboard lit from behind. By means of simple props, he managed to capture the aura of metropolitan life, while at the same time producing a vivid fashion image of the green dress.*

Erwin Blumenfeld worked as an apprentice at a fashion studio in Berlin, where he became acquainted with the poet Else Lasker-Schüler, as well as George Grosz and the Expressionists. In 1918, he deserted from the German army and fled to Holland, where he worked as a bookseller. It was at this time that he became active in the Dada movement, which would inspire him throughout his career. From 1932 onwards, he began to photograph professionally. Early on, he adopted the visual language of Surrealism and incorporated it into his images. He used a variety of techniques and experimented with collages, solarisation, multiple exposures, and he also combined negative and positive printing. His great success as a fashion photographer came in 1941, when he opened up a studio in New York and began working regularly for the magazines *Harper's Bazaar* and *Vogue*, as well as for several advertising agencies.

Wim van Sinderen, Fleur de Carvahlo, Helen Adkins et al., Erwin Blumenfeld: His Dutch Years 1918–1936, *The Hague 2006; Erwin Blumenfeld,* Eye to I: The Autobiography of a Photographer, *London 1999; William A. Ewing (ed.),* Erwin Blumenfeld: A Passion for Beauty, *New York 1996.*

Brassaï (Gyula Halász)
1899 Brassó, Romania – 1984
Beaulieu-sur-Mer, France

Clocharde, Quai des Tuileries (Tramp, Quai des Tuileries), 1930–2, 23.4 × 17.7 cm
Deux hirondelles (Two Policemen), 1931, 29 × 23 cm
Fille, rue Quincampoix (Prostitute, rue Quincampoix), 1930–2, 22.8 × 17.2 cm
Laitier (Milkman), 1930–3, 22.3 × 17.4 cm

Centre Georges Pompidou, Paris. Musée National d'Art Moderne / Centre de Création Industrielle

Untitled, c.1932, 23.7 × 18 cm

→ p.41

Fotografische Sammlung, Museum Folkwang, Essen

'The night makes allusions but doesn't reveal anything. The night disorients and surprises us by its strangeness; it releases forces that are dominated by intellect during the day … I used to love the wonders of the night that were forced by the light to disclose themselves; there is no such thing as absolute night' (Brassaï, Paris, 2000, p.157). One of Brassaï's passions was to go wandering in the nocturnal city. From 1930 this resulted in photographs of empty streets and parks, of dance halls, cafés, bars and of nocturnal figures strolling through the sparsely lit streets of Paris. Brassaï published a selection of these images under the title Paris de Nuit *(1932–3) and later in* Voluptés de Paris *(1934). As can be seen in the uncanny photograph of the two mannequins (Untitled), the night is not only reproduced in the photograph, but can also be generated by photographic means, through adequate lighting and exposure.*

The young Hungarian Gyula Halász, son of a literature professor, studied at art academies in Budapest and Berlin and moved to Paris in 1929, where he initially worked as a journalist for Hungarian and German newspapers. From 1929 he started to illustrate the articles with his own photographs, having been influenced by his compatriot André Kertész and by Eugène Atget. In 1932 he adopted the pseudonym Brassaï, which is based on the Hungarian name of his hometown Brassó. In December of that year, his book *Paris de Nuit* was published with a text by Paul Morand. The book was a huge international success and the journalist Brassaï turned photographer, much sought-after by magazines. He produced numerous portraits and photographs of works in the studios of his artist friends, and undertook a long-term freelance project on graffiti. He published several books, such as *Conversations avec Picasso* (1964) and *The Artists of my Life* (1982).

Brassaï, *exh. cat., Centre Georges Pompidou, Paris 2000; Anne Wilkes Tucker (ed.),* Brassaï: The Eye of Paris, *Houston 1999; Brassaï,* Marcel Proust sous l'emprise de la photographie, *Paris 1997.*

Henri Cartier-Bresson
1908 Chanteloup, France –
2004 Paris

Séville, Espagne (Seville, Spain), 1938, 23 × 34 cm

Fotografische Sammlung, Museum Folkwang, Essen

Taxi Drivers, Berlin, 1931, 24 × 35.7 cm, printed 1980s

Spain, 1933, 19.6 × 29 cm

→ p.208

Fondation Henri Cartier-Bresson, Paris

Mexico City, 1934, 38.5 × 26 cm, printed 1968
→ p.45

The Museum of Modern Art, New York. Gift of the photographer, 1985

Madrid, 1933, 23.2 × 34.7 cm

The Museum of Modern Art, New York. Gift of the photographer, 1947

In 1934 Henri Cartier-Bresson photographed a passer-by, with her newborn baby wrapped in a cloth, on the streets of Mexico City, where he lived for a year in a Barrio Popular. He arranged photographs resulting from this stay into his scrapbook in 1946. They show the French upper-middle-class photographer's fascination with the simplicity of the life he found there: the naked children at play, semi-hidden figures, and again and again, people lying or sleeping on the ground. The recurrent theme of his Mexico images is the 'primitive', in keeping with the crude, uncanny visual world of his early years. At the end of his stay in Mexico, his images were shown, together with works by Manuel Álvarez Bravo, in an exhibition held at the Palacio de Bellas Artes, Mexico City.

At the beginning of Henri Cartier-Bresson's artistic career, he was interested in painting and the spirit of Surrealism. During 1927/8 he studied under André Lhote at his studio in Paris. The 1930s and 1940s were the most definitive years for a figure who was to become one of the most influential photographers of the twentieth century. In 1931 he produced his first photographs while travelling through the Ivory Coast, followed by a journey to Spain in 1933 and his first publications in the magazine *Vu*. After his year-long stay in Mexico, he went to the USA and took film classes under Paul Strand. In 1937 he shot his first documentary film during the Spanish Civil War. In 1940 he became a prisoner of war in Germany but managed to escape in 1943. In 1946 his first retrospective exhibition was held at the Museum of Modern Art, New York. The following year Cartier-Bresson was one of the founding members of the photo agency Magnum and in the following decades predominantly worked as a photojournalist. In 1952 he published his first important book, entitled *Images à la Sauvette*, in which he developed his much quoted theory of the 'Decisive Moment'.

Henri Cartier-Bresson, Scrap Book: Photographies 1932–1946, *exh. cat., Fondation Henri Cartier-Bresson, Paris 2006; Peter Galassi,* Henri Cartier-Bresson: The Early Work, *exh. cat., Museum of Modern Art, New York 1987.*

Martín Chambi
1891 Coaza, Peru – 1973
Cusco, Peru

Señorita en traje de baño (Girl in Bathing Suit), 1932, 30 × 24 cm, printed 2008

→ p.46

Señorita Torera (Girl Bullfighter), 1932, 30 × 24 cm, printed 2008

→ p.210

Archivio Fotografico Martín Chambi / Martín Chambi Photo Archives

In front of a painted floral background in the studio, a woman in a bathing suit poses elegantly and slightly artificially. It is the portrait of a self-confident and modern woman in Peru's paternalistic, pre-modern society. Martín Chambi photographed the different social classes of his time, representing the diverse ethnic identity and the social and historic complexity of Peruvian society. The solemnity and dignity that he bestowed on all his models – from the beggar boy to the aristocratic lady – gives his body of portraits their characteristic sense of magnitude.

Martín Chambi was born into an indigenous Peruvian family. In his teens, he first came into contact with the medium through the photographer at the goldmine where his father worked. In 1908 he became an apprentice to a photographer in Arequipa, and in 1917 opened his first studio, which he relocated to Cusco in 1923. In addition to being a studio photographer for over fifty years, Chambi documented the cultural heritage of his country. He photographed different styles of architecture, including ancient ruins, and landscapes, as well as the inhabitants of the Andes, and published these images in the form of postcards. In 1979 the Museum of Modern Art, New York, honoured him with a solo exhibition.

Amanda Hopkinson, *Martín Chambi*, London 2001; Publio López Mondéjar (ed.), *Martín Chambi 1920–50*, Barcelona 1990.

Alvin Langdon Coburn
1882 Boston, Massachusetts
– 1966 Colwyn Bay, Wales

– From a series of **vortographs of Ezra Pound**, c.1917 –

Three photographs, 20.8 × 15.7 cm, 20.7 × 16 cm, 20.4 × 15.4 cm, printed later

→ p.29

International Museum of Photography at George Eastman House, Rochester, New York. Gifts of Alvin Langdon Coburn

Around 1917 Alvin Langdon Coburn took a number of 'vorticistic' portraits of the American poet Ezra Pound, who had coined the term Vorticism in 1914. Coburn tied together three shaving mirrors to serve as a prism in front of the lens, thus reflecting a segmented image. He created a multiple view of one face, contrary to the classical studio portrait that is idealised and unscathed. Coburn also photographed very simple objects such as pieces of wood or crystals, objects not refering to themselves but to a new kind of vision: 'Why should not perspective be studied from angles hitherto neglected or unobserved? Why, I ask you earnestly, need we go on making commonplace little exposures of subjects that may be sorted into groups of landscapes, portraits, and figure studies? Think of the joy of doing something which it would be impossible to classify, or to tell which was the top and which the bottom!' (Alvin Langdon Coburn, 'The Future of Pictorial Photography', in Photograms of the Year, 1916)

Alvin Langdon Coburn was introduced to photography by his distant cousin Fred Holland Day, and later worked professionally in the medium. He met Alfred Stieglitz early in his career, joining the Photo-Secession in 1902. In 1904 his images were published in *Camera Work* and he became one of the most renowned Pictorialist photographers. In the 1910s some of his images foreshadowed the New Vision of the 1920s. In 1912 he emigrated to Great Britain, where he met George Bernhard Shaw and became friends with English Cubist artists and Vorticists. Later on Coburn was interested in the cultures of the Far East, the influence of which can be seen in the mystical aspects of his work.

Alvin Langdon Coburn, exh. cat., Fundación Pedro Barrié de la Maza, Coruña and Centro Cultural de la Villa, Madrid 2000; Alvin Langdon Coburn: Photographs 1900–1924, Zurich and New York 1998; Mike Weaver (ed.), Alvin Langdon Coburn: Symbolist Photographer. Beyond the Craft, New York 1986.

Joan Colom
b.1921, lives in Barcelona

– From the series **Gente del Raval** (People of Raval) 1958–61 –

Untitled, 23.3 × 12.2 cm

→ p.207

Untitled, 23.2 × 17.5 cm
Untitled, 23 × 12.6 cm

→ p.70

Foto Colectania Foundation, Barcelona
© Joan Colom / Courtesy Foto Colectania

These three photographs of women, probably prostitutes, are part of an extensive collection of images that Joan Colom compiled in Barcelona's Barrio Chino (Raval Quarter) at the end of the 1950s. Colom took the images candidly, from a low camera position and without looking through the viewfinder; the final framing was decided upon when enlarging the image in the darkroom. In view of the authoritarian Franco regime of the 1950s, Raval must have been an shifty quarter. Like other famous metropolitan red-light districts, it is located close to the harbour and yet, in the eyes of many citizens, is an alien, extraterritorial area (see Arnold Genthe). Complementary to Colom's rough fragments of the streets are the star portraits of boxers and variety dancers executed at the FotoRamblas studio at around the same time and place, which show the more glamorous side of the 'immoral city'.

Joan Colom worked as accountant. In 1957, at the age of thirty-six, he developed a fascination for photography and joined the Catalan photographic society. In 1960 he was involved in the founding of the photographers' union El Mussol. A year later he exhibited his photographs of Raval at the Sala Aixelà. Following the controversy surrounding his book *Izas, Rabizas y Colipoterras* (1964), which he co-published with Camilo José Cela, Colom abandoned photography. The social and historic significance of his Raval photographs was rediscovered in the 1990s.

Joan Colom, *Raval*, Göttingen 2006; Joan Colom, *Fotografías de Barcelona, 1958–1964*, Madrid 2004; Camilo José Cela and Joan Colom, *Izas, Rabizas y Colipoterras*, Barcelona 1964.

Baron Adolf (Gayne) de Meyer
1868 Paris – 1949 Los Angeles

The Marchesa Casati,1912, pub. in *Camera Work*, no.40, 1912, photogravure, 23.9 × 18.5 cm

Fotografische Sammlung, Museum Folkwang, Essen

Berthe Modelling, 1918, pub. in *Vogue*, 1 Sept. 1918, 23.8 × 19.9 cm

Haus der Photographie / Sammlung F.C. Gundlach, Hamburg

Mannequin, Elizabeth Arden Advertisement, c.1926, 21.6 × 15.9 cm

→ p.30

Collection of Margaret W. Weston

For some years, Elisabeth Arden promoted her cosmetic products in the pages of Harper's Bazaar and British Vogue with a single face, photographed by Baron Adolf de Meyer in several images in 1926. The softly lit face is bandaged with a white cloth, covered with make-up and retouched in such a manner that it appears to be a doll's head. The surreal beauty of this mask-like face is the result of de Meyer's subtle lighting and the soft tonality of the print, which corresponds perfectly to the image of the advertised product. The Neoclassical austerity of these Elizabeth Arden photographs is characteristic of the style of that time, and yet they also reveal the influence of turn-of-the-century pictorialism in de Meyer's photography.

Baron Adolf Gayne de Meyer took drawing and painting classes under Claude Monet before turning increasingly to photography and specialising in portraits. In 1896 he moved to London and joined the Camera Club and later the Royal Photographic Society. Some of his

photographs were published in Stieglitz's *Camera Work* in 1908 and 1912. In 1910 he produced his first fashion photograph for *Vogue*, and in time he became one of the first renowned and much sought-after fashion photographers. His photographs accompany the transition in the magazines from using fashion drawings to photography. He lived in New York from 1912, and worked for the Condé Nast publishing house until 1922, later for *Harper's Bazaar*. His photographs decisively influenced the image of *Vogue* and *Vanity Fair*.

A Singular Elegance: The Photographs of Baron Adolph de Meyer, exh. cat., International Center of Photography, New York 1994; Robert Brandau (ed.), Baron Adolf de Meyer, London 1976.

Department of Police, Bureau of Identification, Chicago

Mug Shots, 1900–26, sixteen photographs on cardboard, each 7.6 × 11.5 cm

→ p.51

Fotografische Sammlung, Museum Folkwang, Essen

In the second half of the nineteenth century, the French authorities deemed it advisable to respond to rapid urbanisation with new methods of public surveillance. In 1882, eleven years after the Paris Commune was abolished, the Paris police introduced a recording method that drew on the new anthropometric system developed by Alphonse Bertillon: a suspect or delinquent was measured, special characteristics noted, and his face was photographed from the front and in profile. In 1890 Bertillon published a treatise entitled *La Photographie judiciaire*, which was based on an accurate photographic method of identification and classification of the structure of the face (such as the individual form of an ear). His system was adopted worldwide. In 1893 it was presented at the World's Columbian Exposition in Chicago and adopted by the Chicago police a year later. It was followed by other new identification techniques that did not rely on photography, such as fingerprints. Nevertheless, mug shots continue to play an important role in police investigations. Their special aesthetics have also inspired and fascinated many artists.

Police Pictures: The Photograph as Evidence, exh. cat., San Francisco Museum of Modern Art 1997; Identités: De Disderi au Photomaton, exh. cat., Centre National de la Photographie, Chêne 1985; Allan Sekula, 'The Body and the Archive', in October, no.39, 1986, pp.3–64.

Philip-Lorca diCorcia
b.1951 Hartford, Connecticut, lives in New York

– From the series **Heads** –

*#06, **08**, 20*, 2001, C-prints, each 125 × 155 × 4 cm

→ p.116

Galerie Rodolphe Janssen, Brussels

Philip-Lorca diCorcia's series Heads consists of close-ups of passers-by in New York. The very long lens and the flashlight, which illuminates the subject from the side, isolates the unaware pedestrian against the dark background of Times Square and converts him or her into a 'chosen' actor among the many extras in the crowd. The artificial lighting evokes the abrupt changes between sunlight and shadow in the canyon-like streets of the city that had fascinated many previous generations of photographers. With the help of studio equipment, diCorcia quotes, and at the same time stages, the 'candid shot' that provides an unvarnished cross-section of urban society, a longstanding tradition of American street photography.

After having studied photography in Boston and at Yale University, Philip-Lorca diCorcia started to work as a fashion photographer. In the late 1970s he began to take pictures of his friends and family. Some of these were shown in the exhibition *Pleasures and Terrors of Domestic Comfort* at the Museum of Modern Art, New York, in 1991. He later concentrated on photographing passers-by, seemingly chosen arbitrarily, in urban sceneries, images that echo the narrative of film stills. His photography is a symbiosis between snapshot and staged photography and was published in the books *Streetwork* (1998) and *Heads* (2001).

Philip-Lorca diCorcia, *Thousand*, Göttingen 2007; Philip-Lorca diCorcia: *A Story-book Life*, Santa Fe 2003; Philip-Lorca diCorcia, *Streetwork 1993–1997*, Salamanca 1998; *Philip-Lorca diCorcia*, exh. cat., Museum of Modern Art, New York 1995.

Rineke Dijkstra
b.1959 Sittard, Netherlands, lives in Amsterdam

The Buzzclub Liverpool, UK / Mystery-world, Zaandam, NL, 1996–7, two-screen video projection, sound, duration 26 min. 4 sec.

→ pp.132–3

Courtesy Marian Goodman Gallery, New York, and the artist

In March 1995 Rineke Dijkstra took portraits of young girls, dressed up for a night out, in the Liverpool Buzz Club. She returned the following year to make more portraits, this time in the form of short video clips recorded in front of a white wall in a makeshift studio adjoining the club. The set-up is simple: the young models face the camera frontally, and are recorded for a certain period of time. The fixed framing and camera position – whether half-length or close-up from head to shoulders – transforms the image frame into a kind of catwalk, on which the girls, elated by the club's atmosphere and the rhythm of the music, can display the originality of their individual styles. Together with sequences she made six months later at the Dutch disco Mysteryworld, these form a double projection. Dijkstra's first video work exerts an immediate, almost physical pull on the part of the observer to empathise with the self-display of the young girls. This intense experience is largely the result of the straightforwardness of a work that beats a new path on the border between photography and video.

Rineke Dijkstra studied at the Amsterdam Gerrit Rietveld Academy between 1981 and 1986 and later worked as a freelance photographer for magazines. She attracted wide attention in the early 1990s with her *Beach Portraits* of teenagers on the seashore. She often invites people to pose in front of her camera who have recently gone through an existential experience: mothers straight after giving birth, young female Israeli soldiers, bullfighters immediately after the fight, and over and again adolescents in the process of defining themselves. Her images capture moments in which the merging of social imprints with individual expression become visible.

Rineke Dijkstra: Portraits, exh. cat., Jeu de Paume, Paris, Fotomuseum Winterthur, Zurich, La Caixa, Barcelona 2004; *Rineke Dijkstra, Menschenbilder*, exh. cat., Museum Folkwang, Essen 1998; *Rineke Dijkstra: Location*, exh. cat., Photographers' Gallery, London 1998.

Robert Doisneau
1912 Gentilly, Paris – 1994 Paris

La Plus Stricte Intimité (The Very Strict Intimacy), 1945, 32.2 × 21.7 cm

Les Amoureux du Vert-Galant (The Lovers from Vert-Galant), 1950, 29.9 × 37.2 cm

→ p.68

Fotografische Sammlung, Museum Folkwang, Essen

The Very Strict Intimacy, taken in Montrouge in 1945, is just one of the many images made by Robert Doisneau in the Parisian suburbs shortly after the war. In 1949 his book La Banlieue de Paris (The Suburbs of Paris) *was published with a text by Blaise Cendrars. Two years later, Otto Steinert showed* The Very Strict Intimacy *in the first* Subjektive Fotografie *(Subjective Photography) exhibition (1951), where it represented the new camera art from France. Loved by a large audience but derided by connoisseurs for the anecdotal content of his pictures, Doisneau earned a reputation for bringing to light the poetry in everyday life. He often staged and choreographed his little incidents, sometimes using actors, even though at that time, the staged photograph did not comply with the ideal of street photography. The micro-plot and the references in* The Lovers from Vert-Galant *suggest this artifice on the part of the photographer.*

A trained lithographer, Robert Doisneau started to take photographs in the late 1920s. In 1932 he worked as assistant in the studio of André Vigneau, and from 1934 to 1939 he was employed as photographer in the Renault factory in Boulogne-Billancourt. But his definitive photographic terrain was the street. In August 1944 he photographed the liberation of Paris, and in 1946 he joined the French photo agency Rapho. The first five years after the war were his most productive period, when he focused on the pleasures of everyday life, both great and small, after the horrors of the war. Initially his photographs were printed in the glossy magazines of the 1950s; later he published several books together with his friend the poet and journalist Robert Giraud.

Kristina Briaudeau (ed.), *Paris: Doisneau*, Paris 2005; Robert Doisneau, *Un Certain Robert Doisneau*, Paris 1986; Jean-François Chevrier, *Robert Doisneau*, Paris 1983.

Madame d'Ora (Dora Kallmus)
1881 Vienna – 1963 Frohnleiten, Austria

Wiener Werkstätte (Vienna Workshop), 1921, 21.7 × 10.5 cm

→ p.37

Collection Christian Brandstätter, Vienna

Automantel aus Hermelin und Persianer (Ermine and Persian Coat), 1921, 22.3 × 13.5cm

Ullstein Bild – Madame d'Ora

From the mid-1910s the Viennese portrait photographer Madame d'Ora maintained a good relationship with the fashion department of the Wiener Werkstätte (Vienna Workshop), for whom this image was produced. During the 1920s, she became increasingly interested in fashion and dance photography and the growing importance of fashion imagery on her photographs became more evident. Ullstein Bilderdienst alone lists 378 of her works in its archive, thus highlighting the huge demand for photographic illustration at the time. Ullstein's magazine Die Dame (The Lady) *was significant in bringing new fashion creations to the modern woman.*

Aged twenty, Dora Kallmus bought her first camera and started to study at the Graphische Lehr- und Versuchsanstalt in Vienna. Being female, she was only allowed to attend the theory classes and for this reason went to Berlin in 1907 for five months to train under Nicola Perscheid. Back in Vienna that same year, she opened her Atelier d'Ora together with Arthur Benda, which quickly became popular with the upper-middle-classes and the aristocracy. In 1926, she sold her Vienna studio to Benda and moved to Paris, where she dedicated herself to fashion photography. In 1940 she fled the Nazis to Southern France, where she lived hidden in a convent. After the war, in addition

to further fashion photographs as well as society and artists' portraits, she produced a remarkable series of slaughterhouse photographs. In 1961 she returned to Austria.

Sabine Schnakenberg, *Dora Kallmus und Arthur Benda. Einblicke in die Arbeitsweise eines fotografischen Ateliers zwischen 1907 und 1938*, Ph.D., Kiel 2000; Monika Faber, *Madame d'Ora Wien-Paris. Portraits aus Kunst und Gesellschaft 1907–1957*, Vienna and Munich 1983.

Carl Durheim
1810 – 1890 Bern

– From a series of **Swiss Roamers**, 1852–3 –

Joseph Ackermann, 37 Jahre alt (Joseph Ackermann, 37 Years Old), 17.9 × 12.4 cm (London only)

→ p.20

Louis Klemke (37 Years Old), 1852–3, 16.4 × 12 cm (Essen only)

Magdelena Bergdorf, geboren 1835 (Magdelena Bergdorf, Born 1835), 18.9 × 13.3cm (Essen only)

Wilhelm Schobel, 18 Jahre alt (Wilhelm Schobel, 18 Years Old), 18.6 × 14.5 cm (London only)

→ p.204

Salted paper prints
Swiss Federal Archives, Bern

In 1852 Carl Durheim was commissioned by the Swiss General Attorney Jakob Amiet to photograph vagrant, homeless and itinerant people. The images provided the basis for lithographic prints that were distributed among Swiss police stations in order to keep track of the movements of these 'debauched subjects', as they were regarded by the authorities. The photographic style echoed the middle-class studio portrait that had just begun to develop: the subjects are portrayed seated, frontal or semi-profile, sometimes leaning against a table, the background light and extraneous information retouched. Durheim's photographs are among the first documents of photography serving the police. It was only towards the end of the nineteenth century that a systematic method for police identification photography was developed.

In 1827–8 Carl Durheim trained as a lithographer in Paris. He worked in that trade in numerous European countries before settling down in Bern in 1841, where he opened his own studio. Like many other lithographers, he later turned to the photographic reproduction process. In 1845 he started to experiment with the daguerrotype. Between 1849 and 1850 he went to Frankfurt to study the technique of paper photography. In the 1850s, he participated in numerous important photography and industrial exhibitions, among others the Exposition Universelle in Paris in 1855.

Wider das Leugnen und Verstellen. Carl Durheims Fahndungsfotografien von Heimatlosen, exh. cat., Fotomuseum Winterthur, Zurich 1998.

Edizioni Brogi

Maccheronaio, Napoli (Macaroni Factory, Naples), 1880, handcoloured albumen print, 19 × 24.7 cm

→ p.23

Dietmar Siegert Collection

That macaroni noodles are the food of the common people is shown by a genre scene of a Naples street in front of a macaroni factory, which was taken presumably by an operator at Edizioni Brogi. Despite its handcolouring, the photograph is also simple fare (which is not to say anything about its quality).

Whereas a comparable photograph produced in the studio of Giorgio Sommer depicts a clear composition of figures, this frontal shot relies entirely on the vitality of the street. Not only do we see the three pasta eaters in the picture, but a large group of uninvited onlookers has shoved itself into the photo, adding a further dimension to the picture's impression of the hustle and bustle of street life in this southern Italian city.

The lithographer Giacomo Brogi (1822–1881) opened his first photographis studio in Florence in 1866 and was, by the 1870s, already one of the city's most famous portrait photographers. Like many Italian photographers he simultaneously worked in the field of photographic art reproductions and city views. These entailed a picturesque marriage between architectural and genre scenes, as in the above-mentioned photo. Many of his clients were tourists from the North. Giacomo's son Carlo (1850–1925) expanded his father's business into a booming enterprise so that the *Edizioni Brogi* founded branches in Rome and Naples. Up to eighty employees worked in Florence alone during the heyday of the company, among them ten photographers. Notwithstanding the competition of the renowned Fratelli Alinari, the Edizioni Brogi was one of the most important photography enterprises in nineteenth-century Italy.

Im Land der Sehnsucht. Mit Bleistift und Kamera durch Italien, 1820 bis 1880, exh. cat., Kunsthalle Bremen, 1998; *Italien sehen und sterben*, exh. cat., Agfa Foto-Historama, Cologne 1994.

Hugo Erfurth
1874 Halle, Germany – 1948 Gaienhofen, Germany

Maria Carmi, 1914, 44 × 32 cm
→ p.36
Lovis Corinth, 1918, 29 × 23 cm

Oil pigment prints
Fotografische Sammlung, Museum Folkwang, Essen

The portraits that Hugo Erfurth took of the actress Maria Carmi in 1914 and of the painter Lovis Corinth in 1918 exemplify the transition of portrait photography from traditional to modernist, from representing social status to presenting the face of the individual. The head of the actress is depicted in stern profile in front of a completely empty background. The position of the head reminds one of a police photograph, yet the soft tonality and the exquisite outline place the picture in the sphere of Pictorialist photography. The face of Lovis Corinth confronts the observer abruptly and frontally, prompting the writer Alfred Döblin to remark in 1946 that the photograph reminded him of the head of a criminal.

In 1895 Hugo Erfurth, who had been taking photographs since his early teens, started an apprenticeship with the Saxonian court photographer in Dresden and took over the portrait studio of another court photographer only a year later. He participated in several exhibitions and won prizes in competitions. In 1906 he opened a new studio in a large building in Dresden and was now able to photograph his models in two parlours, with artificial lights, and without the traditional studio props. Erfurth became a widely acclaimed portrait photographer in Germany, due to the high quality and psychological intensity of his images. In 1922 he opened the *Graphisches Kabinett Erfurth*, which adjoined his studio, where he presented the work of many important artists from that time. He moved to Cologne in 1934, where his studio and many of his negatives and prints were destroyed during the Second World War.

Portraits of an Age: Photography in Germany and Austria, 1900–1938, exh. cat., Neue Galerie, New York 2005; Bodo von Dewitz et al. (eds.), *Hugo Erfurth. Photograph zwischen Tradition und Moderne*, exh. cat., Agfa Foto-Historama, Cologne 1992.

Walker Evans
1903 St Louis, Missouri – 1975 New Haven, Connecticut

Penny Picture Display, Savannah, Georgia, 1936, 21.9 × 17.6 cm
→ p.50

The Museum of Modern Art, New York. Gift of Willard Van Dyke, 1968

Subway Portraits, 1938–41, sixteen photographs on cardboard, each 6.6 × 4.8 cm, mounted 1959

The J. Paul Getty Museum, Los Angeles

Labor Anonymous, **Detroit**, 1946
→ p.61

Thirty-seven prints, different sizes, average 16 × 11.5 cm
Galerie Thomas Zander, Cologne

'Labor Anonymous – These people walked by a carefully planted camera one afternoon in downtown Detroit last month. None posed; few knew they were being photographed. Fortune prints their images – with thanks to them for serving this visual purpose – as a cross section view of average hard-working people … Machine-oilers or stuck-runners, truckers, loaders, or short-order cooks pass you here. Some may be worried, some just blank in the smooth waters of prosperity. All are – at a safe guess – your anonymous producers' (Unclassified: A Walker Evans Anthology, 2000, p.189). *This unpublished draft by Walker Evans was intended to accompany his series* Labor Anonymous *in the magazine* Fortune *in November 1946. The idea of a 'cross section view of average people' continued to occupy Evans. Between 1938 and 1941 he secretly photographed passengers in the New York subway, only years later starting to work with this material. Before his book* Many Are Called *was published in 1966 he compiled a tableau presenting sixteen head shots of women from New York, all differing in age and social status, which resembled passport or 'Wanted' photographs. An earlier, famous photograph by Evans,* Penny Picture Display, Savannah, Georgia *– of a photo studio's window display – presents in one image a portrait of the city consisting of 225 photographs of its citizens. At the same time, it reflects the significance that Evans ascribed to the simple and everyday use of photography.*

At first, Walker Evans was interested in writing. Fascinated by French literature of the nineteenth century, he spent the years 1926 to 1927 in France and attended seminars at the Sorbonne. From 1928 on, an intense interest in photography began, which resulted in photographs influenced by the aesthetics of the New Vision. From the beginning of the 1930s he developed a descriptive, distant and objective mode of seeing that went on to form a new photographic aesthetic: the documentary style. Concerned about his own artistic freedom, Evans worked only briefly, from 1935 to 1937, for the US-government agency Farm Security Administration. During a stay with the writer James Agee with three poor peasant families in Alabama in 1936, the book Let us Now Praise Famous Men was conceived. In 1938, he exhibited his *American Photographs* at the Museum of Modern Art, New York, which established him as the quintessential vernacular photographer of American society. The accompanying catalogue *American Photographs* has been very influential due to its specific sequential narrative structure. From 1945, he was editor of *Fortune*, in which he also published numerous essays. After 1965 he taught at Yale University.

Jeff L. Rosenheim and Alexis Schwarzenbach, *Unclassified: A Walker Evans Anthology*, Zurich 2000; Walker Evans, *Many Are Called*, New York 1966 (reprint 2004); Walker Evans, *American Photographs*, New York 1938 (numerous reprints).

Samuel Fosso
b.1962 Cameroon, lives in Bangui, Central African Republic

– From a series of **Self-Portraits** –
Untitled, 1976, 15.9 × 15.9 cm
→ p.211
Untitled (Sitting), 1976, 15.9 × 15.9 cm
Untitled (*Standing with Hand on Chin*), 1976, 15.9 × 15.9 cm
→ p.99

Courtesy of Jack Shainman Gallery, New York

Samuel Fosso initially took his self-portraits in order to send them to his family when he was working as an apprentice photographer, and therefore made them without taking into consideration a wider audience. He worked on them at night, when the studio was closed, using a variety of props. He was both photographer and model, and found inspiration for his role-playing in magazines. Meanwhile, in the United States, Cindy Sherman had just graduated from art school and was beginning to develop her own method of self-staging.

From the age of ten, Samuel Fosso lived in Bangui, where he became an apprentice photographer. Aged only thirteen, he opened his first studio, whose name he changed several times: Studio Confiance, Studio Gentil, Studio Hoberau and finally Studio Convenance. Fosso's playful staging of his own identity – in a way also a reference to the African studio tradition itself – is now a central point of reference for a younger generation of African photographers.

Tapping Currents: Contemporary African Art and Diaspora, exh. cat., The Nelson-Atkins Museum of Art, Kansas City 2008; Maria Francesca Bonetti (ed.), *Samuel Fosso*, London 2008.

FotoRamblas

– From series of **Boxeadores, luchadores, varietés** (Boxers, Fighters, Vaudevilles) –
Twelve photographs, 1960s, 60 × 50 cm, printed 2008
→ p.81

Ángels, Barcelona

Mateu is the name of the young boxer who stands poised in the spotlight, fists raised as if to fend off the blow of an invisible opponent. He is but one of the many boxers in Barcelona who, from the mid-1950s, found their way from the ring to the FotoRamblas Studio in search of a shining portrait. Proud, earnest and unflinching, they are imposing figures, positioned in front of a light background. They are of a flawless beauty, not least because of the elaborate retouching.

Apart from Vives, Quimet, Rafael Muñoz, Alberto Fonollosa and José María Cirés – five photographers who, between 1956 and 1985, consistently pursued a FotoRamblas style – an average of fifteen people were employed in the large studio: assistants, workers who finished or retouched negatives and copies, lab workers, salesmen. The chequered performers of the nearby vaudevilles and night clubs frequented FotoRamblas – fighters, vaudeville dancers, comedians, acrobats, transvestites: 'In everyday life these comedians were "the others", different, and would bear for the rest of their life the stigma of difference imposed by the Catholic standards of behaviour of these years' (*FotoRamblas*, 2002, p.21). After the dissolution of the studio, the Spanish photographer Santos Montes took over the archive.

FotoRamblas: Boxadores, luchadores, varietés y otras imágenes de un estudio de Barcelona 1956–1985, exh. cat., Ángels Barcelona, Madrid 2002.

Robert Frank
b.1924 Zurich, lives in Nova Scotia and New York

Doll, 1949, 35.3 × 20.6 cm

→ p.65

Washington, 1961–6, 43 × 64 cm

Fotografische Sammlung, Museum Folkwang, Essen

– From the series ***From the Bus, New York*** –

Six photographs, 1958, 23.5 × 34.3 cm, 33.6 × 22.9 cm, 34.3 × 23.5 cm, 26.1 × 17.8 cm, 34 × 24.5 cm, 26.5 × 17.7 cm

→ p.76

Courtesy the artist

'These photographs represent my last project in photography. When I selected the pictures and put them together I knew and I felt that I had come to the end of a chapter. And in it was the beginning of something new' (Robert Frank, Lines of my Hand, *1972). The new 'chapter' he referred to was film. In the year in which Frank photographed the streets of Manhattan from bus windows, he also started experimenting with a 16 mm film camera. Until then, his photographs had been single shots. From the Bus, however, is conceived as a series, presenting pedestrians in the manner of a travelling movie camera. The bus becomes an extension of the camera, an urban seeing device.*

Between 1947 and 1953 Robert Frank travelled between America and Europe in search of a suitable place in which to live with his young family, as well as the 'right' photography. He decided in favour of the United States, working there as a freelance photojournalist. Between 1955 and 1956, with the help of a Guggenheim grant, Frank travelled across the United States. These photographs resulted in the book *The Americans* (1959), a restless road-movie that influenced generations of photographers with its radical subjective approach. From 1959, together with the Beat poets Jack Kerouac and Allan Ginsberg, he started to make movies such as *Pull my Daisy* (1959) and *Me and my Brother* (1965–6). The films, videos and photographs (mostly Polaroids) that Frank has produced since the end of the 1960s focus on biographical aspects, revolving around themes of memory and loss.

Robert Frank, exh. cat., Tate Modern, London, Museu d'Art Contemporani de Barcelona, Fotomuseum Winterthur, Zurich 2004; *Robert Frank: Hold Still Keep Going*, exh. cat., Museum Folkwang, Essen 2000; Robert Frank, *Lines of My Hand*, New York 1972.

Ron Galella
b.1931 New York, lives in Los Angeles

Woody Allen/Mia Farrow September 18, 1980 New York City, EXCLUSIVE – Woody Allen and Mia Farrow heading for dinner in Greenwich Village, 1980, 25 × 20 cm

→ p.88

Mick Jagger/Jerry Hall, January 16, 1983, Beverly Hills, CA, Mick Jagger and Jerry Hall Arrive at L'Ermitage Hotel in Beverly Hills, California, 1983, 20 × 25 cm

© Ron Galella, courtesy Galerie Wouter van Leeuwen, Amsterdam

Ron Galella's photographs of celebrities span the realms of popular culture, contemporary photography and contemporary portraiture. In reference to the picture of Woody Allen and Mia Farrow he wrote:

'September 18, 1980: NYC. The heretofore-private romance of Woody Allen and Mia Farrow has now been exposed. These are the first pictures of the lovey-dovey twosome clinging to each other in the back seat of Woody's chauffeur-driven Rolls Royce with black tinted windows. The night this was snapped, Woody and Mia had dinner at his favourite restaurant, Elaine's. They employed the same strategy to avoid being photographed together, each making a dash for his Rolls Royce. On their way home, my wife, Betty, and I got out of the car at a stoplight and snapped them from both sides of the car. They were surprised – we got the exclusive' (Exclusive Diary, 2004, n.p.).

Ron Galella started his career as a photographer in the US Air Force during the Korean War. From 1955 he began working for numerous magazines. Today he is widely considered one of the first American paparazzi and has provided a steady stream of immediate and candid images for the pages of hundreds of publications around the world including *Life*, *The New York Times*, *People*, *The Star* and *Vanity Fair*. He once said: 'My passion is to show the world the stars it celebrates in the natural and spontaneous moods that only paparazzo photojournalism can capture. I am interested in printing onto film what is real' (*Exclusive Diary*, 2004, n.p.).

Ron Galella (ed.), *Disco Years*, New York 2006; Ron Galella (ed.), *Ron Galella: Exclusive Diary*, Bologna 2004; Steven Bluttal (ed.), *The Photographs of Ron Galella, 1960–1990*, Los Angeles 2002; Ron Galella (ed.), *Off Guard: A Paparazzi Look at the Beautiful People*, New York 1976.

Galerie Contemporaine, littéraire, artistique

Galerie Contemporaine, vol.4, Paris, 1878, album 37 × 28 cm, with thirty-one Woodburytypes. Open at: Antony Samuel Adam-Salomon (1818–1881), *Charles Garnier*, photographed c.1865

Galerie Contemporaine, vol.5, Paris, 1880, album 37 × 28 cm, with thirty-one Woodburytypes. Open at: Etienne Carjat, *Charles Baudelaire*, photographed c.1863

Photographs on single plates:

Etienne Carjat (1828–1906)

  Jules Simon, pub. 1876–80

  Victor Schœlcher, pub. 1876–80

  Charles Baudelaire, c.1863, pub. 1880

Ferdinand Mulnier (active 1860–1890)

  Henri de Bornier, pub. 1876–80

Nadar (1820–1910)

  François Coppée, pub. 1876–80

  Ferdinand Fabre, pub. 1876–80

Antony Samuel Adam-Salomon (1818–1881)

  Charles Garnier, c.1865, pub. 1878

Emile Tourtin (active 1873–99)

  Théodore de Banville, pub. 1876–80

  → p.21

Woodburytypes, each 35.3 × 27.5 cm
Fotografische Sammlung, Museum Folkwang, Essen

The photographic portrait of the poet Théodore de Banville was printed in the late 1870s in Galerie Contemporaine, littéraire, artistique, *published by Ludovic Baschet. Galerie Contemporaine presented individual personalities: writers, scientists, musicians, actors, painters and sculptors, a unique Who's Who of cultural life in the French Third Republic. From 1876,* individual magazines were published weekly, featuring a large portrait photograph of the featured personality and an insert with biographical texts, illustrations and a facsimile autograph. Every six months, the separate issues of Galerie Contemporaine *were published together in a volume. The portraits were printed as Woodburytypes, fine art prints that were high in quality and tonal range. The original photographs were taken by the most renowned photographers of that time, even if some images dated back more than fifteen years, like the famous portrait of Charles Baudelaire by Etienne Carjat.*

Emile Tourtin, portraitist of Théodore de Banville, remained little known, unlike his model and his famous colleagues Nadar and Etienne Carjat. Active from 1873 to 1899, he maintained for a short time a studio on the exclusive Parisian boulevard des Italiens, an address that appears on the reverse of the Banville portrait. His stamp, which can be found on the back of his *carte-de-visite* photographs, confirms his trade as 'Peinture & Photographie' (Painting & Photography). Tourtin also operated studios in Rouen and Le Havre.

Simone Klein, '…beobachten Sie den Blick, das Lächeln, die Gestik… Die Präsentation berühmter Zeitgenossinnen der Galerie Contemporaine', in *Alles Wahrheit! Alles Lüge!*, exh. cat., Walraff-Richartz-Museum, Cologne 1996, pp.151–62.

Arnold Genthe
1869 Berlin – 1942 New Milford, Connecticut

– From the series ***San Francisco's Old Chinatown***, c.1899 –

Marketing, 26.4 × 33.7 cm

Dead to the World, pub. 1908 as *The Opium Fiend*, 32.2 × 25.1 cm

  → p.205

The Toy Peddler, 34.7 × 26.5 cm

  → p.35

The Street of the Gamblers, by Day, 23 × 30 cm

The Vegetable Peddler, 23.2 × 33.5 cm

Arnold Genthe with Camera, pub. 1908 as *An Unsuspecting Victim*, 33.7 × 23 cm

  → p.14

Late prints, unretouched and undated prints
International Museum of Photography at George Eastman House, Rochester

'Then it was that my Chinatown adventure began. Again and again I went there until I became a familiar figure on its streets. Many days I stood for hours at a corner or sat in some wretched courtyard, immobile and apparently disinterested, as I waited, eager and alert, for the sun to filter through the shadows or for some picturesque group or character to appear – a smoker to squat with his pipe, or a group of children in holiday attire' (As I Remember, 1936, p.36). More than 200 photographs exist of Genthe's excursions to San Francisco's Chinatown. These candid pictures show life on the streets, the bustle of tradesmen and workers, the activity of women and children, the presence of the rich and wealthy, as well as opium smokers. In 1908, just two years after the complete destruction of the quarter by the great earthquake, his book Pictures of Old Chinatown *was published.*

A fascination with the mysterious quarter of the Chinese community first awoke Arnold Genthe's interest in photography, which he then made his profession. In 1906 he was an eyewitness to the catastrophic earthquake in San Francisco, and one of his photographs subsequently became an American icon (*Looking Down Sacramento Street, San Francisco,*

18 April, 1906). In 1911, he relocated his studio to New York. Among his clients were many members of the political establishment of the 1930s and 1940s, as well as numerous renowned actors. Dance was of special importance to his artistic oeuvre, and resulted in the publication *The Book of Dance* in 1916. The cosmopolitan photographer also devoted an extensive photographic series to the old quarter of New Orleans, which was published in book form in 1926.

John Kuo Wei Tchen, *Genthe's Photographs of San Francisco's Old Chinatown*, New York 1984; Arnold Genthe, *As I Remember*, New York 1936; Arnold Genthe, *Pictures of Old Chinatown*, New York 1908.

Arturo Ghergo
1901 Montefano, Macerata, Italy – 1959 Rome

Isa Miranda, 1942, 22.5 × 16.7 cm

→ p.71

Marina Bert, 1946, 23.5 × 17.5 cm

Valentina Cortese, 1945, 22.4 × 16.3 cm

Mariella Lotti, 1940, 22.8 × 16.6 cm

Museo di Fotografia Contemporanea, Cinisello Balsamo, Milan

Arturo Ghergo's portrait of the actress Isa Miranda is staged according to the classical style of the photographic studio: the half-profile portrait is in soft focus and the eyes and lips have been highlighted. The backlight accentuates the blond hair. With the help of retouching, the face has been turned into an immaculate surface. Ghergo stages the Hollywood actress, who had returned to Italy after the outbreak of the Second World War, both as ethereal being and as femme fatale, which corresponded to her official image: the Italian Marlene Dietrich.

Arturo Ghergo learned the technical aspects of photography from his brother. In 1929 he moved to Rome, where he opened a studio at the Via Condotti. Very quickly, the studio became one of the most important in Rome, frequented by the wealthy and aristocratic, by politicians and movie stars. In the 1940s he began to work as a film cameraman. Along with Elio Luxardo, he is one of the most renowned portrait photographers of Italian celebrities of the 1940s and 1950s.

Arturo Ghergo: Fotografia e cinema, exh. cat., Palazzo Reale, Milan 2007; Alberto Pellegrino (ed.), *Arturo e Ermanno Ghergo*, San Severino Marche 1998.

David Goldblatt
b.1930 Randfontein, South Africa, lives in Johannesburg

– From the series ***On Eloff Street, Johannesburg, South Africa*** –

Two photographs, 1966–7, 30 × 42 cm, printed 2008

→ p.77

Courtesy Goodman Gallery, Johannesburg and the artist

In 1966–7, Goldblatt photographed pedestrians on Eloff Street, one of the principal roads in Johannesburg. His street photographs capture the coincidental constellations of people of differing ethnic and social origins. The coexistence of black and white people in this image, which could have been taken on an American avenue, is deceiving and plays on the viewer's awareness of Apartheid in South Africa. Goldblatt wrote: 'I found after a time that in both economics and photography, I was looking for the same sort of thing: a grasp of social reality; the means for comprehending its complexity and of reducing that understanding to communicable statements' (Fifty-one Years: David Goldblatt, 2001, p.417).

David Goldblatt became interested in photography while still in school. After the sale of his family's textile business, he devoted all his energy to photography and started to work as an assistant editor for the British magazine *Tatler*. In the early 1950s, he documented the ways in which the new Apartheid system became visible in urban settings. The portrayal of different social milieus in South Africa was more important to him than the recording of single events. His series were published in numerous books, such as *In Boksburg* (1982), a photographic study of a small-town middle-class white community. Since the mid-1990s he has exclusively used colour and puts more emphasis on a topographic mode of seeing. In a career spanning more than fifty years, Goldblatt has compiled a unique archive on the structure of South African society.

David Goldblatt. Südafrikanische Fotografien 1952–2006, exh. cat., Fotomuseum Winterthur, Winterthur and Centro Internazionale di Fotografia, Rome, 2006; *David Goldblatt: South African Intersections*, exh. cat., Kunstpalast, Düsseldorf and Camera Austria, Graz 2005, David Goldblatt, *Fifty-one Years: David Goldblatt*, Barcelona 2001.

Paul Graham
b.1956 Stafford, England, lives in New York

– From the series ***American Night*** –

Untitled 1999 (New York) #45, 1999, 180 × 228 cm

→ p.115

Untitled 1999 (Memphis) #53, 1999, 189.5 × 238.5 cm, printed 2008

Digital C-prints, Diasec
© the artist, Courtesy of Anthony Reynolds Gallery, London

Paul Graham's project American Night *consists of sixty-three photographs and was published, like many of his other series, in the form of a remarkable book. The majority of the images show isolated figures viewed from a distance, who wander about aimlessly on the periphery of big cities, lost in the type of landscape where only social outcasts are out and about. An artificial, milky haze covers the images. Interspersed with these, single images appear like hyperreal stereotypes of the American dream: colourful architectural photographs of homes with cars and garages. Untitled 1999 (New York) #45 is part of a third type, ten images comprising individual portraits of passers-by or homeless people, living outside the social system of New York.*

By the time he graduated from Bristol University in 1980, Paul Graham had already secured his first solo exhibition, where he presented large-format photographs of modern suburban houses. He was influenced by William Eggleston, Walker Evans and the New Topographics movement. While the 1980s were marked by a photographic response to the social situation in Great Britain under Margaret Thatcher (*Beyond Caring*, 1984–5), after 1988 he started to travel extensively through a Europe that was still under the shadow of its past (*New Europe*, 1988–92) and to the modern Japan (*Empty Heaven*, 1989–95). Again and again, Graham gave new impulses to documentary photography, both in terms of his images and conceptually. Serial components play a central role in his numerous book projects. Since the 1990s his approach to both the combination of images and their visual language has become increasingly experimental and associative.

Paul Graham, *A Shimmer of Possibility*, Göttingen 2007; Paul Graham, *American Night*, Göttingen 2003; Paul Graham, *End of an Age*, Zurich 1999; Paul Graham, *A1: The Great North Road*, Bristol 1983.

Sunil Gupta
b.1953 New Dehli, lives in New Delhi and London

– From the series ***Mr Malhotra's Party*** –

Pavitr, 2007

→ p.134

Bikram, 2007

→ p.211

Inkjet prints, each 111.8 × 111.8 cm
Collection of Rudolph Leuthold

The series Mr Malhotra's Party *by Sunil Gupta subtly plays with the pose as a symbol of self-assertion in the midst of a contingent street life. The photographer writes: 'In the 1980s I made constructed documentary images of gay men in architectural spaces in Delhi (Exiles series). Now people are meeting less in parks etc, and more on the net, and in places like "private" parties, I am trying to visualise this latest virtual queer space by a series of portraits of "real" people who identify their sexuality as "queer" in some way. This time they are willing to identify themselves. They are guests of an imaginary party. I'm calling it Mr Malhotra's Party. Gay nights at local clubs in Delhi are always sign-posted as private parties in a fictitious person's name to get around the law: Section 377, a British colonial law, which still criminalises homosexuality in India. Mr Malhotra is the ubiquitous Punjabi refugee who arrived post partition and contributed to the development of the city' (www.sunilgupta.net).*

Growing up watching Bollywood films in all their glorious colour, Sunil Gupta moved to Montreal with his family in the late 1960s, where his interest in photography began to develop. From the mid-1970s he lived in New York, where he studied photography at the New School for Social Research under Lisette Model. At the end of the 1970s, he moved to London to continue his studies at the Royal College of Art. He was involved in the founding of Autograph (Association of Black Photographers) in London, and he also set up the Organisation for Visual Arts (OVA) to promote a greater understanding of questions regarding cultural differences and their incorporation into the sphere of fine art.

Sunil Gupta, *Pictures from Here*, London 2003; David A. Bailey, *Sunil Gupta: Monograph*, London 1998; Sunil Gupta (ed.), *An Economy of Signs: Contemporary Indian Photography*, London 1990.

Philippe Halsman
1906 Riga – 1979 New York

– From the series ***Jump Photographs*** –

Edward Steichen, 1959, 30.4 × 24.3 cm

→ p.74

Weegee, 1961, 42.6 × 33.5 cm

Grace Kelly, 1955, 42.6 × 33.5 cm

Marilyn Monroe, 1959, 42.6 × 33.5 cm

© Philippe Halsman Estate / Magnum Photos

'In a jump, the subject, in a sudden burst of energy, overcomes gravity. He cannot simultaneously control his expressions, his facial and his limb muscles. The mask falls. The real self becomes visible. One has only to snap it with the camera' (Philippe Halsman's Jump Book, New York 1959, p.8). In the 1950s Philippe Halsman produced large-format portraits of numerous American cultural and political celebrities and also asked them to perform some kind of action for the camera. Halsman considered jumping to be a good way to avoid a frozen pose. He called this philosophy of jump photography 'jumpology'. His

Jump Book, *published in 1959, contains a tongue-in-cheek discussion of jumpology and 178 photographs of celebrity jumpers.*

Philippe Halsman studied electrical engineering in Dresden. In Innsbruck in 1928 he was accused of patricide and, even though the exact circumstances of his father's death remained unclear, he was convicted. His trial provoked many anti-Semitic remarks, but also mobilised an number of prominent advocates across Europe. In 1930 he was pardoned but expelled from the country. He became a photographer in Paris and began to work for fashion magazines such as *Vogue*. In 1940 he immigrated to New York. The following year he met Salvador Dalí, through whom he came into contact with the Surrealist movement. Of particular importance to his career was his long-term and very successful association with *Life* magazine, for which he photographed many celebrities, especially film stars. Halsman holds the record of 101 covers for *Life*.

Philippe Halsman: A Retrospective. Photographs from the Halsman Family Collection, exh. cat., National Portrait Gallery, Washington 1998; *Dalí & Halsman*, exh. cat., Dalí Museum, Cleveland, Ohio 1978; Philippe Halsman, *Philippe Halsman's Jump Book*, New York 1959.

Lewis Wickes Hine
1874 Oshkosh, Wisconsin
– 1940 Hastings-on-Hudson,
New York

Beggar, N.Y., 1910, 11.1 × 16.4 cm
Man Sleeping in Doorway, c.1910, 11.2 × 16.3 cm

International Museum of Photography at George Eastman House, Rochester, New York. Gift of the Photo League, New York

The Mendicants, 1910, 12.7 cm × 10.2 cm

→ p.34

Small Newsie Downtown, St. Louis, 1910, 10.2 × 12.7 cm

National Archives, Washington, DC

Self-Portrait with Newsieboy, 1908, 13.8 × 11.8 cm

→ p.14

The J. Paul Getty Museum, Los Angeles

The name Lewis Hine is inseparably connected to the notion of socio-documentary photography. Besides his photographs of immigrants at Ellis Island, one of his first projects was the fight against child labour, which he led on behalf of the National Child Labor Committee (NCLC). He photographed the working conditions of children in factories, agriculture, the mining industry and especially on the streets, to bring about social and political reform. An example of this is his series featuring child newspaper sellers, Newsieboys (between 1908 and 1912). The careful composition and iconography of some of his images belies their pragmatic use, sometimes cropped or montaged, on posters, in articles and lectures. The image of a blind beggar and a girl (The Mendicants, 1910) has a timeless, almost mythological quality. It is one photograph among countless others in the history of the medium devoted to blind people in the city.

Whilst studying education at New York University, Lewis Hine was already teaching at the Ethical Culture School in New York from 1901. The reform-oriented and socially engaged superintendent of this school, Frank A. Manny, was to play a crucial role in his engagement. In 1903 Hine began photographing at school events and even introduced photography as a school subject. Around this time he commenced his documentation of Ellis Island. From 1906–7, he was active in the NCLC and in 1908 discontinued teaching, becoming a full-time photographer for the magazine *The Survey*. It was during these years that he documented the social life on the streets of New York. In May 1930 he received an assignment to take pictures of the construction of the Empire State Building, which were published in his book *Men at Work* in 1932.

Vicki Goldberg, *Lewis W. Hine: Children at Work*, Munich 1999; Karl Steinorth (ed.), *Lewis Hine: Passionate Journey, Photographs 1905–1937*, Kilchberg and Zurich 1996; Daile Kaplan (ed.), *Photo Story: Selected Letters and Photographs of Lewis W. Hine*, Washington and London 1992; Naomi Rosenblum and Walter Rosenblum (ed.), *America and Lewis Hine*, New York 1977.

George Hoyningen-Huené
1900 St Petersburg – 1968
Los Angeles

Photographer Edward Steichen, Examining a Negative, Surrounded by Photographic Equipment, pub. *Vogue*, 15 June 1941, 24 × 19.2 cm

Courtesy Condé Nast Archive

This portrait by George Hoyningen-Huené, which depicts Edward Steichen at work, can be viewed as a homage to his famous colleague. The image also refers to the canon of modernist photography that Steichen himself had previously introduced to the magazines of Condé Nast. However, the empty space, the clear outlines and the important role of light in this image are more than just quotation; Hoyningen-Huené was also addicted to reduced geometrical forms. When the image of Steichen was published in Vogue in 1941, his work for Condé Nast was a thing of the past.

At the age of seventeen, George Hoyningen-Huené fled from the turbulence of the Russian Revolution to London. He first took up as a painter's apprentice under André Lothe in Paris, before working as a fashion illustrator. He then became the head of photography for French *Vogue* in 1925. Until 1935, Hoyningen-Huené was employed at Condé Nast, but later went to *Harper's Bazaar*, where he worked alongside Alexey Brodovitch for ten years. He was one of the great aesthetes of fashion photography. He intuitively combined an austere classicism with the visual language of modern Constructivism. He also took his carefully planned compositions out of the studio and into a classical, seemingly Mediterranean light. In 1929 his work, exemplary for its highly creative quality, was exhibited in the seminal *Film und Foto* (Film and Photography) exhibition in Stuttgart.

William E. Ewing, *The Photographic Art of Hoyningen-Huene*, London 1986; *George Hoyningen-Huene: Eye for Elegance*, exh. cat., International Center of Photography, New York 1980.

Pieter Hugo
b.1976, lives in Cape Town

– From the series **The Hyena & Other Men**, 2007 –
Abdullahi Mohammed with Mainasara, 2007, C-print, 100 × 100 cm

→ p.142

Courtesy Galerie Bertrand & Gruner and the artist

'In Abuja we found them living on the periphery of the city in a shantytown – a group of men, a little girl, three hyenas, four monkeys, and a few rock pythons. It turned out that they were a group of itinerant minstrels, performers who used the animals to entertain crowds and sell traditional medicines. The animal handlers were all related to each other and were practising a tradition passed down from generation to generation. I spent eight days travelling with them. The spectacle caused by this group walking down busy market streets was overwhelming. I tried photographing this but failed, perhaps because I wasn't interested in their performances. I realised that what I found fascinating was the hybridisation of the urban and the wild and the paradoxical relationship that the handlers have with their animals – sometimes doting and affectionate, sometimes brutal and cruel' (The Hyena & Other Men, 2007, n.p.). In this way Pieter Hugo recalls his first stay with the hyena men. Two years later, in 2007, he returned to Nigeria, where he made more portraits, including Abdullahi Mohammed with Mainasara under the city highway of Lagos.

The South African photographer Pieter Hugo focuses in his works on the liminal activities of society. His series *Looking Aside* (published as a monograph in 2006), shows portraits of Africans who suffer from albinism or other forms of physical difference. His photographic exploration of the city of Musina at the border of Zimbabwe, published in 2007 under the title *Messina/Musina*, investigates the social and economic distortions brought about by Africa's colonial history.

Pieter Hugo, *The Hyena & Other Men*, Munich 2007; Pieter Hugo, *Messina/Musina*, Rome 2007; Pieter Hugo, *Looking Aside*, Rome 2006.

Peter Hujar
1934 Trenton, New Jersey
– 1987 New York

Ethyl Eichelberger as Auntie Bellum, 1979, 50.8 × 40.6 cm
Ethyl Eichelberger as Nefertiti Standing, 1978, 50.8 × 40.6 cm

→ p.98

Courtesy the Peter Hujar Archive and Matthew Marks Gallery, New York

In Peter Hujar's work, the artist's studio becomes a place of self-depiction as well as a location for encounters with other free spirit of the 1970s through the act of portraiture, a place of social emancipation. His models are New York's bohemians, homosexuals and artists. Ethyl Eichelberger was a famous drag performer in New York's subculture. Nefertiti and Auntie Bellum were perhaps characters from the actor's experimental theatre.

Peter Hujar learned the photographic craft as an assistant to several commercial photographers before he began to undertake freelance work in fashion and advertising photography from the mid-1950s to the mid-1970s. During this time, he travelled to Europe extensively and lived for a while in Italy, where, in 1963, he photographed the mummies in Palermo's catacombs, among other subjects. These images, combined with portraits of members of the New York art scene, were included in his book *Portraits of Life and Death* (1976). Through his contact with Richard Avedon he photographed for *Harper's Bazaar* from 1966 to 1970. His static black-and-white portraits are often shot simply, in front of empty walls, and show great empathy for his sitters. Other subjects include male and female nudes, as well as animals and the nocturnal streets of downtown Manhattan.

Peter Hujar, exh. cat., ICA, London 2007; Peter Hujar: Night, exh. cat., Matthew Marks Gallery, New York 2005; Peter Hujar: A Retrospective, exh. cat., Stedelijk Museum, Amsterdam and Fotomuseum Winterthur 1994; Susan Sontag, Portraits in Life and Death, New York 1976.

Sarah Jones
b.1959, lives in London

– From the series **Actor** –
Actor II, 1995, C-print on aluminium, 150 × 150 cm

→ p.124

The MAG Collection

Sarah Jones's four-part series *Actor* shows two people in front of a neutral backdrop. The title indicates that they may be playing some kind of role. Taken as American shots (a portrait from head to knee), the characters stand together without seeming to be aware of each other. At first glance, the poses of the figures appear strange, their gestures and facial expressions mysterious. In fact, Jones based her series on an altarpiece by Pierro della Francesca, located in the Brera in Milan, and the mysterious expression of its character. Her fascination with these highly constructed images is indicative of the tendency in portrait photography since the 1980s to focus on distance rather than on psychological presence.

Sarah Jones earned a Bachelor of Arts at Goldsmith's College in London, where she studied from 1978 to 1981. She completed her Master's degree in 1996. She did not receive a conventional training in photography, but has a background in contemporary art and dance, which might explain the references to theatre and the history of art in her work. These elements become visible in a series of images that show young girls posing in bourgeois interiors or gardens with the same detached absorption as those in *Actor*. With these photographic tableaux, as well as with her previous work *Consulting Room* (1995–8), Jones has contributed an interesting new approach to the directorial mode of photography. She was awarded the 13th Bradford Fellow of Photography in 2007.

Archive, no.10, National Media Museum, Bradford, Oct. 2007; *Sarah Jones*, exh. cat., Le Consortium, Dijon 2001; *Sarah Jones*, exh. cat., Museum Folkwang, Essen 2000; Chris Townsend (ed.), *Sarah Jones*, Salamanca 1999.

Valérie Jouve
b.1964 Saint-Etienne, lives in Paris

– From the series **Les Personnages** (The Characters) –

Sans titre, no.3 (Untitled, No.3), 1994–5
→ p.117

Sans titre, no.4 (Untitled, No.4), 1994–5

C-prints, each 103 × 133 cm

Fotografische Sammlung, Museum Folkwang, Essen

'The city: a machinery, but also a chemistry, a reality that is impossible to embrace or grasp, an irrational sensation. Photography: an abstract inscription, a captivating process, but also a mechanical vision of the world, an authority of verisimilitude and thus a certain authenticity … The city is in the constant process of production: spaces, people who don't move in the same direction – singular bodies that affirm themselves in their simple presence, their posture, their consciousness … "Characters" (in the fictional sense of the word) raise questions and simultaneously invent and construct utopian cities and their own projection' (Valérie Jouve, *2002, p.4*). Valérie Jouve developed her substantial body of work *The Characters* in the 1990s. The images are characterised by a dialectic between foreground and background; a linking middle ground is missing. *The Characters* appear on the stage of the image like faded apparitions in front of a blurred architectural scene.

Valérie Jouve studied sociology in the first half of the 1980s, and in the late 1980s photography at the Ecole Nationale de la Photographie in Arles. In the 1990s, she produced urban landscapes around Marseille, as well as architectural photography and sequences of passers-by, in addition to her series *The Characters*. Her work always deals with the space that people manage to create for themselves in a given urbanistic frame. Between 2000 and 2002, she made her first movie *Le Grand Littoral* (The Great Seashore), also in the urban wasteland of Marseille, followed by her

second film *Time Is Working Around Rotterdam* (2006). In the extensive exhibition *Skulptur Projekte Münster 2007* she showed her work *Münsterlands*.

Dean Inkster, *Valérie Jouve*, Paris 2007; *Valérie Jouve, fotografie. Pont bleu – sorties de bureau*, exh. cat., Sprengel Museum, Hanover 2005; Valérie Jouve and Dean Inkster, *Valérie Jouve*, Vanves 2002.

Marjaana Kella
b.1961 Orimattila, Finland, lives in Helsinki

– From the series **Hypnoosi** (Hypnosis) –

Nainen hypnoositilassa (Hypnotised Woman), 1997, 170 × 125 cm
→ p.118

Nuori nainen hypnoositilassa – 3 (Young Hypnotised Woman – 3), 1999, 165 × 125 cm

C-prints
Marjanna Kella / Courtesy van Zoetendaal Amsterdam

'In hypnosis, a person's inner mental images and outer appearance may be really wide apart. And even if the surface is presented in a lot of detail, we still can't know what is going on in the mind of the pictured person … Hypnosis became a kind of method for dismantling the traditional formula of portrait picturing, where the person photographed often consciously tries to present him or herself for the portrait' (Marjaana Kella, *2002, p.45*). In her series Hypnosis, Marjaana Kella plays with the tradition of the studio portrait, removing its function as a site for representing one's identity, while maintaining its seclusiveness and its technical potential for staging. With subtle irony, she comments on our fascination with the photographic portrait, as a membrane between the inside and outside. It is no coincidence that her series echoes the role of photography as a vehicle for spiritualism around 1900.

Marjaana Kella studied at the Free Art School in Helsinki between 1985 and 86 and later at the University of Art and Design, where she received a Master's degree in 1993. Between 1993 and 1999 she taught at the Academy of Fine Arts in Helsinki. She received a solo show at the Finnish Museum of Photography in 2003, which included both *Hypnosis* and her series *Reversed* – portraits that depict people from the photographer's generation, taken from the back.

Willem van Zoetendaal (ed.), *Marjaana Kella*, Amsterdam 2002; Anna Gashell and Joachim Schmid, *Marjanna Kella*, exh. cat., Hasselblad Center, Göteborg 1999.

Chris Killip
b.1946 Douglas, Isle of Man, lives in Cambridge, Massachusetts

– From the series **In Flagrante, Great Britain** –

Torso, Pelaw, Gateshead, Tyneside, 1978, 50.4 × 39.9 cm
→ p.102

Boy Sitting on a Wall, Tyneside, 1976, 43.4 × 52.7 cm

Fotografische Sammlung, Museum Folkwang, Essen

The upper body and the face are not shown in the torso photograph that Chris Killip took of a person in coat, presumably an elderly man, sitting on a wall, yet it is an arresting image of poverty. The precision of the large format shows every fold in the threadbare coat, every open seam. In Killip's second image in this exhibition, the overly large shoes of the young boy play

a central role: they become a symbol of both the tramp and the street. These two photographs are from the series reproduced in Killip's book *In Flagrante*, which comprises fifty photographs and was published in 1988. Using portraits, scenic images and landscapes, the publication documents the social decay of the working class in the North-east of England.

Chris Killip's professional life as a photographer began in 1964, when he worked as an assistant to the advertising photographer Adrian Flowers in London. Later he began to undertake freelance work. From 1969 on, he developed his own documentary style, influenced by Paul Strand and Walker Evans. In 1970, he returned to the Isle of Man, and the portraits and landscapes that he produced there were published as a book in 1980. Killip's documentation of the English North-east, an area particularly neglected by the Thatcher government, began around 1975. Ten years later, he and Graham Smith exhibited their photographs of this region at the Serpentine Gallery, London. In 1976, he founded the Side Gallery in Newcastle-upon-Tyne. Chris Killip has always been a mediator of photography and an active protagonist of his artistic convictions; since 1991 he has taught photography at Harvard University.

Chris Killip, *Pirelli Work*, Göttingen 2006; Chris Killip, *In Flagrante*, London 1988; Chris Killip, *Isle of Man: A Book about the Manx*, London 1980.

William Klein
b.1928 New York, lives in Paris

– Books –

Life Is Good and Good for You in New York: Trance Witness Revels, Editions du Seuil, Paris 1956, 28.2 × 22.7 cm, 194 pp.
→ p.82

Rome, Editions du Seuil, Album Petite Planète, Paris 1959, 28.4 × 22.7 cm, 194 pp
→ p.83

Moskau, Nannen, Hamburg 1964, 35.2 × 26.2 cm, 184 pp.
→ p.84

Moscow, Crown Publishers Inc., New York 1964, 35.4 × 26.5 cm, 184 pp.

Fotografische Sammlung, Museum Folkwang, Essen / Private Collection, Essen

Tokyo, Crown Publishers Inc., New York 1964, 35.5 × 26.5 cm, 184 pp.

Sammlung F.C. Gundlach, Hamburg

'Traditional photography books put me to sleep: they'd have some sacrosanct image on the right side, and a blank page on the left. They were untouchable, academic, and boring. For me, design, graphics, and layout were almost as important as the photographs themselves. And that's why I did everything I could to create a new kind of visual book – double pages with twenty images on them, all crowded together like comics, as well as facing pages that collided with each other, and double pages with severely cropped images. They parodied product catalogues, with a good dose of Dada' (William Klein, New York, 1954/55, *1995*). This comment describes the driving force behind William Klein's first book, which included the groundbreaking photographs that he had taken in New York in 1954 and 1955.

– Fashion Photographs –

Simone and Olympic Wrestlers, Rome, 1960, 39.8 × 29.8 cm

Simone and Sophia Loren, *Rome*, 1962,
39.9 × 34.3 cm

Mirrors and Roofs, New York, 1961,
43.3 × 35.5 cm

→ p.67

Haus der Photographie / Sammlung F.C. Gundlach,
Hamburg

*When William Klein started organising his first photo
shoots for Vogue in 1957, the street had already been
discovered as a location for fashion pictures. Klein not
only relied on the dynamic vision of the wide-angle
lens, but he also staged images that glowed with
the glamour of a star entering the scene. He often
used props, such as a set of mirrors for Mirrors and
Roofs, and for Simone and Sophia Loren, a life-sized
cardboard photograph, placed in the streets of Rome,
where the young fashion model met upon the icon of
the famous film star.*

William Klein began his artistic career as a painter in
Paris in the late 1940s. Following his geometric Hard-
Edge paintings, he experimented with cameraless
photography. After his return to New York in 1954 he
discovered street photography, and began working in
this new medium. He used his camera as a dynamic
recording device, which he brought to life through his
own body movement among people on the street. His
book *Life Is Good and Good for You in New York*, which
was published in 1956, was received both by critics
and the public as a provocation, but also as something
entirely new. He then embarked on a diverse range
of photography and film projects. In 1958, his first
short film *Broadway by Light* was released, followed
by numerous documentaries such as *Muhammad
Ali, The Greatest* (1964–74) and *Far from Vietnam*
(1967), as well as experimental feature films. During
this time Klein also found time to undertake fashion
assignments, working for *Vogue* from 1957 onwards,
and for *Harper's Bazaar* from 1967.

William Klein: Rétrospective, exh. cat., Centre Pompidou, Paris 2005; William Klein, *New York, 1954/55*, Heidelberg 1995; William Klein, *In & Out Fashion*, Heidelberg 1994.

Suzanne Lafont
b.1949 Nîmes, lives in Saint-Ouen, Paris

Marcheur no.1 *(Passer-by No.1)*, 1995–8,
147.5 × 120 cm

→ p.119

Balayeur (Sweeper), 1997, 153.9 × 122.5 cm

Serigraphies
Collection of the artist

The images Passer-by *and* Sweeper *are part of a
working process that Suzanne Lafont started in 1994–5
and which was first articulated through the image* Le
Défilé *(Parade). Underlying this series of works is the
idea of separation and re-combination. 'How can one
produce a relationship between a human figure and
the world, based on its distance, its being uprooted,
its separation?' asks Lafont (Lecture of the Artist,
1996). She answers by separating the figure and
background in her images and devising two categories
of image types: the 'object unit' (pictures of facades
and advertising signs) and the 'character unit'. Like a
display of cards on a table, Lafont's pictures can be
combined and mounted on the wall in many ways,
resulting in differing narratives. At the same time, they
refer through their expression and the double exposure
to the concept of the grotesque, which has always
been important in Lafont's work. The pictures have
been screen-printed, thus quoting a familiar public
image: the poster.*

Suzanne Lafont, whose background is in philosophy,
produced her first photographic works in 1984. In
France at that time, where the tradition of reportage
was still predominant, her staged images must have
seemed like a provocation. Her series *La Rue* (The
Street), exhibited at the Centre Georges Pompidou
in Paris in 1990, presents staged 'snapshots' of the
faces of passers-by. Her work engages in a dialogue
with other media, such as painting and cinema, whose
influence in the form of the close-up and in methods
of montage becomes visible in different series. After
several solo shows, including the Jeu de Paume, Paris
and the Museum of Modern Art, New York (1992) she
was represented at Documenta X (1997) by her work
Tragedy, a modular system of posters clued on the
walls of a pedestrian underpass.

Suzanne Lafont, *Appelé par son nom*, Arles 2003; Paul Stulzman, *Suzanne Lafont*, Vanves 1998; *Documenta X*, exh. cat., Kassel and Ostfildern-Ruit 1997; *Susanne Lafont*, exh. cat., Musée Departemental d'Art Contemporain, Rochechouart 1997.

Jacques Henri Lartigue
1894 Courbevoie, France
– 1986 Nice

Monte Carlo, 1911, 6.9 × 4.7 cm

Au Champs de courses à Auteuil, *Paris,
juin 1911* (Race Day at Auteuil, Paris, June
1911), 1911, 10.1 × 6.7 cm, modern print

Paris, juin 1911 (Paris, June 1911), 1911,
10.2 × 6.2 cm

→ p.206

Paris, 28 juin 1912 (Paris, 28 June 1912),
1912, 12 × 11.9 cm

→ p.31

*Avenue du Bois de Boulogne, Paris, février
1911* (Avenue du Bois de Boulogne, Paris,
February 1911), 1911, 8.7 × 5.6 cm

Sentier de la Vertu, Paris, mai 1912 (Path of
Virtue, Paris, May 1912), 1912, 7 × 4.8 cm

*Avenue du Bois de Boulogne, le matin,
Paris, février 1912* (Avenue du Bois de
Boulogne, Morning, Paris, February 1912),
1912, 6.5 × 4.8 cm

Paris, juin 1912 (Paris, June 1912), 1912,
12.2 × 9.5 cm, modern print

*Jupes courtes et bottes style 1915, Avenue
du Bois, Paris, juillet 1915* (Short Skirts and
Boots 1915-style, Avenue du Bois, Paris,
July 1915), 1915, 12 × 10.3 cm

Donation J.H. Lartigue – Ministère de la Culture
– France

*At the age of seventeen, Jacques Henri Lartigue took
snapshots of elegant ladies in the Bois de Boulogne.
He commented in his diary: 'This is where I lie in wait,
sitting on an iron chair, camera controls fine-adjusted.
Distance: 4 to 5 meters; speed: shutter screen slit
4mm; aperture: depending on what she arrives from
… She is the lady in all her get-up, very fashionable,
very ridiculous … or very pretty, who knows? Far off,
amongst the walkers, she stands out like a golden
pheasant in a henhouse. She approaches … I'm shy,
trembling a little. Twenty meters… ten meters … eight
… six … and click! The shutter of my big camera makes
so much noise that the lady jumps almost as much as
I do. It doesn't matter a bit, except to the man with a
loud voice accompanying her who, with a furious look,
starts to get hold of me … What does it matter, though,
all that counts is the pleasure of having a new photo'
(Lartigue: Album of a Century, 2003, p.376).*

The child of an affluent French family of entrepreneurs,
Jacques Henri Lartigue started taking photographs at
the age of eight. The family, the pleasures of childhood
and youth, sports events and urban life were among
his initial playful experiments with the camera.
Although his photography was later overshadowed by
his ambition to be a painter, he was an enthusiastic
amateur photographer throughout his life, and his
numerous albums are unique documents of high
bourgeois existence in the twentieth century. His
photographic oeuvre was honoured with an exhibition
at the Museum of Modern Art, New York, in 1963.

Martine d'Astier, Quentin Bajac, Alain Sayag (eds.), *Lartigue: Album of a Century*, Paris and New York 2003; *Diary of a Century: Photographs of Jacques Henri Lartigue*, conceived by Richard Avedon, New York 1970.

Helmar Lerski
1871 Strasbourg – 1956
Zurich

– From the series **Köpfe des Alltags** (Heads
from Everyday Life), 1928–30

Köchin aus Ostpreussen (Cook from East
Prussia), 28.9 × 23 cm

Reinemachfrau (Charwoman), 29.2 × 22.7 cm

→ p.42

Hausangestellte (Domestic Worker),
29.1 × 23.1 cm

Junger Buchhändler (Young Bookseller),
29.1 × 22.6 cm

Bettler aus Sachsen (Beggar from Saxony),
29.1 × 20.9 cm

Metallarbeiter (Metal Worker), 29 × 22.8 cm

Stubenmädchen (Parlourmaid), 28.5 × 23 cm

Näherin (Seamstress), 28.9 × 22.8 cm

Fotografische Sammlung, Museum Folkwang, Essen

*'Just like the Russian film directors who came to the
conclusion that ordinary people are better material
than famous actors, Helmar Lerski finds his models
on the street or has them come from the employment
office. He was of the opinion that every human being
has a face, one just had to make an effort in order to
see it.' The fascination with amateur actors expressed
in Curt Glaser's preface to Helmar Lerski's book
Heads from Everyday Life of 1931 was widespread
among filmmakers and intellectuals during this period.
The photographer and cameraman Lerski believed it
possible to transform the 'unseen people' from the
street into different characters with different moods
by using specific lighting. In his book, Lerski shows as
many as seven face studies of the 'cleaning woman'.*

Having grown up in Zurich, Israel Schmuklerski only
began to work as photographer around 1910, by then
almost forty years of age. Before this, he had led a
bohemian life and was an actor on German-speaking
stages in America, where he changed his name
to Helmar Lerski. From 1916 to 1928, held in high
regard for his expressive chiaroscuro, he worked as a
cameraman on more than forty German films, among
them Paul Leni's *Wachsfigurenkabinett* (Wax Museum)
of 1923. In an attempt to replicate the success of his
earlier photo book *Köpfe des Alltags* (Heads from
Everyday Life), Lerski produced a series of portraits
of *Jewish Faces* in Palestine, with which he hoped to
create a counter image to the hate-campaign of Nazi
propaganda. From 1932 to 1948 he lived in Tel Aviv,
where he made films on behalf of Zionist institutions
and carried out his experiment *Metamorphosis through
Light*, 140 photographs of just one young man, with
which he intended to show the significance of directed
light. Lerski returned to Zurich in the spring of 1948.

Florian Ebner, *Metamorphosen des Gesichts. Die 'Verwandlungen durch Licht' von Helmar Lerski*, Göttingen 2002; Ute Eskildsen and Jan-Christopher Horak (eds.), *Helmar Lerski. Lichtbildner*, exh. cat., Museum Folkwang, Essen 1982; David Mellor, 'London–Berlin–London: A Cultural History. The Reception and Influence of the New German Photography in Britain 1927–1933', in David Mellor (ed.), *Germany: The New Photography 1927–1933*, London 1978, pp.112–31.

Leon Levinstein
1910 Buckhannon, West Virginia – 1988 New York

Broadway and 42nd Street, c.1974, 35.1 × 22.8 cm

→ p.62

Untitled (NYC), 1960, 34.1 × 25.9 cm

Bleekerstreet, 1954, 35.3 × 27.7 cm

Fotografische Sammlung, Museum Folkwang, Essen

Several photographs and prints exist of the lanky young man whom Leon Levinstein photographed on 42nd Street around 1974. They all follow the same principle: the man's body completely fills the vertical image, thus becoming a graphic individual figure. He is typical of Levinstein's wandering characters illustrating the condition humaine, *photographed in the streets of New York over a thirty-year span. The (often strained) metaphor of the chronicler of the street as a mixture of loafer,* flâneur *and stray dog aptly describes his way of working. Towards the end of his life, he ordered his work into several different series.*

In the 1930s Leon Levinstein moved from West Virginia to Baltimore, studying at the Maryland Institute of Art before serving in the Air Force during the Second World War. After the war, he moved to New York, where he worked as an art director in a small advertising agency. At the same time, he took photography classes under Alexey Brodovitch, the art director of *Harper's Bazaar*, as well as under Sid Grossman at the famous Photo League. Levinstein's work became known in the 1950s after having been shown in several important exhibitions at the Museum of Modern Art, New York (*Then and Now*, 1952; *Always the Young Stranger*, 1953 and *Family of Man*, 1955). Until the 1980s, he travelled widely in Mexico, India and Europe. In 1975, at the age of sixty-five, he finally received a Guggenheim Fellowship grant. However, his regular occupation until his death was graphic design. In 1995, the National Gallery of Canada honoured him with a retrospective as an important representative of the New York School of Photography.

Sam Stourdzé, *Leon Levinstein: Obsession*, Paris 2000; *The Moment of Exposure: Leon Levinstein*, exh. cat., National Gallery of Canada, Ottawa 1995; Jane Livingston, *The New York School, Photographs 1936–1963*, New York 1992.

Helen Levitt
b.1913, lives in New York

New York, c.1940, 19.1 × 12.7 cm

The Museum of Modern Art, New York. Purchase, 1942

New York, 1940, 16.6 × 22.5 cm

The Museum of Modern Art, New York. Anonymous gift, 1941

New York, c.1945, 33.8 × 25 cm

The Museum of Modern Art, New York. Gift of the photographer, 1959

New York (Foreign Legion), c.1940, 22.6 × 33.6 cm

→ p.57

Courtesy the artist and Laurence Miller Gallery, New York

Commenting on her numerous photographs taken in the streets of New York in the 1940s, Helen Levitt wrote: 'There were plenty of kids playing on the streets. The streets were crowded with all kinds of things going on, not just children. Everything was going on in the street in the summertime. They didn't have air-conditioning. Everybody was out on the stoops, sitting outside, on chairs' (New York Times, 8 April, 2004). The photographs are unsentimental and dynamic, focusing especially on the children's gestures. Walker Evans once called them 'both dance and affectionate poetry', describing their style as 'anti-journalistic'. Levitt mainly worked in East Harlem and the Lower East Side of Manhattan – the slums, where the African-Americans and Italians lived. She also took a cinematographic view of the street in her documentary film In the Street *of 1947.*

Helen Levitt began her career while working for a portrait photographer in Brooklyn. It was there that she encountered Henri Cartier-Bresson in 1935. Upon meeting Walker Evans, she became his assistant in 1938. In the 1930s and 1940s she photographed life on the streets of New York, as well as children at play, and this became an important subject. She later expanded her repertoire to include the elderly and other ordinary people. With the exception of a trip to Mexico in 1941, her photographic subject always remained New York. When she returned from her travels, she started to work as a film editor for Luis Buñuel, and later shot her own documentary films in collaboration with James Agee, who in 1946 had written an essay for her book *A Way of Seeing*, which was not published until 1965. Her documentary *The Quiet One* was nominated for an Oscar in 1948 and proved groundbreaking for independent low-budget productions. In 1959 and in 1960 she received Guggenheim Fellowship grants and her interest turned back to photography. She took some colour photographs in the 1960s, but in the 1980s she returned to black and white photography.

Helen Levitt: Photographs 1937–1991, exh. cat., Sprengel Museum, Hanover 2008; *Slide Show: The Color Photographs of Helen Levitt*, exh. cat., Museum of Modern Art, New York 2005; Helen Levitt, *Here and There*, New York 2003; *Crosstown*, exh. cat., International Center of Photography, New York 1997.

Madame Yevonde
1893 – 1975 London

– From the series **Goddesses**, 1935 –

Lady Elizabeth Felicia Henrietta Augusta Bridgett Poulett Photographed as 'Arethusa', 42 × 27.5 cm

→ p.55

Vivex colour print
National Portrait Gallery, London

Mrs James Beck as 'Daphne', 37 × 26.5 cm

Lady Milbanke as Queen of the Amazons ('Penthesilea'), 37.2 × 27.9 cm

Vivex colour prints
New Media Museum, Bradford

The competition between various portrait studios for prominent customers in the 1930s was fierce, but the London-based photographer Madame Yevonde was successful, due to her unique imagination. Inspired by eighteenth-century painting and the Olympic Ball that was held in London in March 1935 (and to which the guests had been asked to wear mythological costumes), she conceived her series Goddesses. *For this project she asked high-society women to pose for her with costumes and props representing characters from antiquity, such as Medusa, Europa, Daphne and Venus. The exaggerated artificiality mimicked the kind of society portrait then in vogue, while allowing modern women to adopt the self-confident attributes embodied by antique figures: courage, strength, narcissism and pride.*

In 1911 Madame Yevonde (Yevonde Middleton) began a three-year appren-ticeship under the female society photographer Lallie Charles, and opened up her own studio in 1914. In just a short period of time she acquired a reputation as an excellent portrait photographer. Although colour photography was not widespread at that time, she experimented with the complicated tri-colour process called Vivex. In 1932, she became the first British photographer to exhibit in colour. The magazine *Fortune* commissioned her to document the last days of the building of the steamship *Queen Mary* before its launch. Her preferred Vivex colour process was discontinued with the outbreak of the Second World War, and she was forced to continue her work in black and white. After the war, she worked as a commercial and magazine photographer. In 1971 she gave her life's work to the National Portrait Gallery in London.

Lawrence N. Hole, *Goddesses*, Seattle 2000; *Be Original or Die: Madame Yevonde*, exh. cat., Villa Stuck, Munich 1998; *Madame Yevonde: Colour, Fantasy and Myth*, exh. cat., Royal Photographic Society, Bath and National Portrait Gallery, London 1990.

Hashem El Madani
b.1928, lives in Saida, Lebanon

– From a series of **Palestinian Resistants**, 1968–72 –

Four photographs, 30.5 × 40.5 cm, printed 2006

→ p.101

Musée Nicéphore Niépce, Ville de Chalon-sur-Saône, France

'In the late 1960s, Palestinians started to be armed, and it became very common to see armed men on the streets in Saida. They used to come to the studio with their arms and very often other customers would borrow the guns and pose with them … I consider the act of posing with a gun as an act of showing off – a display of power. It is part of my role as a photographer to photograph them the way they wish. I never interfered and never had judgements on my clients' (Hashem El Madani in a conversation with Akram Zaatari, Studio Practices, *2004, p.15).*

Lebanese-born Hashem El Madani learned the photographic craft from a Jewish photographer named Katz in Haifa in 1947. As a consequence of the Zionist-Arabian war, Hashem El Madani left Palestine in 1948 and returned to Saida. Initially, he worked as an itinerant photographer in the town's streets and beaches. Around 1952, he opened a studio that he named after the adjoining movie theatre Studio Shehrazade and which he maintained for over fifty years. El Madani considers himself a simple portrait photographer. He once expressed a wish to photograph all the citizens of Saida. The 500,000 images comprising his archive are now preserved in the Arab Image Foundation (AIF), in which the artist and filmmaker Akram Zaatari was significantly involved. The members of the AIF analyse through socio-cultural and artistic methods how national (Arab) and individual identity is constituted through the photographic image. Their analysis *Mapping Sitting*, based on studio and street photography from the Arabian region, was pioneering.

Lisa Le Feuvre and Akram Zaatari (eds.), *Hashem El Madani: Studio Practices*, Beirut and London 2004; Karl Bassil, Zeina Maasri, and Akram Zaatari, *Mapping Sitting: On Portraiture and Photography*, Beirut 2002.

Robert Mapplethorpe
1946 New York – 1989 Boston

Lisa Lyon, 1982, 40.6 × 50.8 cm

→ p.93

Joe, NYC, 1978, 40.6 × 50.8 cm

Lisa Lyon won the first Women's World Pro Bodybuilding Championship in 1979, becoming a prototype of the 1980s woman. Lyon and Mapplethorpe met at a party in Soho, and arranged a photo-shoot in the photographer's studio, which resulted in a collaboration from 1980 to 1982, leading to the publication of the book Lady Lisa Lyon *(1983). In countless sessions, which were also sometimes held outdoors or in other cities such as Paris, Lyon took on a variety of roles: the motorcycle woman, circus artist, playgirl and even the 'black widow'. The main focus was on the pronounced staging of the body, translated into the Neoclassical language of Mapplethorpe's black and white photography. 'The images are a little tough, just like us', Lyon once said. A comment by Mapplethorpe suggests that he was interested in stretching the limits of depictions of the body: 'She is like a new animal for me, a third gender maybe'* (Portfolio, *published by the German magazine* Stern, *no.33, 2003, p.10).*

After having completed his studies in art and design at the Pratt Institute of Art in Brooklyn, Robert Mapplethorpe started his artistic career with sculptural work, assemblages and collages from magazines. In 1971 he began experimenting with a Polaroid camera, predominantly taking self-portraits. Later, he mainly worked with a medium-format camera. He names photographers such as Nadar, Alfred Stieglitz and Fred Holland Day as influences on his highly aestheticised style. From the late 1970s he produced nudes and portraits, fragmented body parts, some of them explicitly homoerotic or sadomasochistic in nature. 'I wanted people to see that even those extremes could be made into art. Take those pornographic images and make them somehow transcend the image', he commented (Bart Everly, 'Robert Mapplethorpe' in *Splash*, New York 1988, n.p.). In the mid-1980s Mapplethorpe – under heavy attack from conservative America – was one of the most famous photographers in New York. He produced still lifes of flowers in addition to extensive portrait series of artists, musicians and movie stars.

Germano Celant and Arkady Ippolitov (eds.), *Robert Mapplethorpe und die klassische Tradition*, Ostfildern-Ruit 2004; *Mapplethorpe*, text by Arthur C. Danto, New York 1992; Joan Didion, *Mapplethorpe: Some Women*, Boston 1989; *Mapplethorpe: Portraits*, exh. cat., National Portrait Gallery, London 1988.

Boris Mikhailov
b.1938 Charkov, Ukraine, lives in Charkov and Berlin

– From the project **Case History**, 1997–8 –

Thirty photographs, C-prints (standard photolab prints), each 15.2 × 10.2 cm

→ p.112

Fotografische Sammlung, Museum Folkwang, Essen

'Now it is important for me to say how the West came to the East and why I used colour photos … The colour "express-photo" became for me the thing which mostly correlated with the new time. In each corner a photo-centre – "Agfa", "Konica", "Fuji" – was opened. The appearance of Western technology made a colour album the thing that connects the rich and the poor. Both the rich and the poor wanted to have colour photographs and there was only one distinction: the rich could afford them, the poor couldn't. The colour photo became an image of the new life. And the poor having a beautiful photo can state: "Now we also live nicely" (Case History, *p.9.). The impact of Boris Mikhailov's photographs in the outstanding series* Case History *is attributable to their deliberate and informal straightforwardness, reminiscent of amateur photography, including the 'red-eye' caused by the camera flash. The photographic material shown in the exhibition – the same prints that Mikhailov used for his book – emphasises the importance of cheap prints to the conception, scale and form of the book.*

In the course of the 1960s Boris Mikhailov, whilst employed as an engineer, began to make photographs. In the 1970s he devoted himself entirely to photography and founded the artists' group Vremja (Time). Among his long-term friends is the Conceptual artist Ilya Kabakov. Since that time, Mikhailov has developed one of the most independent positions in contemporary documentary photography, reflecting in a very personal, visually overwhelming manner the breakdown of the Soviet Union and subsequently the exuberant growth of the new capitalist era. Landmarks of this development include the *Red Series* (1968–75), the panoramic street scenes of the 'brown' (*On the Ground*) and 'blue' (*Twilight*) series and as well as the books *Unfinished Dissertation* and *Case History*.

Boris Mikhailov: A Retrospective, exh. cat. Fotomuseum Winterthur, Zurich 2003; Boris Mikhailov, *Case History*, Zurich 1999; Boris Mikhailov, *Unvollendete Dissertation*, Zurich 1998.

Lee Miller
1907 Poughkeepsie, New York – 1977 Chiddingly, England

Lázló Bardossy, Fascist ex-Prime Minister of Hungary, Facing the Firing Squad, Budapest, 1946, 27.4 × 27.4 cm

→ p.59

Lee Miller photographed the execution of László Bardossy, the Fascist collaborator and ex-prime minister of Hungary as she travelled into Eastern Europe, documenting the aftermath of the war. In her words: 'In the yard it was almost light … The whole set up was being changed. Instead of the big beam-like vertical stake, attendants were stacking sandbags against the brick wall. They had changed their minds and were going to give him the dignity of a firing squad. He wore the same plus-fours tweed suit, ankle high shoes with white socks turned over the edges as when he'd been arrested. He held his beaky grey face high and his gestures were taut. The four gendarmes who had volunteered for the execution stood in line awaiting the order to fire. They were less than two yards from him. Bardossy's voice orated in a high pitched rasp, "God save Hungary from all these bandits."' (The Lives of Lee Miller, *1985, p.167*).

Lee Miller began her career on the other side of the camera, posing as a professional model for Edward Steichen, George Hoyningen-Huené and Arnold Genthe. In 1929 she left the United States to participate in the Parisian art scene that was developing around the Surrealists. She was Man Ray's model, partner and assistant before becoming a notable photographer herself. After leaving Paris in 1932, she opened her own commercial and portrait studio in New York, which she abandoned in 1934 to marry the Egyptian businessman Aziz Eloui Bey. Already living in London with the Surrealist artist Roland Penrose when the German bombing began, she became a photojournalist accredited with the US Army and teamed up on many assignments with the American photographer David E. Scherman, a *Life* magazine correspondent. Her remarkable photographs of the war, especially of the liberation of the concentration camps Buchenwald and Dachau, had a significant influence on the American perception of the conflict in Europe. After her marriage to Penrose in 1947, she continued to work for *Vogue* and *Life*, but only on an occasional basis. In 1949, they bought Farley Farm House in Sussex, which during the 1950s and 1960s became a sort of artistic Mecca for visiting artists.

The Art of Lee Miller, exh. cat., Victoria & Albert Museum, London 2007; Katharina Menzel-Ahr, *Lee Miller. Kriegskorrespondentin für Vogue*, Marburg 2005; Richard Calvocoressi: *Lee Miller: Portraits from a Life*, London 2002; Jane Livingston, *Lee Miller: Photographer*, London 1989; Antony Penrose, *The Lives of Lee Miller*, London 1985.

Lisette Model (Elise Amélie Felicie Stern, later Seybert)
1901 Vienna – 1983 New York

Montparnasse, 1933–8, 42.2 × 50.5 cm

→ p.208

Fotografische Sammlung, Museum Folkwang, Essen

– From the portfolio **Twelve Photographs** –

Man with Pamphlets, Paris, 1937, 40 × 49.5 cm, printed 1976

Woman with Veil, San Francisco, 1949, 40 × 49.5 cm, printed 1976

→ p.54

Promenade des Anglais, Nice, 1937, 40 × 49.5 cm, printed 1976

Olbricht Collection

'Photographs of people from the Riviera, from the Bowery, from the sidewalks of New York … Lisette Model has an international reputation for her unusual and truly remarkable photographs. She is on the photographic staff of the magazine, Harper's Bazaar. She does not, however, take the usual fashion photographs, but subjects such as the circus, window reflections, people on the streets; these are now run as special features in the magazine' (Lisette Model, *2000, p.106). This press release issued on the occasion of Lisette Model's exhibition in San Francisco in 1946 points out that she saw herself as a quite different magazine photographer. Three years later, in 1949, she took the photograph* Woman with Veil, *a satirical portrait of a fading bourgeoisie.*

Music was Lisette Seybert's first love. In 1918 she took up piano studies in Vienna and in 1920 she began harmony studies under Arnold Schönberg. In 1926 she moved with her mother and sister to Paris, where she also pursued voice studies. Ending her musical career around 1933, she began taking photographs. Her first images of the promenade des Anglais in Nice date from 1934. A year after their marriage in 1937, Lisette and Evsa Model immigrated to the USA. The 1940s marked years of intensive photographic work, primarily in New York. Not only published in magazines, Model's photographs were shown from early on in numerous exhibitions. In the early 1950s she took up teaching at the New York School for Social Research, to which she was committed until her death. Diane Arbus was her most famous student.

Lisette Model. Fotografien 1934–1960, exh. cat., Kunsthalle Vienna and Fotomuseum Winterthur, Vienna 2000; Ann Thomas, *Lisette Model*, exh. cat., National Gallery of Canada, Ottawa 1990

Daido Moriyama
b.1938 Osaka, Japan, lives in Tokyo

– Books –

Nippon Gekijo Shashincho (Japan: A Photo Theatre), Muromachi-Shobo, Tokyo 1968, 21 × 22 cm, 150 pp., 149 black and white photographs

Sashin yo Sayonara (Bye Bye Photography), Shasin Hyron-sha, Tokyo 1972, 23 × 18.2 cm, 308 pp., 137 black and white photographs

Karyudo (Hunter), Chuo Kolon-sha 1972, 26.5 × 22 cm, 120 pp., 104 black and white photographs

→ pp.84–5

Antoine de Beaupré
Philippe Morane

Japan: A Photo Theatre *is Daido Moriyama's first and most important book. It is representative of the raw, experimental work of the Provoke group of photographers, centred around the short-lived magazine of that name in the late 1960s and 1970s. The expressive, associative visual language of the photographs in the book draws the viewer in, revealing a deeper metaphorical meaning. The photo-historian Gerry Badger describes it as follows: 'The book's core was a series on theatre that Moriyama had made for the magazine* Camera Mainichi *called* Entertainers. *Moriyama … took these theatrical images and combined them brilliantly with images of other types of urban outsiders to make a metaphor of theatre-as-life, and of life-as-theatre. He sought the world of the hipster, the freak, the "other", from the avant-garde Terayama theatre group, which featured nude women, dwarfs and burlesque characters of all kinds, to the more vernacular nightlife of the city, the strip joints, gangster bars and backstreet Kabuki theatres, a fusion of the old and new, high and low, insider and outsider, freak and non-freak' (Martin Parr and Gerry Badger,* The Photobook: A History, *vol.1, 2004, p.288).*

After initial employment as a graphic designer, Daido Moriyama began a photographic apprenticeship in Takeji Iwamiya's studio in Kobe in 1959. In 1961 he moved to Tokyo to join the photographer's group VIVO, which was already about to break up. The work of Shomei Tomatsu was just as important an influence on his pictures as was William Klein's *New York*. From around 1965 Moriyama developed his rough snapshot aesthetic. He was member of *Provoke* magazine group, which published his photographs from second edition on (1969). In 1972 his books *Hunter* and *Bye Bye Photography* were published, the latter of which was particularly radical in its approach to photographic materiality. Since that time he has published numerous books and been involved in many group and solo exhibitions. Today he is regarded as one of the most influential Japanese photographers of the 1970s and 1980s, not just in Japan but also in the West.

Daido Moriyama: Retrospective since 1965, exh. cat., SK-Stiftung, Cologne 2007; Daido Moriyama: The Complete Works, Nishihara 2004; Daido Moriyama: Stray Dog, exh. cat., San Francisco Museum of Art, 1999.

Stefan Moses
b.1928 Liegnitz (now Legnica),
Poland, lives in Munich

Peggy Guggenheim, 1969, 23.5 × 29.7 cm
→ p.75

Collection Thomas Walther

This photo taken by Stefan Moses is of a blackboard on which Peggy Guggenheim had attached portraits, passport photographs and photo-studio images of herself, their stamps suggesting that they were used as official documents. The thirteen photographs span a period of about three decades, from her youth to her maturity. On the one hand, they are references to the eventful life of this famous muse, cultural patron and art collector, and, on the other, they reflect the changing face and self-perception of a woman as she ages.

– From the series ***Deutsche*** (Germans), since 1963 –

Elektrodenschweisser, Bochum (Electrode Welder), 1964

Werkzeugmacher (Toolmaker), Essen 1964

Korrosionsschutzarbeiter, Remscheid (Corrosion Worker), 1964

Each 32.8 × 27.5 cm, printed 2008
Fotografische Sammlung, Museum Folkwang, Essen

For his most renowned series Die Deutschen (Germans)*, which he began in 1963 while travelling through West Germany, Moses followed in the long tradition of por-trait photography by setting up makeshift studios on the streets or other public places. He photographed people in front of a light grey backdrop. These images formed a cross-section of society in that they presented different types and professions, which is reminiscent of August Sander's project, as well as the travelling studio of Irving Penn. After the fall of the Berlin wall, Moses continued his portrait photography in East Germany.*

Stefan Moses was a young apprentice when, after the Second World War, he was employed as a photographer by the National Theatre in Weimar. In 1950 he moved to Munich, where he worked as a photojournalist for newspapers and magazines. Ten years later he was employed at the magazine *Stern*, for which he did numerous reportages. A focus in his work at the time was cultural and political life in Western Germany. In the 1960s, he embarked on a number of Conceptual portrait cycles such as *Spiegelbilder* (Mirror Images), *Künstler machen Masken* (Artists Make Masks) and *Die großen Alten* (The Great Elderly). Moses probably took the photograph when he visited Guggenheim in Venice in 1969. The blackboard photograph is exemplary of Moses's interest in new photographic narratives and conceptual forms within portrait photography.

Ulrich Pohlmann und Matthias Harder (eds.), Stefan Moses. Die Monographie, Munich 2003.

Charles Nègre
1820 – 1880 Grasse, France

Les Ramoneurs en marche (Chimney Sweeps Walking), before May 1852,
15.9 × 21.7 cm
→ p.18

Salted paper
Musée Carnavalet-Histoire de Paris, Paris

Le Petit Chiffonnier (The Little Ragpicker), c.1851, 13.6 × 10.3 cm
→ p.224

Albumen print
Collection Thomas Walther

The photographic sketches that Charles Nègre made of chimney sweeps, ragpickers and hurdy-gurdy men in the early 1850s received wide critical acclaim from the nascent photo community. Essays in the magazine La Lumière *compared his calotypes to drawings by Rembrandt and paintings by Murillo. More than once, he staged his photographs on the patio and on the street in front of the house at Quai Bourbon where his studio was situated. Serving as a basis for his paintings and drawings, these early camera images exhibit a playful use of the still-fledgling medium, which is reflected in the unguarded look of the young ragpicker into the camera or in the staged movements of the chimney sweeps. During that time, his artistic interest in these kinds of characters was multifaceted and went alongside the picturesque description done by other painters and writers. In Baudelaire's poetry, the ragpicker was akin to the modern artist.*

Having received his artistic training in the studio of Paul Delaroche in the early 1840s, Charles Nègre began to work with the new medium of photography. Along with many of his artist friends and other important figures of Parisian intellectual life, he was a member of the Société Héliographique, the world's first photographic society, established in 1851. In addition to his genre scenes on the street he also recorded architecture and its details. Since he was not chosen as a photographer for the Mission Héliographique, which aimed to record France's monuments, he produced a series on Romanesque art in Southern France on his own account.

Françoise Heilbrun, Charles Nègre. Das photographische Werk, Munich 1988; Françoise Heilbrun and Philippe Néagu, Charles Nègre, Paris 1980; Charles Nègre, exh. cat., National Gallery of Canada, Ottawa 1976.

Helmut Newton (Helmut Neustädter)
1920 Berlin – 2004
Los Angeles

– Magazine works –

Courrèges, in *Vogue français*, March 1970, n.p.

Le point de vue de Vogue sur les collections (The Point of View of *Vogue* on the Collections), in *Vogue français*, Sept. 1971, pp.169–70

La Mode piégée (Fashion Caught in a Trap), in *Vogue français*, Oct. 1971, pp.190–1
→ p.104

Haute Couture 1975–1976, in *Vogue français*, Sept. 75, pp.144ff

Beauté Silhouette 1982 (Beautiful Silhouettes 1982), in *Vogue français*, Nov. 1981, pp.160–70
→ p.105

Femme ou surfemme (Woman or Super-woman), in *Vogue français*, Sept. 1977, pp.122–3

von Parish Kostümbibliothek. Abteilung des Münchner Stadtmuseums, Munich

Catherine Deneuve, 1983, C-print, 51 × 36 cm

Helmut Newton Foundation / Permanent Loan Staatliche Museen zu Berlin, Kunstbibliothek

'During my whole life as a photographer the printed page was my dynamo. I realised very early on that the most important factor would be to be published, with a by-line, and that to me was much more important than the money people would pay me for my pictures. Today, clients who commission me to photograph their advertising campaigns insist that I sign the work. In many ways, this is an insurance that I will only accept work that interests me. If any of these photographs end up on gallery or museum walls or in the possession of collectors, well, all the better, and I am delighted, but primarily these pictures are taken for a very definite purpose: to influence, to sell a product, in short for propaganda' (Pages from the Glossies, 1998, p.11). The magazine works from Vogue *stem from the 1970s, a decade in which the innocent youth of the swinging 60s yielded to more offensive and aggressive concepts, as shown in the* Big Nudes.

In 1938, Helmut Neustädter, a German Jew, fled from National Socialist Berlin to Singapore. From late 1936 to 1938 he had already received his initial training in the studio of the Berlin photographer Yva. From Singapore he went to Australia, married the actress June Brunell in 1948 and ran a photo studio. From 1961 onwards, he worked for the French edition of *Vogue* in Paris. This was when Newton, together with the magazine's creative directors, began to make a name for himself through his provocative photo series – whether appropriating the iconography of a secret-agent film, bringing a leopard into the studio, or citing a range of photographic styles. The explicit nudity in his photographic work attracted feminist critique, but, for others, Newton's women represented self-confident femininity. In addition to his fashion photographs, which were later published in numerous books, he created a large collection of scenic celebrity portraits.

The Best of Helmut Newton: aus dem photographischen Werk, exh. cat., Deichtorhallen Hamburg 2007; Helmut Newton, exh. cat., Neue Nationalgalerie, Berlin 2000; June Newton and Walter Keller (eds.), Helmut Newton: Pages from the Glossies, Facsimiles 1956–1998, Zurich 1998.

Ken Ohara
b.1942 Tokyo, lives in Glendale, California

– Book –

One, Tsukiji Shokan Publishing Co. Ltd, Tokyo, 1970, 26.7 × 22 cm, 492 pp., 496 black-and-white photographs

→ pp.86–7

Fotografische Sammlung, Museum Folkwang, Essen

For his book One, *Ken Ohara photographed pedestrians whom he met by chance in the streets and parks of New York during the 1960s. The book comprises close-up portraits of 496 individuals. The photographs were taken using a ring flash, which can be seen in the evenly lit faces and the pin-like reflexes in the eyes. This flat lighting and the uniform tight framing reduce the physiognomic and racial differences between Ohara's subjects, thus focusing attention on the generic qualities of the human face. Like a metaphor for New York as the melting pot, Ohara had chosen the proportions of the Manhattan phonebook as the format for* One.

Ken Ohara studied photography at the Nihon University in Tokyo and moved to New York in 1962. He was an assistant to both photographers Richard Avedon and Hiro and worked as a freelance photographer for *Harper's Bazaar* in later years. In the 1970s he produced several Conceptual portrait projects in which he experimented with aspects of seriality. His book *One* caused a sensation and led to his participation in the exhibition *New Japanese Photography* at the Museum of Modern Art, New York, in 1974. In the same year, he received a Guggenheim Fellowship grant. During the 1990s he worked on a series of portraits that referenced the long exposure times of the early days of photography and which were published in the book *With* (2005).

Ken Ohara. Erweiterte Portraitstudien seit 1970, exh. cat., Museum Folkwang, Essen, Städtische Galerie Wolfsburg, Münchner Stadtmuseum, Munich 2006; Ken Ohara, *ONE*, Tokyo 1970 (Facsimile reprint, Cologne 1997).

Cas Oorthuys
1908 Leiden, Netherlands – 1975 Amsterdam

Vlaglegging. Weteringplantsoente Amsterdam werd door de illegaliteit een vlag gelegd op plaats waar Nederlanders werden neergeschoten (The Resistance Lay a Flag on the Weteringsplantsoen in Amsterdam where Dutch People Had Been Killed), March 1945, 21.4 cm × 20.2 cm

→ p.58

Rijksmuseum, Amsterdam

In the sphere of photography, when the events, conflicts and wars of the twentieth century are captured, it is as if they are presented on a huge stage. Cas Oorthuys (Casparus Bernardus Oorthuijs) experienced the time of the German occupation of the Netherlands during the Second World War as an eye-witness. The blur in his photograph, realised on a plaza in Amsterdam in March 1945, suggests that he took it under conditions of great tension or perhaps candidly. It captures the moment when two figures hurriedly plant a flag to express resistance. Later, Oorthuys published this image in his book 1944–45: Het laatste jaar *(1944–45: The Last Year, 1970). Although twenty-five years had passed between the events photographed and the publication, the sequence of the images in the book still had great immediacy – an impressive document of the lasting trauma of occupation.*

Cas Oorthuys studied decorative arts and crafts at the School voor Bouwkunde, and later architecture at the Bouwkunde van de MTS in Haarlem. In 1930 he was employed as a draughtsman by the City of Amsterdam for two years and began working as an amateur photographer in 1933. A year later, he took over the advertising studio of his friend Cok de Graaff and from 1936 until early 1941 worked for the *Arbeiderspers* (Worker's Press) and freelanced as a reportage photographer for *Het Volk* and *Wij*. During the Second World War he produced portraits for forged passports, for which he was imprisoned in a concentration camp for three months. Between 1951 and 1965 he made over forty photo books about European countries and cities. His photographs were also included in the important exhibition *The Family of Man* (1955).

Willem van Zoetendaal (ed.), *Cas Oorthuys: Guaranteed Real Dutch, Congo*, Rotterdam 1992; Sybrand Hekking, *Cas Oorthuys fotograaf 1908–1975*, Amsterdam 1982; Cas Oorthuys, *Rotterdam. dynamische stad, 1950–1990*, Rotterdam 1959 (reprinted 1990).

Adrian Paci
b.1969 Shkoder, Albania, lives in Milan

– From the series **Back Home** –

Back Home 2, 2001, digital C-print, Diasec, 105 × 125 cm

→ p.126

Courtesy the artist and Galerie Peter Kilchmann, Zurich

In the series Back Home, *Adrian Paci photographed his Albanian friends, who – just like him – had left their homeland to make a new life for themselves as migrants in other European countries, many of them in Italy. Paci travelled to Albania and photographed their former houses. He then used each of these images as the basis for a large painted background, and asked each former owner to pose in front of it. In this sense, he was following in the tradition of studio photography, but he took it a step further: the backdrops do not depict an exchangeable, idealised landscape, but a 'memoryscape' of the life of the person portrayed.*

Adrian Paci studied at the Art Academy in Tirana, Albania. During the civil war of 1997 he moved to Italy with his family. His work is influenced by his autobiography, and this is reflected in the choice of individuals he depicts, and his interest in political shifts caused by war and migration. He also reveals the ways in which our lives are interconnected, and how we are shaped and conditioned by our environmental boundaries, as well as by the global socio-economic apparatus.

Still Moving UT: Adrian Paci, exh. cat., Museum am Ostwall, Dortmund 2007; Kurt Wettengl, *Adrian Paci*, Pirma 2007; *Adrian Paci*, exh. cat., Galleria Civica di Modena, Milan 2006.

Norman Parkinson
1913 London – 1990 West Indies

Wenda, Times Square, NYC, September 1949, Cibachrome, 61 × 50.5 cm, later print

→ p.73

Courtesy Norman Parkinson Archive

Norman Parkinson was one of the first to take fashion photography to the street in the 1940s. This picture shows the model and actress Wenda Rogerson, who is often present in his photographs, and who had become his wife two years earlier. The image was commissioned by American Vogue, *and was published on 1 September 1949. It was produced through double exposure: in the first image, the focus was on the model in the foreground, so that both she, and especially her clothes, were well lit. The second exposure focused on the neon signs on Broadway, and the irradiation caused by the shifting focus creates additional dynamics that underscore the pacey atmosphere of the urban scenery.*

As the assistant of a court photographer, Norman Parkinson was first trained in portrait photography before opening his own studio aged twenty-one. From 1935 to 1940 he worked for *Harper's Bazaar* and *The Bystander*. During the Second World War, he was a commissioned photographer for the British Air Force. From 1945 to 1960, he was employed as a photographer for *Vogue*, for whom he took not only fashion photographs, but also shots of many celebrities. From 1960 to 1964, he worked for the Queen, eventually becoming a court photographer.

Norman Parkinson: Portraits in Fashion, exh. cat., National Portrait Gallery, London 2004; *Norman Parkinson: Photographs 1935–1990*, exh. cat., National Portrait Gallery, London 1994; *Norman Parkinson: Fifty Years of Style and Fashion*, exh. cat., National Portrait Gallery, London 1981.

Martin Parr
b.1952 Epsom, England, lives in Bristol

– From the series **Autoportraits**, 1999–2001 –

Bangladesh, Dhaka, 36 × 32 cm

→ p.128, bottom right

Cuba, Havana, 57 × 47 cm

Holland Amsterdam, 35 × 31 cm

Thailand, Bangok, 33 × 28 cm

Singapore, New Ming Chun Photo Studio, 24 × 19 cm

Portugal, Santa Cruz, 30 × 25 cm

→ p.128, bottom middle

England, Tac Studios, London, 19 × 24 cm

→ p.128

Argentina, 15 × 20.5 cm

Italy, Rome, 11 × 9 cm

→ p.128, upper left

North Korea, 26 × 20.5 cm

→ pp.15, 128, bottom left

C-prints
© Martin Parr / Magnum Photos

In addition to creating his own documentary photography, Martin Parr is highly interested in the history and culture of the medium, a pursuit that can be seen in his series Autoportraits. *On countless travels, Parr had his picture taken in portrait studios and Photobooths, in improvised studios and by street photographers in amusement parks, at tourist sights, beaches and airports. This resulted in an amusing and sometimes bizarre collection of images, where Parr poses with a friendly smile against the backdrop of the diverse sceneries with which photographers worldwide try to improve the originality of their offer and the image we have of ourselves. 'As different as they are, one from the next, these portraits reveal more about photography and contemporary culture than they do about Martin Parr' (Marvin Heifermann, 'In His Own Image', in* Autoportrait, *2000, n.p.).*

Martin Parr studied photography at Manchester Polytechnic, his interest in the medium having been encouraged from a young age by his grandfather, a keen amateur photographer. In 1975 Parr was given an award for his work *Home Sweet Home* by the Arts Council of Great Britain. Very early, he broke with the tradition of black and white photojournalism, and in 1982 he began working exclusively in colour, often using an additional fill-in flash. In this sense, his work stands in stark contrast to that of many of his colleagues at the photo agency Magnum; Parr was admitted to the agency after a long debate in 1994. His documentary work is marked by its ironic view of everyday behaviour in Western consumer societies, and has been published in numerous books, such as *The Cost of Living* (1989) and *Home and Abroad* (1993). His many activities attest to his broad interest in popular photography and photographic culture: he has published anthologies of found images such as *Boring Postcards* (1999), as well as a two-volume history of the photo book (with texts by Gerry Badger).

Val Williams, *Martin Parr*, London 2002; Martin Parr, *The Last Resort*, Stockport 1998 (first ed. 1986); Martin Parr, *Small World*, Heidelberg 1995.

Irving Penn
b.1917 New Jersey, lives in New York

– From the series **Small Trades**, Paris, 1950 –

Les Garçons-Bouchers (Butcher's Boys), 32.6 × 24.8 cm, printed 1951

Le Marchand de concombres (Cucumber Seller), 33.6 × 25.3 cm, printed 1951

→ p.63

Le Balayeur de rue (Street Sweeper), 34.2 × 23.8 cm, printed 1951

Télégraphiste (Telegraphist), platinum print 48 × 35.9 cm, printed 1976

Le Vitrier (Glazer), platinum print, 43 × 27.6 cm, printed 1976

Les Pâtissiers (Pastry Cooks), platinum print, 49.8 × 36.7 cm, printed 1976

Rempailleurs (Chair-rushers), platinum print, 34.9 × 32.6 cm, printed 1976

Musée Carnavalet-Histoire de Paris, Paris

– From the series **Small Trades**, New York, 1950 –

Portrait of a Street Photographer, 1951–2, 43.2 × 40.6 cm

Courtesy Pace/MacGill Gallery New York

'I began an extended series of photographs of workmen and people in the Small Trades for Vogue *in Paris in the summer of 1950. During the vacation months, it was possible to rent the daylight studio of an old photography school on the top floor of a house on the Rue Vaugirard. As the studio was also a school classroom in the disappearing subject of daylight photography, it came close to the ideal of what such a studio should be' (Irving Penn,* Worlds in a Small Room, *p.16). In the course of that year, Penn also continued the series* Small Trades *in London and New York. For more than twenty-five years, he realised projects as an ambulant studio photographer, beginning in the Peruvian city Cusco in 1948. Worldwide, Penn invited various ethnic groups and tribes (among others in Morocco, New Guinea and Cameroon) in front of the camera of his improvised daylight studios.*

In 1936, Irving Penn began his studies at the Philadelphia School of Industrial Art under Alexey Brodovitch, whom he assisted at *Harper's Bazaar* in 1937 and 1938. After initially having worked as designer, he started to do commissioned photographic work for *Vogue* in 1943 and continues to do so today. Parallel to this, he began a close cooperation with the editorial director Alexander Liberman, which has lasted for more than fifty years. As well as the ambulant studio photography, he became famous for his portraits, in particular his novel staging of well-known characters, as well as his fashion photography. His images of Lisa Fonssagrives, his favourite model and later his wife, influenced the fashion photography of the 1950s. His minimal object and still-life photography revolutionised applied commercial photography in the 1950s and 1960s.

Irving Penn, *Objects for the Printed Page*; Göttingen 2002; Irving Penn, *Worlds in a Small Room*, New York 1974; Irving Penn, *Moments Preserved*, New York 1970.

Photobooth / Photomaton

120 photographs of **German Women**, 1928–45

→ p.52

Sulphur silver prints, varying sizes 5.1 × 3.8 cm
Günter Karl Bose, Berlin

In 1925 the Russian immigrant Anatol Josepho received the US Patent Number 16656995 for a 'coin-in-the-slot-machine which would automatically photograph the sitter, develop the photographs, dry them and deliver them'. When, two years later, he sold the patent for $1,000 to a group of investors led by the banker Henry Morganthau, the history of Photomaton Inc. began. The machines that were initially set up in New York's theatre district quickly spread to all large cities across the USA. As early as 1928, the cubicles began to appear in Europe, the first among them in Berlin. After a wait of eight minutes, the customers received a strip of eight pictures, which they could cut up and use as they pleased. The images created were no longer the result of the photographer's inspiration or judgement, but were the product of the human subject interacting with the technical apparatus. The process of Photobooth portraiture abolished the separation between subject and object inherent in the photographic act, and posing face to face with the mirroring glass thus represented a moment of self-objectification. At the same time, this new technique invited a playful means of both portraying and inventing oneself, which was exploited by the French Surrealists. Since the late 1950s, various artists have used the Photobooth cubicle as an intimate platform for their photographic work. In 1989, Andy Warhol's legendary Photobooth Pictures *were exhibited in New York for the first time in their entirety.*

Nakki Goranin, David Haberstich, *American Photobooth*, New York 2008; Babette Hines, *Photobooth*, New York 2002; *Andy Warhol: Photobooth Pictures*, exh. cat., Robert Miller Gallery, New York 1989; Bern Boyle and Linda Duchin, *Photomaton: A Contemporary Survey of Photobooth Art*, Rochester, New York 1987; Klaus Maas and Ellen Maas, 'Das Photomaton', in *Fotogeschichte 1*, Frankfurt 1981, pp.60–72.

Richard Prince
b.1949 Panama Canal Zone, lives in New York

Untitled (The Same Man Looking in Different Directions), 1978, Three C-prints, each 50.8 × 61 cm

→ p.106

Courtesy Gladstone Gallery, New York

The source material of Untitled (The Same Man Looking in Different Directions) *consisted of three different advertising photographs, which Prince re-photographed, enlarged, and then combined, in order to make visible the constructs of advertising and consumerism. The title refers to the different directions in which the man is looking, ironically ignoring the more obvious feature of the original images: the stereotypical worlds of business quarter, exclusive interior and marina that surround him. These might well be faked worlds, back-projected in a photo studio.*

Richard Prince reflects on the visual and symbolic world of American consumer society and vernacular culture. In the latter half of the 1970s he developed his 'rephotography' – the photographic reproduction of published magazines images – as a method of appropriating images and putting them into a new context. Of these, his *Cowboys*, images of the Marlboro Man, are his most famous. Prince also adopts popular photography as found in biker magazines. In the mid-1980s he took up painting again, and a recurrent subject is jokes presented against a monochrome background. Prince is considered a central figure of postmodern appropriation art. His work has been shown recently in his retrospective *Spiritual America* at the Guggenheim Museum, New York (2007).

Richard Prince, exh. cat., Guggenheim Museum, New York 2007; Michael Newmann, *Richard Prince (Untitled)*, London 2006; *Richard Prince, Photographien*, exh. cat., Kestner Gesellschaft, Hanover 1994; *Richard Prince: Untitled*, exh. cat., Barbara Gladstone Gallery, New York 1988.

Timm Rautert
b.1941 Tuchel (now Tuchola), Poland, lives in Essen

– From the series **Deutsche in Uniform** (Germans in Uniform), 1974 –

Herr Kurt Bischoff, 29 Jahre, Oberfeldwebel (Mr Kurt Bischoff, 29 Years Old, First Sergeant)

→ p.100, left

Fräulein Dorothee Oppermann, 20 Jahre, Schwesternschülerin (Miss Dorothee Oppermann, 20 Years Old, Nursing Student)

→ p.100, right

Herr Bernhard Weichselgartner, 36 Jahre, Verkehrsmeister, Kontrolleur bei der Rheinischen Bahngesellschaft AG, Düsseldorf (Mr Bernhard Weichselgartner, 36 Years Old, Traffic Master, Inspector of the Rhein Course Company AG, Düsseldorf)

C-prints, each 29 × 32 cm, printed 1990s
Courtesy galerieKleindienst, Leipzig

'The choice of uniforms as a subject has no immediate link to [August] Sander, but it was important to explore Sander's principle. However, I was interested in Germanness too, otherwise I would have called my series "people". I was attracted by the attitude that I saw in uniform wearers: that people feel safe in their uniforms. I did not want to disturb this sense of security. The uniform became somehow touching in this way. For all the similarity and clarity in the pictures – at least I hope so – you can still see that one person sees another person' (Timm Rautert in conversation with Wolfgang Brückle, Camera Austria, *no.98, 2007, n.p.). The thirty-three photographs comprising the series* Germans in Uniform *were taken in the photographer's studio in Düsseldorf in 1974. A selection of these images was published in an edition of Zeit magazine (3 July 1975).*

From 1966 to 1971 Timm Rautert studied photography with Otto Steinert at the Folkwang School in Essen. In addition to independent projects, such as his *Picture-analytical Photography* (1968–74), he worked as a photojournalist in the 1970s and early 1980s. His collaboration with the journalist Michael Holzach resulted in numerous reportages for *Zeit* magazine. The focus of his work is the human being, be it in the situational context of reportage or in the classic portrait genre. The changing world of work is another recurrent theme, as exemplified by his book *Gehäuse des Unsichtbaren* (Housing of the Invisible) 1992. Since the mid-1990s, Rautert has been working on the series *Koordinaten* (Coordinates) and *Artwork*, both of which can be seen as an extension of his 'picture-analytical interest'. From 1993 to 2007, Rautert taught photography at the Academy of Visual Arts in Leipzig.

Timm Rautert, *Deutsche in Uniform 1974*, Göttingen 2006; Timm Rautert, *When We Don't See You, You Don't See Us Either: Photography 1966–2006*, Göttingen 2007; Wolfgang Brückle and Timm Rautert, 'Der Mensch: Erscheinung und Verschwinden', in *Camera Austria*, no.98, 2007, pp.24–37.

Henri Rivière
1864 Paris – 1951
Sucy-en-Brie, France

– From a series of street scenes, Paris 1885–95 –

Passagers sur l'impériale d'un omnibus (Passengers on the Upper Deck of a Bus), 9 × 12 cm (London only)

Personnages, deux chiens et voitures à impériale sur le pont du Louvre (People, Two Dogs and Cars on the Louvre Bridge, 9 × 12 cm (London only)

Un Couple rentrant dans un bâtiment public (A Couple Entering a Public Building), 9 × 12 cm (London only)

→ p.19

Femmes portant de grands paniers, quartiers des Halles (Women Carrying Large Baskets in Les Halles), 9 × 12 cm (London only)

Madame Rivière marchant en compagnie de deux chiens devant la gare Saint-Lazare (Madame Rivière Walking Accompanied by Two Dogs in Front of Saint-Lazare Train Station), 12 × 9 cm (Essen only)

Madame Rivière portant un fardeau sur l'épaule, marchant dans une rue (Madame Rivière Carrying a Load on her Shoulders, Shopping in the Street, 12 × 9 cm (Essen only)

Personnages assis sur des banc publics (People Sitting on Benches), 12 × 9 cm (Essen only)

Personnages de dos marchant sur le pont de l'Alma (People from behind Walking on the Alma Bridge), 9 × 12 cm (Essen only)

Musée d'Orsay, Paris

The photographs that Henri Rivière took between 1885 and 1895 on the streets of Paris are full of urban atmosphere. The introduction of fast gelatine silver plates at the beginning of the 1880s permitted the photographing of moving subjects – passers-by, market-women, omnibuses and carriages. Rivière's pictures, cut out of the perceptive flow correspond to the en passant observation of the flâneur. They represent the contingent constellations of the street, where blurred figures – casting long shadows or appearing as sillhouettes against the backlight – are only half shown or conceal each other.

Henri Rivière made his entry into the art world in 1882, when he became a member of the editorial staff of *Le Chat Noir*, journal of the bohemian Montmatre cabaret of the same name. From 1886 to 1896, he staged more than forty shadow theatre plays for *Cabaret du Chat Noir* using painted colour backdrops. As an artist who later made a name for himself with woodcuts, etchings and lithographs in the Japanese style, he probably did not consider his photographs to be of artistic value in their own right. He was interested in the medium as a document, the basis of other images for, for broadening the perception of modern life. Around 350 of his photographs have been preserved and are now located in the Musée d'Orsay.

Henri Rivière, graveur et photographe, exh. cat., Musée d'Orsay, Paris 1988.

Thomas Ruff
b.1958 Zell am Hammersbach,
Germany, lives in Düsseldorf

Portraits, 1981–5, forty C-prints, each 24 × 18 cm
→ pp.108–9

Fotografische Sammlung, Museum Folkwang, Essen

'With the portrait series, I wanted to create a gallery of my generation – I wanted to make a whole lot of images and 24 × 18 cm seemed to be a good format for that. In between, I tried to enlarge the portraits on a scale of 1:1 but didn't like it in comparison with reality … In 1986 I had the money to produce three really big photographs and that convinced me. It was not just a "blow up" from a small image, but an entirely new image' (Thomas Ruff in conversation with Ute Eskildsen, Thomas Ruff, 2001, p.166). Thomas Ruff started working in the portrait genre with a small standardised print format and a correspondingly conventional portrait format: the ID photo. The first series of forty portraits, which plays with the idea of representation by portraying Ruff's generation in the Düsseldorf art world of the 1980s, already suggested what would become the characteristic of his later works: the suppression of any psychological dimension. In these later works, faces are presented on large surfaces (mostly 210 × 165 cm).

Ruff began his studies at the Düsseldorf Art Academy in 1977, and in 1978 was admitted into the class of Bernd Becher, where he worked on his first series *Interieurs* (Interiors). In 1986–7, his international breakthrough came with his large-format portraits. At the same time, he was also working on the series *Häuser* (Houses). Since then, he has investigated various aspects of photographic culture, whether producing the photographs himself, appropriating them from elsewhere or digitally retouching them. His series reflect diverse technical and scientific modes of seeing (*Stars, Nights, Stereo Photographs*), social usages (*Other Portraits, Blue Eyes*), the published image (*Newspaper Photos*), the history of photography and art (*l.m.d.r., Machines, Poster*) and the internet (*Nudes, Substrat*). Together with other graduates of the Becher class, Ruff established a new type of the photo artist.

Thomas Ruff, *Fotografien 1979 – heute*, Cologne 2001; *Thomas Ruff*, exh. cat. Essor Gallery, London 2001; Thomas Ruff, *Nudes*, Munich 2003.

August Sander
1876 Herdorf, Germany –
1964 Cologne

– From his project on the **People of the Twentieth Century** –

Hotelpersonal (Rezeption) in Hamburg (Hotel Reception Staff in Hamburg), 1928, 27.7 × 20.5 cm, reprint 1982

Erwerbslose in Hamburg (Unemployed People in Hamburg), 1928, 28.8 × 20.6 cm, reprint 1976

Kriegsinvalider (War Invalid), 1928, 28.7 × 20.1 cm, reprint 1982

Drehorgelspieler in Wien (Organist in Vienna), 1930, 28.8 × 22.1 cm, reprint 1976

Waschfrau in Wien (Washerwoman in Vienna), 1930, 27.7 × 21.3 cm, reprint 1982

Arbeiterkinder, Köln (Worker's Children, Cologne), 1932, 27.7 × 22 cm, reprint 1982

→ pp.53, 210

Fotografische Sammlung, Museum Folkwang, Essen

'People of the Twentieth Century (A Culture Work in Photographs) by August Sander, Cologne Lindenthal, divided into seven sections, arranged by profession and comprising of 45 portfolios with 12 photographs each' – this was the title that, according to a concept of 1925–7, August Sander wanted to give his ambitious work, which was to form a picture of German society through portrait photographs. According to the reconstruction of Sander's monumental project by Gunther Sander and Ulrich Keller (1980), the six photographs presented here come from portfolios in Section VI, The City: portfolio 40, Youth of the City; portfolio 41, Servants; and portfolios 42 and 43, Figures of the City. In Sander's cyclic model of society, the metropolis stands for the decline of civilisation.

After having learned the photographer's craft and spending some years wandering across Germany, August Sander worked in a portrait studio in Linz, Austria. In 1909 he moved to Cologne, where he ran a studio in the neighbourhood of Lindenthal until the destruction of the city in 1944. Even the portraits that he took outside his studio were characterised by the static poses of his subjects. From the beginning of the 1920s he was in contact with the Group of Progressive Artists and began to conceive an outstanding collection of German types. This resulted in the publication of *Face of our Time* in 1929, containing sixty photographs, which was widely received and controversially discussed. During the era of National Socialism, the portrait project came to a halt. Sander took extensive series of landscape photographs along the river Rhine and architectural photographs in Cologne. His work was rehabilitated and honoured in the 1950s and 1960s. He is considered a central point of reference for documentary-style photography.

Susanne Lange and Gabriele Conrath-Scholl (eds.), *August Sander, Menschen des 20. Jahrhunderts*, Cologne 2001; Olivier Lugon, *Le style documentaire. D'August Sander à Walker Evans, 1920–1945*, Paris 2001; Gunther Sander (ed.), *August Sander, Menschen des 20. Jahrhunderts*, Munich 1980.

Friedrich Seidenstücker
1882 Unna, Germany – 1966
Berlin

Zwei Arbeiter beim Asphaltieren der Straßenbahnschienen (Two Workers Asphalting the Tram Rails)

Zertrümmerung alter Bordsteine (Smashing of Kerbstones)

→ p.43

Aufstemmen des betonierten Straßenbelages (Prying Open Concrete Pavement)

→ p.43

Straßenarbeiter beim Steineschaufeln (Roadmen Stone Shovelling)

→ p.43

Kohlenträger beim Transport des Koks für das Gaswerk (Coal Heaver at the Coke Transport for the Gasworks)

Kokslieferung (Coke Delivery)

→ p.43

Transportarbeiter beim Nickerchen auf seinem mit einem riesigen Koffer beladenen Handkarren (Transport Worker Taking a Nap on a Handcart Loaded with a Gigantic Suitcase)

Schaufensterputzer (Window Cleaner)

Each 18 × 13 cm, printed 1930s

Bildarchiv Preussischer Kulturbesitz, Berlin / F. Seidenstücker

Among the countless photographs that Friedrich Seidenstücker took of everyday scenes in Berlin in the 1920s and 1930s is a number depicting diverse professions and occupations. The roadworker for instance – being one of the emblematic heroes of modernism, for paving roads was an important premise for the acceleration of modern life – is shown in Seidenstücker's photographs performing the different activities of his profession. Seidenstücker paid special attention to a concise depiction of the gestures of work. This is where he differs from other photographers, who focused on the form of the portrait when photographing characters of the street. These images were often used for illustrating reports on aspects of public life in newspapers and magazines and derive from countless walks through the metropolis by this quiet and humorous observer. He was especially drawn to the young modern woman. Seidenstücker's keen perception was sharpened by his continuous photographic activity in the zoological garden of Berlin.

In 1904, Seidenstücker moved to Berlin in order to continue his engineering studies. Within a year, he was studying sculpture at the Royal Academy of Fine Arts in Berlin. Disrupted by various study visits, jobs and military service, his studies continued from 1919 to 1923. In the beginning of his stay in Berlin, he discovered his passion for photography, with which he had already experimented in his childhood. From 1923 to 1929, he worked as a freelance sculptor and photographer, taking up in1930 to 1939 assignments from Ullstein Bilderdienst. After the war, he took many photographs of the destroyed Berlin. In the 1970s, Seidenstücker was rediscovered by photo historians as an important chronicler of the interwar years.

Antje Schunke, *Friedrich Seidenstücker. Zwischen Ruinen und Vergangenheit – Berliner Fotografien 1945–50*, Goethe-Institut, Nancy 2007; *Friedrich Seidenstücker, Der humorvolle Blick. Fotografien 1923–1957*, exh. cat., Sprengel Museum, Hanover, 1997; *Der faszinierende Augenblick. Fotografien von Friedrich Seidenstücker*, ed. Bildarchiv Preussischer Kulturbesitz, Berlin 1987.

Bruno Serralongue
b.1968 Châtellerault, France, lives in Paris

Manifestations du collectif des sans-papiers de la Maison des Ensembles, place du Châtelet, Paris (Demonstrations of the Maison des Ensembles Group of Immigrants, Place du Châtelet, Paris), 2001–3, 28 individual photographs, first part of a series of 45, Cibachrome, each 31.5 × 39.5 cm
→ pp.120–1

Collection Frac Nord-Pas de Calais, Dunkerque, France

'Demonstrations by the Maison des Ensembles group of immigrants who are denied proper legal recognition, began in 1999. Since then, every Thursday and Saturday from 17.00 to 19.00, they marched around the fountain of the Place du Châtelet, with a banner calling for regularisation of all immigrants in their position … The first photo is dated September 8th 2001. The last photo [was] taken on January 11th 2003. The series includes 45 photographs' (cf. www. airdeparis.com/artists), These kind of events, which Bruno Serralongue photographed over the course of sixteen months, are generally mentioned little in official press coverage. His persistent observation of the ongoing demonstrations highlights how current events are either exposed or concealed by the media.

In the 1990s, Bruno Serralongue studied photography and fine art at the Ecole Nationale de la Photographie in Arles and at the Villa Arson in Nice. Since then, he has been pursuing a documentary approach in many works, which has helped to bring the event, a classic subject of photography, back into contemporary photography

– not as a 'decisive moment', but rather as a political and social category. He works like a commissioned photojournalist, but with a different approach. He combines a conceptual attitude with an anachronistic style of documentary, using a large-format camera to attain a more deliberate perspective.

Bruno Serralongue, *Rapport de Forces*, Paris 2004; Bruno Serralongue, *Spillover*, Chatou 2004; *Bruno Serralongue*, exh. cat., Centre National de la Photographie, Paris 2002.

Andres Serrano
b.1950, lives in New York

– From the series ***Nomads***, 1990 –
John Paul
→ pp.113, 204
Pete
Gussie
→ p.5

Cibachrome, silicone, Plexiglas, each 152.4 × 125.7 cm
© Andres Serrano. Courtesy of the artist and Paula Cooper Gallery, New York

Andres Serrano's series Nomads *was first exhibited in the gallery Stux, New York, in November 1990. It comprises thirteen stately, large-format portraits that the artist took in the New York subway in an improvised studio. His models were homeless people, among them numerous Afro-Americans – poverty stricken, shadowy figures who often remain unseen. It is symptomatic of Serrano's provocative methods that he exhibits this series together with photographs of seven masked members of the Ku Klux Klan. 'The idea of showing the Klan and the homeless pictures together was exciting. I like the tension between the two. They are about extreme poverty and extreme prejudice … [T]he average gallery-goer is probably somewhere in the middle, and he has to reconcile his feelings for one group with his feelings for the other.' (Andres Serrano in conversation with Coco Fusco, www.communityarts. net/readingroom/archivefiles/2002/09/shooting_the_kl.php, 26 February 2008)*

Between 1967 and 1969, Andres Serrano attended the Brooklyn Museum Art School. From the beginning, he included within his images topics and objects from Christian iconography, whose combination with bodily fluids like blood and urine (*Piss Christ*, 1987) caused considerable cultural conflict in the United States during the 1990s. Another series commenting on a different urban aspect, *The Morgues*, also provoked controversy. The images in his subsequent body of work, *A History of Sex*, 1996 combine the explicit depiction of physicality, sexuality and age with the classical form of the tableau. His latest project, *America*, is an extensive collection of studio photographs depicting a diverse range of American characters.

Andres Serrano, *America and Other Work*, Cologne 2004; Andres Serrano, *Body and Soul*, New York 1995.

Cindy Sherman
b.1954 Glen Ridge, New Jersey, lives in New York

– From the series ***Bus Riders***, 1976 –
#2, #4, #6, #7, #9, #10, #13, #14, #15
each 25.4 × 20.3 cm, printed in 2000
→ p.107

Hamburger Kunsthalle

In Cindy Sherman's series Bus Riders, *viewers of today can sense that here is a young and still unknown artist*

who is starting to develop a method of working through playful experimentation. Shortly after graduating from art school in 1976, Sherman converted her artist's studio into a photo studio. In front of a white wall, she photographed various characters whom she had seen on public transport – but her only model was herself, impersonating them all. In these images, Sherman's love of popular culture and everyday topics, as well as her keen sense of observation, are already evident. The absorption of the passengers – who represent a social class not privileged enough to own a car – is emulated with great attention to detail. Sherman does not try to conceal the fact that these images are taken in a makeshift studio setting, which emphasises the typological character of the images.

Cindy Sherman, who studied painting at Buffalo State College, used the camera initally only in documenting her extensive role-playing, an activity she already engaged in as a child. Her work *Untitled (Film Stills)* (1977–9), the early series *Bus Riders and Mystery Murder People* (1976), were internationally acclaimed, leading to her first solo exhibition at the Museum of Contemporary Art in Houston. Her work is thematically extremely diverse, and it has often been read as a comment on the (de-)construction of femininity. Today, she remains the only protagonist in her work, making use in her elaborate and complex stagings of props such as dolls and artificial limbs. With her *Sex Pictures* (1992), she commented on the controversy surrounding the censorship of an exhibition of Richard Mapplethorpe's photographs by the NEA (National Endowment for the Arts). Sherman's works are paradigmatic of the postmodern practice of staged photography.

Cindy Sherman: A Retrospective, exh. cat., Museum of Contemporary Art, Los Angeles 2006; Johanna Burton (ed.), *Cindy Sherman*, Cambridge, Mass. 2006; *Early Work of Cindy Sherman*, exh. cat., New York 2000; David Frankel (ed.), *Cindy Sherman: The Complete Untitled Film Stills*, New York 2003.

Malick Sidibé
b.1935 Soloba, Mali, lives in Bamako

– From his ***studio portrait photographs*** –
Monsieur Dembelé agent secret (Monsieur Dembelé Secret Agent), 1964
→ p.80
Voici ma montre et ma bague (Here Are my Watch and my Ring), 1964
L'Amateur surnommé Kala (The Amateur Nicknamed Kala), April 1966

Modern prints from the original negatives, uncropped, each 28 × 28 cm
Gwin Zegal, St Brieuc

Immediately after opening in 1962, Malick Sidibé's studio became one of the most popular portrait studios in Bamako. The majority of its clients were young people, proud of their new social status and possessions, which, for many citizens of the new capital, came with Mali's independence in 1960.

– From his ***portraits at dance evenings*** (Les Chemises [hanging folders]) –
Babengo Club, Médina Coura, 26-12-64, 1964

Soirée Mariage, Seydou Doumbia, 2-11-68 (Evening Wedding, Seydou Doumbia, 2-11-68), 1968

Nuit du 31-12-69 (Night of 31-12-69), 1969

Nuit du 16-9-72 (Night of 16-9-72), 1972

Each 32 × 48 cm
Fotografische Sammlung, Museum Folkwang, Essen

Nuit du 1-1-73 (Night of 1-1-73), 1973
Nuit du 7-7-73 (Night of 7-7-73), 1973

Each 32 × 48 cm
Gwin Zegal, St Brieuc

At the same time, Sidibé also photographed Bamako's young people dancing or posing with friends at parties in private houses and in small clubs. As early as the following day, guests and partygoers were able to order their portraits by choosing from photographs attached to hanging folders. Encouraged by the success of his portraits taken as an intinerant photographer at official evenings or parties

After an apprenticeship as a jeweller at an arts and crafts school in Bamako, Malick Sidibé, son of Malian peasants, learned the photographic trade under a French photographer who operated a studio in Bamako. Encouraged by the success of his portraits taken as an intinerant photographer at official evenings or parties, he opened his own *Studio Malick* in 1962. Until the emergence of amateur and colour photography and the introduction of mini-labs at the end of the 1970s, Sidibé worked as portrait photographer, after which he moved into camera repair. On the occasion of the photography festival *Rencontres africaines de la photographie* in Bamako in 1994, his photographs, as well as those of his older fellow countryman and friend Seydou Keïta, were rediscovered. In 2007, Sidibé was awarded the Golden Lion at the Venice Biennale for lifetime achievement.

Chemises, Göttingen, St Brieuc 2008; *Malick Sidibé – André Magnin*, Zurich 1998; *Malick Sidibé – Bamako 1962–1976*, exh. cat., Fondation Cartier pour l'art contemporain, Paris 1995.

Camille Silvy
1834 Nogent-le-Rotrou – 1910 Saint-Maurice, France

Declaration. L'Ordre du jour de l'Empereur à l'armée pour aller en Italie, Paris (Declaration. The Emperor's Order of the Day for the Army for Italy, Paris), 1859, Albumen silver print, 25.7 × 18.8 cm

→ p.17

Collection Thomas Walther

The men who have gathered around the poster are pointing demonstratively at the posted news, as if unable to believe what they are seeing. The man on the far right has already grasped the message, and another is affirming his solidarity by placing his hands on the shoulders of the man standing in front. Camille Silvy's photograph was taken in connection with the Austro-Sardinian war of 1859. However, the picture does not really show the first reaction to the Emperor's order, in the sense of a natural snapshot, which would not have been possible due to the long exposure time required for images in those days. It is a choreographed photograph of an event, a staged picture of what the reaction of these men might have been.

Camille Silvy initially studied law before becoming a diplomat. He took up photography after a visit to Algeria, and in the 1850s was involved in both landscape photography and genre portraits such as his image of two young musicians in the street. As a 'paysagiste' he already revealed a certain pre-Impressionist sensibility for atmospheric effects. In 1859, he moved to London, where he ran a large studio in Porchester Terrace, Hyde Park. As far as portrait photography was concerned, he specialised in exquisite *cartes de visite*, the invention of his countryman André-Adolphe-Eugène Disdéri. In the late 1870s, he returned to France.

Mark Haworth-Booth, *Camille Silvy: River Scene, France*, Malibu 1992.

Giorgio Sommer (Friedrich Sommer)
1834 Frankfurt – 1914 Naples

Mangiatori di maccheroni, Napoli (Macaroni Eaters, Naples), c.1885, albumen print, 24.2 × 18 cm

→ p.22

Dietmar Siegert Collection

Macaroni Eaters was one of the most popular subjects of the Neapolitan scenes that Giorgio Sommer staged in his studio. Exclusively composed for the camera, the folkloric genre pictures he constructed against neutral backgrounds – of chestnut-sellers, knife-grinders, cobblers, water-sellers, guttersnipes and petty thieves – bear little relation to real events on the street. Being an accomplished businessman as well as a talented photographer, Sommer had his eye on tourists and their appetite for the picturesque types of street life in Naples, images of which proved much sought-after souvenirs even in the form of staged studio photography.

Not much is known about the early life of Giorgio Sommer. He was born Friedrich Sommer in Frankfurt, and discovered the new medium of photography after having completed a merchant apprenticeship. After 1856–7, he worked in Italy. Together with his partner Edmondo Behles, he opened a studio in Rome and from the 1860s maintained a studio in Naples. From there he went on photographic excursions to the North as well as through Mezzogiorno and Sicily. The Vesuvius district was interesting for him in many respects: its architecture, its inhabitants, its antiquities, the excavations at Pompeii, the landscape near the Gulf and not least Vesuvius itself, whose eruption in 1872 he documented in striking images.

Giorgio Sommer in Italien. Fotografien 1857–1888, exh. cat., Fotomuseum im Münchener Stadtmuseum, Munich 1992.

Edward Steichen
1879 Luxemburg – 1973 West Redding, Connecticut

Jack Donahue, 1928, 24 × 19 cm

→ p.49

Walter Winchell, 1929, 24.1 × 19.1 cm

Frank Lloyd Wright, c.1932, 24 × 19.2 cm

Fotografische Sammlung, Museum Folkwang, Essen

An inscription in the margin of the photographic portrait of Jack Donahue, a contact sheet from a large-format glass negative, reads: 'Vanity Fair. Jan. 24. 1928'. Donahue was a Broadway actor, forgotten today. The archives of Broadway list the world premiere of the musical Rosalie as taking place on 10 January 1928, Donahue playing one of the leading roles. Very likely, the image was published in the magazine Vanity Fair shortly after the premiere, communicating the event to a broad audience. This picture is one of countless portrait and fashion photographs that Edward Steichen produced for the Condé Nast publishing house in the 1920s and 1930s, introducing the visual language of modernism to Vogue and Vanity Fair. Simple geometrical forms and clear outlines structure the largely empty stage of the studio; the use of directed electric light stages the models in front of the camera.

Edward Steichen's professional career reflects the changing roles of the photographic medium from its early claim to art to its later pretention as a universal visual language. After a two-year stay in Paris, Steichen, who worked in advertising but had ambitions as a painter and had taught himself photography, opened a portrait studio at 291 Fifth Avenue, New York, in 1902 where Alfred Stieglitz's renowned gallery, 291, opened three years later. In the 1910s, Steichen and Stieglitz were two of the leading spokesmen for Pictorialist photography. At the end of the First World War, Captain Steichen – he had joined the US Army Air Service in July 1917 – was head of the photographic aerial reconnaissance. In 1923, as successor to Baron Adolf de Meyer, he became head of photography at Condé Nast in New York. With the rising significance of photography in magazines, Steichen increased his output of portraits of celebrities from the worlds of politics, culture and sport, as well as fashion and advertising photography. In his later curatorial career he dedicated himself to the ambitious exhibition project. As the head of the photographic department at the Museum of Modern Art, New York, he conceived the famous touring exhibition *Family of Man*, widely acclaimed by an international public but criticised by some for its simplistic Western vision of the world.

Steichen, une épopée photographique, exh. cat., Jeu de Paume, Paris 2007.

Otto Steinert
1915 Saarbrücken, Germany – 1978 Essen

Ein-Fuß-Gänger (One-Legged Pedestrian), 1950, 28.5 × 39 cm

Gallery Kicken, Berlin

Appell (Roll Call), 1950, 60 × 47 cm

→ p.66

Private Collection, Montana, USA

Both Roll Call and One-Legged Pedestrian were taken in Paris in 1950; both experiment with exposure time. Yet the mood of each of these two iconic images by Otto Steinert is entirely different: one is surrealistic and uncanny in nature and the other formal and precise. For Steinert, Paris at the beginning of the 1950s seemed the appropriate place to continue and to reconcile the diverse tendencies of the New Photography of the 1920s. From the German point of view – after the interruption by the Nazis – the formal inventions of the avant-garde presented still a fertile laboratory of modernism. Rather than depicting the reality of the city, Steinert instead takes the street as a vantage point from which to experiment with these different approaches.

In 1947 the medical doctor and enthusiastic amateur photographer Otto Steinert decided to open a Studio for Fine Art Photography in Saarbrücken. A year later, he became professor of the public School for Arts and Crafts. Together with three young like-minded photographers, he founded the influential group fotoforum in 1949. Its exhibition *Subjektive Fotografie* (Subjective Photography), two years later, was highly influential for European photographers. Steinert's most important photographs originate from the early 1950s, many of which were taken in Paris. Besides his photographic practice, Steinert was a successful teacher, firstly in Saarbrücken until 1959 and later in Essen. With his collection of prints he laid the foundation for the Fotografische Sammlung at the Museum Folkwang in Essen.

Otto Steinert, *Parisian Shapes*, Göttingen 2008; Ute Eskildsen (ed.), *Der Fotograf Otto Steinert*, Göttingen 1999; Otto Steinert (ed.), *Subjektive Fotografie*, Bonn 1952.

Bert Stern
b.1929, lives in New York

Veruschka von Lehndorff and David Bailey, 1964, pub. in Vogue, 1 March 1965,

50.8 × 40.6 cm, printed 2008

→ p.79

Courtesy Staley-Wise Gallery, New York

Bert Stern's first cover photo for Vogue *in 1960 was a huge success, and he received many more assignments on account of it. In 1964 he produced his well-known photograph of David Bailey and Veruschka von Lehndorff, which depicted the photographer lying on the ground to snap the model towering over him. It is possible that this image inspired a famous scene in the history of cinema. In his film* Blow Up *(1966), which also features Veruschka in the role of the model, the director Michelangelo Antonioni interpreted the sequence between photographer and model in another way and turned the pose upside down. The photographer, whose character was based on Bailey, is seen kneeling over the prone model, as if penetrating her with his camera, turning the photo studio into an eroticised combat zone.*

At the age of seventeen, Bert Stern began working in the mailroom of the magazine *Look*. In 1949 he became an art director for *Mayfair* magazine. While deployed in Tokyo during the Korean War, he began taking photographs. In the 1960s his focus shifted from advertising photography to portrait photography of film stars. He worked for *Life*, *Vogue* and many other magazines. In 1958 he produced a documentary film entitled *Jazz on a Summer's Day*, and in 1962 he began making television commercials. His most famous photographs are his portraits of Marilyn Monroe of 1962, which were commissioned by *Vogue*. They were taken only six weeks before her death, and were given the title *The Last Sitting*.

Bert Stern, *Adventures*, Boston 1997; Bert Stern, *Marilyn Monroe: The Complete Last Sitting*, Munich 1992.

Joel Sternfeld
b.1944, lives in New York

A Lawyer with Laundry, Corner Bank and West 41st Street, NYC, October, 1988, C-print, 138 × 111 cm

→ p.114

Fotografische Sammlung, Museum Folkwang, Essen

The distinguished lawyer depicted in this image does not seem to mind being photographed with his dirty laundry. He stands casually on a slightly shabby street, and the photographer subtly includes a New York Times *vending machine. Joel Sternfeld's photographs all seem to be snapshots, and yet in reality they were diligently taken employing a large-format camera and a tripod. The lawyer is just one of sixty* Strangers Passing, *whom Sternfeld photographed in a variety of places across the United States between 1985 and 2000. This project can be seen as a cross-section of society, but Sternfeld never categorises his models in the way that August Sander did, and nor does he seek out the average face as Walker Evans did. Instead, he demonstrates a certain empathy for his models in his attempt to focus on their disparity.*

Joel Sternfeld is known for his documentary work on the United States, and is a representative of the New Topographics and New Color photographers. He studied at Dartmouth College, New Hampshire. His most important book, *American Prospects*, was published in 1987, and features fifty-five images of the contemporary landscape. Ten years later, he published *On this Site: Landscape in Memoriam* (1997), fifty photographs of ordinary places in America where violence has occurred. In 1978 and in 1982, he was awarded Guggenheim Fellowship grants.

Joel Sternfeld, *When it Changed*, Göttingen 2008; Joel Sternfeld, *Joel Sternfeld, Sweet Earth: Experimental Utopias in America*, Göttingen 2006; Joel Sternfeld, *Strangers Passing*, Boston 2001; Joel Sternfeld, *Walking the High Line*, Göttingen 2002.

Louis Stettner
b.1924 New York, lives in Paris

Le Ménage (Household, *also known as* Family Walking), Paris, c.1950, 30.3 × 22.4 cm

→ p.64

Fotografische Sammlung, Museum Folkwang, Essen

'Most important was the outdoor studio that was Paris. I would take long daily walks with my camera, leaving myself open to whatever happened around me. Sometimes I am asked why I did it. There was no economic basis and the possibility of recognition was slight. I suppose I was driven by a great need and love to get close to the world around me. Each photograph was a way of reaching out, an act of discovery' (Wisdom Cries Out in the Street, *1999, p.22*). Louis Stettner's memory of his early time in Paris sketches the humanitarian, postwar attitude to life that found photographic expression in poetically condensed street scenes.

Louis Stettner studied engineering at Princeton but soon became interested in photography. When he moved back to New York, he became a member of the Photo League. In 1939 he came into contact with Alfred Stieglitz, Paul Strand, Lewis Hine and Weegee. In 1947 he went to Paris to study film at the Institut des Hautes Etudes Cinématographiques (IDHEC). There, he became acquainted with Brassaï and Robert Doisneau, who were to influence his work. From 1949 to 1965, he worked as a freelance photographer for numerous magazines. In the 1970s Stettner taught at different American universities and published texts on photography in the magazine *Camera 35*.

Louis Stettner, *Wisdom Cries Out in the Streets*, London 1999; Louis Stettner, *Photo poche*, Paris 1998; Louis Stettner's New York 1950s–1990s, exh. cat., Suermondt-Ludwig-Museum der Stadt Aachen, New York 1996.

Alfred Stieglitz
1864 Hoboken, New Jersey – 1946 New York

A Snapshot, Paris, 1911, Photogravure, 13.7 × 17.4 cm, pub. in *Camera Work*, no.41, 1913

→ p.27

Fotografische Sammlung, Museum Folkwang, Essen

In 1911, Alfred Stieglitz, editor and founder of Camera Work, *published in his magazine a series of photographs of New York where, the modern city appears as the* City of Ambition: *the large harbour, the ships, the avenues and the construction sites. The two street scenes that Stieglitz published in* Camera Work *two years later under the title* A Snapshot *are more restrained; their modernity lies rather in the mode of seeing and they seem to reflect an immediate observation, a spontaneous moment. Twelve years later, the Hungarian Constructivist László Moholy-Nagy expressed his disapproval of this style of atmospheric photography, commenting (on the image of a female passer-by on the street) in his manifesto* Painting, Photography, Film: *'The victory of Impressionism or photography misunderstood. The photographer turned painter instead of using his camera photographically.'*

Alfred Stieglitz's career was characterised by his ambition to establish photography as a emancipated and contemporary medium of Fine Arts. Having studied mechanical engineering in Berlin in the 1880s, he went on to become a leading spokesperson for American photography in the 1890s. With his magazines, especially *Camera Notes* (1897–1902),

Photo-Secession (1897–1902), and later *Camera Work* (1903–17), as well as his legendary gallery Fifth Avenue 291 (1905–17), he succeeded in creating a forum for his ideas regarding Pictorialist photography. Under the influence of the European avant-garde, and as a reaction to the modern reality of the city, his photographic stance later shifted towards straight photography. After the implementation of modernist positions, he refocused on his own photographic practice, in which the city had always played a central role.

Pam Roberts (ed.), *Alfred Stieglitz: Camera Work. The Complete Illustrations 1903–1917*, Cologne 1997.

Paul Strand
1890 New York – 1976 Orgeval, France

New York (later titled *Wall Street*), 1916, 12.8 × 16.3 cm, pub. in *Camera Work*, no.48, 1916

→ p.28

Photograph – New York (later titled *Portrait, Washington Square Park*), 1916, 22.7 × 16.5 cm, pub. in *Camera Work*, no.49/50, 1917

The Museum of Modern Art, New York. Anonymous gifts, 1966

– Published in **Camera Work**, no.49/50, 1917 –

Photograph – New York (later titled *Man in a Derby Hat, New York*), 1916, 22.6 × 17.1 cm

Photograph – New York (later titled *Blind Woman, New York*), 1916, 22.6 × 16.7 cm

→ p.4

Photograph – New York (later titled *Woman Wearing Hat, New York*), 1916, 23.6 × 17.1 cm

Photogravures
The RPS collection at the National Media Museum, Bradford. Purchased with the assistance of the Art Fund

'I wanted to see if I could photograph people without their being aware of the camera … [W]here [the idea] came from, I don't know exactly' (Paul Strand: An American Vision, *1990, p.37*). *In this way, Paul Strand laconically describes the motivation for his series of six portraits, among them* Blind Woman, *which he started taking candidly in 1916, at first with the help of an attached lens dummy and later with a prism viewfinder. With these candid shots, Strand introduced the radical* New Photography: *intimate close-ups that conveyed the authenticity of the moment. In the last two issues of* Camera Work, *Alfred Stieglitz featured seventeen of Strand's photographs, including the famous picture of people rushing to work in Wall Street.*

During his schooling at the Ethical Culture School in New York (1904–9), Paul Strand met the dedicated teacher and photographer Lewis Hine. At the same time, the young photographer was becoming drawn to the aethetics of pictorialism. His images of New York, which in Stieglitz's eyes were 'pure photography', originated from the mid-1910s. Strand was the first photographer to be given a solo show in the 291 gallery in 1916. After his first movie *Manhatta* (1921, with Charles Sheeler) and other commissioned film work, he made several documentaries from the late 1920s until the early 1940s. In his photographic practice, Strand began to focus on rural areas and their people, starting in Mexico in the 1930s. He went on to publish numerous books combining portraits and landscapes, among them, *Time in New England* (1950), *La France de Profil* (A Profile of France, 1952), *Un Paese* (A Village, 1955)

Paul Strand: Circa 1916, exh. cat., Metropolitan Museum of Art, New York 1997; Sarah Greenough, *Paul Strand: An American Vision*, Washington DC 1990.

Street Photographers

Portraits by Makeshift Studios in the Street, Europe and South America, c.1920s, Five photographs, each c.14 × 9 cm

→ p.33

'Surprise Photographs', Europe and South America, c.1920–40, Fourteen photographs, each c.14 × 9 cm

→ p.32

Souvenir with Berlin Bear, Berlin, c.1960s, Five photographs, each c.14 × 9 cm

→ p.14

Private Collection, Paris

Nineteenth-century travelling photographers who set up transportable backdrops and arranged props in small town market squares rapidly helped spread a new type of image – the photographic portrait. Due to the rapidly growing number of professional studios as well as a boom in amateur photography at the end of the century, photographers needed to offer something original in order to stay in business. Setting up small studios at fairs, lidos and tourist sights was a way to attract hilarious clients. In addition to makeshift studios, 'surprisers' appeared on the scene who 'accosted' passers-by with their cameras in front of a well-lit urban scenery, hoping that their startled models would agree to purchase their portraits. After 1920, a camera was even developed that was able to take several images in rapid succession, which resulted in almost film-like sequences; this helped to ensure that among the captured images there should be at least one capturing the passer-by perfectly. Even now 'surprisers' exist in a multitude of forms, such as photographers who take children's pictures at the zoo. The Berlin souvenir photo of the 1960s and 1970s, where people could pose with a fake bear, is just one example of many different local specialties that have existed or still exist today. Many famous photographers, such as Robert Frank, Walker Evans, Stefan Moses and Martin Parr have paid homage to their anonymous colleagues by photographing them or by incorporating elements of these street photographers' practice into their own work.

Clément Chéroux, 'Portraits en pied de nez, l'introduction du modèle récréatif dans la photographie foraine', in *Études photographiques*, no.16, May 2005, pp.88–107; Karl Bassil, Zeina Maasri, and Akram Zaatari, *Mapping Sitting: On Portraiture and Photography*, Beirut 2002; Michel Frizot, 'Anonyme ambulant', in *Historie de voir. De l'invention à l'art photographique (1839–1880)*, Paris 2001, p. 80.

Beat Streuli
b.1957 Altdorf, Switzerland, lives in Brussels

Porte de Ninove, Bruxelles (Porte de Ninove, Brussels), 2007, two-screen digital slide show

→ p.136–7

Galerie Conrads, Düsseldorf-Berlin

The images – the faces of pedestrians, fragmentary views of cars – are projected onto two flat screens as a digital slide show. Beat Streuli produced Porte de Ninove, Bruxelles in 2007, at one of the busiest city gates in Brussels, isolating the individuals from the urban space surrounding them with his telephoto lens. Streuli has also created a large-scale wallpaper installation in which vertical format images of passers-by form an uninterrupted frieze of figures. Despite his use of different media, his recent works all have the same focus: they depict a multicultural society.

When Beat Streuli began photographing in the early 1990s, he established his own recognisable style, giving his street photography both a conceptual and a serial framework. His subject matter, whether in the form of slide projections, videos, books or public installations, has always been urban passers-by, captured against blurred backgrounds with a sculptural attention to detail, and documenting the visible phenomena of globalised Western culture. 'The young people that I photograph in European and American cities', he has said, 'don't seem to differ very much from each other. I think there is a kind of standardised look that young people in the Western world have' (Barcelona lecture, May 1996).

Beat Streuli, *New York City 2000–02*, Ostfildern-Ruit 2003; Beat Streuli, *Rom*, Baden 1990; Beat Streuli, *City*, Ostfildern-Ruit 1999.

Antanas Sutkus
b.1939 Motiejaus Kluoniskiai, Lithuania, lives in Vilnius

Melody of Loneliness, Vilnius 1977, 37 × 39 cm, printed 2000

→ p.103

Fotografische Sammlung, Museum Folkwang, Essen

When viewed out of context, this photograph depicting an old accordion player with his hat askew might be read as an allegory of the street. It seems as if this street musician is the errant wanderer who has seen it all on his travels. But viewed in a historical context, the melancholy exuded by this image becomes a political dimension. Following the photographer's reading of his own image 'that man was probably Russian according to his clothes and accordion. He is not a working man, he likes to drink. Just a free man … possibly a soldier who stayed in Lithuania after the WWII' (Antanas Sutkus, email correspondence, 6 April 2008). Sutkus's depiction of such a figure certainly did not correspond with the idealised image of productive socialist workers promoted in the Soviet Union. Beyond its picturesque appearance, it is also an image personifying the loneliness of the outsider.

Between 1958 and 1964 Antanas Sutkus studied journalism at Vilnius University. In 1969 he co-founded the Photographic Art Society of Lithuania (PASL), the first photographic association in the Soviet Union. At that time he also became committed to promoting artistic photography in the Baltics. In 1965, as a young man, he accompanied Jean-Paul Sartre and Simone De Beauvoir on their travels through Lithuania. In 1976 he began his project *People of Lithuania*, in which he documented the changes occuring in his home country. Sutkus has stated that he hopes his photographs will help future generations to understand the psychology of Lithuania during that time in its history.

Antanas Sutkus, *Daily Life Archives: 1959–1993. Unpublished Photographs*, Vilnius 2003; Antanas Sutkus, *Photographs: 1959–1999*, Vilnius 2000.

Mitra Tabrizian
b.Tehran, Iran, lives in London

– From the series ***Beyond the Limits***, 2000 –

Untitled, C-print, 125.2 × 183.4 cm (Essen only)

→ p.123

Collection Sparkasse Essen

Untitled, C-print, 120 × 180 cm (London only)

Fotografische Sammlung, Museum Folkwang, Essen

Set in the future, Beyond the Limits constructs fragments of everyday life, each portraying an event in which something has gone 'wrong'. 'I was interested in the work of French sociologist-philosopher Jean Baudrillard, in particular his theory of "implosion", the point where things turn in upon themselves and produce the opposite effects to those intended. I was looking at what is happening now and pushing it one step further. For instance, in the image of the crowd "networking", what's gone "wrong" is the disappearance of art!' (Mitra Tabrizian, email correspondence, 18 March 2008). The project explores the crisis of contemporary culture by reframing the genre of street photography in particular within a critical perspective.

Mitra Tabrizian studied at the University of Westminster in London in the early 1980s. At this time, the discourse on photography in Great Britain was concerned with conceptual notions, due to the influence of the prominent figure Victor Burgin, who incorporated the theories of semiotics into photography. Tabrizian's extensive work combines photography, text and film, developing political narratives. Her first important work came out of her collaboration with Andy Golding on the photographic series *The Blues* (1986–7), and *Surveillance* (1990). She has published and exhibited widely, and currently teaches at the University of Westminster.

Mitra Tabrizian: Beyond the Limits, exh. cat., Museum Folkwang, Essen 2004; Mitra Tabrizian, *Correct Distance*, London 1990.

Juergen Teller
b.1964 Erlangen, Germany, lives in London

– From the series ***Go-Sees*** –

Carmel, 9th September, 1998

Ana, 30th September 1998

Sophie Dahl, 20th October, 1998

Desire and Candice Neil, 22nd May 1998

Christie Foley, 20th October 1998

→ p.131, right

Eva Bodenhoff, 20th October 1998

→ Cover image and p.130, right

Mak, 9th October, 1998

→ p.131, left

Romilly, 14th January, 1999

→ p.130, right

Eight C-prints, each 30.5 × 24 cm
Courtesy of the artist and Lehmann Maupin Gallery

Girls Who Come Knocking On My Door is the laconic caption of the first photographs of over 400 images in Juergen Teller's book Go-Sees. From May 1998 to April 1999, Teller photographed young women at 'go-sees', an informal presentation of a model to a photographer. Central to these meetings are test shots, for which Teller had the models pose on the spot, in the entrance area of his London studio. The limited space of the hallway, the frame of the door and pavement form the improvised catwalk on which the young women have to prove their talent. At the same time, this area functions as a gate between street and studio and makes believe that the medial paradise of supermodels and stars are within reach. In the early 1930s, the photographer Yva expressed in photo narratives this longing of young women to enter the world of magazines. Seventy years later, the sheer number of Teller's photographs proves the undiminished lure of modelling.

After his training at the Bayerischen Staatslehranstalt für Fotografie in Munich (1984–6), Juergen Teller moved to London. At the end of the 1980s, his first images were published in British life style and fashion magazines like *i-D*, *The Face* and *Arena*. No matter whether he portrayed musicians such as Kurt Cobain,

Courtney Love and Björk or photographed fashion campaigns with Linda Evangelista and Kate Moss, Teller is among those formal versatile photographers, wishing to explore the duplicity of illusion and reality in the world of fashion and pop culture; for example, his photo sequence with the model Kristen McMenamy, shot in a studio dressing room and published in 1996 for *Süddeutsche Zeitung* magazine. Teller He is part of a generation of young photographers who blur the demarcation line between the printed page in magazines and showrooms in galleries and museums.

Juergen Teller, Märchenstüberl, exh. cat., Folkwang Museum, Essen 2002; Juergen Teller, *Go-Sees*, Zurich 1999; Juergen Teller, *Tracht*, Göttingen 2001; Juergen Teller, *Nurnberg*, Göttingen 2007; Juergen Teller, *Louis XV*, Göttingen 2004.

John Thomson
1837 Edinburgh – 1921 London

– Book –

Street Life in London, Low, Marston, Searle & Rivington, London, 1877–8, Decorative cover embossed with gold leaf, 28 × 21.5 × 3 cm, 1878; Pamphlet with Essay, Part three, 2 April 1877, 27.7 × 21.5 cm

– Photographs –

London Nomads, 10.8 × 8.5 cm

Covent Garden Flower Women, 11.1 × 8.2 cm

Recruiting Sergeants at Westminster, 11.3 × 9 cm

Public Disinfectors, 11.1 × 9 cm

Street Doctor, 11.3 × 9 cm

Street Advertising, 11.2 × 8.6 cm

'Caney' the Clown, 11.5 × 8.8 cm

The Temperance Sweep, 9 × 5.8 cm

→ p.24

The Dramatic Shoe-Black, 9 × 11.7 cm

Covent Garden Labourers, 11.5 × 8.7 cm

Woodburytypes
The RPS Collection at the National Media Museum, Bradford. Purchased with the assistance of the Art Fund

---

In February 1877 the first of twelve monthly issues of Street Life in London *appeared, edited by the photographer John Thomson and the journalist Adolphe Smith. Each of these issues comprised three photographs with accompanying texts. The photos were reproduced as Woodburytypes, which, in contrast to the engravings typical of contemporary book publications, lent the pictures a greater degree of realism.* Street Life in London *appeared in book form in 1878, followed a year later by an abbreviated version entitled* Street Incidents. *Thomson's thirty-six photographs depict London's lower classes, their different trades and labours, but also their hardship. Henry Mayhew's lengthy series of articles on 'London Labour' and 'London Poor' of the 1850s, to which Thomson and Smith referred, along with the stories of Charles Dickens, had aroused a sensitivity to such themes. Although the traditional context of Thomson's photographs echoes the lithographs* Cries of London, *their means of publication, including the textual commentary, make them an early example of socio-documentary photography.*

Thomson studied chemistry, an important qualification for early photography. Guided by geographic and ethnographic pursuits, he left England in 1862 for almost ten years on a voyage to explore the Far East. He travelled to Singapore, India, Siam (Thailand), Cambodia and Indochina. In 1868 he settled in Hong Kong and opened an improvised photo studio, in order to realise a large project on China and its inhabitants for which, from 1870 onwards, he travelled 8,000 kilometres across the country, returning to London in 1872. *Illustrations of China and its People* appeared in four volumes in 1873–4. From 1876 onwards he devoted himself to photo safaris through London's poorer quarters and, in 1878, he photographed in Cyprus. He ran a portrait studio in London in the 1880s. In 1917 he was named Honorary Life Fellow of the Royal Geographic Society for his life's work.

Sylvia Sukop, 'Die soziale Wirklichkeit als Bild: John Thompson's Street Life in London', in *Alles Wahrheit! Alles Lüge!*, exh. cat., Agfa Foto-Historama, Cologne 1996; Stephan White, *John Thomson: Life and Photographs*, London 1985.

Wolfgang Tillmans
b.1968 Remscheid, Germany, lives in London

Piccadilly Line

→ p.135, left

Circle Line

→ p.135, upper right

Victoria Line

→ p.135, bottom right

Central Line

→ p.135, bottom left

Central Line Suit, Jubilee Line, 2000

C-prints, each 40.6 × 30.5 cm
Courtesy Galerie Daniel Buchholz, Cologne

'This was a project I had in mind for long time, which I finally realised last year when I guest-edited an issue of the London homeless magazine The Big Issue. *I have always associated the Underground with incredible intimacy among people, without them wanting to be intimate with each other. It's a weird phenomenon, whereby men and women standing incredibly close to each other and looking into each other's shirts and ears and hair is acceptable, and we've all decided not to think of it a sensual experience, because a taboo is at work. I find it fascinating how shifting that one little parameter makes everything else shift. The Tube pictures are also ultimately about how negotiable social behaviour is; but initially, of course, I was fascinated by what I saw' (Wolfgang Tillmans in conversation with Nathan Kernan, Wolfgang Tillmans, 2002, p.137).*

In his first exhibition *Approaches* (Hamburg and Remscheid, 1988), Wolfgang Tillmans worked with laser copies, already demonstrating his appetite for experimentation. He studied at the Bournemouth & Poole College of Art & Design, at the same time supplying style magazines such as *i-D* and *Spex* with his photographs. The series with Alex and Lutz and their childlike play with sexuality, published 1992 in *i-D*, is already part of the photohistory of the 1990s. These early pictures take their inspiration from his 'family' – the youth and subcultural techno scene. Since then Tillmans's subject matter has broadened. It doesn't fit anymore into a single category, combining pictures of friends with photographs of celebrities, the still life on the window sill with the appropriated image material of his artist's books, the layout of the magazine with a seemingly random hang on the gallery wall, his own life with political engagement such as the fight against Aids. This fusion of different photographic practices with the authenticity of his personal attitude makes Tillmans one of the most influential artists of today. He won the Turner Prize in 2000.

Wolfgang Tillmans, *manual*, Cologne 2007; Wolfgang Tillmans, *Freedom from the Known*, exh. cat., P.S.1. and the Museum of Modern Art, New York 2006; Wolfgang Tillmans, *If one thing matters, everything matters*, London and Cologne 2003; Jan Verwoert et al., *Wolfgang Tillmans*, London 2002.

Lee To Sang
b.1939 Hong Kong, lives in Amsterdam

To Sang Photo Studio Amsterdam, c.1995, printed 2007

→ p.127

.*To Sang Photo Studio Amsterdam*, c.1980, printed 2007

To Sang Photo Studio Amsterdam, c.1980, printed 2007

C-prints, each 40 × 30 cm
Lee To Sang / Courtesy Van Zoetendaal Amsterdam

The clientele of a photo studio, whether in a city or a village, is usually composed of people from the local community. Lee To Sang's photo studio is no different, except that the lively Amsterdam quarter de Pjip in which it is situated unites people from every corner of the globe. In addition to coloured-paper backgrounds and stage curtains, To Sang's studio features a backdrop of the Alps, and a Chinese garden. His models are from diverse ethnic and social backgrounds, thus resulting in an interesting cultural mix – a friendly 'clash of civilisations'. The ideal landscape is part of the tradition of studio portraiture: in the early days of photography it was very popular among the European bourgeoisie to transport themselves into classical scenarios by means of painted backgrounds and crumbling columns.

Lee To Sang comes from a Chinese family of painters based in Hong Kong. In 1979, he moved to Amsterdam, where he opened his own photo studio in Albert Cuypstraat No.5. Apart from the local Dutch people, his clients included the many immigrants of that neighbourhood – Surinamesi, Pakistani, Chinese and Kurdish. 'I don't usually ask clients what they do, so sometimes it doesn't happen until later that I realise that they were famous. I've photographed some old mayors of Amsterdam, and Lurch from the movie *The Addams Family*' (*Colors Magazine*, Oct./Nov. 2003, p.83). To Sang became known through Johan van der Keuken's documentary film *To Sang Fotostudio* of 1997, which, following his previous film *Amsterdam Global Village*, showed yet another facet of multicultural Amsterdam.

Stefan Ruiz (ed.), 'Photo Studio/Studio Photo', *Colors Magazine*, Oct./Nov. 2003; Willem Van Zoetendaal (ed.), *To Sang Fotostudio*, text by Jaffe Vink, Amsterdam 1995.

Umbo (Otto Umbehr)
1902 Düsseldorf – 1980 Hanover

Schattenwunder (Shadow Miracle), 1928, 28 × 20.6 cm

→ p.39

Galerie Kicken, Berlin

Umbo's Shadow Miracle, Mysterium *(Mystery) and* Unheimliche Straße *(Uncanny Street) are three surveys that were taken from a window of the agency Deutscher Photo-Dienst (DEPHOT, German Photo-Service) in 1928 – scenes that seem to have captivated the photographer. Even if this elevated camera position is part of the radical New Vision adopted by modernist photography in the late 1920s, these images poetically transform the street in a manner similar to Surrealist sensibility. Compared to Friedrich Seidenstücker's contemporaneous typological portrayals of street workers, for instance, the workers depicted here are cast in the far less tangible role of shadow figures.*

In the autumn of 1921, Umbo began to study at the new Bauhaus in Weimar, attending the preparatory course under Johannes Itten, as well as the metal workshop. In the summer of 1923 he moved to Berlin, where he made ends meet with miscellaneous jobs in the art world. After having made his first photo-montages, Umbo turned to photography towards the end of 1926, producing close-ups of faces, images of Berlin bohemians and street scenes. In 1928, he co-founded the photo agency DEPHOT. By the early 1930s he was one of the most renowned photographers in Berlin. The major exhibition *Film und Foto* (Film and Photography) of 1929 included thirty-nine of his photographs. When the Nazis seized power, DEPHOT was prohibited. Later, Umbo supplied images to the syndicated press, for instance the movie magazine *Der Stern* and the propaganda publication *Signal*. After 1945, he lived in Hanover, attempting to re-establish himself as a photojournalist and documenting the devastations of the war. Towards the end of his life, as a simple employee of the Kestnergesellschaft (Kestner Society), he lived to see the recognition of his early work.

Herbert Molderings, *Umbo: Otto Umbehr, 1902–1980*, Düsseldorf 1996.

Ed van der Elsken
1925 – 1990 Amsterdam

Young Woman in Cheong-San Dress,
Hong Kong, 1960, sequence of eight photographs, each 24 × 18 cm (varying horizontal and vertical format)

→ p.97

Leiden University Library

On his journey around the world in 1960, Ed van der Elsken photographed the sequence Young woman in Cheong-San Dress, *in Hong Kong. Reminiscent of a tracking shot from a movie, it appears on a double page in his famous book* Sweet Life *(1966). He describes his subject as: 'A very nice, nice-looking young woman in the typical local costume, the cheong-san, with that great side split … I followed this babe around for a while. She knew I was doing it, and didn't like it one bit'* (Sweet Life, *New York 1966).*

Apart from some classes at the Nederlandse Fotovakschool in Den Haag, Ed van der Elsken was an autodidact. From 1950, he lived for four years in Paris and developed a liking for bohemian life on the Rive Gauche that resulted in his most renowned book *Love on the Left Bank* (1956), the first of more than twenty books that he was to publish during his lifetime. His many travels led him to places such as Tokyo, Hong Kong and Africa, where he also took colour photographs for the magazine *Avenue*. His 'stream-of-consciousness' style was very influential on European postwar photography. From the 1960s he also shot short films, mostly about his own life, and later worked in television. His last movie is about his battle with cancer before his death. His body of work was presented posthumously to a large audience at Documenta X in 1997.

Ed van der Elsken: Sweet Life. Fotografie + Film 1949–1990, exh. cat., Kunstmuseum Wolfsburg, Göttingen 2000; *Once upon a Time*, exh. cat., Stedelijk, Amsterdam 1991; *Ed van der Elsken*, exh. cat., Stedelijk, Amsterdam 1966; Ed van der Elsken, *Sweet Life*, New York 1966.

James van der Zee
1886 Lenox, Massachusetts
– 1983 Washington DC

Stroll in the Park, c.1925, 30.4 × 25.4 cm
Father and Son, 1924, 30.4 × 25.4 cm

Courtesy Donna Mussenden van der Zee

American Legioneer, District of Columbia, 1937, 24.4 × 20.3 cm

→ p.48

Fotografische Sammlung, Museum Folkwang, Essen

The American Legioneer *who has taken a seat at the small round table in James van der Zee's studio is completely surrounded by images and signs: the medals carefully pinned to the shirt of his uniform, the photograph of a young boy (possibly himself) wearing a scout's uniform, at which he gazes with great absorption, and the many other symbols in the background that fight for our attention, including the American flag, visual fragments of a military parade and of a mourning soldier at a comrade's grave. The painted backdrop, widely used in studios at this time, has been replaced by photographic means; with the help of several negatives van der Zee has copied the different visual elements into the image. The American identity of this young black man is thus forcefully inscribed into his portrait. As a symbol of his pride and success he holds a cigar, which the photographer has made appear to be lit by retouching the photograph and adding smoke rings.*

James van der Zee began to photograph when he was a boy of fourteen. From 1909 to 1915 – being a gifted musician – he earned his money by playing in various orchestras. In 1915 he moved to Newark, New Jersey, to work as a lab technician in a photo studio. Only a year later, he opened up his own studio Guarantee Photos (later known as GGG Photo Studio) in Harlem, New York. He thus became a chronicler and exponent of the Harlem Renaissance, a manifestation of the new self-confidence of African-American culture. Whether he was photographing show-business celebrities or the emancipated middle classes, his images are full of life, glamour and pride. In 1967 the Metropolitan Museum discovered his extensive archive and two years later his images were included in the exhibition *Harlem on My Mind*.

Colin Westerbeck (ed.), *James Van Der Zee*, Chicago 2004; Deborah Willis-Braithwaite (ed.), *Van der Zee: Photographer: 1886–1983*, Boston 1998; *James Van Der Zee*, exh. cat., National Portrait Gallery, Washington DC 1994.

Louis Vert
1865 Paris – 1924 Epluches,
France

– From the series featuring *Small Trades and Clochards*, 1900–06 –

Vitrier (Glaser),1900–02, 23.5 × 17.4 cm
Etameur (Tinsmith), 1900–02, 23.5 × 17.4 cm

→ p.25

Clochard endormi sur un banc (Tramp Sleeping on a Bench), March 1905, 14.3 × 21.4 cm

Clocharde assise sur un banc (Female Tramp Sitting on a Bench), March 1905, 14.3 × 21.1 cm, printed c.1930

Musée Carnavalet-Histoire de Paris, Paris

In 1932, an amateur photographer gave a collection of '88 photographs – street scenes, small trades, etc. … taken by Monsieur Vert in Paris between 1900 and 1906' to the Musée Carnavalet in Paris. As a museum presenting the history of Paris, whose collection also contains photographs by the far more famous Eugène Atget, the Carnavalet seemed the appropriate venue. Around 1900, many photographers captured the hawkers of the city, urban characters who were already considered picturesque denizens of Paris similar to the clochards. *Unlike Atget's photographs of 1899, which show the tradesmen posing, Louis Vert succeeded in isolating his subject for a brief moment from the bustling street life using a short exposure time and a longer focal length.*

Primarily, Louis Vert worked in his father's print shop, but all his free time was devoted to photography. From 1904 until his death in 1924, he was a member of the Société d'Excursions d'Amateurs de Photographie and took part in their events, excursions and monthly slide shows. The bulletins of the society show that in 1906 and in 1921, Vert presented slides of his images of the *Petits Métiers* (Small Trades). On the occasion of the second evening, the writer acknowledged: 'But the highlight of the evening was the presentation of the Small Trades of Paris. Some of those that were once part of our picturesque streets and walks have now disappeared' (*Atget, Géniaux, Vert*, Paris 1984, p.57).

Atget, Géniaux, Vert. Petits métiers et types parisiens vers 1900, exh. cat., Musée Carnavalet, Paris 1984.

Tom von Wichert
1909 Riga – 1985 Munich

New York – Volkswagen, c.1954,
Cibachrome, 31 × 41.8 cm, printed 1983,

→ p.69

Fotografische Sammlung, Museum Folkwang, Essen

New York – Volkswagen *is a commissioned advertising photograph taken for Volkswagen in 1954. Due to the challenging lighting technology required, it was only possible to realise its very elaborate staging at a film studio, employing both stage design and painted backgrounds. Tom von Wichert was one of the first postwar advertising photographers to bring the street into the studio through the painstaking staging of images.*

Before working as a foreign correspondent in the Baltics, Tom von Wichert was a trainee at the *Riga Review*. He studied history, economics and sociology, and he was also employed as an editor at the Ullstein Bilderdienst in Berlin, where he first came into contact with photography. After the war he worked as a freelance photojournalist for several magazines until the mid-1950s, when he switched to fashion and studio photography.

Fotografie+Werbung, exh. cat., Museum Folkwang, Essen 1989.

Jeff Wall
b.1946, lives in Vancouver

The Arrest, 1989, 120 × 145 × 4 cm
→ p.122

Transparency in lightbox
Collection Sebastien Janssen, Brussels

In his work, Jeff Wall makes a distinction between cinematographic photographs and documentary photographs, with The Arrest *belonging to the first category. This distinction conceals the long tradition of staged images in 'documentary' photography. The term 'cinematographic', however, gives some clue as to Wall's method: each of his images of this kind is based on a scenario, and is shot after a location and cast have been selected, followed – in most cases – by digital post-production. The Arrest quotes from the iconography of historical painting, especially of lust and violence, as well as recalling Caravaggio's chiaroscuro. One of the police officers is searching the trouser pocket of the detained Hispanic man, an example of the ambivalent and yet significant details within Wall's theatrical images that he has referred to as 'micro-gestures'. The Arrest was produced in Vancouver in 1989, a city in which Wall also has realised numerous other works, that frequently enact the social tensions and economic power structures of the modern city.*

Jeff Wall studied art history at the University of British Columbia in Vancouver from 1964 to 1970, followed by studies at the Courtauld Institute of Art in London until 1973. After working experimentally in the 1960s, his international breakthrough came with works such as *Destroyed Room* (1978), *Young Workers* (1978–83) and *Picture for Women* (1979). Wall has consistently searched for a contemporary interpretation of Baudelaire's concept of the 'painter of modern life'. His open, conceptual method of staging photographs, as well as their presentation in light boxes taken from commercial advertising, are attributes of a photographic paradigm shift iniciated by the conceptual art in the 1960s.

Jeff Wall, exh. cat., White Cube, London 2007; *Jeff Wall*, exh. cat., Tate Modern, London 2005; Jeff Wall, *Transparencies*, Munich 1986.

Gillian Wearing
b.1963 Birmingham, lives in London

– From the series ***Album*** –

Self-Portrait as my Mother Jean Gregory,
2003, C-print, 135 × 116 cm

→ p.129

Collection Maureen Paley

Self-Portrait as my Father Brian Wearing,
2003, C-print, 164 × 130.5 cm

Collection Greatford Estates Limited

Self-Portrait as my Mother Jean Gregory is part of the series Album, for which Gillian Wearing re-enacted photographs of members of her family and also of herself as a teenager by posing in the location dressed up in masks, wigs and costumes. In these portraits, Wearing sought to examine the psychological imprint that relatives make on individuals using the rhetorics of photographic family pictures.

Photographer and a video artist Gillian Wearing studied art and design at Chelsea School of Art, London (1985–7), and fine art at Goldsmith's College, London (1987–90). One of her most important works is her series *Signs that say what you want them to say and not signs that say what someone else wants you to say* (1992–3), comprising nearly 600 portraits of people expressing themselves through the signs they hold up. Her video installation *Drunk* (1997–9), in which she transfers inebriated street people into the white cube of her studio, is also characteristic of her approach. She explores the disparities between public and private life, between individual and collective experience and between belonging and exclusion.

Gillian Wearing, exh. cat., Serpentine Gallery, London 2000; Russell Ferguson, *Gillian Wearing*, London 1998; *Turner Prize 1997*, exh. cat., Tate Britain, London 1997.

Weegee (Usher Arthur Fellig)
1899 Zloczew, Austria – 1968 New York

Transvestite, 1940s, 21.7 × 18.6 cm

→ p.205

Their First Murder, 9 October 1941, 1941, 30.4 × 27.1 cm

→ p.56

Open-Air Canteen, Broadway and 47th Street at Five in the Morning, 1940s, 34 × 26.9 cm

→ p.209

Corpse with Glasses, 11 August 1941, 1941
25.6 × 33.5 cm

Self-Portrait, Working in the Trunk of his Chevrolet, 1942, 24 × 19.3 cm; (back cover)

Galerie Berinson, Berlin

'My car became my home. It was a two-seater, with a special extra-large luggage-compartment. I kept everything there, an extra camera, cases of flash bulbs, extra loaded holders, a typewriter, fireman's boots, boxes of cigars, salami, infra-red film for shooting in the dark, uniforms, disguises, a change of underwear, and extra shoes and socks. I was no longer glued to the teletype-machine in police headquarters. I had my wigs. I no longer had to wait for crime to come to me, I could go after it. The police radio was my life line. The camera – my life and my love – was Aladdin's lamp' (Weegee by Weegee, 1975, p.52). *This passage from Weegee's autobiography reads like a comment on his famous self-portrait as frantic photo journalist, a staged representation of his photographic vocation.*

The son of Jewish immigrants, Usher Fellig was eleven years old when he reached New York, where his name was Americanised to Arthur. The family settled down in Manhattan's Lower East Side. He left school at the age of fourteen and started to work in a studio for advertising photography. At the age of eighteen, he made a living as a street photographer and later worked in a studio producing passport photographs. In 1925 he was employed as lab worker in the photo agency Acme Newspictures. Fellig went freelance in 1935, adopting his pseudonym and starting to produce the photographs on which the 'Weegee' myth was founded. By tuning in to police radio signals, he was able to reach the scene of crime or tragedy in time to capture it first. He photographed anything worth reporting in a very direct style and not without cynical humour. In addition to the *Sex and Crime* images, he took many photographs reflecting the social contrasts and phenomena of the metropolis, among them the people who slept rough in the city. His book *Naked City* (1945) established his reputation as a photographic author.

Weegee: Dans la collection Berinson, exh. cat., Musée Maillol, Paris 2007; Weegee, *Weegee by Weegee: An Autobiography*, New York 1975.

Garry Winogrand
1928 New York – 1984 Tijuana, Mexico

– From a series of photographed women in the public space –

London, c.1967, 35.6 × 28.9 cm

New York, n.d., 35.6 × 28.9 cm

→ p.89

New York, n.d., 35.6 × 28.9 cm

Galerie Thomas Zander, Cologne

'Whenever I've seen an attractive woman, I've done my best to photograph her. I don't know if all the women in the photographs are beautiful, but I do know that the women are beautiful in the photographs. By the term "attractive woman", I mean a woman I react to positively. What do I react to in a woman? I do not mean as a man getting to know a woman, but as a photographer photographing.' Winogrand's comment in the preface of his book Women Are Beautiful reminds one of his famous maxim 'I photograph to find out what something will look like photographed.' Do his words reveal the passion of the photographer, or is he hiding his passion for women behind his camera? It was always young women, dressed in summer clothing whom Winogrand photographed at parties or in parks, and above all, on the street. Nevertheless, he was no invisible agent stalking his victims in secret, but looked for direct confrontation with his subjects.

Garry Winogrand corresponds to the American proto-type of a street photographer, a lonesome transient in the canyonesque streets of the city, armed with his Leica and a wide-angle lens. In 1948 he studied painting at Columbia University, New York, where he also began to photograph, attending the classes of Alexey Brodovitch at the New School for Social Research from 1949. In 1951, he received his first assignment from *Harper's Bazaar* and in 1964 the first Guggenheim Fellowship Award for 'photographic studies of American life'. The exhibitions *Toward a Social Landscape* at George Eastman House, Rochester, New York, in 1966 and *New Documents* at the Museum of Modern Art, New York, in 1967 established Winogrand as one of the most important chroniclers of American society. Besides the street, his preferred sites of photographic study included the zoo, the airport and the rodeo, as well as media events, demonstrations, press conferences and parties. When Winogrand died in 1984, he left behind countless unedited images, among them 2,500 rolls of undeveloped film and 6,500 rolls of film of which no contact sheets had yet been made.

Garry Winogrand: Figments from the Real World, exh. cat., Museum of Modern Art, New York 1988; Garry Winogrand, *Women Are Beautiful*, New York 1975.

Yva (Else Ernestine Neuländer-Simon)
1900 Berlin – 1942 Majdanek, Poland

Max Liebermann, 22 × 16 cm

→ p.40, right

Lil Dagover, 22.5 × 17 cm

Asta Nielsen, 22 × 16 cm

→ p.40, left

Ullstein Bild – Yva

In 1930 the August edition of UHU, the magazine of the Berlin Ullstein Bilderdienst, presented an entertaining photographic rebus titled: 'Who Are They? An Unfamiliar View of Celebrities'. The puzzle shows ten personalities of the Weimar Republic – but seen from behind. 'Facial expression and look can be mastered with great self-control, and many celebrities seem to be very different in real life from their familiar photographic faces. The back view, however, more often than not tells the truth: it is often more telling how one sets one's foot, bends or straightens one's neck or holds arm and head.' This series of photographs consists of six studio portraits by Yva, including the three mentioned above, and street scenes taken by photographers from an agency, showing the back view of Gerhart Hauptmann und Albert Einstein.

Under the pseudonym Yva, Else Neuländer opened her first photo studio in Berlin in 1925. After a brief collaboration with the artist Heinz Hajek-Halke, she turned her main focus towards commercial photography for the glossy magazines: portraits, fashion photography and advertising images. Friedrich Korner, editor in chief of *UHU*, proved an invaluable partner. For this magazine, Yva photographed photo narratives in the early 1930s that reflect the longings of young shop girls. By 1934 her studio had acquired an excellent reputation in the area of fashion photography, and employed eight members of staff, among them the young Helmut Newton (1936–8). Discrimination against Jewish citizens had already started by the time the Nazis seized power. In 1936 a female friend became the official head of the studio, but in 1938 Yva was prohibited from working. In 1942 she and her husband Alfred Simon were deported to Majdanek concentration camp and murdered.

Marion Beckers and Elisabeth Moortgat, *Yva. Photographien 1925–1938*, Tübingen 2001.

The Pose: Its Troubles and Pleasures
Susanne Holschbach

More than any other era, the age of photography, as the media theorist Marshall McLuhan once wrote, has directed attention to our physical and psychic postures.[1] He was thinking of the fleeting gestures, the emotional expressions and movements captured as snapshots by journalists and street photographers alike, and which, in this way, entered public consciousness. But beyond these snapshots that have helped to stake out the world of the visual unconscious, it is the pose of portrait photography that has added to the enormous, ever-growing store of images of corporeal expression – images that fascinate and continue to be regarded, compared and interpreted. Building up a number of relations over time, both street and studio photography have not only changed our image of ourselves, but have also influenced the way in which we portray ourselves.

Showing oneself in front of the camera – be it in the street or in the studio – has to do with the notion of the pose. Generally speaking, the pose refers to an arbitrary posture seen to be stilted or artificial. This essay will look at the pose from another perspective, reading it as the nuanced interaction between photographer and photographed subject, between the camera and the body, an interaction transforming human into photographic expression.

Striking a pose

By staging the pose, photography took a lead from the fine arts. But the photographic portrait was not merely, from day one, a continuation of painting with different means. Photography democratised the portrait: it offered many people a first-time opportunity to witness themselves as an image. And not only that: as early as the nineteenth century, celebrity portraits of all kinds were purchased, collected in albums and compared. Do artists, for instance, look any different from authors? Which poses are typical for scientists, and which ones for politicians or actors? Similarities as well as differences became apparent, not least because members of the royal family visited the same studio and stood in front of the same camera as did wealthy citizens. However, photography was not only used for the purposes of self-representation or remembrance. People were literally taken from the street into the studio in order to retain their image for later identification, to study their physiognomy and classify it according to a given 'type'. The contrary poles of the photographic portrait in the nineteenth century are shown directly facing each other on a double page of this catalogue (pp.20–1).[2] Both images stem from the early days of photography, the 1850s, when being photographed was still an unaccustomed and often strenuous procedure for the model, who had to maintain his or her pose for several seconds, if not minutes, before the photographer could close the shutter. This was easier to accomplish when seated, as shown by the two men in our examples. Although they are contemporaneously similar in motif and aesthetics, we instantly note the differences in pose between the two men. The one, clad in a buttoned wool coat, folds his hands in front of a portly stomach; his attentive, albeit reserved, gaze is not directed into the camera, but into an indefinite distance. Upon closer scrutiny, we can barely see the back of the chair on which the man is seated, since he appears to rest within himself, as if denying any form

1 See Marshall McLuhan, *Understanding Media: The Extensions of Man*, Corte Madera, California 2003, p.262.

2 In his seminal text *The Body and the Archive* Allan Sekula refers to this as the 'honorific and the repressive pole of portrait practice'. See Allan Sekula, *The Body and the Archive* (1986), in *October* 39, Winter 1986, p.7.

of external support. The pose adopted for the camera corresponds to a demeanour that has become second nature for him. The other model, by contrast, is dressed in a threadbare open jacket as he crosses his arms over his lap; he seems to shrink into himself on an uncomfortable wooden chair that he will quickly leave again. With a gaze intently directed at the camera, his posture expresses both the discomfort generated by the event of being photographed and the challenge of giving a good picture.

The first photograph depicts the French poet Théodore de Banville and is part of the Galerie Contemporaine, a collection of portaits of famous personalities of the time, of the range of types already mentioned. The photographer Emile Tourtin seems to have relied entirely on the personal aura of his model, renouncing any kind of embellishment. The other example shows a travelling salesman, or 'roamer', held and photographically registered by Swiss authorities working in the service of a national demographic programme to control the 'homeless'.[3] It ended up in police archives, where, if needed, it could later be used for a warrant poster. Carl Durheim, the photographer in charge, portrayed his model according to the conventions of contemporary studio photography; the small round table on which the cap is placed therefore appears as a humble alternative to the standard furnishings of a commercial photo studio. We should note that the strict front-and-side views of police photography had not as yet been invented, which would not only deny the photographer any attempt to stage the shot, but would above all suppress the pose as a form of self-portrayal.

Both examples emphasise the core principle of the pose in a staged portrait. The pose allows a person to reveal something about his self-perception and his social status; the pose is at once a conscious attitude and an involuntary expression of psychic dispositions and social norms. It can intimate the conditions under which the portrait was created, and it can bear signs of agreement as well as resistance. The pose is at the interface between the individual and society, between inside and outside, the conscious and the unconscious.

To pose means to show oneself as one wishes to be perceived. It was the studio photographic portrait that, for the first time, made it possible for a larger section of society to put this ideal self-perception into a picture. In the nineteenth century, the aspiring middle classes, in particular, saw photography as the suitable medium to flaunt what they had attained and still wanted to attain. The photographic studios in the large cities were equipped with parlour furniture, mock pillars and heavy curtains, thus setting the perfect scene in which to present oneself and allude in a grand fashion, baroque style, to the assumption of 'having arrived'. Similar modes of self-portrayal were still to be found in photo studios of the twentieth century. A photographer such as James van der Zee also relied on a representational style for his Harlem studio, which, in its heyday of the 1920s and 1930s, was frequented by members of the black middle class who had acquired financial prosperity during the interwar years.[4] The opportunity of staging one's portrait was of central importance to van der Zee's customers. In that

3 See Martin Gasser, Thomas Dominik Meier and Rolf Wolfensberger (eds.), *Wider das Leugnen und Verstecken. Carl Durheims Fahndungsfotografien von Heimatlosen 1852/53*, Zurich 1998.

4 See Colin Westerbeck (ed.), *The James Van Der Zee Studio*, Chicago 2004.

they gave the best possible image of themselves, they were able, with the help of the photographer's conscious arrangements, to fix their image for posterity, thus creating a positive, self-authored black image that stood in contrast to the negative stereotypes, the degrading images of the 'other' to which Afro-Americans continued to see themselves exposed (p.48).[5]

The middle-class notions of honour and respectability fundamental to van der Zee's staged portraits also reappear in the studio photographs of Caribbean immigrants to Great Britain dating from the 1950s, which Stuart Hall reads as an alternative history of blacks in Great Britain: 'They document where people were, at a certain stage of their life, and how they imagined themselves, how they became "persons"'[6] – a statement that altogether refers to the traditional studio portrait.

Outwitting the pose

We show ourselves in a pose, but we also hide behind a pose. Indeed, it is repeatedly assumed that the staged photographic portrait encourages the pose, an assertion primarily based on the studio work of the nineteenth century with its theatrical means of choreographing the photo shoot. In her famous book *Photography and Society,* Gisèle Freund[7] criticised, for instance, the very successful portrait photographer A.A.E. Disdéri for depicting 'character masks' instead of individuals because of his employing stereotypical attributes for each profession and social class which disguised any form of individual personality. Disdéri himself, who introduced the *carte de visite* format in the 1850s and who, in doing so, unleashed a veritable passion for portrait collecting, believed that the tendency of the sitter to adopt a 'masquerade' was more to do with the customers' imagination than with what the photographer offered. His instructions for portrait photographers state that the clientele tended to imitate role models and would stand in front of the camera in 'rehearsed formal poses' and 'appropriated faces'.[8] He therefore advised his colleagues 'to study, deliberate and find a means of ridding the subject from preconceived ideas, and to observe meticulously those fleeting moments in which – oblivious – the subject poses in a natural, uninhibited manner'.[9] Even to the present day, generations of portrait photographers have tried to outwit the 'masquerade' of the pose in all possible ways, to look behind the facade and to bring a person's authenticity to the surface. The American photographer Philippe Halsman developed a particularly original method of doing so in the 1950s; he portrayed high-ranking politicians, judges, entertainers, actresses, industrialists – people from all strata of society who were used to showing an 'official face'. Intent on looking behind this representative facade, he had the idea of asking his customers to jump into the air, often towards the end of a sitting. As Halsman explains: 'In a jump the subject, in a sudden burst of energy, overcomes energy. He cannot simultaneously control his expressions, his facia and his limb muscles. The mask falls. The real self becomes visible. One has only to snap it up with the camera.'[10] Hardly anyone denied him this wish; almost two hundred jumping portraits were taken. Analysing these, Halsman developed what he called a 'Jumpology', a psychology of the jump. In a jump, for instance, with both arms stretched upwards, as in the portrait

5 Dawoud Bey has described the affect these portraits had on him as a young political activist when he saw them exhibited for the first time in the late 1960s: 'What was also striking to me at the time was how little resemblance these pictures bore to the image of Harlem that even I, growing up in the black middle-class suburbs of Queens, New York, had come to imagine. Van Der Zee's photographs became for me, at that moment, a wonderful window through which an unseen past and a largely unseen black subject were made vividly and immediately accessible'. See Dawoud Bey, *Authoring the Black Image: The Photographs of James Van Der Zee*, in *The James Van Der Zee Studio*, p.29.

6 See Stuart Hall, *Reconstruction Work*, Ten-8, no.16, 1984, p.5.

7 Gisèle Freund, *Photography and Society*, Boston, Mass. 1979.

8 See André-Adolphe-Eugène Disdéri, *Die Photographie als bildende Kunst*, Dr. A.H. Weiske, Berlin 1864, p.282.

9 Ibid.

10 See Philippe Halsman's *Jump Book* (1959), New York 1986, p.8.

of New York Governor Thomas E. Dewey, Halsman read single-mindedness and ambition; in a jump with closed eyes, as in photographer Edward Steichen's case, he saw a vivid inner life (p.74); and in a jump with both legs bent backwards, such as Marilyn Monroe's, he saw a girl, rope-skipping.

Halsman used the jump to create a liminal situation – literally, a transient state – in which his customer's sense of self-control was not entirely gone, but in which the intended pose revealed other aspects of his personality. Contemporary art photography investigates comparable liminal conditions. The Dutch photographer Rineke Dijkstra, for instance, made a series of portraits of young people photographed on the beach against the horizon of the open sea.[11] In this way, Dijkstra is able to foreground the tension between the site of the photograph (representing leisure, freedom and the release from societal pressure) and the elaborate act of taking photographs with a large-format camera (which requires the subject to adopt a pose, as in the studio). In other series, she photographs women immediately after childbirth and toreros in the arena following a bullfight – images in which the after-effect of an existential, physical experience lives on, in which the self as 'image' becomes unimportant. Finally, Dijkstra also makes use of the video as a medium that takes place in time, so as to undermine the rigidity of the pose. She films girls in the foyer of a Liverpool club, who, under the influence of alcohol and the excitement of dance, still wish to look decent in front of the camera: what we see here is the very act of posing (p.132).

Becoming a picture

Posing is an act that is both active and passive. The female clubbers act for Dijkstra's camera, but not like an actress who re-enacts previously rehearsed gestures. Instead, they adapt their behaviour to resemble the image with which they identify themselves – an image, for instance, of sexiness, glamour and femininity. This process of becoming-a-picture, which can be regarded as a form of mimicry, is not limited to the specific situation of being photographed or filmed; it takes place in the street as much as in public places, even in one's own four walls, because it is a fundamental mechanism of intersubjectivity: in order to be perceived and recognised as a person at all, I need to allow myself to be identified within the framework of a series of possible pictures. The film theorist Kaja Silverman refers to this as 'screen'. She states that 'ever since the inception of cave drawing, it has been via images that we see and are seen'.[12] What is specific to our epoch are the terms of this 'specular foundation', which, in spite of the technologies of cinema and video, are essentially *photographic*; they are expressed through the media images that flood us on a daily basis and which, to a greater or lesser degree, influence us consciously, but the image we have of ourselves is also determined by the manifold photographs that accompany us from birth. Historically unique, this process of not just seeing oneself in the mirror but through the eyes, in a way, of others caused irritation in the early days of photography.[13] For us it has meanwhile become commonplace. If we reconstruct the process by which the image of our body was transformed into a 'photographic' one, then we inevitably need to go back to the photo studio. It

11 See Rineke Dijkstra, *Menschenbilder*, Essen 1998.

12 See Kaja Silverman, *The Threshold of the Visible World*, New York and London 1996, p.195.

13 In this context, Roland Barthes speaks of 'the disturbance (to civilization)'. See Roland Barthes, *Camera Lucida: Reflections on Photography*, trans. Richard Howard, London 1993, p.12, emphasis R.B.

is here where poses are not merely 'captured', but are in fact created through the photographic act. In order to be as successful on photo paper as in a classic oil painting, the body must adapt to the conditions of the photographic setting; in other words, it must be made 'photogenic'.[14] The photo studio of the nineteenth century was the first locale in which to experiment with the photogenic: by trying out various poses, optimising light and focus, new images of the body were gradually modelled.[15]

In the twentieth century it was, above all, fashion photography that took the lead as a laboratory for staging the body. The art of fashion photography is, of course, also based on the pose, but this pose is no longer tied to a person in particular and their self-expression, since the model is nothing but an accidental personification. The pose of fashion photography could become inventive. It initially served the purpose of displaying particularities of clothing, but quickly emancipated itself and became a carrier of meaning. It can exude an aura of eroticism, extravagance, aggression or naturalness; it can evoke a certain type, atmosphere, situation or action. Fashion photographers use the pose as a convenient tool; it can be 'isolated' and carry the picture as much as it can become a pure ornament incorporated into an overall composition of clothing, light and space.

Fashion photography creates perfect images of the body because it can, as in a laboratory, direct all means of production: the model and the surroundings are determined accordingly, the light conditions are changed at will, an individual cut, perspective and focus are chosen, thus allowing a very nuanced image of the body. Any wish to conform to these pictures is inevitably doomed to failure, and not only because attaining the 'perfect' body is impossible. Never, or only rarely, do we appear in a perfect light in real life, in a perfect environment in which everything fits together flawlessly. But this failure can also be seen as a form of resistance: the resistance of the real body, of the real person, to dissolving in the medial image.

Playing with the pose

In his famous work on photographic portraiture *Camera Lucida*, towards the end of the passage in which he reflects upon the notion of 'being photographed', Roland Barthes speaks of the 'mortiferous layer of the Pose'.[16] He describes the moment of being photographed as a mortification, as the transfer from subject to object in which the former becomes a ghost. By freezing into a pose, the subject who is about to be photographed anticipates the arresting shot of the photographer; it is the last bit of resistance that he can muster before he becomes 'Total-Image, which is to say, Death in person.'[17] Barthes's formulation culminates in negative attributes long associated with the posed photograph – even after the exposure time had been shortened and elaborate fixation methods were no longer necessary. It reminds us of Walter Benjamin's description of one of his childhood photographs, an image of the times of 'those studios which – with their footstools and tripods, tapestries and easels – put you in mind of both a boudoir and a torture chamber'.[18] The ten-year-old Walter stood in such a studio in front of a 'crudely painted prospect of the Alps

14 In the chapter 'He Who Is Photographed', Barthes expresses such a desire: 'If only I could "come out" on paper as on a classical canvas, endowed with a noble expression – thoughtful, intelligent, etc!' See Barthes, p.11.

15 See Susanne Holschbach, *Vom Ausdruck zur Pose. Theatralität und Weiblichkeit in der Fotografie des 19. Jahrhunderts*, Berlin 2006.

16 See Barthes, p.15.

17 Ibid., p.14.

18 Walter Benjamin, *Berlin Childhood around 1900*, trans. Howard Eiland, Cambridge, Mass. and London 2006, p.132.

… surrounded by folding screens, cushions, and pedestals which craved my image much as the shades of Hades craved the blood of the sacrificial animal'.[19] One also thinks of Siegfried Kracauer's reflections on a portrait of his grandmother as a young woman which, without the stories told by relatives about the woman in the picture, is nothing but an 'archaeological mannequin', a 'doll in historic dress'.[20] Any reference to real life appears to be totally missing in this kind of portrait; the people are enclosed in a space and time of their own.

The advent, in the late nineteenth century, of handheld cameras for amateur photographers meant an escape from the artificial world of the photo studio and professional photographers. Handheld cameras could be taken anywhere and could even 'capture' movements. The child-photographer Jacques Henri Lartigue, for instance, continually photographed people as they jumped into the air or down steps – in moments of spontaneity and vitality that formed a stark contrast to the poses in front of a large-format camera. Even the ladies in their latest haute couture of the season and their escorts in tails, whom Lartigue caught strolling through the parks or at the races, hardly resemble lifeless mannequins, but are vivid examples of contemporary history (pp.31, 206). Amateurs such as Lartigue were the pioneers of a movement that increasingly spread in the first half of the twentieth century. Photographers went out into the streets in order to take pictures of people in moments when they thought themselves unnoticed in the anonymous crowd. Fashion photographers, too, left the artificial world of the studio and used the cityscape as a backdrop to infuse the models with life. The widespread domestic use of snapshots ultimately made a visit to the commercial photo studio redundant, so that the snapshot came to substitute the staged photograph, the ideal of being natural replacing that of being representative.

Interestingly, a modernisation of the studio portrait took place not in Europe, but in Africa, where commercial portrait photography continued to hold its ground well into the 1990s.[21] Its creative use of props, requisites, costumes and poses opened a new perspective onto staged European photography, which had found its way into African studios in colonial days and which subsequently evolved into an independent culture. The work of Malik Sidibé from the 1960s and 1970s, for instance, still conveys a true sense of contemporary life. The young people of Bamako, the commercial centre of Mali, met in Sidibé's street studio to exchange the latest news and to be photographed in their newest club attire. Their poses emanate confidence and assertiveness, filling the sparse studio space, which Sidibé managed to transform with very little means into a stage for his clients' self-portrayals (p.80).[22] Other photographers developed their work to a high artistic degree by using painted backcloths. The colourful stage props of Philip Kwame Apagya, for example, who has been running a photo studio in the Ghanaian harbour town of Shama since the early 1980s, are a response to his clientele's dream of a modern lifestyle. Urban motifs such as skylines, airports and apartment blocks transport the customer into a modern metropolitan environment. Room dividers with hi-fi and television sets as well as refrigerators full of food symbolise the epitome of consumerism. In this case, the poses are emblematic gestures through

19 Ibid., p.131.

20 See Siegfried Kracauer, *Die Photographie* (1927) in Siegfried Kracauer, *Der verbotene Blick, Beobachtungen, Analysen, Kritiken*, Leipzig 1992, p.187 (English translation by A. Kossack).

21 African studio photography was made available to the German public through exhibitions and publications such as Tobias Wendl and Heike Behrend (eds.), *'Snap me one!' Studiofotografen in Afrika*, Munich and New York 1998. In 2004, an interesting example of studio photography from 1960s and 1970s Beirut was shown in the Photographers' Gallery, London. See Lisa Le Feuvre and Akram Zaatari (eds.), *Hashem El Madani: Studio Practices*, Beirut and London 2004.

22 See André Magnin (ed.), *Malick Sidibé*, Göttingen 1998.

which the subject associates himself with his surroundings, seeing his ambitions fulfilled in the very photograph (p.111).

The studio can be a site of social control, discipline and normalisation – both African and European studio photography testify to this. But it can likewise liberate fantasies and create a space in which to adopt different roles and fictional identities. In the nineteenth century, many customers had their photograph taken either in exotic dress or historic costume, as worn at popular fancy dress balls of the time, or they chose an outfit from the photographer's stock of available costumes. But the playful potential of the pose – in which clothing and disguise are essential elements – best comes into its own when the subject is alone in the studio, is both model and photographer. The young artist Samuel Fosso, who opened a studio in Bangui, Nigeria, in the late 1970s, only needed a cloth for his backdrop, with a curtain left and right, to enact his self-portraits. Posing either as a cool hipster with spotlights to his left and right or as a shy boy half-hidden behind the curtain, or else grouping various requisites around him, Fosso not only continues to stage himself anew, but he performs this very self-enactment (pp.99, 211).[23] As for Cindy Sherman, she does nothing else when she slips into the role of different bus riders in front of a simple white wall – and, in doing so, demonstratively includes the cable of the camera's release (p.107). Sherman's work underlines the exemplary extent to which pose, masquerade and photography interact, how much it is beyond a mere game of dressing-up, how little it has to do with the self-portrait as such. Yet it shares a fundamental passion for posing that has accompanied photography since its very early days. The tiny space of the photo booth is at times sufficient to satisfy this passion for the pose, thus making the entire photo studio, its photographer included, totally superfluous.

23 See *Samuel Fosso, Seydou Keïta, Malick Sidibé: Portraits of Pride. West African Portrait Photography*, Stockholm 2003, pp.76, 81–103.

La Foto Chiari: Some Thoughts towards a Neorealist Photography
Jeremy Millar

If we consider the studio to be a place of creation – a place for the invention of selves, if not actual self-invention, a place of display and of demonstration too – then hasn't the street been the most important studio of all? Certainly it was the studio of modernity, from which much of modernism's fractured suddenness, its abrupt cacophony, its discordant renderings ruptured the Academic spirit of the age. Charles Baudelaire, that most provocative botaniser of the asphalt, promptly recognised the increasing value of the street to the artist of modernity, and it was in 'Loss of a Halo' (1865), one of his *petits poèmes en prose*, that his belief found perhaps its most fabulous expression. Here, the poet loses his aureole in the shifting chaos of the boulevard, but rather than attempt to retrieve it, he leaves it upon the ground and in doing so finds himself liberated; in the 'mire of the macadam' – both literal and moral – he discovers an array of experiences that had hitherto escaped him, and in submitting himself to them he is able to create an art that shares its dangerous energy. Indeed, such an act – a surrender to the anarchy of the street – becomes a necessity for any serious artist; it is only a bad poet who would concern himself with salvaging a tarnished and second-hand sanctity.

I cannot help but think here of two fictional characters, a writer, and a photographer, both of whom 'commit foul acts, and indulge in debauchery' as Baudelaire's poet hoped to do. It is the writer Marcello Rubini in Federico Fellini's *La dolce vita* (1960) that is by far the more complex of the two: a society journalist who enjoys the allure of Rome's decadent elite, yet looks longingly (or so he almost convinces himself) towards the 'halo' of being a serious writer. The photographer we barely know, since he seems barely to know himself, and yet it is his name that we remember: Paparazzo. 'Interesting work. Artistic, in a way', remarks Marcello's father to the photographer when they first meet, yet the older man's ignorance blinds him from Paparazzo's methods more effectively than the flash bulbs that these street photographers then toss, wasted, from their cameras (their subjects treated likewise). They chase film-stars and later squat in dusty gutters, waiting for a friend of Marcello's to arrive by bus before surrounding her with empty smiles and Graflex snarls. 'What's all this?' she asks, 'Do you think I'm some actress?' No: they know, instead, that she is about to be told by the police that her husband has taken the lives of their children, before taking his own. Another face on the street, and another photograph.

The manner in which these *raggazzi* act suggests why many people now view street photographers with a certain contempt. When real-life paparazzo Ron Galella repeats that 'You're either somebody or nobody', it is clear in whom he is interested; a photographer such as Garry Winogrand was, in this regard at least, somewhat less discerning, and allowed himself to impose upon the nobodies too. The attitude of the street photographer can, as a consequence, seem intrusive and aggressive and, with cold, clear eyes and ruthless effectiveness, more lupine than human (when Marlon Brando knocked out four of Galella's teeth with a single punch, the actor's hand became infected as a result).

Some photographers have been more withdrawn in their pursuit, although scarcely less relentless. In 1960, Ed van der Elsken followed a woman through the streets of Hong Kong – his presence would be too apparent to the woman for this activity to be described as 'stalking' – her bright white dress acting as a beacon for his camera amongst the grey of the city (p.97). Of course, van der Elsken's gaze is sexually charged – it follows a slim young woman in a tight-fitting Cheong-san dress, split up the thigh – and this might make viewers feel ill at ease. We learn nothing of the woman, unnamed and unknown, the whiteness of her clothing offering an undefined blankness that acts as a screen upon which the photographer – and by extension the viewer – can project his or her own thoughts, wishes and desires. Of course, this might be a projection in itself, and we could consider the woman less an object of desire than the personification of objective chance, much like the unwitting subjects of Vito Acconci's *Following Piece*, 1969, or Sophie Calle's *Suite Venitienne*, 1979. In this sense, the woman becomes an Oriental Nadja, who, like the eponymous heroine of André Breton's 1928 novel, is less a person than a state of mind, or a means by which one might try to understand the surrounding world.

As suggested above, one can always mitigate one's desires by making them appear more noble, or inconsequential, than might actually be the case, and in Laurie Anderson's *Fully Automated Nikon (Object/Objection/Objectivity)*, 1973 we can see this process of sublimation at work (p.104–5). The project was suggested while Anderson was eating in a seafood restaurant in Virginia, where she was mistaken for an actress in a long-running television serial. As her denials came to be taken, increasingly, as proof of this identity by the middle-aged woman who had approached her, Anderson asked if she could photograph her as a means of taking control of the situation. 'As I shot the photograph, I realised that photography is a kind of mugging, a kind of assault. I was shooting her, then stealing something.' Anderson continued this form of self-assertion upon her return to New York, deciding to photograph men who made comments to her on the street: 'I had always hated this invasion of my privacy and now I had the means of my revenge.' One need not be a student of the male psyche to predict that, upon being challenged by Anderson, the men acted as if victims themselves, although they recovered their sense of self-composure, and were soon posing for her camera 'like taking their picture was the least I could do'. Perhaps mindful of the legal consequences of publicly exhibiting these photographs, especially when they had often been coaxed with charm and untruths – 'I said he looked like my uncle and I wanted him to see his double' – Anderson then placed a strip of white card over the eyes of her subjects. The effect of this, however, is less one of legal protection or of guarding the privacy of those upon whom the camera had been turned, than, on the contrary, of a form of attack, a symbolic blinding. (Blinding is an act that has often been considered as a symbolic castration, and historically both blinding and castration were sometimes seen as equal and alternate punishments to the death penalty.) As such, the camera becomes considered as a judicial (even judicious) tool, albeit one that enacts a symbolic retribution.

A belief in the camera as a means of delivering social justice, or of social betterment, has long been held, however naively. For the burgeoning bourgeoisie of the nineteenth-century, a visit to the photographer's studio acted as a form of social confirmation; for others further down the social ladder, the visit of a camera-carrying activist might have presaged an act of progressive social or political change; for the most part, however, any direct causal connection between the making of a photograph and any social effect was almost impossible to establish. However, such a connection was explicitly made in a little-known film by Roberto Rossellini, *La macchina ammazzacattivi* (The Machine To Kill Bad People), begun in 1948 although not completed and released until four years later. The postwar period was a time of profound social, political and economic change in Italy, and many filmmakers were attempting to create an authentic native cinema in reaction to Fascism, and the popular 'white telephone' comedies that had dominated the 1930s (the white telephone being a desirable luxury item at the time). Whereas these earlier films had been characterised by the high production values that were to become embedded in the state-of-the-art Cinecittà studios, opened by Mussolini in 1937 – luxurious sets, perfect lighting and high cinematic style – the films that became known as 'neorealist' had a quite different, albeit equally distinctive, visual style. This was partly a technical necessity – Cinecittà had been stripped by the retreating Germans and Italian Fascists in the late summer of 1943 – and partly a moral necessity: the realities of war and its attendant hunger, poverty and destruction gave these filmmakers a subject – and sense of moral urgency – that overwhelmed all other concerns. The street was to become the studio.

In its use of location shooting, non-professional actors, natural light, non-interventionist direction, and the avoidance of complex editing and other post-production techniques, neorealist film owed far more to the documentary filmmaking of someone like Robert Flaherty than to the lush social comedies of earlier Italian cinema; as Rossellini himself remarked, 'Things are there. Why manipulate them?' This was cinema *contra* cinema, or, as the critic André Bazin wrote of Vittorio De Sica's *Ladri di biciclette* (Bicycle Thieves, 1948), one of the most important neorealist films: 'There are no more actors, no more story, no more mise-en-scène, that is to say finally in the aesthetic illusion of reality – no more cinema.' Of course, this was not an attempt to destroy cinema *completamente*, and no one closely involved in the movement was naive enough to believe in the possibility of a cinema of unmediated reality; rather, their intervention was to move beyond the merely cinematic, even the merely real, towards a cinematic reality that was somehow even more real than reality itself.

Reality, of course, is never so easily contained, and even as critics attempted to define the emergent neorealist cinema, its directors were already subverting it from within, and Rossellini's *La macchina ammazzacattivi* is a prime example of this. Certainly, it is not the director's finest film, and, sitting uneasily between the completion of *L'amore* (1948) and the release of *Europa '51* (1952), it has been considered little more than a *commedia dell'arte* aberration for those committed to Rossellini as a realist master, yet it is its exploration of the destructive power of the photographic portrait that justifies our attention here. As is typical of the genre, the plot itself is convoluted, and its minutiae need not detain us unduly. The film opens in a town on the Amalfi coast, and follows the seemingly miraculous events that occur the day after the appearance of a barefoot old man who, it is clearly suggested, is the town's patron saint, Andrew. The fishing boats return laden, and a grant of eleven million lire is received from the central government, although the only supernatural act that we actually see him perform is on the day previously, in the studio of Celestino Esposito, the town's photographer and the film's central character. The old man arrives at the studio – La Foto Chiari – asking for a chair in which to spend the night and, after being led inside, enters into a conversation with the photographer about the town and the events that had occurred earlier on this, the Saint's festival day. Celestino remarks that Saint Andrew seems to have forgotten the town, to which the old man replies that good men must act to eradicate those who do evil. Having earlier witnessed Celestino arguing with a policeman while photographing the festival procession – an antipathy that goes back to an earlier quarrel over a shared love – the old man asks the photographer to bring him a portrait of the policeman, and then to photograph it with his camera. 'It's done', Celestino says. 'Done?' the old man replies, 'I'd say it's his undoing.' Rushing outside to find out what has happened, Celestino comes across a crowd gesturing at the policeman, who is standing stiff and lifeless, his arm outstretched in a Fascist salute, frozen in the pose he held in the picture that Celestino has just photographed. Returning to the studio, Celestino finds that the old man has disappeared; the blessed – or cursed – camera, his means of combating evil, remains.

Suitably empowered, Celestino begins to take up what he believes to be the Saint's good work, re-photographing portraits and thereby freezing those who are attempting to benefit personally from the town's good fortune, most notably the wealthy – and corrupt – politicians and businessmen who make up the town's council. It soon becomes clear, however, that it is not just the rich who are susceptible to avarice: the priest wants the money to be spent on new faux-Byzantine mosaics, and even the poor – who had been portrayed in many a neorealist film as blameless victims – are blinded by self-interest. Celestino's indignation at the evil and selfishness of those around him leads him to freeze more and more of the town's citizens – 'I have to exterminate the wicked!' he declares – until, in a moment of remorse, he decides to turn the camera upon a portrait of himself, but only after he has destroyed the old man who had started the trouble. He reappears in the photographer's studio and is revealed not as Saint Andrew but as a minor demon, who had hoped to make a name for himself 'down there' with his new invention. (It is interesting to note that in his seminal study on light and shadow *Ars Magna Lucis et Umbrae* (1646), Athanasius Kircher explains the principle of the *camera obscura* by using an illustration in which the image is associated with the devil.) Celestino forces him to make the sign of the cross and everything is restored to as it was before.

While some critics have dismissed the film as being socially conservative – the status quo, with all its ills, is re-established after all – I would suggest that Rossellini is attempting something more subtle than simple condemnation, something that we would do well to consider when we look at, and think about, the photographs gathered here. At the beginning of the film, the camera − and its related forms of filmic representation − is presented as a means of moral and ethical apprehension, the means by which profound truths can be captured and then understood. Suitably equipped, Celestino considers himself as possessing a vision somehow more penetrating than that of his fellow citizens, certainly a vision that can break through the surface appearance of reality and reveal the actual substance of that which surrounds him; indeed, it is the burden of this gift, and his frustration with the moral blindness of the others, that seems to exacerbate his self-righteous indignation and further intensifies his photographic vengeance. It is important to remember, therefore, that Celestino's camera does not act directly upon people when they are photographed by it, but only when their portraits are photographed; of course, this has a certain comic advantage (when certain figures are frozen with no apparent cause), and it also removes Celestino from the scene of the crime, but I would suggest that such a separation is more meaningful than that. In taking a photograph of another photograph, Celestino is not moving towards a supposedly higher form of reality as he believes, but, as any Platonist might offer, is moving further away, producing instead a representation of a representation of our own shadow of reality. The connection between art and reality is not strengthened but weakened.

To paraphrase Roland Barthes (who, like Jean-Luc Godard, knew two or three things about portraits and cities), Celestino's machine is not just a camera, but it is hardly a just camera either. This is made even more apparent when we consider that he does not actually use it to reveal the truth of a person − their relative good or evil − but rather to enact a punishment based upon no more than his own conviction. One cannot look to the mechanical procedure of the making of a photograph − or indeed a film − to provide meaning or value, whether aesthetic, intellectual, moral or otherwise; one must look instead to the broader context in which the photograph or film is being made, including the intentions of the maker (which is why Rossellini argued that neorealism was 'above all moral position from which one looks at the world. It then becomes an aesthetic position, but it begins as a moral one'). The two photographs − the original portrait and Celestino's copy − might, for all intents and purposes, be identical, but if the intentions and purposes of each image differ, then the meanings of the photographs must differ too. The original photograph of the mayor as a baby, for example, was made to celebrate the gift of life, whereas its copy was made in order to remove that gift; the meanings of these two identical portraits could scarcely be more different.

This brief discussion on an old − and obscure − Italian film might seem rather obtuse, particularly in response to the wealth of photographic imagery that surrounds us here, but it is hoped that it might encourage a richer engagement with these works. Who is being photographed, and by whom? Why is the photographer making these pictures, and for which other reasons might they then become valuable, meaningful or important? At times the answers to such questions are not so clear. In Richard Avedon's tripartite portrait of the Chicago Seven, for example, taken in 1969, we see the protesters − Rennie Davis, David Dellinger, John Froines,

Tom Hayden, Abbie Hoffman, Jerry Rubin and Lee Weiner – who were charged with conspiracy, inciting to riot and other charges related to violent protests at the Democratic National Convention held in Chicago the previous year (pp.94–5). It is a strange and awkward portrait, not least because of the relatively disparate appearance of those within the group, from the outward respectability of Dellinger's jacket and tie to Hoffman's skinny-jeaned indifference. Avedon emphasises this sense further by making the image unbalanced, leaving gaps between figures, even slicing and repeating parts of Hoffman and Rubin where the separate exposures join, and indicating that this is a shift in time as well as space as their poses alter slightly between the two. Avedon developed this frieze-like format earlier in the year, photographing Warhol and members of his Factory in a similarly empty white space, with the actor Joe Dallesandro moving from the left to the right-hand frame, as we would usually read it; he used it again a year and a half later, photographing not those protesting against the Vietnam war but rather those implementing it, the Mission Council, the highest-ranking military and civilian managers on the American side of the conflict. It was in the two works taken later, on both sides of the Sixties' ideological divide, that Avedon withdrew somewhat, preferring to adopt an attitude that is disinterested rather than indifferent, as though preparing a police line-up with no sense of who, if anyone, might be guilty.

We might consider some of Bruno Serralongue's photographs with a similar sense of uncertainty, especially the series of photographs of the weekly protests of the 'sans-papiers' (immigrants without the necessary legal papers) (p.120–1). These photographs are testament to the determination and dignity of a group of men who were demanding the right to a life of decency in France, and valuable for this, but do they look so very different from photographs that the police might take to document the demonstration for their own rather different (and ultimately disruptive) reasons? (We might, in turn, be reminded of the celebratory photographs taken by the Communards in Paris, 1871, which were subsequently use to condemn them, or similarly the photojournalism of Tereza in Milan Kundera's novel *The Unbearable Lightness of Being* which was used by the invading Soviet authorities to identify Czechoslovakian protesters). This is not to belittle Serralongue's photographs, certainly not, but rather to emphasise the inescapable complexity involved when we photograph anything, and people more than all else. Bazin remarked that Rossellini 'directed facts', and one might ask how many of these photographers act likewise, and how different these photographs might look if we considered them thus: these teenagers in doorways, intermittently aware of being beautiful, or the Ukrainian *bohmzes* posing naked in wastelands, and wasted themselves. And what of the Japanese woman in Araki's *Tokyo* (1973)? How different in would be to see her walking, instead, in the photographs of Philip-Lorca diCorcia, where light surges into the city's gloaming, or down the streets that float and fade upon Beat Streuli's projection screens, as if in a film whose mind has begun to wander. Perhaps our minds should wander too, so that we might return to these photographs later to see how much they have changed, while staying the same, and how much of ourselves remains within them.

Urban Characters, Imaginary Cities
Florian Ebner

Pictures of sleepers and slumbering images

A century both defines a given stretch of time and demarcates discrete historical eras. As a term, 'turn of the century' not only refers to a calendar change, but also suggests a world in the process of transformation. Yet a glance at the works of two photographers – one working at the turn of the nineteenth century, the other at the turn of the twentieth – suggests that the worlds they reveal have changed very little. There are a surprising number of similarities in their imagery. Indeed, both men – the one, Louis Vert, a Parisian printer's employee and an amateur photographer, the other, Francis Alÿs, a trained architect and artist living in Mexico City – dedicate a series of photographs to the 'public sleepers' in their respective societies, who make their beds in the street, on park benches or in the entrances of houses. Another series by each photographer centres on the subject of city hawkers, who are shown, with all their goods and chattels, as unremarkable, natural figures in these environments. Both photographers – the member of the Société d'Excursions d'Amateurs de Photographie as well as the internationally exhibited artist – present their work as slide projections and, thus, overtly to their respective public.[1]

1 For further information on the photographers and works discussed in this essay, see the related sections in the Index.

Upon closer scrutiny, however, it turns out that these very similarities in subject matter reveal a world that has indeed changed. In *Sleepers* 1999–2006, a series of eighty photographs, Alÿs juxtaposes the homeless or stranded people lying in the streets of Mexico City with just as many stray dogs – a seemingly provocative combination (see pp.138–9). The deep perspective – the camera is almost on ground level – suggests a certain solidarity or intimacy, directly referring to a place that the megalopolis has reserved for its drop-outs: the asphalt of the street. In contrast to these laconic recordings, part of Alÿs's extensive exploration of urban characters, the photographs of clochards (tramps) taken about a hundred years earlier by Louis Vert on the quays of the Seine in Paris, bear more picturesque nuances. Vert was only one of many photographers, who took an interest in this subject, profoundly appreciated by painters and travellers.

The French amateur also photographed the representatives of the *petits métiers* (small trades) between 1900 and 1902, apparently sensing that these livelihoods might soon disappear from the cityscape in a rapidly modernising Paris (p.25). Similarly, the *Ambulantes* or hawkers, captured by Alÿs between 1992 and 2006 document the countless, makeshift 'shadow economies' nestled into the nooks and crannies of Mexico's metropolis. More interesting than a socio-historical commentary on changes in the global field over time, however, are other questions raised by these photographs. Which characters of the city did photography seek out to document or even create? What was it about them that fascinated the photographer, influencing his choice to depict them in a certain way? Which urban archetypes have we stored in our collective subconscious?

Encounters on the boulevard

Interest in street life and city promenading place both Vert and Alÿs within the long modernist tradition of urban *flâneurs*. The contemporary artist Alÿs may have adopted a faster pace, regarding modern life from the end of all urban utopias, and he may perhaps regard the *bourgeois* concept of the *flâneur* as dated, yet, like his historic precursors, his is a sensibility that defies the progressive commercialisation of all aspects of life.

The roots of the *flâneur* lie in the inexhaustible reservoir of images and stimulating experiences offered by the streets of nineteenth-century Paris. In his text *Le Peintre de la vie moderne* (The Painter of Modern Life), Charles Baudelaire wrote that the *flâneur*'s: 'passion and profession is to be one with the crowd. For the true *flâneur*, for the impassioned observer, it is a great pleasure to feel at home in the waves of the crowd, in movement, in the fugitive and the infinite.'[2] Baudelaire defines the transitory, the fleeting and the contingent as the aesthetic principles of the avant garde, exercised in the bustling activity of the boulevard, in the parks and at the race course.

The *flâneur* has many faces: not only does he pursue a veritable passion for collecting the oddities of the streets – as in the case of Louis Vert who gathered the pictures of hawkers and tramps – but he is also interested in novel encounters with the opposite sex. In his poems *Les Fleurs du mal* (The Flowers of Evil), Baudelaire captures the fleeting beauty of such moments. The sonnet *A une passante* (To a Woman Passing By), first published in 1860 in the journal *L'Artiste*, makes the modern reader think of a snapshot. The narrator's encounter with an unknown woman in the street appears fixed or frozen, concretised in a few visual fragments. This quality of frozen time lends the *flâneur*'s vision a photographic aura. But it is a pre-photographic one, since instantaneous photography would not be possible for three decades, with the introduction of faster emulsions and more manageable hand cameras. In Baudelaire's eyes, the young medium of photography that, through the studio portrait, provided a means of self-adulation for the bourgeoisie, was still, at best, a 'humble servant' of the sciences and arts. Thus, the representation of contingency as the epitome of the photographic has not been invented by photography, but stems from an urban sensitivity that was later to find its ideal form of expression in that medium.

From the 1890s onwards, amateur photographers began to fill their photo albums with images of metropolitan street life. Henri Rivière, for instance, was a graphic artist as well as a passionate photographer, who used his camera to capture the hustle and bustle of Parisian boulevards and of pedestrians rushing past him (p.19). By the early 1910s, one young amateur no longer had faith in chance encounters on the boulevard: the seventeen-year-old Jacques Henri Lartigue had to scout the Bois de Boulogne in order to capture the bourgeois daughters of Paris, out on their leisurely strolls, and take them home with him as photographic trophies (pp.31, 206).

The photographic apparatus was a precious instrument for the *flâneur*; with it, he could capture the fleeting encounter and give concrete form to the gaze of desire, yet it was a weapon that betrayed his voyeurism. Conversely, his status as a secret observer – 'the observer is a prince who celebrates his incognito everywhere'[3] – allowed the *flâneur* to become a widely used metaphor for the street photographer, appearing in numerous publications on this subject.[4] Thus, the figure of the *flâneur*,

2 Charles Baudelaire, *Le Peintre de la vie moderne* (1859), *Figaro*, 3 Dec. 1863 (translation by Ariane Kossack).

3 Ibid.

4 See Colin Westerbeck and Joel Meyerowitz, *Bystander: A History of Street Photography*, Boston 1994.

the observer who both writes and takes photographs, is just as much a product of the city as the *clochard*, the prostitute, the ragpicker or the dandy. At the same time, however, he was and is their chronicler.

Picturesque scenes and candid shots

When, in the mid-nineteenth century, photographers took to the streets, illustrators and painters were there already. They were responding to a growing interest in the illustration of urban figures. In the early 1850s, Charles Nègre, an academically trained painter, began to produce photographic genre scenes of organ grinders and ragpickers. His photographs of *Les amoneurs en marche* (Chimney Sweeps Walking), staged at the Quai Bourbon in Paris around 1851 (p.18), remind us of urban scenes in paintings by Honoré Daumier or the later lithographs of Gustave Doré.[5] Upon close scrutiny, the photographic dimension of his shots – their seemingly frozen movement – turn out to be fake; put differently, these are imagined instantaneous photographs. Nègre's moving figures only simulate the gestures of a walker, thus revealing one of the paradoxes of early photography: that the impression of naturalness in movement could only be transmitted by the artificial pose of a frozen gesture. In the eyes of Nègre's contemporaries, this may not have been a paradox, since the styles of early documentary photography developed out of the tradition of staging common both to portrait and photo studios.[6] John Thomson's photographs in his book *Street Life in London* (1877–8) are to be read in this vein (p.24). These thirty-six pictures are carefully structured genre compositions featuring odd characters like *Caney the Clown*, *Street Doctor* or *The Crawler*, a photograph of painful poverty. Thomson's depiction of the life of ordinary people continues yet another, and this time iconographic, tradition: the *Cries of London* or the *Cris de Paris* (i.e. the market criers of London or Paris). This picturesque series of lithographed and handcoloured drawings introduces the many urban actors of the city, the small traders, in the form of individual portrait figures.

By 1900, there was an expansive collection of photographic material translating these lithographic genre portrayals back into the reality of urban life. Eugène Atget's renowned photo portraits of the *petits métiers* and *clochards*, which he collected in the series entitled *Paris Pittoresque*, as well as Vert's contemporaneous unstaged (straight) photographs (p.25), or the later work of the Berlin photographer Willy Römer, are all examples of the appropriation of this genre by photography. Apart from locating figures within a detailed cityscape, photography's novel contribution to visual urban culture was its wide and inexpensive distribution in the form of postcards. But even more, photography conferred a face to the representational tradition of types depicting its subjects as true characters in contrast to the illustrated stereotypes of the lithographic prints: the knife-grinder, the shoe-shiner, the tinker, the broom-maker, the street musician, the balloon vendor, the bird dealer, the coal man – they were, at the same time, human beings with individual traits and features.

To supplement the visual archive of old Europe before the First World War, we find a different critical view of street characters simultaneously emerging in the 'new

5 See Françoise Heilbrun, *Charles Nègre. Das photographische Werk*, Munich 1988.

6 See Monika Faber, 'Die Tradition der Inszenierung', in *Das Auge und der Apparat*, Ostfildern 2003, pp.16-23.

world'. The beggars photographed by the American social reformer Lewis Hine in the streets of New York around 1910 no longer possess the picturesque romanticism of a *clochard* on the banks of the Seine. Children are not depicted watching the organ- or knife-grinder in rapt fascination, since it is the paperboys themselves who are now the subjects of the photos, which Hine used in his battle against child labour (p.34). These photographs have become visual documents in the social debate and are a far cry from the 'Documents pour artistes' that Atget created. Even if Hine makes use, in part, of a traditional iconography to anchor his compositions of figures, these images lay claim to another reality: 'Look at this! I have seen it!' This is the political side to the 'straight photography' that Paul Strand was soon to capture with the immediacy of his candid shots.

In 1917, issue 49/50 of the American avant-garde journal *Camera Work* shook the established milieu of art photography with an abrupt invasion of reality. As its editor Alfred Stieglitz observed: 'The work is brutally direct. Devoid of all flim-flam; devoid of trickery and of any 'ism' … These photographs are the direct expression of today.'[7] The 'brutal directness' of the photos, taken with a hidden camera in the streets of New York by a twenty-six-year-old Strand, derives from the fact that they show people of the street – a yawning market woman, a blind peddler (p.4), a sandwich man – in an uncanny proximity to the lens never before seen, and entirely devoid of poses. Following modernistic pictorial language, the models are partly truncated in the pictures, appearing as a bust or a half-torso, comparable to a representational studio portrait. Yet they still depict the 'Man of the Crowd'. Photography's artistic borrowings from painting, pursued for over seventy years, have faded into the background. In Strand's images, photography seemed to have come into its own. Admittedly, there is something fundamentally teleological in such a claim, yet one cannot help seeing them as the dawning of a new era.

A photographic editing of society

In 1931, Walker Evans, a young photographer and intellectual, introduced the American reading public to photo books from Europe in the journal *Hound & Horn*. He included a publication by his colleague August Sander, stating: '*Antlitz der Zeit* is more than a book of 'type studies' … It is a photographic editing of society, a clinical process.'[8] Sander's famous project, which aimed to be a comprehensive atlas of portraits of German society, of which *Antlitz der Zeit* (Face of our Time) 1929 was but a first excerpt, is much more than a simple collection of character types (p.53). It is a narrative in pictures that expresses a wariness of civilisation and which would be unimaginable without the cult of physiognomy that had apparently taken hold of a polarised society in the German Weimar Republic. If we were to try to understand the metropolis of that time through these images only, as arranged by the photographer in his metropolitan portfolios, it would appear to us as a gathering of the artistic *bohème*, of vagrants and stranded souls. Sander's monumental oeuvre is of a clinical beauty; nonetheless, it stems from two traditions: the 'ordinary' photographic studio portrait, and the picturesque character study of the street.

7 Alfred Stieglitz: 'Our Illustrations', in *Camera Work*, nos.49/50, June 1917, cited in Pam Roberts, 'Alfred Stieglitz, 291 Gallery and Camera Work' in *Alfred Stieglitz: Camera Work, The Complete Illustrations 1903–1917*, Cologne 1997, p.28.

8 Walker Evans, 'The Reappearance of Photography', in *Hound & Horn*, no.5, 1931, cited in Jeff L. Rosenheim and Alexis Schwarzenbach (eds.), *Unclassified: A Walker Evans Anthology*, Zurich 2000, p.84.

Evans's concept of the 'editing of society' reminds us of a new form of visual culture that flourished in the early 1930s: namely, the world of the illustrated magazine, which displayed the entirely new reality of urban life. The flashy pages of the tabloids both reproduced and constructed modern character types such as the 'new woman', a socially emancipated figure imaginable only in the liberating environment of the modern city. Yva's fashion photos and photo stories for the Ullstein press (p.40) and Edward Steichen's celebrity portraits for *Vogue* and *Vanity Fair* (p.49) helped to mass-circulate the role models of a new urban lifestyle, which the promenading bourgeoisie, a few years earlier, could only find in the window displays of the photo studios along the wide city boulevards. Therefore, the shop windows and the illustrated magazines are related media in the dialectical relationship between the production of images and their reception, a relationship constantly upheld between street and studio.

Evans's concept of the 'editing of society' also refers to his own work. The American photographer does not investigate his society according to principles of originality, as seen in the European urban figures of Sander and his precursors. Instead, he seeks the face of the ordinary Joe, the average American. Evans's own embodiment of the *flâneur* allowed him to remain incognito in the crowd, yet his approach reflects the continuing mechanisation of society's cultural fabric. Between 1938 and 1941, he used a hidden camera to photograph the passengers sitting opposite him in the New York subway. When experimenting with his material later, at the end of the 1950s, Evans isolates the passengers' heads as if they were pictures taken in a photo booth or even mug shots for the police. In 1946, his camera indiscriminately registered the passers-by rushing through the streets of an industrial zone in Detroit – his is a fixed, hidden point of view, which maintains a deep perspective. It is Evans's typology of passing workers that lends visual expression to the contemporary experience of the Tayloristic zeitgeist.[9] In the same year, Evans published a selection of photographs under the title 'Labour Anonymous' on a double-page spread of the journal *Fortune*, having suggested 'A cast of characters in an industrial city, 1946' as an alternative title (p.61).[10]

Evans's recourse to photographic techniques (serial uniformity, neutral background and standardisation) is reminiscent of the practice of studio portraiture. After the Second World War, a number of photographers rediscovered the traditional (or improvised) studio as a site for taking photos, in order to rid the urban figures and social types of their everyday surroundings and to give them a stage on which to present themselves as individuals. For *Vogue*, Irving Penn undertook a large-scale, fifteen-year project as photographer in charge of an itinerant photo studio. In his series of urban characters photographed in Paris, London and New York in 1950, it is again the representatives of the *petits métiers* who epitomise their respective cities (p.63). Penn finds his models in the street and invites them into his rented daylight studio in their work clothes. The studio backdrop serves as a rolled-out platform on which his subjects can stage their presence. Ultimately, however, it is the photographer's eye and his choreographic talent that not only allow his models to represent their trade, but also enable each one of them to emerge as an original character. Penn's work breathes the humanistic spirit of the 1950s.

9 Taylorism refers to the principles expressed in Frederick Taylor's *The Principles of Scientific Management* (1911), relating to the organisation of labour in the workplace.

10 Evans, 'The Reappearance of Photography', p.189.

The face of the other half

If we consider the photo studio as a locale that not only reproduces civic identity, but constructs an 'image' as well, then it is not a neutral space, but one of social metamorphosis. The photographer and film cameraman Helmar Lerski confirms this assertion in his series *Heads from Everyday Life*. In the late 1920s, he invited his protagonists into his Berlin studio: the *Charwoman* (p.42), the *Receptionist*, the *Metal Worker* or the *Beggar from Saxony*, all of them transformed under his spotlight into soulful figures or rebellious characters. These portraits, reminiscent of close-ups of the silver screen, polarised ideological debates among his contemporaries in Germany. Kenneth Macpherson, editor of the British film-journal *Close Up*, defended Lerski's idealised approach against conservative criticism in an issue of 1931, arguing that dreams of social advance clearly found more legitimisation in the fictitious world of contemporary film than in the reality of the photo portrait: 'One has to ask oneself … what might the distinctive features of a washerwoman be? … May she never transcend the washtub, her face be never anything, but steamily puffy and pink? … According to our Berlin critic, however, it would appear that the virtue of film is the vice of photography.'[11]

When, in 1990, the American artist Andres Serrano set up an itinerant photo studio in a New York subway station, replete with artificial light and colourful backdrops, it was not the anonymous subway riders whom he asked to sit as models for his camera, but rather the homeless people dwelling there, the 'faceless and nameless people whom we don't even ordinarily look at'.[12] Serrano's *Nomads* are large-format photographs that exchange Lerski's pictorial language of the silent film for the iconography of painted portraits of monarchs (p.113). For a postmodern artist, Serrano's approach is marked by a surprisingly clear social engagement, yet at the same time, the use of the photographic medium places him in a long tradition of portraiture, which has taken an interest in the face of the 'other' for entirely different reasons.

The nineteenth century relied on studio photography to develop a somewhat dubious science that concerned the categorisation of delinquents. At the turn of the century, driven by a more innocent inquisitiveness, many photographers began to explore the dark and unknown quarters of the city. The German private tutor Arnold Genthe photographed with a hidden camera San Francisco's exotic Chinatown, a world he found fascinating for its vibrant culture and characters such as *The Toy Peddler* (p.35) or *The Opium Fiend* (p.205). Sixty years later, the Catalan Joan Colom ventured into similar extraterritorial areas in his hometown of Barcelona. Armed, like Genthe, with a hidden camera, he roamed the red-light district of Raval in search of furtive glances, gestures and poses in a street culture governed by prostitution (pp.70, 207). In contrast to Colom's crude photo fragments, we find that Brassaï's lonesome figures in nocturnal Paris in the 1930s resemble protagonists on a theatre stage: the prostitute, the suitor, the trickster, the cop, the ragpicker. One of the greatest usurpers of the nocturnal urban drama was the reporter Weegee, who used a harsh flash to illuminate the criminal abysses of New York City, presented to us in the book *Naked City* (1945).

11 Kenneth Macpherson, 'As Is', in *Close Up*, 1931, p.220.

12 Coco Fusco, *Shooting the Klan: An Interview with Andres Serrano*, http://www.communityarts.net/readingroom/archivefiles/2002/09/shooting_the_kl.php

In her essay 'Melancholy Objects', published in her book *On Photography*, Susan Sontag wrote: 'The photographer is an armed version of the solitary walker reconnoitring, stalking, cruising the urban inferno, the voyeuristic stroller who discovers the city as a landscape of voluptuous extremes. Adept of the joys of watching, connoisseur of empathy, the *flâneur* finds the world "picturesque".'[13] In this text, the photographer-*flâneur* has lost his innocence: as a member of the bourgeoisie, his interest in the shady environs of the city – 'an unofficial reality behind the façade of bourgeois life that the photographer "apprehends" as a detective apprehends a criminal' – arouses suspicion.[14] Yet Sontag's reproach goes further still, arguing that photography essentially amasses images of the world without truly comprehending it. 'The camera makes everyone a tourist in other people's reality',[15] but is itself indifferent towards it. Sontag's essay reflects a criticism of the media typical of the 1970s, which she was to revise in a later text. However, it is due to photography's compulsion to collect in an apparently indifferent manner that it has provided the very bedrock of our visual memory of the city.

Scenarios and archetypes

There is a certain sculptural allure to the character types in Lisette Model's photographs. The scrawny old woman of the Lower East Side clad in a threadbare coat (p.54), the shouting newspaper vendor, the fat tourists on the Promenade des Anglais, or yesterday's bourgeoisie on the American boulevards. The photographer's tight framing of the shot and her chosen lens isolate the figures from their scenery as if cut out in front of a urban decor, their shapes entirely filling the picture. We see them as archetypes today, as emblematic figures of the street. Model also photographs the sleepers of the city; the photo of a female *clocharde* taken in Paris in the 1930s has a strangely archaic quality, and its deep perspective creates a sense of intimacy (p.208). The recumbent body not only dominates the picture's horizontal axis, but also *signifies* it: the horizontal line alludes to the existential condition of all those who are out of sync with the city's operating system. It is no coincidence that the *clochard* has been the most photographed urban subject since the advent of the handheld camera. In contrast to the reclining *clochard*, we notice the verticality of the pedestrian whose gait is upright, energetic, rushed, confident, and who is framed by an urban architecture stretching skyward. This formulation is the result of a kind of somatic knowledge fed and stored by our constant visual appropriation of still images. According to theories of cognitive science, a child understands the world in terms of a scenario: a visit to the restaurant entails a waiter, guests, table manners and, finally, the bill.[16] Thus, our concept of unfamiliar urban sites such as the slum, the brothel or the stock exchange may well derive from a number of photographic and filmic images of spaces, actions and people. Indeed, from a historical point of view, our acculturation to the modern metropolis coincided with the young medium of photography. Amidst the rapidly growing number of public images in magazines and books, on postcards, billboards and in exhibitions – through which photography has fashioned our visual conception of the modern city – the view of the individual has become particularly important. Photography – whether due to the remnants of a humanist tradition of allocating a name and role to every

13 Susan Sontag, *On Photography*, London 1978, p.55.

14 Ibid., p.56.

15 Ibid., p.57.

16 See George Lakoff, *Women, Fire and Dangerous Things: What Categories Reveal about the Mind*, Chicago 1987.

individual in society, or to photography's empathy as a medium that always incorporates the other – has brought together an imaginary ensemble of characters without which it would be impossible to visualise the urban spectacle. In this respect, photography has contributed, both in quantity and in quality, to the legacy of painting and its portrayal of character types. As a pictorial medium, photography also provides a link to the performative arts – in the street as in the studio. Not without reason are Brassaï's protagonists reminiscent of the cast list, for instance, of a play by Bertolt Brecht, or Cindy Sherman's *Bus Riders* (p.107) similar to that of a Martin Scorsese film.

Different approaches in contemporary photography reflect how these figures have survived and left their indelible mark on our perception of the city. Even if 'straight photography' has in recent years gone back to the archetypes of the street (especially the pedestrian), often emphasising seriality, another phenomenon should be mentioned here: since the 1980s, the street has again become the showplace for a form of staged photography partly produced under the technical conditions of the studio. As stated earlier, photography followed the tradition of staging from its earliest beginnings. Yet now it is a 'directorial photography' – Jeff Wall's light boxes, illuminating different forms of social conflict (p.122), or the errant figures of Valérie Jouve (p.117) for example – that enacts a 'culture of the street'. Last but not least, urban street characters have also found refuge in the studio. The encounter with the other in the street has now been exchanged for a certain allegorical play. In Suzanne Lafont's photographs, staged between 1995 and 1998, figures move in front of a black background like *revenants* of a bygone culture. The elements that Lisette Model managed to extract from the contingent flux of the street are here illuminated under a spotlight; the essence of movement, activity and attitude leaves traces of a melancholic flow of 'afterimages'. Lafont's *Le Marcheur* (Passer-by) has not yet lost the rhythm of the modern city; he might be an allegory for the pace of the sidewalk, an uncontrollable automaton overexposed by the photographic apparatus (p.119). As for the *Balayeur* (Street Sweeper), he must quickly brush away the last traces of the past, since machines now clean the boulevards, and the utopias of the city are being written elsewhere.

The Narrative City:
Image, Glamour and Isolation
Michael Bracewell

'Starlight open wide. Everybody is a star!'
Lou Reed, Songs for Drella, 1990

I Let a writer introduce the modern city

For the young, handsome, successful American novelist F. Scott Fitzgerald, wearing a good English suit and with a snappy spring in his step, there was little doubt that the streets of his adopted New York City were the place of infinite stories.

On his premature death in 1941, Fitzgerald's friend Edmund Wilson would write: 'he was better than he knew, for in fact and in the literary sense he invented a generation'. And when one thinks of that act of invention now – the incapsulation in prose of a new, technologically enabled epoch, the Jazz Age, gift-wrapped in glamour and rendered imperial by the combined forces of money and mass production – one might compare its visceral intensity to the simultaneously expanding and accelerating medium of photography. As Hollywood later came to provide Fitzgerald with some of his greatest fiction, so throughout his career he was a writer obsessed with the construction of image, be that personal or literary.

This was a fascination that had begun in his adolescence, and would become all but obsessive during his years as a student at Princeton. How did one define oneself through one's demeanour and appearance? Half a century before the pundits of the British style press had begun to invent sophisticated, partially ironic, periodic tables of trend, individualism and fashionability, Fitzgerald was compiling an index of social types that was both profound and flippant – an intellectual balancing act that would accompany the tragic drive to self-destruction at the centre of both his fiction and his own chaotic career. The perilous, fathomless depths of image, and the mirroring and manipulation of image within the new, commercial industries of film and advertising, would be explored with a lucidity and psychological acuity that were as visual as they were literary.

The era so seductively chronicled by the earlier Jazz Age writings of Fitzgerald is similarly brought to life by both social realist and 'society' photographers. Streets scenes, poignant moments of urban life, are matched by, for example, Cecil Beaton's dazzling portraits of the wealthy, fashionable, bohemian and aristocratic. In Beaton's portrait photography from the years between the First and Second World Wars, one is shown the sartorial and narcissistic extravagance of a class and generation whose poised flamboyance would become a key model for the dandys and dolly birds of the Pop age, forty years later. It is entirely within the focus of a Fitzgeraldian vision, however, to set such glamour, in all of its surrealistic aggression, beside the realities of life for the new consumer classes, weighed down with long hours and financial depression.

Here, for instance, is a scene from *The Beautiful and Damned*, first published in 1922:

> Anthony and Gloria, seated, looked about them. At the next table a party
> of four were in process of being joined by a party of three, two men and
> a girl, who were evidently late – and the manner of the girl was a study
> in national sociology. She was meeting some new men – and she was
> pretending desperately. By gesture she was pretending and by words and
> by the scarcely perceptible motionings of her eyelids that she belonged to a
> class a little superior to the class with which she now had to do, that a while
> ago she had been, and presently would again be, in a higher, rarer air.
> She was almost painfully refined – she wore a last year's hat covered with
> violets no more yearningly pretentious and palpably artificial than herself.

In its cruelty as much as its clarity, this is a scene that reads in almost entirely photographic terms: a representational description of a social group, nuanced and framed, as regards the reader's empathetic relationship with the image, by a forceful confluence of emotive details. In effect, although we are taken to this cheap, New York cabaret bar by Fitzgerald's characters – two upper-class young Americans in the first flush of romance – we are seeing the scene from the author's point of view, as through a lens. The constant slide within the routines of urban life – routines circumscribed by tireless consumption – between work and pleasure, giving rise to moments of startling individualism as much as common anonymity, is studied in its American context by the photography of Lisette Model and Helen Levitt. For both of these photographers, intimacy and vulnerability, presence and transience, become key themes within the quotidian drama their work reveals. The tension between overt and covert subjectivity, detachment and poise, would be a further strand in Fitzgerald's writing that enabled his capturing of the eloquent image; hence Jay Gatsby will be seen standing on the extravagant garden steps of his mansion on Long Island Sound, dressed in 'a gorgeous pink rag of a suit'; hence at the Gare du Nord, an alcoholic American reveller will arrive at the platform so nervous with withdrawal that the wad of bank notes he is carrying has become a sweat-sodden, screwed up ball, deep in the grip of his fist.

Fitzgerald was the dazzling, Art Deco update – T.S. Eliot described him as making the greatest advances in American fiction since Henry James – of the founding modern novelists of the middle years of the nineteenth century: the great European naturalists, such as Honoré de Balzac, Gustave Flaubert, Ivan Turgenev and Leo Tolstoy. And in the lineage of those writers, Fitzgerald recognised the city as foremost a narrative, in which social strata corresponded to architecture, fashions, manners and topography with a tenacity that was all the more rigid for being so unquestioned. In this, just as Balzac could introduce a volume of his 'Human Comedy', set in the early decades of the nineteenth century, with a meticulously detailed description of both the appearance and the situation of a Parisian boarding house of derelict gentility, so for Fitzgerald, the monolithic, brutal, thrilling, teeming thoroughfares of New York could present an entire social cosmography – a narrative city in which the workings of fortune and destiny were as inviolable and manifold as they had been in Chaucerian England.

The search in this city of stories – a quest that would later be described in the opening voiceover to each episode of the popular American television series, *Naked City* – would seem always to acknowledge the presence of epic truth within quotidian detail; the proximity of life to death, that overwhelming indifference of nature to human suffering that W.H. Auden had described, and the defining synonym of finitude between mortality and the city limits. In an essay not published until after his death, 'My Lost City', the older Fitzgerald saw what was perhaps an intimation of looming death from the roof garden of the Plaza hotel:

> I had discovered the crowning error of the city, its Pandora's box. Full of vaunting pride the New Yorker had climbed here and seen with dismay what he had never suspected, that the city was not the endless succession of canyons that he had supposed but that it had its limits – from the tallest structure he saw for the first time that it faded out into the country on all sides, into an expanse of green and blue that alone was limitless. And with the awful realization that New York was a city after all and not a universe, the whole shining edifice that he had reared in his imagination came crashing to the ground.

Such, perhaps, would be the quieter message of mature modernism's clamour for urban truth; a moment of twinned apostasy and epiphany, as revelatory as any philosophical encounter within the Sublime landscapes of earlier Romanticism, and providing above all a brief respite from the crash and clatter of the streets, the bars, the shops and the trains; a moment of fresh air, so to speak, sudden, startling, somewhat concussive, before the inevitable return to the worn-out thoroughfares of public space, and the gathering roar of machinery.

II Fast, faster … Pop

In the long hot summer of 1964, a young English art student called Mark Lancaster – tall, gay, striking looking, originally from Yorkshire – could be found in the library of the Museum of Modern Art, New York, where he was researching his degree thesis on the photography of Alfred Stieglitz, the 291 gallery, and Stieglitz's magazine, *Camera Work*. It would be an activity that would lead, in its configuration of interests, personnel, time, place and incident, to the summary of a new age – or, at least, to the passing of the baton of a particular sensibility from one distinct era to another.

Lancaster was a star pupil at Newcastle University Department of Fine Art, of the English Pop artist, Richard Hamilton; and it was through Hamilton, and more particularly by way of Hamilton's friendship and collaboration with Marcel Duchamp, that Lancaster had gone to America that summer, and, moreover, to the studio of Andy Warhol. There must have been a degree of mutual understanding in the air, for as Lancaster pursued his research for his thesis, he was also admitted to the mythic coterie of street stars, misfits, addicts, casualties and charismatic bohemian artists who comprised the milieu of Warhol's first 'Silver' Factory. Within a matter of weeks, Lancaster had found his feet sufficiently in this new environment (and one can only imagine how dizzily glamorous the white-hot core of American Pop art must have seemed to a student from the industrial north-east of England, only recently delivered from the austerity measures of the immediate post-war years), to take a 'starring' role in Warhol's film *Kiss* 1964 – his on-screen partner being Gerard Malanga.

Photographers of the early Pop age – the period between the middle years of the 1950s and the 1960s – such as Bert Stern, William Klein and Irving Penn, would all make studies of the new, mass commodification of glamour. The latest fashion lifestyles and models for aspirational celebrity would share above all a sense of acceleration: that the stories they told were fables of boundless exuberance and honed sophistication. In this, the iconic photographic portraiture of the period might be called pre-Lapsarian – that Pop's state of grace was still intact, the party still in full swing. Premonitions of collapse – of which there were few greater examples than Stern's last portraits of Marilyn Monroe – were perhaps the more chilling for being felt in the midst of what Tom Wolfe (with only partial irony) would describe as 'a happiness explosion'.

But, back in the summer of 1964, the social dimension of Warhol's studio began to open up to the young British art student, and embodiment of sophisticated Pop cool, Mark Lancaster. Having heard that Lancaster was researching the photography of Stieglitz, the ever-helpful Warhol remarked that he should meet with his friend at the Metropolitan Museum of Art, Henry Geldzahler – who would not only be able to show Lancaster the Stieglitz holdings there, but could also introduce him to the vibrant, event filled, Jazz Age, urban paintings of Florine Stettheimer, known as 'The Cathedrals of New York'. ('She's my favourite artist', Lancaster would later recall Warhol enthusing, 'She's soooo great.')

In art-historical terms, however, there would be a triangular development of events in Lancaster's experience of the New York 'underground' art scene of the early 1960s that relates to the developing – darkening – ideas of image, portrait, celebrity and the city. As the work of Stieglitz is possessed of a beauteous austerity, steeped in what appears to be the textural and pictorial equivalent of emotional integrity, so Lancaster's role in *Kiss* can be seen to enact a totally new idea not just of portraiture, but of image making *per se*. A coldness exudes from Warhol's 'movies', their mood wavering between bored detachment and nervous tension. One might add to this heady encounter of artistic ideas, as experienced by Lancaster, the over-arching significance of the city itself, and of the relationship between Warhol's early 'stars' and their roles as both urban characters and photographic subjects.

In the second paragraph of his memoiristic essay 'Goodbye To Berlin', published in 1939, Christopher Isherwood provides an account of himself that might easily apply to Warhol, and to Warhol's notion of photography: 'I am a camera with its shutter open, quite passive, recording, not thinking.' This chimes exactly with Warhol's famous pronouncement that he would like 'to be a machine', and sets in place the idea of a new urban landscape and technological environment in which everyone and everything is in a constant state of mediation. Somewhat different in approach from Hamilton's more intellectual, art-historical concept of Pop, the thinking behind Warhol's 'Screen Test' series, for example, appears deceptively simple. Faced for some minutes with the blank eye of a rolling cine camera, the subjects have no choice but to reveal themselves in some way – the test becomes one of nerve, as much as anything. At the same time, within the conceits of cultural and aesthetic status, the subject is temporarily elevated to the position more usually held – at this point in the 1960s – by an actor (better, a star) auditioning for a role in a big glamorous film. Finally, there is a sense in which the image-making process is both forensic and domestic. Are these subjects offering themselves up to be little more than pictorial name entries in a log book? Or are they more flattered by the medium, and the heightened notion of attention that it proposes? In both of these possibilities, we are introduced to a new epoch of urban portraiture, and one in which the mass manufacture and consumption of image will be of paramount importance.

Incident and vista, object and action, the delicate, proprietorial relationship that a glimpsed stranger appears to maintain with his surroundings – all are presented with such intensity and heartfelt eloquence in the street scenes and portraits of the late nineteenth and early twentieth centuries, that there is always the forceful sense that one is being shown the universe in miniature: a cosmic incident refined to a glance, a hem, a chair, a passer-by lost in thought or entranced by something only he can see.

In the burgeoning Pop age, as transposed from the broader world of modernist culture, a key theme within the narrative city would be its election of archetypes and heroes on a scale and complexity that updates the chronicles of classical myth. Such chemistry of image and circumstances will formulate the notion of modern glamour, not just in its wider, more secular reading as the manifestation of heightened wealth and beauty, but in its deeper, historical and etymological definition as derived from the conflation of 'language' and 'magic'. Proceeding from such a potent confluence of human and supernatural phenomena, this profound understanding of glamour brings with it a key to the seemingly locked or inscrutable constitutions of modern stardom – the entire apparatus of aspirational image as it takes its place as both a social force of formidable urgency and as the workings of a vast, commercial industrial complex.

One might usefully date the modern Pop age from the week in May 1956, when Elvis Presley's single 'Heartbreak Hotel' hit the top of the US charts. This was also the year, in Great Britain, that the Whitechapel Gallery held its exhibition *This Is Tomorrow*, and the *Daily Mail* created its 'Home of the Future' for the Ideal Home exhibition. At the Institute of Contemporary Arts in London, then based in Dover Street, the loose-knit group of artists, theorists and critics known as The Independent Group had already proceeded some way down its socio-philosophical analysis of American 'Mass Age', commercial artisan culture. A key result of the group's enquiry was the letter written by Hamilton to the husband and wife architectural team, Peter and Alison Smithson in 1957, in which he submitted his iconic: 'Pop art is …' list of qualities defining 'popular art' (no such movement as 'Pop art' being in existence at this time.)

For an art student of Lancaster's generation, these events and activities would comprise a new, America-focused avant garde, and stand in strict contrast to the Francophile or London School enthusiasms of many art teachers of the period. And as such, the findings of what would become known as Pop art took their place alongside the equally important business of being a consumer, and, vitally, a fan of Pop products themselves – movies, fashions, magazines, records. All the commercially created and mass-produced insignia of this new Pop age.

With regard to photographic portraiture, too, an entire new world was being pioneered, in which aspirational image was empowered by sub-cultural style as much as by the accelerated, intoxicating rhythms of new music, from skiffle and rockabilly to 'trad' jazz and Rhythm and Blues. One further refinement of this new image consciousness would be the trend amongst the young to recreate themselves through Pop styling as mythic versions of themselves – not in itself an original activity, but one that became supremely heightened and democratised by the commodity culture of the latest stars and media of the Pop world.

From this, one can divine that the founding formula for Pop itself was the fusion of technology and sex: the processes of industrial design and mass production being brought into the service of heavily stylised and eroticised romanticism. Such was the world that Warhol would later note in his account of his drive across America with Taylor Mead at the very beginning of the 1960s – had already created a total Pop environment for 'kids who had never known anything else'.

In a fast forward through time to the rave music culture of the 1990s, we can see the descendants of these first children of the total Pop age. They possess, as we can see, for example, in the club-based work of Rineke Dijkstra or Wolfgang Tillmans – a certain quality of science fiction. The young inhabitants of a vast social ghetto, are seen to pursue drug, music and style codes that have become endless variations on a well-worn theme. Richard Hell's punk slogan 'I belong to the Blank Generation' – which might acquire such poignancy if applied, for instance, to the social realism of Paul Graham – appears emptied of meaning. The quality most heightened in such photographs is an ancient, bared and fragile subjectivity, neither enhanced nor defended by the best efforts of either aspirational cultural materialism and postmodern pop sub-cultures.

Inculcations of 'la vie deluxe' – luxury product fantasies of wealth and celebrity, devolving in sedimentary manner from the empyrean of high fashion to the day dreams of the new suburban classes – would in their turn provide pictorial splendour and clever quirks of styling. The narrative city was on course to make the late twentieth-century shift from being a place of production to being a centre of consumption, serviced by a myriad style codes, the steadily mounting torrent of which would become increasingly homogenised, eventually reaching a critical mass that rendered all attempts at sartorial individualism equally meaningful and meaningless. The finitude that Fitzgerald had recognised from the roof garden of the Plaza hotel, half a century earlier, would find its postmodern equivalent in the realisation that the industrial manufacture of image and celebrity, and its mass mediation, did little more than render image transparent and fame commonplace. Warhol had predicted this world in the early 1960s, presenting in his art a chilling dichotomy between glamour and wealth on the one hand, and a death-like, discursive void on the other.

In his 1976 film adaptation of Walter Tevis's science fiction novel, *The Man who Fell to Earth*, director Nicholas Roeg portrayed the stranded alien Thomas Jerome Newton – played by David Bowie, then at the height of his avant-pop superstardom – as becoming alcoholic, isolated and addicted to binging on random multi channels of American television. Addressing the postmodern relationship between viewer and image in the late 1990s, the historian and biographer Jon Savage remarked, 'Now we're all Thomas Newton – and isn't it a bore?'

The ubiquity of image-making has created the visual equivalent of white noise. Yet there continues within the rising roar to be moments of silence, during which, it seems, the subjects of portraiture look back at the viewer with a gaze or a countenance – however impassive or withdrawn – that is above all questioning. Our meaning, it seems, is reflected in their image; and the passing young man with the world at his feet, who seemed to be there just a minute ago, leaves nothing more behind him than the memory of a shadow.

Typologies

Typologies

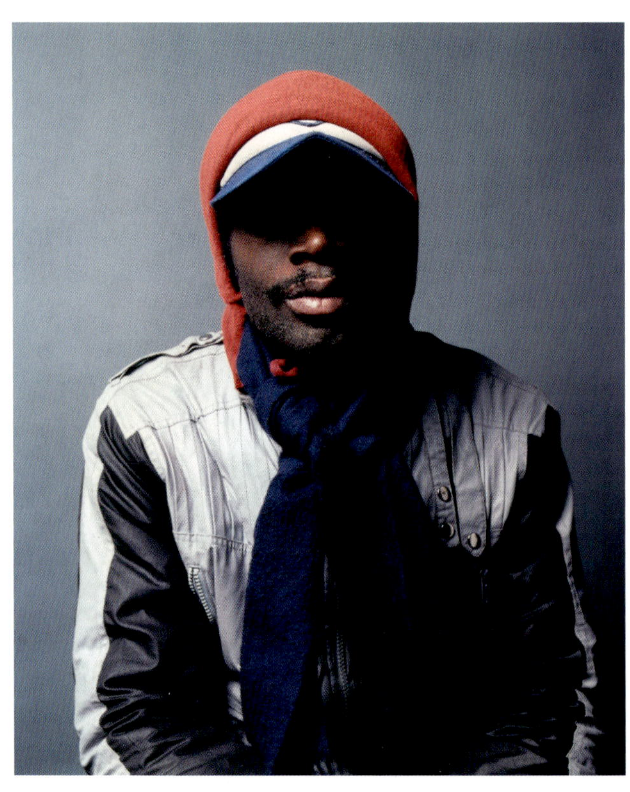

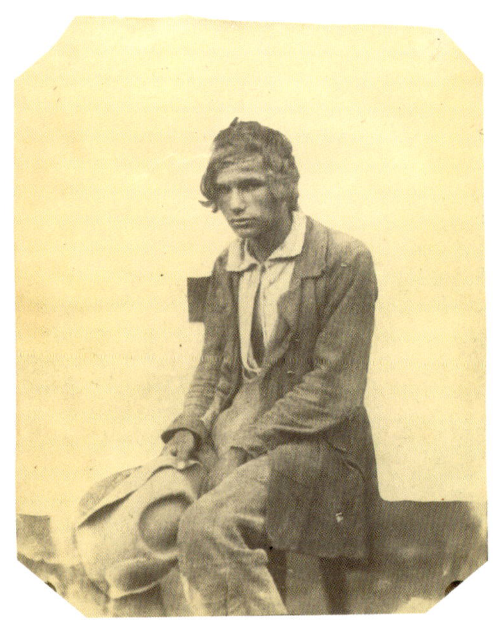

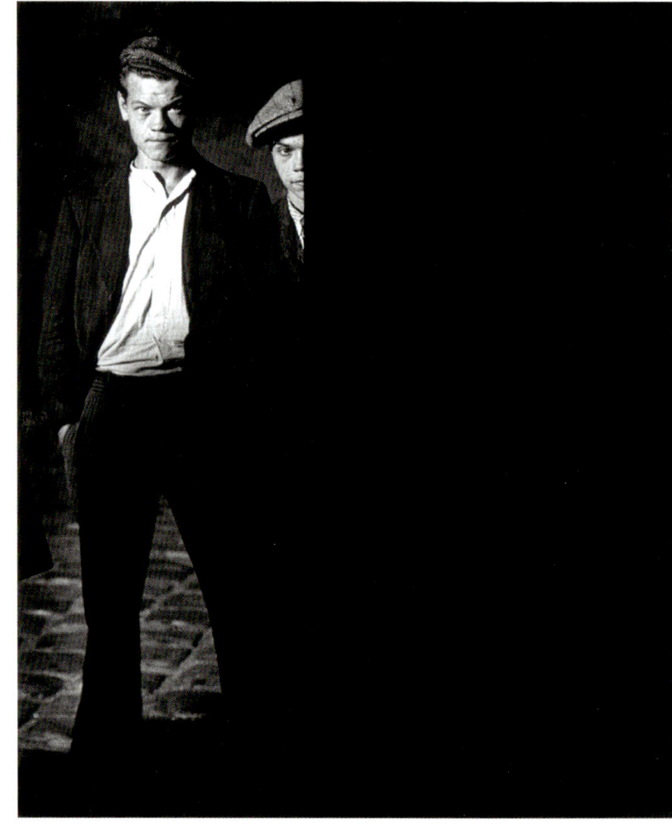

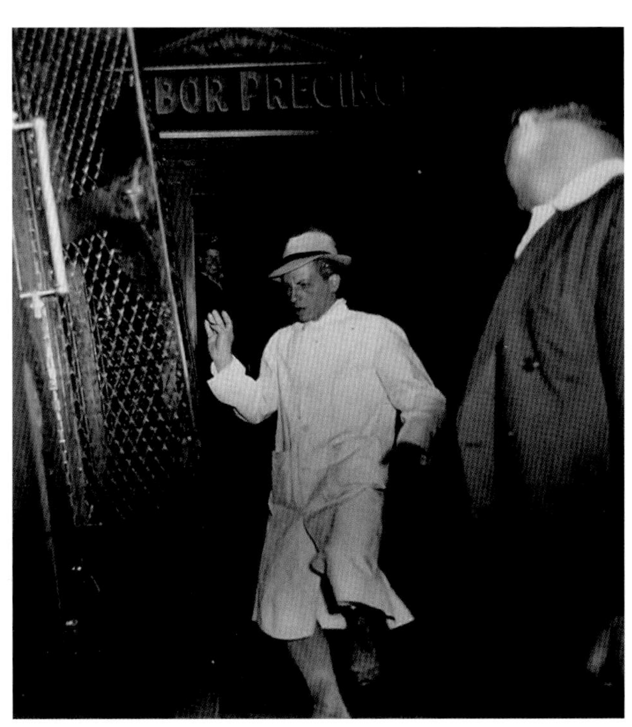

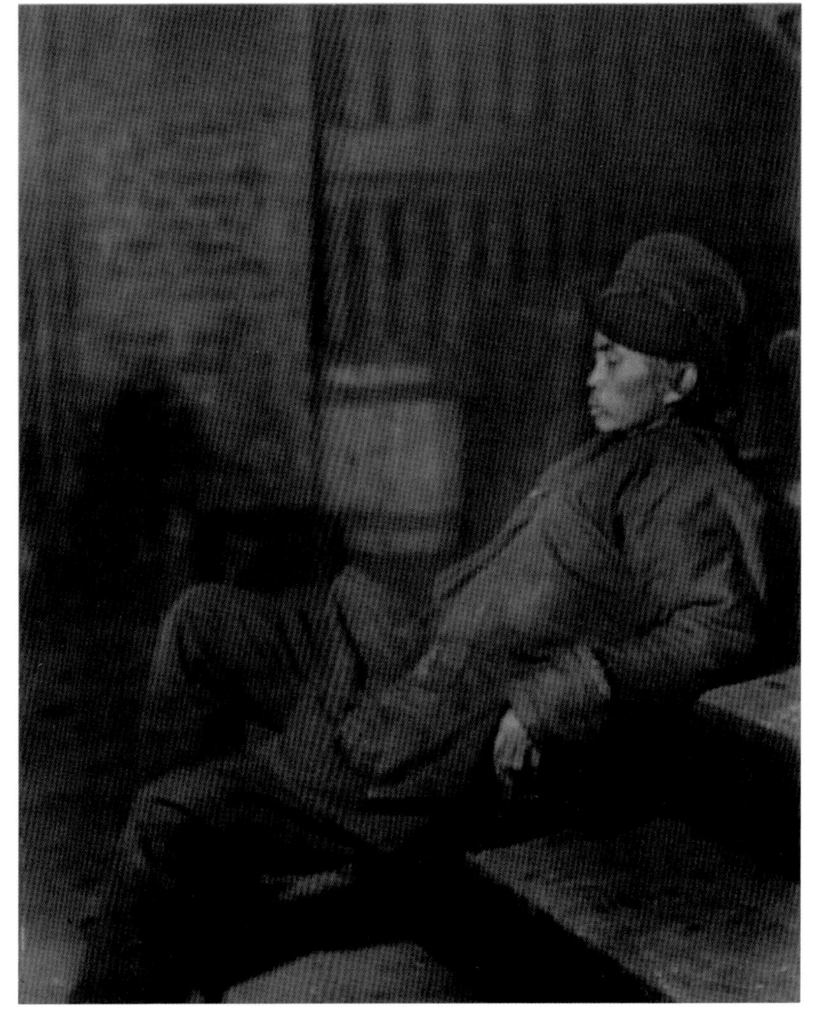

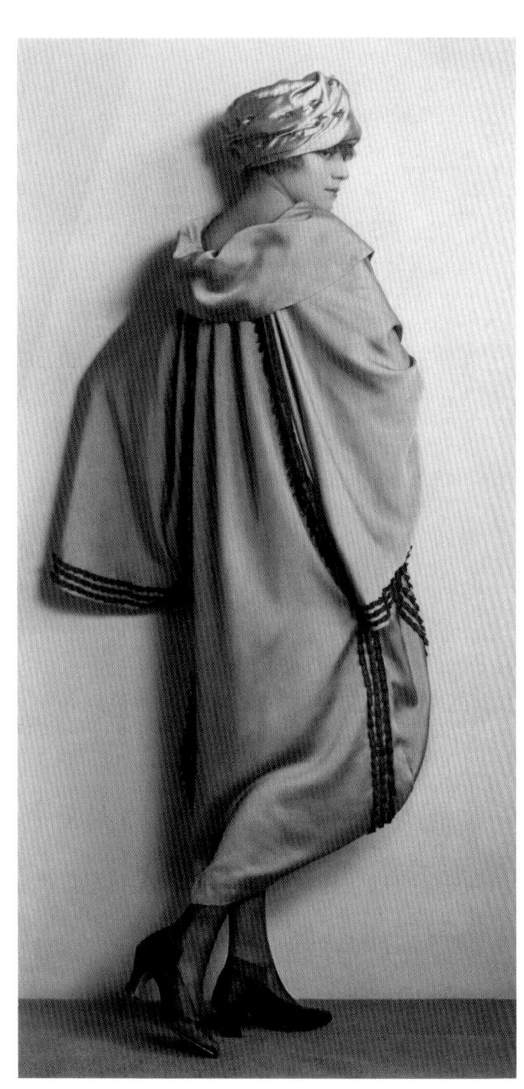

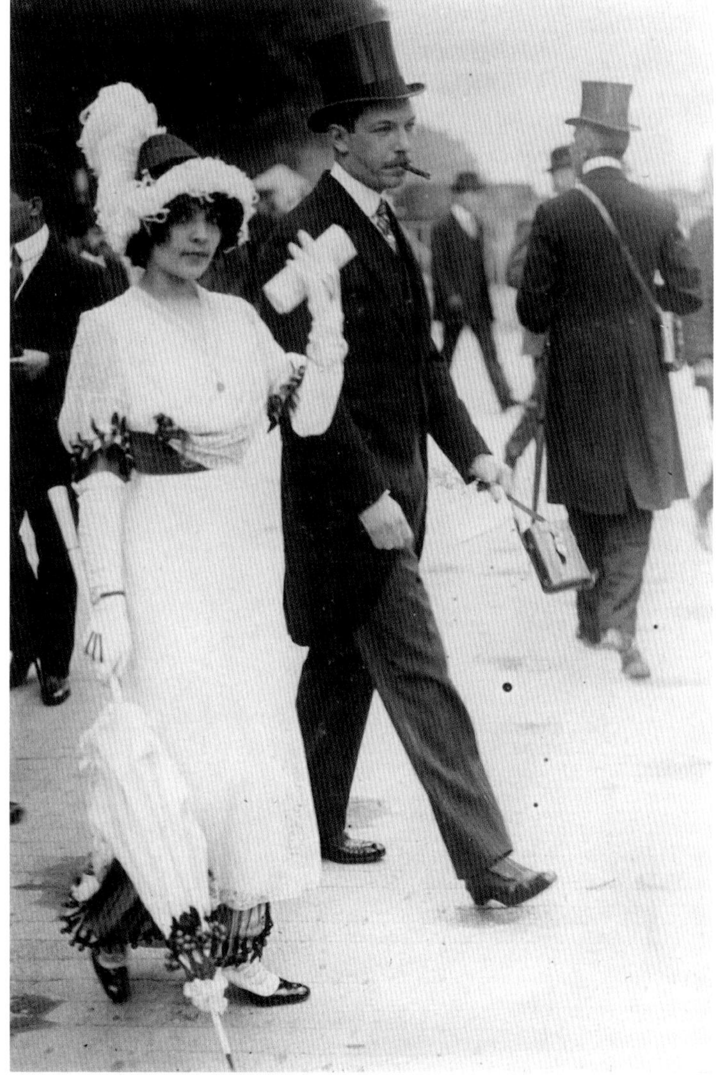

Peeping and Posing

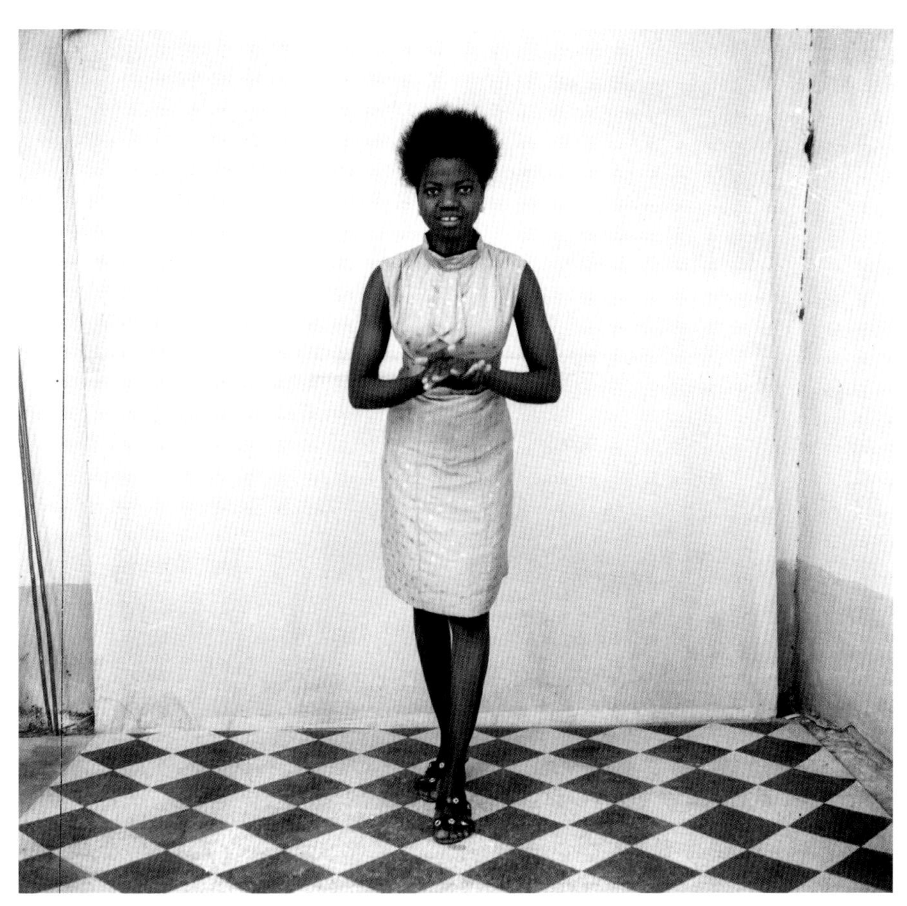

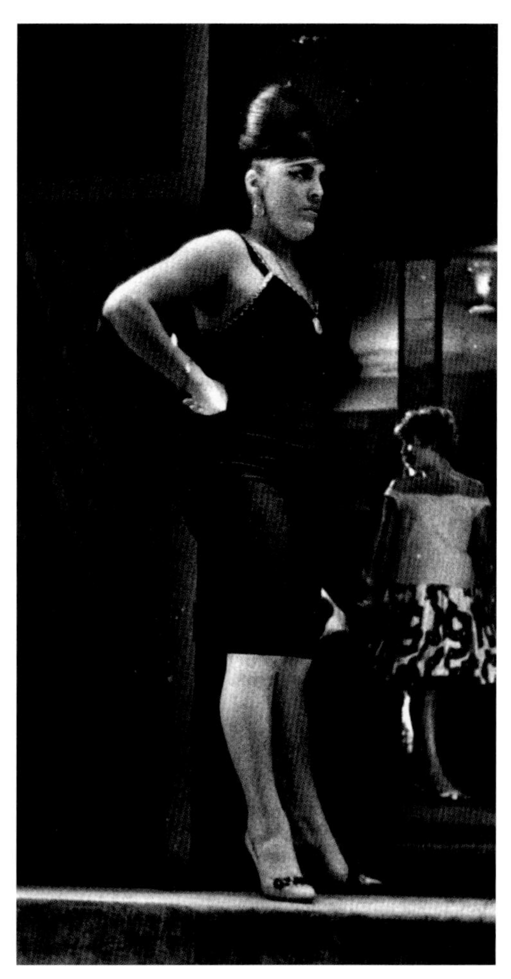

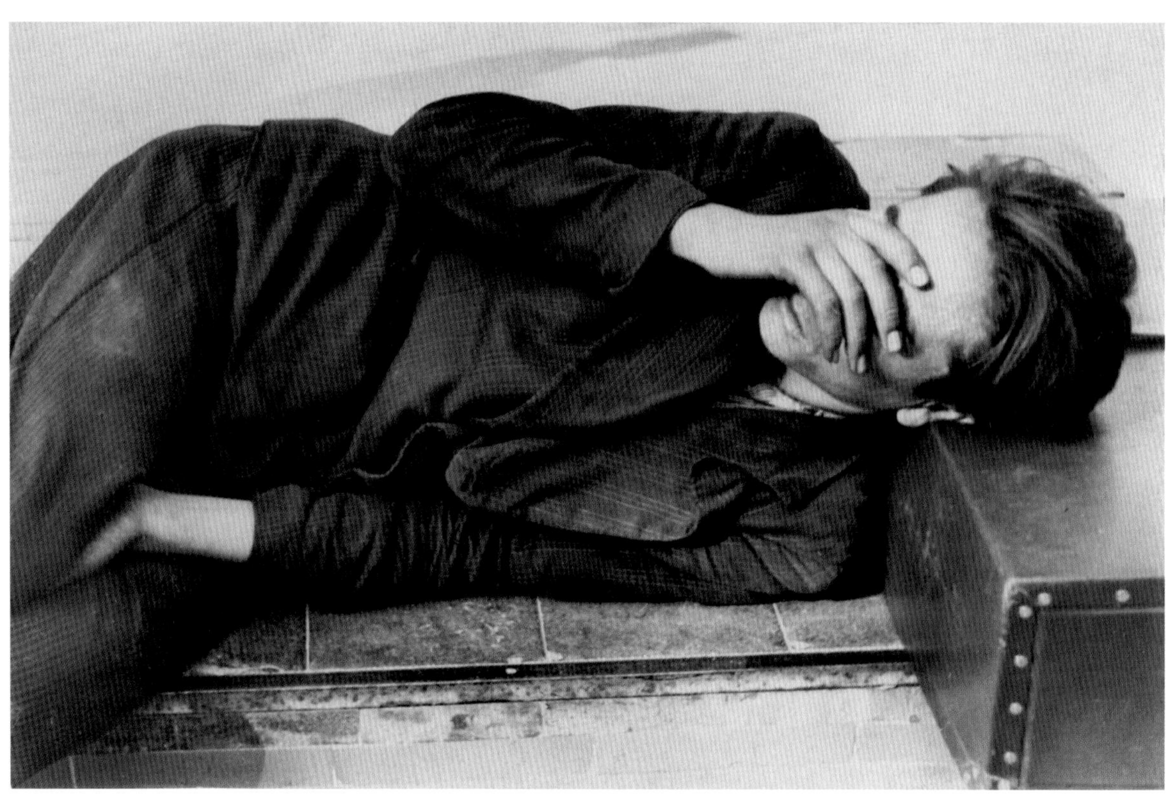

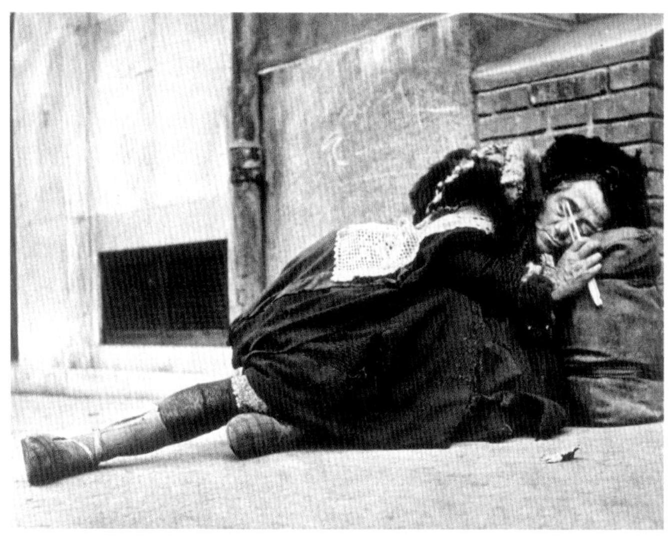

City Sleepers

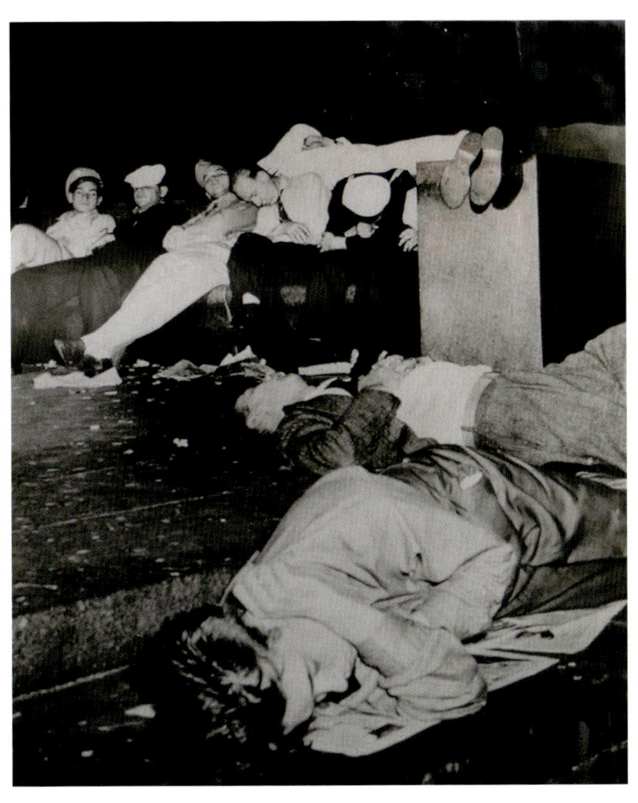

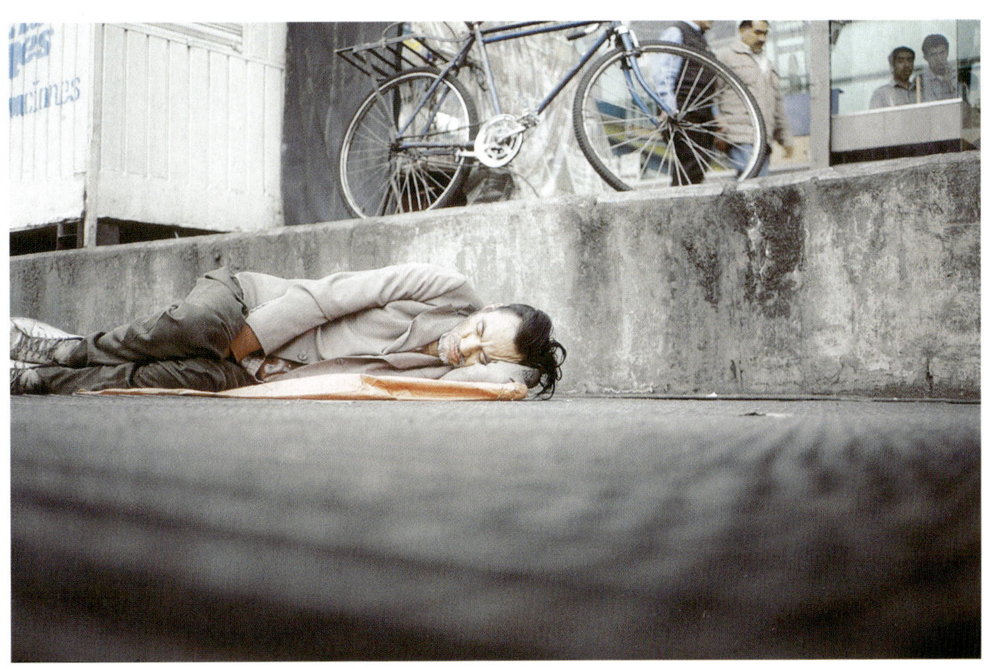

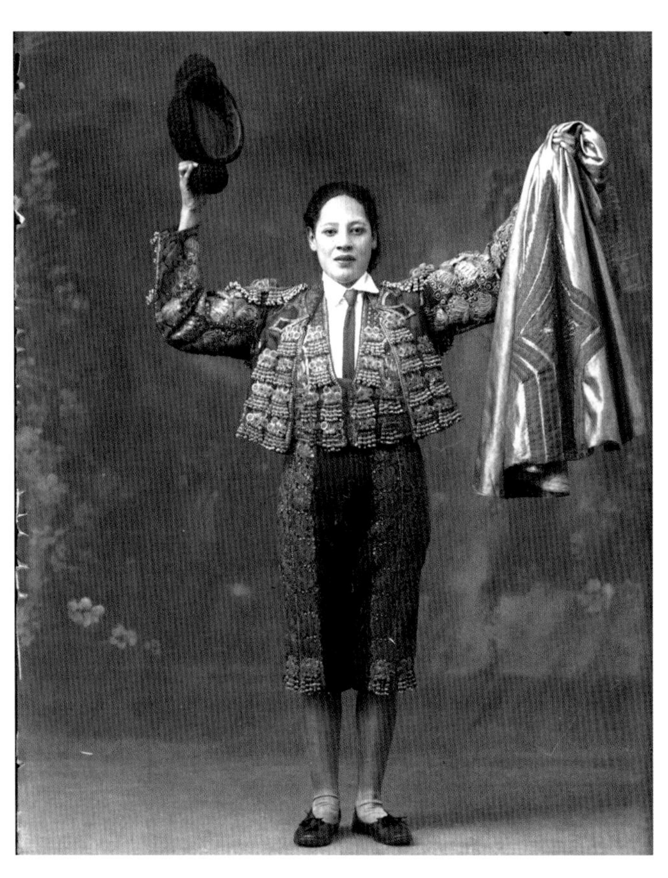

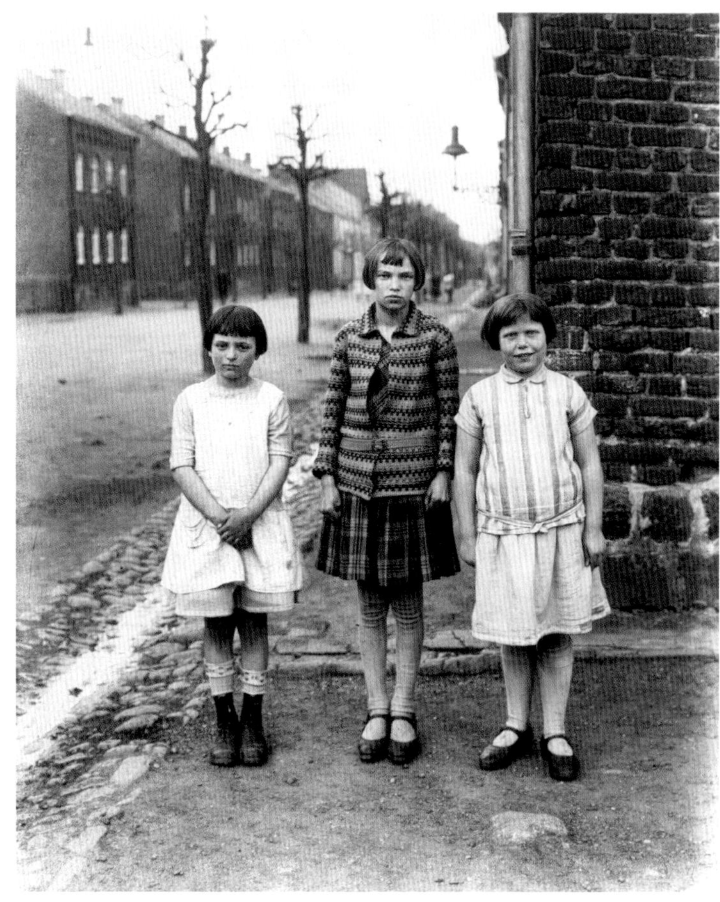

Portraits of Pride

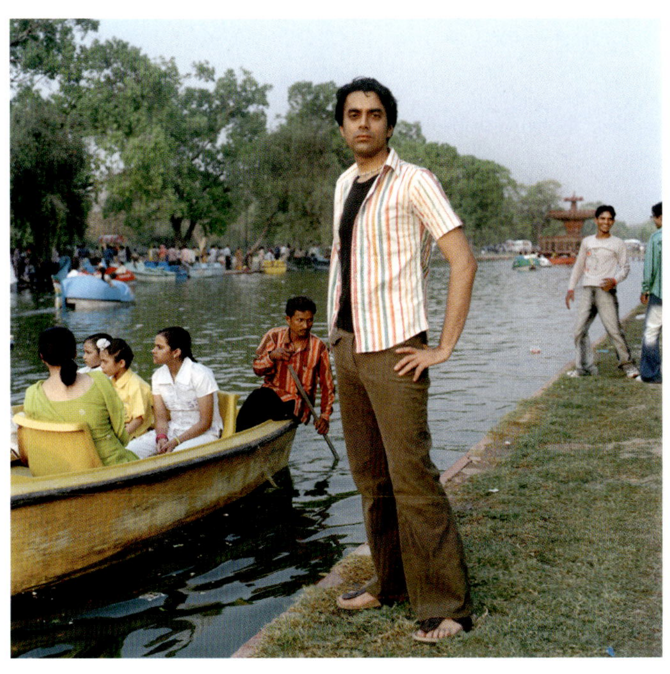

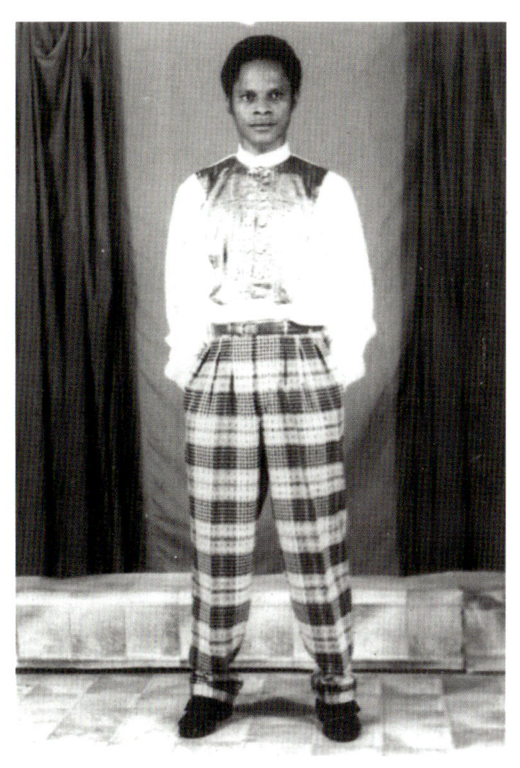

Blind

Pages 4–5,
clockwise from top left:

Paul Strand, *Photograph – New York* (later titled *Blind Woman, New York*), 1916

Andres Serrano, *Gussie*, from the series *Nomads*, 1990

Paul Graham, *Untitled 2000 (Memphis) #36*, 1999
(Not exhibited / Courtesy of Anthony Reynolds Gallery, London)

Photographers at Work

Pages 14–15,
clockwise from top left:

Robert Frank, *Street Photographer*, 1950
(Not exhibited / Courtesy of the artist)

Lewis Hine, *Self-Portrait with Newsieboy*, 1908

August Sander, *Straßenphotograph* (Street Photographer), c.1930
(Not exhibited / Fotografische Sammlung, Museum Folkwang, Essen)

Richard Sudden, *Andres Serrano Photographing a Klanswoman in Georgia*, 1990
(Not exhibited / Courtesy of Paula Cooper Gallery, New York)

Martin Parr, *Pyongyang*, from the series *Autoportraits*, 1999

Edward Steichen, *Self-Portrait with Photographic Paraphernalia*, 1929
(Not exhibited / Fotografische Sammlung, Museum Folkwang, Essen)

Stefan Moses, *Straßenfotograf* (Street Photographer), Berlin 1963
(Not exhibited / Fotomuseum im Münchner Stadtmuseum)

Arnold Genthe, *Arnold Genthe with Camera* (pub. 1908 as *An Unsuspecting Victim*), c.1899

Fear of the Other

Pages 204–5,
left to right:

Andres Serrano, *John Paul*, from the series *Nomads*, 1990

Brassaï, *Voyous de la bande du Grand Albert, Paris XIVe* (Rogues of Grand Albert's gang), 1932
(Not exhibited / Fotografische Sammlung, Museum Folkwang, Essen)

Carl Durheim, *Wilhelm Schobel, 18 Jahre alt* (Wilhelm Schobel, 18 Years Old), 1852–3

Weegee, *Transvestite*, 1940s

Arnold Genthe, *Dead to the World* (pub. 1908 as *The Opium Fiend*), c.1899

Peeping and Posing

City Sleepers

Portraits of Pride

Pages 206–7,
left to right:

Madame d'Ora, *Wiener Werkstätte* (Vienna Workshop), 1921

Jacques Henri Lartigue, *Paris, juin 1911* (Paris, June 1911), 1911

Malick Sidibé, *Simulation de marche* (Walking), 1967
(Not exhibited / Courtesy of Gwin Zegal)

Joan Colom, from the series *Gente del Raval* (People of Raval), 1958–61

Pages 208–9,
left to right:

Henri Cartier-Bresson, *Spain*, 1933

Lisette Model, *Montparnasse*, 1933–8

Weegee, *Open-Air Canteen, Broadway and 47th Street at Five in the Morning*, 1940s

Francis Alÿs, from the series *Sleepers*, 1999–2006

Pages 210–11,
left to right:

Martín Chambi, *Señorita Torera* (Bullfighter Girl), 1932

August Sander, *Arbeiterkinder, Köln* (Worker's Children, Cologne), 1932

Sunil Gupta, *Bikram*, from the series *Mr Malhotra's Party*, 2007

Samuel Fosso, *Untitled (Self-Portrait)*, 1976

Charles Nègre, *Untitled*, also known as *Le Petit Chiffonnier* (The Little Ragpicker), c.1851

Copyright Credits

The publishers have made every effort to trace copyright holders.
We apologise for any omissions that may inadvertantly have been made.

Manuel Álvarez Bravo © Colette Urbajtel

Francis Alÿs © Francis Alÿs / Courtesy David Zwirner, New York

Laurie Anderson © Laurie Anderson / Courtesy Sean Kelly Gallery

Philip Kwane Apagya © Philip Apagya / Courtesy Fifty One Fine Art Photography, Antwerp

Nobuyoshi Araki © Nobuyoshi Araki / Courtesy Pinakothek der Moderne, Munich

Diane Arbus © The Estate of Diane Arbus 2008

Richard Avedon © 2008 The Richard Avedon Foundation

Cecil Beaton © Cecil Beaton Archive, Sotheby's

Frank Berger © Frank Berger 2008

Erwin Blumenfeld © ADAGP, Paris and DACS, London 2008

Brassaï © The Brassaï Estate – RMN

Henri Cartier-Bresson © Henri Cartier-Bresson / Magnum Photos

Martin Chambi © Archivo Fotográfico Martín Chambi, Cusco, Peru. www.martinchambi.com

Alvin Langdon Coburn © Estate of Alvin Langdon Coburn / George Eastman House, Rochester

Joan Colom © Joan Colom / Courtesy Foto Colectania Foundation, Barcelona

Philip-Lorca diCorcia © Philip-Lorca diCorcia / Courtesy David Zwirner Gallery

Rineke Dijkstra © Courtesy the Artist

Robert Doisneau © The Estate of Robert Doisneau & Agence Rapho Agence Rapho / Camera Press

Hashem El Madani © Hashem El Madani / Courtesy Arab Image Foundation

Hugo Erfurth © DACS 2008

Walker Evans © Walker Evans Archive, The Metropolitan Museum of Art, New York

Samuel Fosso © Samuel Fosso / Courtesy Jack Shainman Gallery, New York

FotoRamblas © FotoRamblas

Robert Frank © Robert Frank

Ron Galella © Ron Galella, courtesy Galerie Wouter van Leeuwen, Amsterdam

Arnold Genthe © Estate of Arnold Genthe / George Eastman House, Rochester

Arturo Ghergo © Cristina Ghergo

David Goldblatt © David Goldblatt / Courtesy Goodman Gallery, Johannesburg

Paul Graham © Paul Graham

Sunil Gupta © Sunil Gupta

Philippe Halsman © Estate of Philippe Halsman / Magnum Photos

Pieter Hugo © Pieter Hugo, Courtesy Yossi Milo Gallery, New York

Peter Hujar © The Peter Hujar Archive / Courtesy Matthew Marks Gallery, New York

Sarah Jones © The Artist/ Courtesy Maureen Paley, London

Valérie Jouve © Valérie Jouve

Marjaana Kella © Marjaana Kella / Courtesy van Zoetendaal Amsterdam

Chris Killip © Chris Killip

William Klein © Les Editions Condé Nast SA

Suzanne Lafont © Suzanne Lafont

Jacques Henri Lartigue © Ministère de la Culture et de la Communication, France / AAJHL

Helmar Lerski © Estate Helmar Lerski / Courtesy Fotografische Sammlung, Museum Folkwang, Essen

Leon Levinstein © Estate of the Artist / Courtesy Howard Greenberg Gallery

Helen Levitt © Helen Levitt / Courtesy Laurence Miller Gallery, New York

Photo Credits

ADAGP, Paris, 72
Àngels Barcelona, 81
Courtesy the artist, 4, 114-15, 119, 120-1, 130-1, 132-3, 134,
136-7, 140-1, 211, front cover
The Richard Avedon Foundation, 94-5
Collection of Foto Colectania Foundation,
Barcelona, 70, 207
Galerie Berinson, Berlin, 56, 205, 209
bpk Berlin / Photo: Friedrich Seidenstücker, 43
Courtesy Christian Brandstätter, Vienna, 37, 206
Archivo Fotográfico Martín Chambi, 46, 210
Condé Nast SA, 63
Paula Cooper Gallery, New York, 5, 111
Haus der Photographie / Deichtorhallen, 47, 67
Museum Folkwang, Essen, 21, 27, 36, 41, 42, 48, 47, 51, 53, 54,
62, 64, 65, 66, 68, 69, 92, 102-3, 108, 112, 109, 114, 117, 204
Fifty One Fine Art, Antwerp, 111
George Eastman House, Rochester, 29, 35, 205
The J. Paul Getty Museum, Los Angeles, 34
Barbara Gladstone Gallery, New York, 106-7
Courtesy Fay Gold Gallery, 15
Goodman Gallery, Johannesburg, 77
Marian Goodman Gallery, New York, 122
Courtesy Association Gwin Zegal, 80, 211
Courtesy of the Internet, 125
Sean Kelly Gallery, New York, 104-5
Gallery Kicken, Berlin, 39
Galerie Peter Kilchmann, Zurich, 126
Achim Kukulies, Düsseldorf, 54
Donation Jacques Henri Lartigue, 31, 206
Galerie Wouter van Leeuwen, Amsterdam, 88
National Portrait Gallery, London, 55
Robert Mapplethorpe Foundation, 93
Courtesy Matthew Marks Gallery, New York, 98
Magnum Photos, London, 45, 49, 128, 208
Museo di Fotografia Contemporanea / Cinisello Balsamo,
Milan, 71
Laurence Miller Gallery, New York, 55
Lee Miller Archives, 59
Yossi Milo Gallery, New York, 36
Fotomuseum im Münchner Stadtmuseum, Munich, 75
Munich, Pinakothek der Moderne. Photo: Bayer & Mitko /
ARTOTHEK, 96
Maureen Paley, London, 124, 129, 135
Norman Parkinson Archive, London, 73

Nederlands Fotomuseum, 97
Musée Nicéphore Niépce, Chalon-sur-Saône, 101
Pace/MacGill, New York, 65
Rijksmuseum, Amsterdam, 58
© Photo RMN / © Hervé Lewandowski, 19
Ulf Saupe, 17, 75, 224
Scala London, 50
Science and Society Picture Library, London, 4, 12, 24, 28
Jack Shainman Gallery, New York, 99
Sotheby's, New York, 30
Staley-Wise Gallery, New York, 79
Steidl Verlag, Göttingen, 61, 100
Courtesy Swiss Federal Archives, Bern, 20, 206
Tate, 107
Ullstein Bilderdienst, 40
© V&A Images / Victoria and Albert Museum, London, 44
Roger Viollet Agency, Paris, 18, 25
National Archives and Records Administration,
Washington, DC, 34
Galerie Thomas Zander, Cologne 89
van Zoetendaal, Amsterdam, 118, 127
David Zwirner Gallery, New York, 116, 138-9

Lenders

Public Collections

Rijksmuseum, Amsterdam

Bildarchiv Preussischer Kulturbesitz, Berlin

Helmut Newton Foundation / Staatliche Museen zu Berlin, Kunstbibliothek

Swiss Federal Archives, Bern

National Media Museum, Bradford

The Royal Photographic Society Collection at the National Media Museum, Bradford

Musée Nicéphore Niépce, Chalon-sur-Saône

FRAC Nord-Pas-de-Calais, Dunkerque, France

Fotografische Sammlung, Museum Folkwang, Essen

Hamburger Kunsthalle, Hamburg

Haus der Photographie / Sammlung F.C. Gundlach, Hamburg

Leiden University Library

National Portrait Gallery, London

Victoria and Albert Museum, London

The J. Paul Getty Museum, Los Angeles

Museo di Fotografia Contemporanea, Cinisello-Balsamo, Milano

Pinakothek der Moderne, Munich

von Parish Kostümbibliothek, Department of Münchner Stadtmuseum, Munich

Museum of Modern Art, New York

Centre Georges Pompidou, Paris Musée National d'Art Moderne / Centre de Création Industrielle

Musée Carnavalet-Histoire de Paris, France

Musée d'Orsay, Paris

George Eastman House, Rochester

National Archives, Washington, DC

Private Collections and Galleries

Ángels, Barcelona

Archivio Fotografico Martín Chambi − Martín Chambi Photo Archives, Cusco

The Avedon Foundation, New York

The Cecil Beaton Studio Archive at Sotheby's

Frank Berger, Leipzig

Galerie Berinson, Berlin

Galerie Bertrand & Gruner, Geneva

Kristleifur Björnsson

The Estate of Erwin Blumenfeld

Günter Karl Bose, Berlin

Collection Christian Brandstätter, Vienna

Galerie Daniel Buchholz & Christopher Müller, Cologne

Fondation Henri Cartier-Bresson, Paris

Condé Nast Archive, New York

Galerie Conrads, Dusseldorf-Berlin

Paula Cooper Gallery, New York

Antoine de Beaupré

Rineke Dijkstra

Fifty One Fine Art Photography, Antwerp

Fundacio of Foto Colectania, Barcelona

Barbara Gladstone Gallery, New York

Goodman Gallery Johannesburg

Collection Greatford Estates Limited

Sunil Gupta, London

Gwin Zegal, St Brieuc

Philippe Halsman Estate − Magnum Photos

Collection Galerie Rodolphe Janssen, Brussels

Collection Galerie Sebastien Janssen, Brussels

Sean Kelly Gallery, New York

Galerie Kicken, Berlin

Galerie Kilchmann, Zurich

Suzanne Lafont

The MAG Collection, London

Magnum Photos London, London

Lee Miller Archives

Robert Mapplethorpe Foundation, New York

Matthew Marks Gallery, New York

Laurence Miller Gallery, New York

Philippe Morane

Olbricht Collection

Pace/MacGill Gallery, New York

Collection Maureen Paley

Norman Parkinson Archive, London

Timm Rautert

Anthony Reynolds Gallery, London

Jack Shainman Gallery, New York

Sammlung Sparkasse Essen

Dietmar Siegert

Collection of Margaret W. Weston

Staley-Wise Gallery, New York

Juergen Teller, London

Ullstein Bilderdienst, Berlin

Donna Mussenden van der Zee

Galerie Wouter van Leeuwen, Amsterdam

Willem van Zoetendaal, Amsterdam

Thomas Walther

Galerie Thomas Zander, Cologne

David Zwirner Gallery, New York

and other private collectors, who wish to remain anonymous

Acknowledgements

In addition to acknowledgements made elsewhere in the catalogue, we would like thank the following individuals for their invaluable contributions to the success of this project:

Joree Adilman; Anthony Allen; Laurie Anderson; Martine d'Astier; Torsten Barabaß; Steve Bello; Frank Berger; Sébastian Betrand; Arianna Bianchi; Emily Bierman; Beatrix Birken; Kristleifur Björnsson; Jesse Blatt; Katrin Bomhoff; Mattie Boom; Achim Borchardt-Hume; Manuel Borja; Günter Karl Bose; Toni Booth; Ami V. Bouhassane; Nadia Blumenfeld-Charbit; Evelien Bracke; Christian Brandstätter; Federico Braun; Maureen Bray; Frauke Breede; Karin Breuer; Justina Budd; Cian Burke; Carole Callow; Teo Allain Chambi; François Cheval; Clément Chéroux; Susanna Chisholm; Donna Chu; Tom Cole; Paula Cooper; Judith Czernichow; Marko Daniel; Amy Davila; Antoine de Beaupré; Jenny de Roode; Rineke Dijkstra; Christiane Dole; Harald Dubau; Peter Ellis; Karla Ebner; Oliver Evans; Luciano Fasciati; Rachel Fendler; Gretchen Fenston; Peter Fleer; Monika Faber; Katie-Marie Ford; Eric Franck; Michelle Franco; Martine Franck; Robert Frank; Daniela Friebel; Frank Frischmuth; Matthew Gale; Barbara Galasso; Philippe Garner; Susanne Gattineau; Arno Gisinger; Andrea Gohl; David Goldblatt; Jens Grädtke; Inka Graeve Ingelmann; Paul Graham; Ulrike Graul; Jessie Green; Katya de Grunwald; Romain Gruner; Sunil Gupta; Irene Halsman; Patricia Hämmerle; Matthias Harder; Vicki Harris; Halley Harrisburg; Lauren Haynes; Françoise Heilbrun; Lorenz Helbling; Elisabeth Heller-Winter; Karen Hellman; Tom Heman; Steve Henry; Maartje van den Heuvel; Ruth Hibbard; Ching Tai Ho; Carole Hubert; Wula Ifantidis; Mary Ilario; Jane Jackson; Sebastien Janssen; Rodolphe Janssen; Kimberly Jones; Sarah Jones; Sabine Kaufmann Staub; Marjaana Kella; Christina Kerkenrath; Michael Kerkmann; Indra Khanna; Peter Kilchmann; Conor Kilroe; Susan Kismaric; Chun-Ju Ko; Christiane Kuhlmann; Suzanne Lafont; Jörg Lampertius; Katie Latona; Cliff Lauson; Hans-Jürgen Lechtreck; Shinae Lee; Brian Liddy; Billie Lindsay; Joanna Ling; Rose Lord; Sophie Lugon; Monika McConnell; Brad MacDonald; David McNeff; Paula Medrano; Irene Mendoza; Santos Montes; Gabriela Moragas; Santiago Muñoz Bastide; Wataru Okada; Erin O'Toole; Barbara O'Connor; Wataru Okada; Alfred Pacquement; Erica Pajerowski; Maureen Paley; Gesine Pannhausen; Lauren Panzo; Martin Parr; Christian Passeri; Jeffrey Peabody; Richard Prince; Aude Raimbault; Katie Rashid; Timm Rautert; Livia Ratcliffe; Valentina Ravaglia; Annemarie Reichen; Arne Reimer; Françoise Reynaud; Anthony Reynolds; Pascal Riviale; Petra Roettig; Fiona Rogers; Jenny de Roode; Naomi Rosenblum; Benita Röver; Helen Sainsbury; Barbara Scheuermann; Jos Schmid; Ina Schmidt-Runke; Sabine Schnakenberg; Antje Schunke; Elke Schwichtenberg; Jean-Pierre Scialom; Mark Sealy; Jasmin Seck; Thomas Seelig; Francisco Serrano Martínez; Andree Sfeir-Semler; Jack Shainmann; Agnès Sire; Elizabeth Smith; Jérôme Sother; Jules Spinatsch; Petra Steinhardt; Urs Stahel; Bert Stern; Lisa Sutcliffe; Roger Szmulewicz; Mitra Tabrizian; Katja Tallner; Rachel Taylor; Hilde Teerlinck; Juergen Teller; Wolfgang Tillmans; Jacqueline Tran; Stephan Urbaschek; Roberta Valtorta; Jacques Van Daele; Maartje van den Heuvel; Wouter van Leeuwen; Willem van Zoetendaal; Karin Waitl; Kirsty Wesson; Paul Wilson; Jacques Van Daele; Kirsty Wesson; Jean-Baptiste Woloch; Sophie Wright; Gunilla Zedigh; Donna van der Zee; James Zeender; Shari Zolla; Bettina von Zwehl.

Authors

Ute Eskildsen
is director of the photographic collection at Museum
Folkwang, Essen. In her curatorial and publishing work she
has been focusing on twentieth-century history, contemporary
practice and the relationship of art and applied photography.

Florian Ebner
is an artist, writing regularly on photography; he works as
interim curator at Berlinische Galerie.

Bettina Kaufmann
is an art historian specialising in nineteenth- and twentieth-
century art and works as a curator at Tate.

Michael Bracewell
is a writer, novelist and cultural commentator.

Jeremy Millar
is an artist. He is an AHRC Research Fellow at the Ruskin
School of Drawing and Fine Art, Oxford.

Susanne Holschbach
is a media and art historian. She is author of *Theatralität und
Weiblichkeit in der Fotografie des 19. Jahrhunderts* and editor of the
module 'Photo/Byte' for the *Media Art Net*.

Colophon

First published 2008 by order of the Tate
Trustees by Tate Publishing, a division of Tate
Enterprises Ltd, Millbank, London SW1P 4RG
www.tate.org.uk/publishing

On the occasion of the exhibition at

Tate Modern, London
22 May – 31 August 2008

Museum Folkwang, Essen
11 October 2008 – 11 January 2009

Designed by Oliver Klimpel
at Büro International London

Printed and bound
in Belgium by Die Keure

Cover
Front: Juergen Teller, *Eva Bodenhoff,
20th October 1998*, from the series
Go-Sees 1998–9 (detail)
Back: Weegee, *Self-Portrait, Working
in the Trunk of his Chevrolet*, 1942

© Tate 2008

Essays © The Authors 2008

A catalogue record for this book is available
from the British Library

ISBN 978 1 85437 778 4

Distributed in the United States and Canada
by Harry N. Abrams, Inc., New York

Library of Congress Control Number:
2008926214

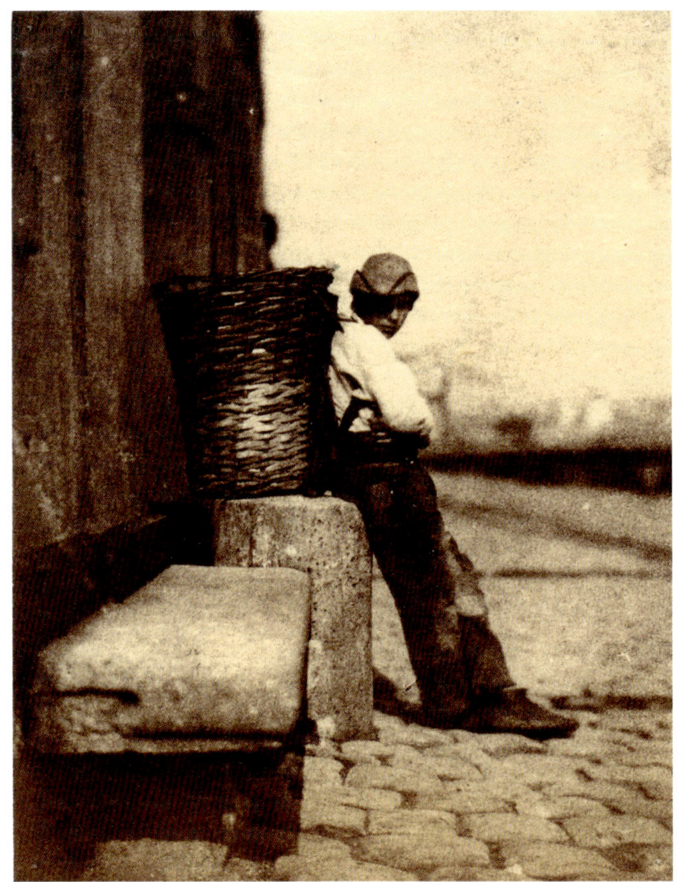

Charles Nègre, *Le Petit Chiffonnier* (The Little Ragpicker), c.1851